BISON
BOOKS

For Tom Edwards —

Westerner —

Dick Etulain

D0958160

THE AMERICAN WEST

SECOND EDITION

A Modern History, 1900 to the Present

Richard W. Etulain and Michael P. Malone

Preface and new chapter for the Bison Books edition by
Richard W. Etulain

UNIVERSITY OF NEBRASKA PRESS
LINCOLN & LONDON

©1989 by the University of Nebraska Press
Preface © 2007 by the Board of Regents of the University of Nebraska
Chapter 8 © 2007 by the Board of Regents of the University of Nebraska

∞

First Nebraska paperback printing: 1989

Library of Congress Cataloging-in-Publication Data
Etulain, Richard W.
The American West: a modern history, 1900 to the present / Richard W. Etulain and Michael P. Malone; preface and new chapter for the Bison Books edition by Richard W. Etulain. — 2nd ed.
p. cm.
Malone's name appears first on the earlier edition.
Includes bibliographical references and index.
ISBN 978-0-8032-6022-1 (pbk.: alk. paper)
1. West (U.S.)—Civilization—20th century. 2. West (U.S.)—Civilization—21st century. 3. West (U.S.)—History—20th century. 4. West (U.S.)—History—21st century. I. Malone, Michael P. II. Title.
F595.E88 2007
978'.033—dc22
2007022081

To Joyce and Kathleen
To the memory of Michael P. Malone and Earl Pomeroy

Contents

Illustrations

Olympia

WASHINGTON

Salem

OREGON

IDAHO

Boise

MONTANA

Helena

NORTH DAKOTA

Bismarck

SOUTH DAKOTA

Pierre

WYOMING

Cheyenne

NEBRASKA

Lincoln

Sacramento

NEVADA

Carson City

Salt Lake
City

Denver

COLORADO

Topeka

KANSAS

UTAH

CALIFORNIA

ARIZONA

Santa Fe

OKLAHOMA

Oklahoma City

Phoenix

NEW MEXICO

The Twentieth-Century American West

TEXAS

Austin

Preface

The existence of this volume is a testament to the extraordinary energy and persistence of the late Michael P. Malone. After coauthoring a splendid state history of Montana (*Montana: A History of Two Centuries*, 1976), Mike began planning a full-scale history of the American West. He had an extensive project in mind, a comprehensive overview of the West from the region's initial landscapes and first human inhabitants to the end of the twentieth century. He wanted other authors to help him with this demanding task. He turned to me as one possible coauthor, but I turned him down in the early 1980s, when he first approached me about joining him in this immense endeavor. I was convinced that I did not have the time or necessary background to jointly author the proposed western history. Undeterred, Mike talked another western historian into writing most of the pre-1840 sections of the book. Then he came back to me, urging me to write the social-cultural chapters about the post-1840 period. This time I agreed to become part of the western triumvirate writing a new history of the West. It was nearly impossible to turn a deaf ear to boyish, enthusiastic Mike Malone.

Changes in the authors' careers delayed completion of our western history. When the third member of the trio bowed out, unable to complete his assigned chapters in the early portion of the book, Mike and I pushed ahead with our sections. It soon became clear that we could publish the third part of the project—from 1900 to the present—because Mike and I had written those chapters. The jointly authored book moved along smoothly, and the University of Nebraska Press quickly published the handsomely done up book in the fall of 1989. We were immensely pleased that *The American West* was named a Main Selection of the History Book Club, received many positive reviews, and gained wide adoption in college history courses. So strong were the sales that the cloth edition soon sold out, and the paper edition quickly went into a second printing. As the years zipped along, we began to consider preparing a second edition of the book.

The second edition was delayed because of unexpected circumstances. In the late 1980s Mike Malone gradually worked his way up the administrative ladder at Montana State University in Bozeman and found less time to carry out his research. I was increasingly buried with editorial and administrative assignments at the University of New Mexico. Then in 1990 Mike Malone, Professor of History, became President Mike Malone at MSU. Still, we began planning how the second edition of *The American West* would look. Then tragedy struck. Mike died suddenly from a heart attack in 1999, and plans for a second edition were put on hold.

But my early retirement from teaching and administration allowed me to move ahead with the revision. This second edition includes the full text of the original, with only minor corrections and additions, because I wanted to retain what Mike Malone wrote in the mid-1980s. There are two changes of note, however. First, I have added a new, extensive chapter, covering the period from the mid-1980s to 2005. This section examines the economic and political topics Malone discusses in earlier chapters, and it also treats social-cultural subjects, which I dealt with in the first edition. Second, all the appended chapter bibliographical essays have been revised and updated and a large section of pertinent readings for the new chapter added. These essays list the books and articles Malone and I utilized in preparing *The American West* as well as those useful to scholars, students, and general readers interested in the post-1900 American West.

Younger scholars coming to the fore since the mid-1980s often viewed the West from a perspective quite different from that of earlier generations of western historians. During these two decades the New Western history took root and flowered. New Western historians saw much about the western past they did not like. Similar to novelists such as Joan Didion, Larry McMurtry, and Leslie Silko, New Western historians pointed to the racism, pioneer greed, and environmental destructiveness that misshaped much of the western past. They also criticized the ideas of frontier historian Frederick Jackson Turner and his disciples as too "triumphalist," as too inclined to see western history as un-flawed adventure and success. Much of the New Western history gained wide acceptance among specialists in western studies.

This volume follows a middle course between the Turn-erians and the New Western historians. Mike Malone and I agreed that earlier western historians were too often blind to the ill treatment of minority groups and settlers' excessively extractive uses of land, water, and other natural resources. Those misadventures needed to be addressed. But to focus only—or even primarily—on these limitations and to over-look the building of western cities, the expansion of farms, and the millions of jobs and homes secured and built in the West was to present only a partial, rather negative picture. So we chose to emphasize complexity—to deal with limita-tions *and* successes. Malone and I were convinced that our approach was the most realistic and convincing path to take in presenting the western past. I still am, as the new chapter in this second edition clearly reveals.

I wish to thank Kathleen Malone and also several editors at the University of Nebraska Press for encouraging the prep-aration of this second edition. I am also pleased to thank editors at the University of New Mexico Press and the University of Arizona Press for allowing me to utilize phrases and sentences from my previously published books for this volume. I am grateful, too, for my colleagues and students in western history for stimulating so much of my thinking and writing about the American West in the past twenty years and more.

Dick Etulain

Acknowledgments

In writing any such broad-gauged volume, authors accumulate many debts. We certainly have. From Michael Malone, special thanks to three fine professors and friends, Father William Bischoff, Elmo Richardson, and David Stratton, who introduced him to western history; to Earl Pomeroy, William Lang, and Richard Roeder for their helpful advice and professional friendship; and to Sue Bender, Diane Arnold, Patsy Culver, and JoAnn Amend for their exceptional assistance in preparing the manuscript. From Richard Etulain, special thanks go to Bob Woodward, Ed Bingham, and Earl Pomeroy, teachers and friends who introduced him to western history; to Jerry Nash, Frank Szasz, and Bob Swanson, colleagues, for their stimulating conversations about the modern West; to Pat Devejian for bringing order, so cheerfully and competently, to his scrambled prose; and to Karen Schwehn for reading galleys.

Together, we owe much to our friend and colleague Kenneth Owens, who helped us to design this project; it benefited considerably from his criticism and assistance. Finally, as the dedication indicates, we offer special thanks to our wives, Kathleen Malone and Joyce Etulain, for all their support over many years.

Introduction

THE 1890s:
A TURNING POINT IN WESTERN HISTORY?

When the young American Historical Association met in Chicago in 1893 as part of the World Columbian Exposition celebrating the discovery of the New World, little did that small gathering of historians realize that a paper presented to them would launch a new discovery of another kind. An exuberant young professor of history from the University of Wisconsin, Frederick Jackson Turner, read on that hot July 12 evening his momentous essay "The Significance of the Frontier in American History." Although the paper neither startled his audience that evening nor immediately stunned the historical profession, it did within a few years dramatically change the way historians looked at both the American past and the American West. Turner had, in fact, presented the most significant and influential interpretation yet advanced concerning American history and culture.

The "frontier thesis," or "Turner thesis" as it became known, frontally challenged established views of American civilization that pointed to European legacies as the most notable formative influences in American history. Turner asserted, to the contrary, that the American frontier—not European traditions—had done the most to spawn the democracy, individualism, and nationalism he saw and celebrated in American society. In one of the boldest sentences of

1

his pathbreaking essay, Turner exclaimed that "the existence of an area of free land, its continuous recession, and the advance of American settlement westward, explain American development." But, he added pessimistically, this frontier sweep across the continent had now come to an end, for the census of 1890 clearly indicated the closing of the frontier. A line of scattered settlements stretched across the previously open spaces of the interior West. The final sentence of Turner's essay stated the significance he saw in the frontier's passing: "And now, four centuries from the discovery of America, at the end of a hundred years of life under the Constitution, the frontier has gone, and with its going has closed the first period of American history."

For Turner, and for many other historians who followed him, the 1890s thus seemed a true watershed in time, the end of the great frontier and the beginning of a new era in which the United States would face an uncertain future without the bounties and the beneficial influences of its pioneer past. Looking back nostalgically, they saw several trends of the nineties, all of which seemed to signify the closing of an era.

The Indians of the West, for example, no longer roamed free. Instead, they now found themselves defeated and confined to forlorn reservations; and the newly enacted Dawes Act of 1887 called for their assimilation as farmers into the American mainstream. Cowboys and open-range stockmen similarly seemed headed for oblivion. Only shrinking stretches of open range remained by the close of the decade, as ranchers fenced off their limited ranges and raised and bought hay for winter feed and as new waves of homesteaders entered their domains. As for the farmers themselves, they too faced hard times in the depressed 1890s—severe droughts and low prices caused by world overproduction.

For others who harvested the bounties of western resources, the nineties also seemed a time of transition. That oldest of western industries, metal mining, experienced profound changes. Except for a few choice locales, such as Homestake, South Dakota, or Cripple Creek, Colorado, few high-grade gold deposits now remained. And the other key precious metal of the region, silver, had collapsed in the termination of federal silver purchases that came with the devastating Panic of 1893. In effect, precious-metal mining drastically declined as a primary regional industry during the 1890s. Henceforth, these metals would derive mainly from the extraction of what was now the key western metal, copper, from the mines of Arizona, Utah, Nevada, and Montana, mines that were by far outproducing those of America's previous copper kingdom, Michigan.

Like copper, big-time lumbering migrated westward from the upper Midwest during the years just before and after 1900, primarily from the cutover forests of the Great Lakes region to the pristine stands of the Pacific Coast running north from San Francisco Bay, reshaping the economy of the Far Northwest. In southern California and the Southwest, another immigrating industry, oil, brought even more dynamic waves of change, as the center of gravity of this burgeoning industry migrated westward from the Mid-Atlantic states to the raw postfrontier lands of Texas, Oklahoma, and California.

Politically, the turbulent 1890s seemed especially a time of drastic upheaval. The Panic of 1893 brought an abrupt end to the political calm of the 1880s and triggered sharp interregional confrontations between the industrial East and the underdeveloped South and West. In both the South and the West, the Populist party emerged as a genuinely radical vehicle of protest against an eastern-based capitalist exploitation carried westward by railroads, banks, and extractive corporations. Drawing their rank and file primarily from agriculture and mining, the western Populists demanded inflationary coinage of silver dollars, democratic reforms like the initiative, the referendum, and the popular election of U.S. senators, and more sweeping federal regulation of industry, even nationalization of railroads. They failed, beginning with the defeat of the Populist-Democratic presidential candidacy of Nebraska's William Jennings Bryan in 1896 at the hands of conservative Republican William McKinley. By 1901, the party was clearly headed for extinction.

3

Although usually less emphasized, shifting sociocultural patterns also seemed to signify the nineties as an era of transformation. Travelers to the West frequently pointed to newly sprouting western cities, especially inland rail centers and Pacific seaports, as signs of a changing West. They noted the increasing numbers of women and families as portents of advancing civilization and culture. And fiction about the region shifted directions too at the close of the nineteenth century, as the earlier local-color writings of Bret Harte, Joaquin Miller, and Mary Hallock Foote gave way to the realism of Hamlin Garland, Jack London, and Frank Norris.

Other, less specific or tangible indicators seemed as well to herald a portentous closing of the frontier. Beginning with the dime novels of the post–Civil War decades, the Buffalo Bill Wild West shows in the 1880s, and later with the first popular western novels (e.g., Owen Wister's *The Virginian*, 1902) and the first western films (*The Great Train Robbery*, 1903), Americans were inundated with countless renderings of popular culture dramatizing the end of the Old West.

Yet, to other observers over the years, the bonds of continuity between the West of the nineteenth century and the West of the twentieth century seemed more significant than did the departures. Just as the pioneer West had been a cosmopolitan meeting place of Indians, Hispanics, Asians, and Anglos, so too has been the modern West. Furthermore, if frontier Westerners relied heavily upon the federal government to provide them with inexpensive land, modes of transportation, and protection, twentieth-century westerners have proved equally solicitous of Uncle Sam for reclamation and freeway projects, defense installations, and many other federally funded enterprises.

Some events and trends of the 1890s that seemed, at first glance, to mark breaks with the past portended, on second glance, continuing traditions. For example, although the Populist party collapsed within a decade of its defeat in 1896, many of its key ideas and adherents reemerged later under the banners of western progressivism, the Nonpartisan League, the New Deal, and other political reform movements. Moreover, although homesteaders seemed to have claimed about all the arable lands the region had to offer by the 1890s, new technologies, land policies, and promotions resulted in the taking of more land under the Homestead acts during the twenty years after 1898 than during the thirty years before. Nor were the apparent breaks in western cultural traditions so sharp in the 1890s as contemporaries believed. The literary regionalism of the local-color writers blossomed again between the two world wars, and educational and religious trends of the early twentieth century were less truly innovative than they were extensions of late-nineteenth-century trends. Thus, Patricia Nelson Limerick makes a valid point in urging historians, "Deemphasize the frontier and its supposed end, conceive of the West as a place and not a process, and Western American history has a new look."

Clearly, the 1890s represented both a break with the pioneer past and a bridge of continuity between the old and new Wests. In fact, the blend of change and continuity that characterized the crossroads 1890s continued as a hallmark of the twentieth-century West. Viewed in broader context, the 1890s appear as a seam in the historical garment of the region, much as the expansionist 1840s and the New Deal–World War II years do as well. To contemporaries at the turn of the century, the nineties seemed a precipitous break with precedent. From the perspective of nearly a century later, that troubled decade appears to have been a key point of transition yet not unique—in truth, quite similar to the times of transition that had occurred a half-century earlier and that would occur again a half-century later.

THE MODERN WEST: A LOOK FORWARD

Looking backward in time offers a vertical perspective on the evolution of the modern West; equally important is the horizontal vantage, from which to view the West in its relationship to other American regions and to the world at large. Turner himself pioneered this approach with his essay "The

Significance of the Section in American History" (1925), which, although less heralded than his frontier thesis, offers a better paradigm for interpreting the West in the modern era. Like his younger contemporary, the gifted Texas historian Walter Prescott Webb (*The Great Plains*, 1931), Turner argued that the rich social, cultural, and political varieties of the United States and its history could be understood only by studying the continuities and differences of its great regions. Over time, the kaleidoscopic patterns of innovation and replication, of national conformity and regional distinction, have molded the American West into a fascinating land of many contours.

At the dawn of the new century, many if not most westerners believed they inhabited a region that was a de facto colony of the East. As producers of raw materials for eastern markets, as captive consumers of eastern manufactured products, as investors hungry for eastern capital, they believed their region to be what journalist-regionalist Bernard DeVoto called a "plundered province." Many political leaders of the West voiced these concerns, but they made little headway in alleviating them. How, after all, was the rest of the United States to be persuaded to take the region seriously when hosts of novels, movies, and other art forms were busily depicting it as a land of adventure and romance?

And yet, other happenings indicated that the West was in fact developing a distinct culture. Even as Oregonians named such towns as Portland, Salem, and Medford after New England cities, they also pioneered the Oregon System in politics, a system that profoundly influenced progressives across the country with its direct democracy. The rapid urbanization of Los Angeles, with its hundreds of thousands of automobiles and resulting networks of highways and later freeways, likewise seemed to herald a new way of national life. And between the world wars, historians Webb and James Malin, novelists Willa Cather and John Steinbeck, and artists John Steuart Curry and Peter Hurd portrayed the West as a region with a unique history and culture, different from those of other regions.

Meanwhile, the economy of the region underwent profound changes. During the period from 1900 to 1930, the West became more than ever before the nation's cornucopia of natural resources. The last great homestead rushes brought western agriculture to new heights of productivity; and, similarly, new technologies swelled outputs in the extractive oil, lumber, mining, and fishing industries. As a result, by the 1920s, the regional economy stagnated under heavy product surpluses and low prices, a problem that became a crisis with the advent of the Great Depression.

The years of depression, New Deal, and World War II, from 1930 to 1945, brought perhaps the most profound wave of change in the history of the West. First with the myriad of federal spending and regulatory programs of the New Deal and then with the massive defense spending programs of wartime, Uncle Sam remade the regional economy, breaking the old bonds of eastern colonialism and setting the West on a path toward parity with its sister regions to the east. During the years since the war, federal investments in science, defense, reclamation, highways, and many other endeavors continued to propel the West's industrialization and urbanization. By the 1970s, large expanses of the region, especially California, Texas, and the southwestern Sunbelt generally, had risen to the vanguard of the American socioeconomic order on a rising tide of federal expenditures, energy profits, and high-technology industries. The recession of the 1980s dampened this situation considerably, but it did not reverse it.

During the postwar years, the West similarly matured and diversified as a region in the realms of society and culture. California led the way, in both region and nation, pioneering in new suburban and youthful life-styles, in new informal clothing styles, in a fast-paced automobile culture based on ribbons of freeways, and in a state system of higher education that drew much admiration and imitation. Religious developments across the southern belt of the West, notably the growing numbers of Hispanic Catholics and a myriad of rising evangelical-fundamentalist groups, also

7

attracted nationwide attention. In a certain sense, as Walter Webb noted, the modern West evolved into the most cosmopolitan of American regions, the homeland of nearly all the country's Indians, most of its Hispanics and Asians, and rapidly rising numbers of blacks. Ethnic voices such as Native American writers N. Scott Momaday and Leslie Silko, Hispanic fictionalist Rudolfo Anaya and dramatist Luis Valdez, and Asian writers John Okada and Maxine Hong Kingston joined a diverse and growing number of other western writers and artists in producing a rich and impressive new regional culture.

Not all the subregions of the West, however, marched in unison through these colonial, regional, and postregional stages of western development. Indeed, the northern plains and Rockies and dry expanses of the Great Basin and interior Pacific Northwest remain largely unpopulated and tied to continuing dominant influences from outside their borders, sometimes as much to California, Texas, and other western power centers as to eastern and international cores of power. For every instance of yeasty sociocultural advancement in the West, there is a corresponding example of imitative and bland conformity.

Thus, the modern West blends pacesetting and imitative tendencies; it is a section or region of the United States that, at the same time, breaks *from* as well as adheres *to* the patterns of the nation at large. Most of all, the overriding feature of modern western history is a persistent barrage of change. More than any other American region, the West has been buffeted by a high velocity of social and economic change, in wave after wave. Time and again, just as western society seemed to be settling into stable regional patterns, a new shift in the world economy, a new cycle of federal activity, or a new wave of newcomers brought sudden disruptions, disruptions that thwarted western nurturings of a true regional identity and culture. In this sense, the land west of the ninety-eighth meridian is more notable for the diversity than for the homogeneity of its geographic, economic, social, and cultural landscapes.

PARAMETERS AND PURPOSES

Yet, the West is truly, in broad definition, a region with certain common characteristics. What are these characteristics that form the region that is the subject of this book? The West, as here defined, is the United States west of the ninety-eighth meridian, a line passing through the eastern Dakotas down the Great Plains through central Texas. Actually, this book will address the entirety of that tier of states embracing the ninety-eighth meridian, including their eastern portions, since state boundaries do not coincide with geographic boundaries and since it makes no sense to speak only of the western and less populous portions of those states, states that are truly a part of the West.

The significance of the ninety-eighth meridian is that it forms, generally speaking, the dividing line between the humid plains to the east and the increasingly arid plains to the west. And it is aridity, as historian Walter Webb so forcefully argued, that constitutes the most basic regional characteristic of the American West. Although the region has expanses of humid lands along its eastern and western peripheries—the green eastern zones of the Great Plains tier of states from North Dakota to Texas and the lush western reaches of the three Pacific Coast states—most of the West is dry, and water is the key factor to life and society. The West is, as Webb aptly said, an "oasis civilization."

Aridity as a core feature of western regionalism is one reason this volume does not group the noncontiguous "western" states of Alaska and Hawaii as part of the region. These states are not arid, nor do they exhibit another key factor of western regionalism: a commonly shared history. All of the West shared a frontier experience; in fact, the frontier did not end in a wave-like movement on the Pacific Coast but, rather, on the long-avoided western Great Plains and in the forbidding deserts of the interior Southwest. A primary aspect of the West's history as a region has been an exploitation of its resources and a relationship toward the East often spoken of as "colonialism." Some states, such as California,

Washington, or Texas, escaped the bonds of economic and political colonialism long ago. Others, such as Montana and Wyoming, still live in its shadow.

Still other bonds, related to these, serve to unite the West-as-region. Outside of Alaska, the West holds the great majority of federally owned lands in the United States; and this federal custodianship, which mandates a twin reliance on and resentment of Uncle Sam at the same time, underscores the truth that this region is and long has been more dependent on federal spending and management than are any of its sisters. In the realms of memory and mythology, the subregions of the West share a common attachment to the mystique of the "Wild" frontier past, with its romanticized cowboys, Indians, and other noble frontiersmen fighting out their struggles of good versus evil against a larger-than-life backdrop. In fact, this mystique, more than any other factor, has hindered coming to terms with the real past and present of this large part of the United States.

In the following pages, we attempt to move beyond the West-as-frontier, and beyond the West-as-wild too. In so doing, we also attempt to avoid the errors incumbent on a directly opposite approach, namely, interpreting the modern West simply by reading national trends and events into a regional application. For, just as much as it was during the frontier period of the nineteenth century, the modern West of the twentieth century is a dynamic and fascinating place, similar to yet different from other parts of the country—a place that cries out for the serious historical study that our many colleagues in the field are now directing to it. Drawing on their scholarship and support, we proceed.

Chapter One

The Emerging Postfrontier Economy, 1900-1930

T he closing of the frontier during the decades following 1890 brought with it an economic transition, away from the rampant exploitation of the
West's seemingly limitless resources and toward the modern, regulated economy that has developed during the past
half-century. During this key formative period, which ended
with the terrible depression of the 1930s, the western economy continued to stand fundamentally on agriculture and
on older extractive industries like mining and lumber, as
well as on newer extractive industries like oil and gas. As
the new century unfolded, the pluses and minuses of such
reliance became increasingly obvious. On the positive side,
the rise of a modern transportation network and the developing Industrial Revolution brought new technologies
and mechanization, which allowed the West to produce ever
greater bounties of wealth for the nation and the world, as
well as for itself. On the negative side, the region's exploitative economy, dedicated overwhelmingly to the production
of unfinished natural products, doomed it to a roller-coaster
cycle of booms and busts and a lingering "colonial" relationship to the financial and industrial capitals of the East. By
the 1920s, a decade of prosperity for most of the nation, the
postfrontier West found itself in a paradoxical position, the
victim of its own riches. All of its key industries—agricul-

ture, lumbering, mining, and petroleum—were drastically overproducing, which meant huge market surpluses, disastrously low prices, chronic recessions, and wasted resources. Westerners, even more than most Americans, would thus enter the modern era searching for methods of controlling production and of mastering their own destiny.

AGRICULTURE—THE CLIMACTIC YEARS

As the West entered the twentieth century, in most of its subregions agriculture remained very much the dominant livelihood and premier source of income. As agriculture went, so went the West. Thus, in part because agriculture set the regional pace and in part because agriculture reflected greater forces at work in the national and international spheres, the cyclical trends in the farm-ranch economy found accurate reflection in the overall economy as well: unprecedented prosperity during the years up to and through World War I (1900–1918), a sharp recession after the war, hard times melding into an interval of prosperity during the 1920s, and then the cataclysm of the Great Depression.

As the nation began to recover, just before the turn of the century, from the deadening effects of the Panic of 1893, American agriculture entered the greatest period of sustained prosperity in its history. With expanding national and international markets, commodity prices soared, luring farmers and ranchers out onto the last remaining open spaces of the West. In addition to good markets and prices, a number of other factors worked to produce this result. These were, generally speaking, years of abundant rainfall. From 1899 through 1916, for instance, North Dakota precipitation registered above average in all but three years. Along with other promoters, western railroads, eager to populate their routes with more consumers, promoted their domains with unprecedented enthusiasm. New and hardier plant varieties, like hard spring wheat from northern and eastern Europe, and heavier and sturdier crossbred cattle were introduced to the plains and other arid regions of the West. Two factors,

A four-horse binder
cutting grain near
Dallas, South Dakota,
1908. Courtesy of the
Wyoming State Ar-
chives, Museums and
Historical Department.

especially, joined to set off this last and greatest surge of
the farming frontier: a new system of mechanized "dryland
farming" and new forms of federal support.

The keys to dry farming lay in conserving moisture in
the soil through deep plowing, which served to draw up
precious water, in compacting the surface to hold down
evaporation, and in intensive cultivation, which similarly
retarded moisture loss by forming a dust mulch. Among
many apostles of the new agriculture, the most renowned
was Hardy Campbell of South Dakota, who had by 1902
won railroad support to publicize his "Campbell System."
Dry farming required large acreages, since crop yields per
acre were low in the arid regions. It also required new machinery to work these larger acreages. American farm implement manufacturers, particularly J. P. Morgan's new International Harvester trust, rose to the occasion, mass-producing
an array of new machines at lowering prices: cumbersome,
steam-driven threshers and tractors, large grain drills for

seeding, harrows and discs to work the hard ground, and headers and binders to cut the crops.

Uncle Sam also contributed to the promotion of the rush to the dry lands with two generous new homestead laws. In 1909, Congress enacted the Enlarged Homestead Act, which doubled the size of the initial homestead grants to a half-section (320 acres) in certain designated semiarid states; and in 1912, it added a further benefit by reducing the "prove-up" time from five to three years for securing full ownership. The lawmakers contributed another bonanza in 1916 with passage of the Stock Raising Homestead Act, which granted homesteads of a full 640-acre section in those marginal areas deemed suitable for no better use than mere grazing. This law proved highly valuable to western stockmen, as they continued their conversion from open- to closed-range operations in which they no longer had access to public lands. To down-on-their-luck farmers "back East," struggling to scratch out a living on a forty-acre wetland farm, these huge, nearly free homesteads out West seemed heaven-sent, even if the lands were parched.

And so, for all these reasons, the last great American land-taking began with the new century, as the farmers' final frontier surged beyond the ninety-eighth meridian—long considered the westernmost limit of adequate rainfall—out onto the high and dry Great Plains sloping upward toward the Rockies. Ranchers watched in amazement as lands deemed usable only for grazing fell before the plow, then joined in themselves by taking up farming and the selling of real estate. During each of the peak years between 1902 and 1910, more than ninety-eight thousand homesteaders filed original entries; and in the latter year, a record eighteen million acres were filed on. In all, as Robert Athearn notes in *The Mythic West*, during "the first two decades of the twentieth century, more lands were taken up under the Homestead Act than all that had been disposed of in the nineteenth century." And, it must be remembered, farmers purchased millions of acres more from railroads and other realtors.

The homesteaders flocked to many subregions of the interior West, but the dry western Great Plains saw the greatest activity. By 1910, agriculture had surpassed mining as Montana's foremost industry; the state's population more than doubled between 1900 and 1920, mainly because of the invasion of its northern and eastern plains expanses by "honyockers," as the homesteaders were called there. Kansas gained roughly three hundred thousand inhabitants during these years, even as many of its eastern counties declined in population due to the rush of farmers to the new wheatlands of the West. Nebraska witnessed the same phenomenon: a net gain of 230,000 population as the eastern corn region sagged while the so-called Kinkaiders—named after the congressman who championed local homestead legislation—flocked to the drylands of the West. On the plains of West Texas, similarly, trainloads of speculators and realtors were on the scene by 1908, buying up farmlands for twelve to twenty-two dollars per acre. Inexorably, the winter wheat belt, anchored by credit and rail lines to Kansas City, spread across western Kansas, Oklahoma, and eastern Colorado, reaching south into the Texas panhandle.

Meanwhile, as the federal government promoted dryland farming, mainly on the semiarid plains, it also subsidized another agricultural program more important to the Southwest—reclamation. Even in prehistoric times, the Indians of this region had irrigated croplands, and in the 1840s the Mormons began large-scale irrigation in the Great Basin. By 1880, a million acres of western lands received some sort of irrigated watering, most of it by simple diversion and all of it by private investment. Clearly, however, major efforts at reclamation would require massive investments in dams and canal systems, and this in turn would necessitate state assistance.

Serious federal interest in reclamation began with the publication in 1878 of John Wesley Powell's *Report on the Lands of the Arid Region of the United States*. Powell, a zealous and in many ways prophetic reformer, called for the development of the West's irrigable lands and won creation of the U.S. Geological Survey, which he directed for thirteen years. Moved by Powell and other apostles, such as William Smythe, proponents of western reclamation formed the Irrigation Congress in 1891 and began issuing a journal, *Irrigation Age*. In 1894, they achieved a first, fleeting victory when Wyoming Senator Joseph Carey pushed through Congress the Carey Act, which offered to each arid state or territory up to one million acres of land if it presented a workable program for developing reclamation. Except in Wyoming, where imaginative state engineer Elwood Mead made it work, the Carey Act had little effect. The state governments simply lacked the resources to tackle the problem.

The reclamationists now focused their efforts directly on the federal government, winning the support of both political parties and of President Theodore Roosevelt. In 1902 they secured from Congress the landmark Newlands Reclamation Act, sponsored by Nevada Representative Francis Newlands and North Dakota Senator Henry Hansbrough. The Newlands Act provided for direct federal construction of reclamation projects, with funding derived in part from the sale of arid and reclaimed lands. The irrigated lands would be reserved for real "family" farmers, not for corporations. To do the work, Congress created an agency destined to become a bulwark of the West, the Reclamation Service (Bureau) within the Department of the Interior, under Powell's able protégé Frederick Newell.

Originating some projects and taking over others already begun, the Reclamation Bureau immediately made its presence felt throughout the arid West. The foremost of its early ventures included the great Roosevelt Dam on Arizona's Salt River, which dispatched water through the forty-mile Arizona Canal to develop the Phoenix area; the Arrowrock Dam near Boise, which underwrote the rise of irrigation in southern Idaho; the Imperial Dam on the Colorado, diverting water to California's Imperial and Coachella valleys; Elephant Butte Dam on the Rio Grande; and the Truckee-Carson Project in Nevada. As the years passed, the Bureau of Reclamation evolved into a mainspring of western development. Western representatives in Congress soon learned to trade their votes on issues near and dear to other regions in return for federal appropriations for their pet reclamation projects. By the 1920s, these large projects tended more and more toward "multiple use," that is, toward flood control, the generation of electricity, and interstate agreements for the allocation of water, like the Colorado River Compact of 1922, as well as simply for providing water for irrigation.

Like oases in the desert, reclamation districts blossomed to transform much of the arid West: green swaths of irrigated haylands along narrow Rocky Mountain river valleys, potato and vegetable crops along the broad Snake River Plain in Idaho, apple and cherry orchards in the Yakima Valley of central Washington, vast acreages of sugar beets in Colorado and Utah, orange and grapefruit groves in the Rio Grande Valley, and expanding fields of citrus crops, cotton, and alfalfa across the breadth of New Mexico, Arizona, and southern California. In West Texas, irrigation combined with the advent of power-driven machinery to extend the cotton kingdom far out into the arid regions. As a result, Texas became the nation's leading cotton producer, with its eastern humid lands part of the Old South cotton empire, based on black labor, and its new west the salient of a new kind of cotton agriculture. By 1910, cotton grew on roughly one-half of all the cultivated acres in the state.

Reclamation and water development seemed the way of the future for much of the West, and few critics emerged in those early years to question such expenditures or environmental dangers. In hindsight, however, portents of trouble did exist. For example, Los Angeles developers led by Fred Eaton and the brilliant William Mulholland seriously compromised the young Reclamation Service by successfully campaigning to divert the waters of the Owens River to underwrite their city's growth and to feed their investments in the parched San Fernando Valley. This episode, as much as the great new dams and canals, signaled the way of the future in western water development.

The big agricultural boom, of both dryland and reclamation farming, soared to greater heights with the outbreak of World War I in 1914—which soon drove up world commodity prices—and soared even higher with American entry into the war in 1917. Desperate to feed and clothe its own armies and those of its allies, the administration of President Woodrow Wilson formed the federal Food Administration in 1917, ably managed by Herbert Hoover and endowed with sweeping new powers. The Food Administration propagandized the public that it was their patriotic duty to eat sparingly and lectured U.S. farmers and ranchers that it was their patriotic duty to produce to the utmost. The agency featured the slogan "Food Will Win the War!" In fact, Hoover offered agriculturists more than sermons: the Food Administration guaranteed basic prices for all prime commodities, for instance a handsome $2.20 per bushel for wheat. Even then, farmers complained that, with high wartime demands, a free market would have paid them more.

The great wartime boom, with its huge export markets and artificially high prices, climaxed the three-century frontier expansion of American agriculture. Total numbers of U.S. farmers and ranchers reached their zenith at this time. Gambling on several years of war at high profits and taking advantage of easy credit, agriculturalists took out mortgages and more mortgages, going far into debt. For a time, they prospered spectacularly. Between 1914 and 1918, their net profits in constant dollars more than doubled, from $4 to $10 billion annually. The frenzied boom affected all the West, but the newly settled areas most of all. During the five years after 1914, the nation's wheatlands increased by twenty-seven million acres, over half of them on the central and northern plains. The rural West had never known such prosperity before. Nebraskans, for instance, purchased $240 million in war bonds, more per capita than any other state's citizenry—a measure of their prosperity as well as of their patriotism.

And then, suddenly, it ended. The war closed abruptly, with Germany's collapse, in November 1918, much sooner than anticipated; and within a year came the closing of the bonanza export markets and the fall of the sky-high farm prices. From 1919 through 1921, U.S. farm prices fell by 40 percent, and the boom descended into a deep agricultural depression. Droughts, dust storms, and locust invasions, resulting in part from the intensive cultivation promoted by the dry farming advocates, compounded the misery. Wheat prices plummeted from over $2.20 per bushel in 1919 to $1.01 in 1921, cotton from thirty-seven cents a pound in 1920 to fourteen cents a year later. Many farmers could not make their mortgage and tax payments and lost everything. North Dakota and Montana were hardest hit. Over half the banks in each state failed during 1919–26. At least seventy-five thousand North Dakotans departed, and Montana lost approximately the same number.

This post–World War I depression marks a major turning point in the history of American agriculture and of the West. With the collapse of this last and greatest of land booms, the West witnessed the real, final closing of the frontier and the dawn of a new era. The 1920s, a period of vaunted prosperity for most of the nation, were a time of stark depression and fundamental upheaval for the agrarian West. A long-term trend began, as hundreds of thousands of dryland farmers, lured onto impossibly small landholdings, failed and fled. After peaking in 1917–18, America's farm population began to decline: 31,393,000 in 1920, 30,216,000 in 1940, 23,077,000 in 1950. As the farmers left, the small towns supporting them also dwindled; and the 1920 census revealed for the first time an urban majority in the nation.

Those farmers and ranchers who stayed on the land had to make hard adjustments. They had to buy or lease more land to acquire enough to achieve workable units, and they needed to secure more capital to buy both the land and the sophisticated new machinery to work it. To succeed, the farmer by now clearly had to mechanize for cost efficiency. In 1915, only 25,000 trucks existed on American farms; by 1945, there were 1,490,000. By 1930, 58 percent of U.S. farmers owned cars. Lightweight, internally geared "Fordson" tractors came into general use during the 1920s; and their low cost, mobility, and pulling power made them very

Steam plow breaking the prairie near Douglas, Wyoming, 1910. Courtesy of the Wyoming State Archives, Museums and Historical Department.

popular. By the close of the decade, these and other tractors were beginning to pull mobile wheat combines and corn and cotton pickers. Farmers could now retire their horses and mules. As they did, the croplands that had grown forage for the animals were sown with crops for market, adding to what was clearly becoming the nation's number one farm problem—overproduction and low prices.

Thus the twenties initiated the modern profile of the agricultural West: fewer farmers and ranchers, fewer but larger and more highly mechanized farms, chronic overproduction, and resultant low prices. Bewildered and angry at the abrupt failure of their prosperity, the farm population once more lashed out, as they had back in the 1890s. They flocked into new organizations, like the militant Farmers Union of smaller operators or the more conservative and businesslike American Farm Bureau Federation. Their congressional representatives, led by Kansas Senator Arthur Capper, formed a determined "Farm Bloc" to press for governmental relief. The Farm Bloc had some successes. Twice it even engineered passage of the controversial McNary-Haugen bills, which aimed at easing the crop surpluses by dumping them on foreign markets. But President Calvin Coolidge vetoed the measures each time. The western agricultural community was learning a hard lesson. Even as they won some concessions, their political influence eroded with their eroding numbers, and businessmen gained greater control of government.

In one final sense, the postwar collapse of agriculture also signaled the close of the frontier. By now, the modern taxonomy of western agriculture was clearly discernible. Along the easternmost periphery of the "West," thrusting out onto the Great Plains up to the rainfall line of the ninety-eighth to one hundredth meridians, southern and midwestern forms of humid area, intensive agriculture prevailed. In Texas, the southern cotton belt, with its heavily black labor force, spread westward across the fertile bottomlands of the Sabine, Trinity, and Brazos rivers. On the central plains, the midwestern "Corn-Hog Belt" spanned the Iowa-Missouri line into eastern South Dakota, Nebraska, and Kansas. To the feedlots of this region came the range cattle of the western plains and mountains for finishing. In the far north, in the broad and fertile Red River Valley of eastern North Dakota–western Minnesota, lay one of the richest and most densely settled granaries of the world.

Moving westward into the semiarid Great Plains and mountain foothills, one entered the fabled heartland of the agrarian West, a region of dryland cereal crops and livestock production. By the 1920s, Kansas and North Dakota ranked as America's foremost wheat states, producing one-fourth to one-third of the nation's crop between them. Large herds of cattle, now fenced in and hay-fed during winters, ranged the entire expanse of the region. Cattlemen dominated whole subregions of the plains, like western South Dakota, the Sandhills of Nebraska, and the Flint Hills of Kansas; but the quintessential cattle state was Texas, which grazed 6.6 million head in 1930, fully one-tenth of all cattle in the United States.

Grazing also predominated in the more marginal agricultural economy of the Rocky Mountain region. Here, typically, cattle and sheep ranchers owned irrigable hay and grazing lands in the valleys and bought or leased mountain uplands for summer grazing. Scattered, large-scale farming produced wheat and barley; but in truth, farm-ranch units here were few and far between after the failed homesteading experiment: by 1930, there were fewer than two hundred thousand in the five-state region of Montana, Idaho, Wyoming, Colorado, and New Mexico.

Farther west, on the parched plateaus and deserts lying between the Rockies and the Cascades-Sierras, agriculture seemed a study in contrasts. Expanding reclamation projects made certain areas, like the cotton-fruit-hay lands of Arizona's Salt and Gila valleys or the vegetable-hay lands of Idaho's upper Snake River Plain, rich and verdant. More commonly, though, sheep and cattle cropped the scablands of the deserts. Here and there—most notably in the remarkably fertile volcanic hills of the Palouse and lower Snake River basins—farmers produced in such abundance that Washington came to rank as one of the nation's leading wheat states.

In the lush valleys of the Pacific coastal states, farmers produced a wide variety of grain, fruit, and vegetable crops, as well as dairy and meat products. Oregon's Willamette Valley ranked as one of America's richest farming locales. In California, the dry and broad Central Valley experienced a transition of signal importance to region and nation. During the 1920s, with increasing irrigation, wheat rapidly gave way to cotton; and the valley gradually became America's greatest fruit-vegetable producer. By 1930, California supplied the nation with three-fourths of its oranges, one-seventh of its grapefruits, and vast tonnages of other fruits, nuts, vegetables, and wines. It ranked, by this time, second only to

Texas among the forty-eight states in the value of its agricultural products. Soon it would rank first.

Such were the strengths and weaknesses, the incredibly broad margins, of western agriculture. By 1900, the Northeast and Mid-Atlantic regions had already found themselves unable to compete with the West for national markets in staple crops. Now, by the late 1920s, the opening of new croplands and the watering of others with federal subsidies further tilted the scales of agricultural production westward.

EXTRACTIVE INDUSTRIES

The West's basic extractive industries resembled its agriculture in that, with the revolutionary application of new technologies, they surged in productivity during the first two decades of the twentieth century and then faced serious problems of overproduction and low prices by the 1920s. In that oldest of the region's extractive industries, metal mining, the earlier focus on highly valuable precious metals—gold and silver—increasingly gave way to an emphasis on the industrially important base metal, copper.

In the wake of the Panic of 1893, precious metals faced a dreary future: the best high-grade veins had, for the most part, been mined out, and silver had lost its primary market when the federal government stopped coining silver dollars. At select locations, precious metal mines still worked on a large scale, as at the Homestake gold district in the Black Hills, the Coeur d'Alene silver district in north Idaho, the Cripple Creek, Colorado, and Mercur, Utah, gold operations, or the new, post-1900 Nevada boomtowns of Tonopah and Goldfield. The cyanide process of gold extraction now made lower-grade ores profitable to work; and in California and elsewhere, mining outfits continued to extract surface gold by such environmentally disastrous methods as blasting away stream banks with large hydraulic hoses and digging up stream beds with floating dredges.

In 1899, Henry Rogers of Standard Oil and other mil-

lionaire speculators formed the American Smelting and Refining Company in an effort to merge the West's silver-lead
smelters into one great "super-trust." They soon lost control
of ASARCO to the powerful family of Meyer Guggenheim
and his seven sons, who had started out in Colorado and
Mexico. The Guggenheims prospered, extracting metals fortunes from Alaska to Latin America; but ASARCO never succeeded in monopolizing this increasingly marginal industry.

Western copper came to command U.S. and world markets during the 1890s in the wake of the Butte, Montana,
district's ascendancy over the formerly dominant Michigan
mines. As the "red metal" expanded in usage with the rising
electrical and telephone industries, first Montana, dominated
by the Anaconda Copper Mining Company, and then Arizona, led by Phelps Dodge, boomed as copper provinces.
In 1899, the diabolical Rogers of Standard Oil and others
who were collaborating in the founding of ASARCO formed
the Butte-based Amalgamated Copper Company in a similar
effort to corner the production of this metal. However, the
Rogers group got into a nasty political fight with independent Butte operators W. A. Clark and F. Augustus Heinze;
and though Amalgamated Copper (later reverting to Anaconda again) did gain control of the Butte district, it failed
to corner the American copper market.

The main explanation for Amalgamated's failure to become the U.S. Steel of copper lay in new technologies, which
so inflated production that no one firm could control it. The
use of electricity made mining machinery, both above and
below ground, much more efficient. And whereas the concentration of copper ores by the new "flotation" method of
releasing them in oil vats made it much easier and cheaper
to reduce lower-grade ores, so did the application of elec-
trolysis to refining simplify the process of removing the final
impurities from smelted copper.

By far the most important innovations took place at the
old Bingham Canyon mining district, near Salt Lake City.
Here, a dynamic group of engineers and investors led by
Daniel Jackling formed the Utah Copper Company and in

The giant Bingham Canyon copper mine in the Oquirrh Mountains of Utah. Courtesy of the Utah State Historical Society.

1903–4 proved a dramatic new way of mining very low grade (as low as 1 percent, or even less) ores. Employing giant steamshovels to dig and rails to haul the ore, and erecting giant concentrators and smelters to reduce it, Jackling demonstrated that huge amounts of previously worthless low-grade ores could be mined profitably in open pits. Bingham Canyon prospered and grew into what John D. Rockefeller once called "the greatest industrial sight on Earth." The Guggenheims gained mounting control over Utah copper, and in 1915 they pulled it into their Alaska-born Kennecott Copper Company.

Open-pit mining clearly represented the wave of the future, and though labor-intensive tunnel mines continued to deepen where rich veins prevailed, pit mining spread rapidly across the interior West. The new methods paid off in a similar fashion at the nearby Robinson District of eastern Nevada, which rejuvenated the town of Ely and also came under the tutelage of Kennecott Copper; at the old Santa Rita, New Mexico, site; at Ray, Miami, Ajo, Bisbee, and Clifton-Morenci, Arizona. By 1907, the deep mines of Butte had lost their preeminence as Arizona, with its many mining centers, became the nation's copper leader. Soon Utah too surpassed Montana to occupy the number two position.

The extent to which copper now dominated the glamorous old precious metals can be seen in two interesting facts. For many years, Bingham Canyon ranked as America's second-greatest gold mine, behind the Homestake; and Anaconda similarly ranked number two in silver, behind the Coeur d'Alenes. Copper, in other words, reigned supreme, and the precious metals faded in importance to become in large part by-products of copper operations. Mining of all kinds boomed during World War I. With a government-guaranteed price of twenty-three cents per pound, the copper industry paid huge dividends during the war, even despite angry confrontations with labor. After the war, though, the copper miners, like the farmers, faced glutted markets and low prices, due especially to portentous, cheap imports from new mines in South America and Africa. As the price of their product fell toward a disastrous five cents per pound, they too fretted about the future of their uncontrolled industry.

Another extractive industry, lumber, also underwent revolutionary changes at the turn of the century. Commercial timbering dated from fur trade and gold rush days, and some early firms like Pope & Talbot and A. M. Simpson Company grew into West Coast powers. In the lush pine, fir, spruce, cedar, and tamarack forests of the western coastal states, and in the less valuable pine and fir stands of the Rockies, frontier lumbering grew up in conjunction with industrial mining and the railroads. Even after the railroads opened midwestern and eastern markets, western lumbermen operated in the shadow of the dominant lumber industry of the Great Lakes region. Their operations were wasteful in the familiar frontier manner: employing the "cut-out-and-get-out" approach, building dams to gorge the logs downstream on floodwaters, exploiting and endangering vulnerable employees in wretched work camps.

The big change began in the 1890s. With the depletion of the splendid forests of the upper Midwest, the established Great Lakes lumbermen began migrating toward the perennial, hardwood forests of the South and the humid, evergreen timberlands of the Pacific Northwest and California. Southern lumbering, featuring black labor, already ranked as a major industry in the piney woods of East Texas by 1899, when mills centered at Orange and Beaumont first surpassed the billion-board-feet-per-year total. Texas rose to sixth rank among lumber states; and its giant Kirby Lumber Company, formed in 1901, became the state's first multimillion-dollar corporation. In 1907, Texas lumber output crested at 2.5 billion board feet and then declined with depleted woodlands, but the state continued to rank among the top national producers.

In January of 1900, the American lumber industry moved dramatically westward with the announcement that a syndicate of midwestern investors led by Jim Hill's Minnesota friend Frederick Weyerhaeuser had purchased 900,000 acres of prime western Washington woodlands from the Northern Pacific Railroad, forming the Weyerhaeuser Timber Company. The Weyerhaeuser group continued buying timberlands and forming new companies, such as Potlatch Lumber in north Idaho. By 1914, it owned 26 percent of Washington's privately held timber stands. Together with the Northern Pacific, Weyerhaeuser owned nearly half of that state's privately possessed standing timber; and together with the Southern Pacific, nearly one-fourth that in Oregon.

By 1905, Washington ranked as the number one lumber state in the nation. Oregon, whose magnificent southwestern pine forests drew increasing attention, came to rank second, and eventually first. California, with its stupendous redwood groves and fully 15 percent of U.S. forestlands, climbed to third place. By 1940, these three states yielded 40 percent of total American lumber production. In the Pacific Northwest, the lumber industry now rivaled agriculture as the primary

27

Lumbermen in a forest of western Washington State. Courtesy of The Huntington Library, San Marino, California.

economic mainstay of the region, responsible for 55 percent of its payrolls and 38 percent of total manufactured values by 1914.

The industry evolved rapidly. Power saws and steam donkeys quickened the efficiency of cutting and yarding timber. First spur rail lines and then trucks made it easier to penetrate the remote backwoods and to operate throughout most of the year. Giant, mechanized mills sawed and planed wood for markets throughout the country. Meanwhile, to the anger of regional boosters but usually to the satisfaction of the big operators, the federal government withdrew millions upon millions of woodland acres into national forests (see below, pp. 67–69), in effect raising the values of the acreages in private hands. The lumber industry prospered during World War I. Following a brief downturn afterwards, it continued to thrive with the big building boom of the 1920s, which lasted until 1926.

By the 1920s, this industry too began to display its modern profile. Western lumbermen, previously among the most wasteful of environmental exploiters, now began salvaging their waste products in the interest simply of widening profit margins. They built pulp mills to process former wastage into paper, manufactured new and cheaper wood products like plywood and fiberboard, even extracted chemicals like formaldehyde. In the language of the business, the lumber industry was evolving into a true "wood products" industry.

Two threats of catastrophic wastefulness, meanwhile, continued to haunt both lumbermen and environmentalists: forest fires and the specter of logged-out and ruined timberlands. Only the hideous dust storms of the 1930s ever rivaled early-day forest fires as environmental disasters. In September 1902, the Oregon City–Tillamook fire incinerated several towns and thirty-five people, immolating over two billion board feet of timber. In the late summer of 1910, an awesome fire whipped by gale winds laid waste to the northern Idaho–western Montana border country, burning over 3.3 million acres and killing more than eighty-five people. The fear of these infernos, as we shall see, did much to convince westerners of the need for federal controls.

The threat of depletion, and the final realization that no more frontiers of virgin lands awaited them, caused lumbermen, federal and state authorities, and thoughtful conservationists to abandon the old ways and to begin treating private and government-owned timber stands as renewable resources—in other words, as agricultural crops. Led by farsighted individuals like lumber consultant David Mason, George Long of Weyerhaeuser Timber, and William Greeley of the West Coast Lumbermen's Association, the Pacific Coast industry pioneered the concept of what came to be known as "sustained-yield forestry" during the late 1920s. By replanting as they harvested, the leaders of this previously most wasteful of frontier industries led the way, ironically, in developing an intelligent use of natural resources that planned for the future.

The Pacific Northwest stood at the forefront of another extractive industry that also harvested a renewable resource, fishing. On the mighty Columbia River, the remarkable salmon runs early attracted a fishing and canning industry, by 1881 producing an annual 530,000 cases valued at $2.6 million. Robert Hume, the "salmon king of Oregon," dominated the enterprise and extended his realm to other rivers of the region; low-paid Chinese workers prevailed in the canneries until "iron chink" canning machines displaced them after 1903. With the new century, Puget Sound fisheries rose rapidly to supersede those on the Columbia; and by 1908, Washington ranked fourth in the nation, behind three Atlantic states, in the value of its fish products. The Puget Sound fishermen harvested not only salmon but also a rich variety of oysters, crabs, and clams. As Atlantic yields of halibut declined, fishermen steamed far into the North Pacific in pursuit of that fish as well.

Texas also developed an important and diversified Gulf Coast fishing industry, operating out of ports like Galveston and Corpus Christi, and so did California. The Californians caught and marketed a wide range of seafood, but the most important fish were tuna and sardines. By World War I, the annual harvest of each stood at over two hundred million pounds. The 1920s found this enterprise in a situation similar to that faced by mining and lumber: disastrously low prices due to overproduction and the threat of squandering its resources to the point of exhaustion. By 1929, for instance, California's world-leading sardine harvest, at three hundred million pounds per year, had so sated the market that sardines were being ground up for fertilizer; and tuna fishermen worried about dangerously declining fish populations. Throughout the decade, Americans and Canadians led in the calling of international conventions to limit Pacific catches and to preserve the fish populations of river and sea.

Just as agriculture transformed the economy of the western plains, mining that of the interior West, and lumber that of the Pacific Coast, so did that most dynamic of the new extractive industries, petroleum, transfigure the Southwest. Since the opening of the first important Pennsylvania wells before the Civil War, oil had risen steadily in commercial importance, mainly in the form of petroleum for illumination but increasingly also as fuel and lubricants for the new

The "iron chink," or Smith Butchering Machine, initially installed at the Pacific American Fisheries Cannery, Fairhaven, Washington, in 1903. Courtesy of the Whatcom Museum of History and Art, Bellingham, Washington.

motor vehicles. Even by the 1880s, John D. Rockefeller's feared and reviled Standard Oil Company dominated the key oil states of Pennsylvania, Ohio, and West Virginia and was consolidating its monopolistic hold on the entire industry.

Out West, naturally enough, oil development came later. Westerners had made some usage of oil ever since Spaniards had applied it for waterproofing and early-day wagoneers had skimmed it from surface pools to lubricate their axles. Southern California led the way in major commercial drilling and refining. Union Oil of California, a sizable concern, took shape in 1890; and in 1892, the calloused frontier promoter Edward Doheny made his landmark strike right in Los Angeles, where within three years an ugly strip two miles long by six hundred feet wide was belching up seven hundred thousand barrels yearly. More booms followed in rapid succession in Los Angeles, the San Joaquin Valley, the Santa Barbara area, and elsewhere.

31

The Spindletop oil field in 1903. Photo by Fred A. Schell, courtesy of the American Petroleum Institute.

Oil refining surged to become California's chief manufacturing industry; and San Pedro Harbor in Los Angeles, newly dredged with federal aid, emerged as one of the world's foremost oil ports. Sensing the threat that this Pacific Rim oil posed to his monopoly, Rockefeller moved in quickly, buying out local developer Demetrius Schofield and forming Standard Oil of California (SoCal) as the West Coast arm of his empire. Standard of California towered over the coastal oil industry and continued to grow as a fully integrated corporation.

The great western threat to Standard Oil's monopoly came not from California, however, but from Texas, a state that the Rockefeller behemoth had earlier avoided because of its tough antitrust policies. Following an initial oil excitement at Corsicana in 1894, the big boom that changed everything came in January 1901 at Spindletop, a forlorn salt dome near Beaumont on the East Texas Gulf Coast. For six remarkable days, Anthony Lucas's derrick spouted a black geyser that signaled a new day in the world oil industry. In a remarkable frenzy, developers jammed rigs nearly atop one another, and land in the field sold for up to $900,000 an acre. Spindletop produced over twelve million barrels of oil in 1902, nearly one-fourth of U.S. output; and new fields nearby—Humble, Sour Lake, and Goose Creek—shot total Texas yields to over twenty-eight million barrels in 1905. The neighboring cities of Houston, Beaumont, Port Arthur, and Baytown boomed to become the mid-American center of oil finance, oil equipment manufacture, and also oil exporting when improvements in the Houston ship channel allowed heavy vessels to move inland from the Gulf.

Spindletop shook the American oil industry to its foundations. Lucas had obtained financial backing from the powerful Mellon family of Pittsburgh, whom Standard Oil had, ironically, earlier forced out of Pennsylvania oil. Now the Mellons formed Gulf Oil in 1901 and took over a large part of the Texas trade. Other major firms also emerged to dominate the Houston-Beaumont complex, such as Joseph Cullinan and Arnold Schlaet's Texas Company (Texaco), which captured an impressive 5 percent of the market and built a towering thirteen-story headquarters in Houston. Two other major companies, both formed in 1911, would likewise play major roles on the American energy scene: Humble Oil and Magnolia Petroleum. As D. W. Meinig comments in *Imperial Texas*, oil "proved to be a prodigious economic multiplier for Texas," producing gigantic reserves of local capital that would be reinvested to yield future bonanzas.

The flood of western oil swamped the national industry, and as the use of motorcars spread, gasoline refineries pouring out cheap fuel underwrote a new way of life for Americans. No longer could the Standard Oil monopoly, based mainly on eastern oil, control the market. In 1900, the trans-Mississippi West produced only 9 percent of U.S. petroleum; by 1911, it produced a whopping 72 percent. In the latter year, the U.S. Supreme Court broke up the Standard Oil monopoly into independent parts, one of which was Standard of California. But even before that, the new western fields had shattered forever Standard's hold on the marketplace.

By 1911, the top six U.S. oil states included three in the West: Texas, California, and Oklahoma. Soon, all three would stand at the top. Oklahoma's experience closely followed that of neighboring Texas. Here, the first commercial well came in at Bartlesville in 1897, followed by a sweep of others across Indian Territory. By 1907, as statehood approached, Indian Territory boasted 255 producing wells. A colorful group of independent "wildcatters" built the Oklahoma oil business: the rapacious Harry Sinclair; the eccentric J. Paul Getty, who would one day become the world's richest man; the future governor E. W. Marland; the boy-wonder Thomas Slick; the three Phillips brothers, Frank, Lee, and Waite; and the mixed-blood Creek Tom Gilcrease, who opened the shallow and sensational Glenn Pool near Tulsa.

Standard Oil moved into Oklahoma with its Prairie Oil and Gas Company, which captured the Glenn Pool and helped to build Tulsa into a major center of oil finance and development. Meanwhile, new fields like those at Cushing and Healdton continued to fuel the big Oklahoma excitement. And here, as in Texas, natural gas, which had at first been wasted as a troublesome nuisance, was now captured and marketed via pipelines for home and business heating. Between 1908 and 1915, Oklahoma's oil and gas fields nearly tripled, and so did its refining capacity. Like their brethren to the south, the new state's oilmen also seized control of more than their share of the political establishment.

On a lesser scale, the oil and gas industry moved into other western states too. The Midcontinental Field, which underlay Oklahoma, extended northward into southern Kansas, where an oil boom, based on such big fields as those at Independence, Chanute, and Butler County, paralleled those to the south. Standard Oil moved north to Kansas with its Prairie Oil and Gas and Forest Oil subsidiaries and built a major refining complex at Neodesha. Lightly populated Wyoming sprouted an oil industry that, relative to its tiny population, influenced the state's development at least as much as did the oil industries of its larger sisters. The main action occurred at Salt Creek in central Wyoming, and nearby Casper emerged as the primary refining center. By World War I, Wyoming claimed twenty-three fields and five refineries and produced annually over twelve million barrels of oil.

The petroleum industry continued its spectacular growth with inflated wartime prices of $3.50 per barrel for crude oil and then with the rising demand for gasoline caused by the rapid increase in car traffic during the 1920s. A wave of new discoveries across the West not only met the escalating demand for oil but actually exceeded it. During the 1920s, California saw a succession of rich new strikes, mainly SoCal's at Huntington Beach, Union Oil's near Whittier, and Shell Oil's at Long Beach. By 1923, these three new fields yielded almost three-fourths of the 263 million barrels produced yearly by the state. Major new discoveries also occurred in Oklahoma, most colorfully the Greater Seminole Field, which sprawled across five counties, and the big boom at Oklahoma City, which sprouted rigs right in the heart of town. The opening of the Burbank Field made the Osages the nation's richest Indians.

Texas, which had been lagging behind California and Oklahoma in production, now once again revolutionized the situation. At Ranger in 1917, then at Burkburnett, Breckenridge, Desdemona, and a succession of West and North Texas sites, such a bounty of new wells came in that Texas held the potential of outproducing all the rest of the country combined. The opening of the enormous Panhandle gas field in 1927 had the same effect on that industry. The crowning discovery came in 1930 with "Dad" Joiner's strike in the immense and shallow East Texas Field near Kilgore.

Joiner sold out to the enigmatic H. L. Hunt, the quintessential oil plunger, who made one of the world's greatest fortunes from the field. The East Texas Field ranks as the biggest in U.S. history. It made many Texans wealthy, boosted Dallas's rise to parity with Houston and Tulsa as a premier petroleum center, and so flooded the market with cheap oil that the price fell to an incredible ten cents per barrel. Even more than the West's other extractive industries, the oil industry entered the Great Depression awash in its own overproduction, racked by ruinously low prices, and shamefully wasting what would one day be reckoned a critically important national resource.

A number of other extractive industries also figured in the West's evolving economy. Coal mining grew up at various locales throughout the region, primarily as an adjunct of coal-burning railroads and mining smelters. Some of the coal operations were truly substantial. Based at Pueblo, the Colorado Fuel and Iron Company owned sixty-nine thousand acres of coal land and mined twelve thousand tons daily by the 1890s. However, coal mining went into a steep decline after World War I, as cheap and clean oil and natural gas stole away its prime markets. New Mexico led the nation in potash production, and Death Valley's borax trains became an enduring symbol of the arid West. Excluding coal, by 1929 the West supplied more than 90 percent of all U.S. mineral production. The region was, truly, America's cornucopia of raw wealth.

RAILS, ROADS, AND TOURISTS

During these years of transition from a frontier to a new economic order, the West also acquired its modern transportation system. The rail network, which had taken shape during the later nineteenth century and had then fallen on hard times in the Panic of 1893, now expanded to its zenith in World War I. Even by then, however, the vital railroad industry was beginning to decline under the competition of a powerful new force that was transforming the American way of life, the automobile.

With the return of prosperity in the late 1890s, the last great epic of American railroad building ensued, raising total national mileage to 193,000 in 1900 and then to a historic peak of 254,000 in 1916–17. Most of this new construction took place in the West, as the region experienced the final surges of the frontier, and most of it represented branch lines built into remote areas. In addition, three new trunk lines built westward to the coast during these years, rounding out the transcontinental network.

In 1905, the Chicago, Milwaukee, St. Paul and Pacific Railroad, an established midwestern line facing tough competition from transcontinentals on both flanks, began a fourteen-hundred-mile westward extension from South Dakota to Seattle. The Milwaukee completed its line in 1909; but, saddled by heavy construction debts and facing the implacable competition of Jim Hill, it failed to prosper. To the south, also in 1905, a group of investors led by Montana Senator W. A. Clark completed the $25 million San Pedro, Los Angeles and Salt Lake Railroad, linking the "City of the Saints to the City of the Angels." The Salt Lake Line opened a major new route through the mining regions of southern Utah and Nevada to the newly improved San Pedro harbor, founding the modern Las Vegas en route. Finally, in 1910, Jay Gould's son George, who had inherited a rail empire from his late father to which he had added the Denver and Rio Grande, finished the building of his Western Pacific Railroad—west from Salt Lake City through the Feather River Canyon to Oakland. Californians welcomed Gould's competitive inroad on the hated Southern Pacific, but the heavily indebted Western Pacific languished just like the Milwaukee.

These new trunk lines seemed, outwardly, to threaten the older, established trunk lines with a renewed competition. In fact, however, the real trend after the turn of the century was twofold: toward a consolidation of railroads into regional empires and toward a more effective system of federal regulation. Three major railroad constellations blanketed the West after 1900. Of these, the least imposing was that assembled by George Gould with allies that included the powerful Rockefeller and Sage interests. This new "Gould System" reached from the Great Lakes to St. Louis and on to Pueblo via the Missouri Pacific, thence to the West Coast via the Denver and Rio Grande and Western Pacific lines.

James J. Hill, flanked by banking associates Charles Steele and George Baker, in Portland, 1910. Courtesy of the James J. Hill Papers, James Jerome Hill Reference Library, St. Paul, Minnesota.

It dominated much of the Southwest, controlling such substantial carriers as the Missouri, Kansas and Texas and the International and Great Northern, but lacked the dynamism of its two major rivals.

In the Northwest, the team of James J. Hill and J. P. Morgan rounded out its empire, based on the Great Northern and Northern Pacific transcontinentals, into a system that by 1906 totalled twenty-one thousand miles of track. The remarkably dynamic Edward H. Harriman led a group of investors in assembling an even larger, though less stable system to the south. In 1897, the Harriman syndicate bought up the decrepit Union Pacific and poured millions into making it a paying enterprise. Following the death of old Collis Huntington, they also acquired control of the Southern Pacific and added the Salt Lake Line to a vast system that by

1906 totalled twenty-five thousand track miles. The rising Hill and Harriman railroad empires aroused fears throughout the West of unrestrained monopoly and rate gouging. The two systems did come into head-on competition at times, as in Oregon, where the Union Pacific and Northern Pacific networks overlapped.

Their key rivalry centered on the strategic and profitable Burlington Road, which Hill needed to access Chicago and which posed a dire threat to Harriman's Union Pacific. After Hill and Morgan had gained control of the Burlington, and Harriman countered with a near-successful raid on the Northern Pacific, the two sides compromised—mainly on the former's terms—by grouping the Northern Pacific, Great Northern, and Burlington into one mighty firm, the Northern Securities Company. Since this holding company represented an obvious regional monopoly (the Milwaukee Road had not yet built west), a public outcry arose that it be prosecuted as an illegal restraint of trade.

With great fanfare, the Roosevelt administration did so, winning a 1904 Supreme Court decision that broke up the Northern Securities Company. In truth, for all Theodore Roosevelt's acclaim as a "trustbuster," the heralded breakup of Northern Securities meant little, since the three roads in question remain to this day under a common corporate leadership. Harriman's empire proved less durable. Soon after his death in 1909, the Supreme Court determined that the joining of the Union Pacific and Southern Pacific was illegal and ordered the two roads separated.

The rail barons' awesome and unrestrained power prompted a renewed public demand, especially from the West, that the Interstate Commerce Commission, which the courts had long since rendered ineffective, be strengthened to regulate the roads effectively. In a series of major enactments, from the Hepburn Act of 1906 to the Railroad Valuation Act of 1913, Congress greatly enhanced the ICC's powers to establish fair rates based on the carriers' true valuation and limited the railroads' ability to secure overrulings of the agency's decisions from conservative courts. Finally, an angry public had thus wrung from Congress a long-sought, truly effective regulation of the railroads.

During World War I, the public importance of the railroads was severely underscored when the federal government seized control of them in order to integrate their management for efficiency. But by the 1920s, the irony of the whole situation began to emerge. The government had finally established a system of tight controls on the railroads just in time to hinder, with limits and delays on rate increases, the ability of the railroads to compete with the new automobiles and trucks that traveled on publicly built roadways. By the postwar era, therefore, the railroads—which had seemed so all-powerful in 1900—were already in decline.

Few, if any, developments ever so revolutionized the American way of life as did the rapid rise of the automobile and the highway systems that served it. By the turn of the century, small and durable cars, powered by gasoline engines and riding on inflatable tires, were appearing in sizable numbers, developed by men like Walter Chrysler, who grew up on a Kansas farm, and Ransom Olds and Henry Ford, who pioneered in mass-producing them. At first, the cars seemed best suited to adventure, as in 1903 when a Packard car made the first transcontinental journey, from San Francisco to New York, in fifty-two days. The autos quickly proved their utility, though, not least during the aftermath of the San Francisco earthquake of 1906, when the city's small numbers of cars and trucks were crucial in ferrying people and supplies. Ford revolutionized the industry when, in 1908, he began mass-producing the fabled Model T on assembly lines, each year bringing lower-priced cars into price ranges available to the millions. The nation counted two million motor vehicles by 1915 and, after the war underscored the practical value of cars and trucks alike, ten million by 1920.

The remarkably quick spread of automobile usage forced an equally rapid expansion and improvement of the national road system. Farmers and cyclists first led the crusade, focusing their efforts on the National League for Good Roads in 1892. Progress came only slowly, however. In 1904, a national "highway" census counted more than 2.1 million miles of "roads"; but only 7 percent of these miles were actually "improved" by gravel, macadam, or concrete. But mass-produced autos forced the hand of government, as organizations like the Lincoln Highway Association, formed in 1913 to lobby for a transcontinental highway along the old Central Overland Route, led the charge. The "good roads" movement swept the country.

In 1916, Congress responded with the Federal Aid Road Act, which inaugurated the enduring policy of providing federal matching dollars to the states for highway building and improvement. The 1916 law authorized the secretary of agriculture to expend $75 million to match state funding for rural road improvement. Congress took a larger step in 1921 with passage of the Federal Highway Act, which provided fifty-fifty matching funds to all the states so that each could designate up to 7 percent of its roads as "primary" and thereby as part of a national, interstate highway system totalling two hundred thousand miles. As a result of this epochal measure, the United States initiated a highway construction program of such proportions as the world had never seen: a continental network of graded and hard-surfaced, two-lane highways designated by even numbers on an east-west axis and odd numbers north-south.

The 1920s, which in so many ways signaled the beginnings of modern America, witnessed a spectacular increase in automobile manufacturing and purchases and an equally spectacular increase in road construction. Annual automobile production rose from two million units per year in 1920 to five and one-half million in 1929. Car-truck registrations totalled over twenty-six million by 1929, enough to carry the entire American population at the time. By 1929, three million trucks traveled the American road, bringing a new efficiency to farm work and a more facile system of hauling freight to remote areas. Buses began robbing trains of passenger fares. Out West, the Santa Fe Railroad's subsidiary Pickwick Corporation initiated in 1925 the nation's first long-distance bus line, linking Portland to El Paso via California; and in 1928, the Yelloway Bus Line started transcontinental service between New York and Los Angeles. As John Jakle observes, in the more egalitarian West—much of it barely a generation removed from the rigors of frontier travel—buses did not carry the low-class stigma that they did "back East."

With its wide-open spaces and paucity of people, the West led the nation in embracing the mobility of the automobile. On a per capita reckoning, the region led all others by a wide margin in car ownership. By the same standard, California, by 1929, led all states; and Los Angeles, with its pathbreaking, "miracle" shopping mile along Wilshire Boulevard, led all cities. California was visibly pioneering a new "suburban" life-style, which the car made possible by permitting the more affluent city dwellers to live happily beyond the crowded urban centers. Other westerners also pioneered in the new age of the automobile. Oregon first developed, in 1919, a gasoline tax, exclusively devoted to funding road construction; and in 1924, Dallas's Pig Stands Company gave America its first "drive-in" restaurant, complete with "curb service."

The undergrown humps of old 1920s highways look impossibly narrow and inadequately graded to us where we can still see the remnants of them snaking around hills in switchbacks. But they represented a marvelous innovation to westerners of that day, anxious to escape the confines of their isolation. Truly, the coming of the automobile and the modern highway had, by the mid-twenties, revolutionized the western life-style even more than had the coming of rails a half-century before.

Among its greatest western impacts, the car transformed a business that grew to become one of the region's leaders, tourism. Defined as sight-seeing or hunting, tourism dates back to the earliest white presence; but genuine tourism really began with the railroads, which joined with other regional promoters to advertise travel. Those whom they lured

Touring cars of the 1920s in Glacier National Park, Montana. Courtesy of the National Archives and Records Service, Washington, D.C.

west were generally wealthy and generally came to two types of places, dude ranches and luxury resorts. Howard Eaton is usually credited with starting the first dude ranch, in Dakota in 1881, and he and many others soon learned that money could be made from treating eastern and European "dudes" to a "genuine" western experience. The luxury resorts usually tried simply to import a bit of high-priced, continental class to a handsome western setting. Among the best were the Broadmoor at Colorado Springs, the Saltair on the Great Salt Lake, and a number in sunny southern California: the Del Coronado at San Diego, the Glenwood at Riverside, the Raymond at Pasadena, and the many fine hotel-resorts at Monterey, Santa Cruz, Santa Monica, and Long Beach.

Mass-produced cars, selling as low as $290 for a Model T touring Ford in 1926, now made it possible for middle-class families to head west, with burlap water bags slung over their radiators, to see the splendors of the sunset region. They came to enjoy the mountains and beaches, to take in the world's fairs at Portland in 1905, Seattle in 1909, San Francisco and San Diego in 1915–17, and especially to tour the new national parks (see chapter 2). From the beginning, National Park Service Director Steve Mather saw the parks

43

as meccas for tourists and contracted with private concessionaires to provide them services. The Park Service began allowing cars into Mount Rainier National Park in 1908, Crater Lake in 1911, Glacier in 1912, Yosemite in 1913, and Yellowstone in 1915. As a result, park visitations climbed from 199,000 in 1910 to 920,000 in 1920 to 2,775,000 in 1930. Millions more flocked to the national forests.

The droves of tourists, as well as routine business travelers, created a major new market for roadside businesses, especially service stations, roadside restaurants (seemingly always with the sign "EAT" in the window), and what came to be known as "motels." At first, the motorists could choose only between downtown hotels and campgrounds for overnight lodging; but the West pioneered in evolving a new alternative. The first recorded campground with cabins appeared at Douglas, Arizona, in 1913. Such "cabin camps" were common by a decade later, usually providing lodging for an extra fifty to seventy-five cents per night. These, in turn, soon evolved into "bungalettes" with individual baths and "motor courts" with individual units under one roof, which were the true beginnings of what is now an American institution, the motel. In these ways, and in many others, car-borne tourism soon became a mainstay of the western economy.

Finally, the aviation industry evolved parallel with the automotive, but more gradually. Even more than the car, the plane seemed at first to be primarily a stunt device. Americans soon came to take aircraft more seriously, however, as planes proved themselves—for instance, with the first transcontinental flight from New York to Pasadena in 1911 or, more important, with their usage during World War I. In 1921, the Post Office Department initiated a transcontinental airmail service, from New York to Chicago and then westward via Omaha and the old Central Overland Route to San Francisco. Then, in the important Kelly Air Mail Act of 1925, Congress followed a precedent set back in overland mail days by authorizing the government to contract with private carriers to deliver the mail, thus using mail subsidies to promote air passenger and freight service. Seattle-based Boeing Air Transport, a part of William Boeing's enterprise that had already built the B-40 biplane, secured the prime Chicago–San Francisco contract. Other firms operated branch-feeder lines that linked to central route termini, such as Western Air Express, operating between Los Angeles and Salt Lake City, or Pacific Air Transport, which flew the length of the Pacific Coast.

At first, air carriers handled only mail and express, but most of them were soon flying passengers as well. Charles Lindbergh's electrifying transatlantic flight of 1927 generated enthusiasm for all forms of flight and led directly to the appearance of modern airlines. For example, in 1930 Boeing Air Transport merged with affiliate lines Pacific Air Transport, National Air Transport, and Varney Air Lines to form United Airlines. Trans-America Air Transport, flying between St. Louis, Albuquerque, and Los Angeles, became Trans-World Airlines; and Universal Aviation, operating from Cleveland across Texas to southern California, became American Airlines.

By 1932, the airlines employed day and night flights to ferry passengers across the continent in twenty-four hours, with stops; by 1935, the trip took thirteen to fifteen hours. By the late 1930s, Boeing 314 Clipper "flying boats" were running luxury flights from coastal cities to the Orient. Lindbergh's and other "barnstorming" pilots' antics set off a rage for private aviation too. Here, again, the wide-open West took the lead in this new form of transportation. California, for instance, surpassed all other states with 20 percent of American pilots and more than 14 percent of all American private planes. More even than most other Americans, westerners flocked to the plane and the car, the newest and greatest instruments of modern mobility.

COMMERCE AND LABOR

During these years the West developed other, varied industries, in addition to those described above; but most of these also related to or served the basic extractive industries, for instance, the sprawling stockyards and meat-processing works that arose at Omaha and Fort Worth, the flour mills at Kansas City, or the port shipping complexes that grew up along the coasts. By the early twentieth century, Galveston ranked for a time as America's second-greatest port and as the world's greatest cotton export center. Houston, with its federally improved, fifty-five-mile ship channel, then surpassed Galveston to rank as the country's second- or third-largest port and as the world's foremost oil port. From the fine natural harbors of the West Coast—San Diego, San Francisco, and Puget Sound—and from those that were federally improved—Houston, San Pedro, and Portland—came a growing bounty of exported raw wealth, much of it headed for Asia or for the new Panama Canal: oil, metals, lumber, cotton, wheat, and beef.

Compared with World War II a generation later, World War I brought relatively little lasting change to the West. This war, unlike its successor, was overwhelmingly European; so the West did not become a staging area for a Pacific theater of operations. The region did house some very large training bases, like Camp Funston–Fort Riley, Kansas, and Camps McArthur, Logan, Travis, and Bowie in Texas. But with the quick folding down of the military after the war, the camps atrophied following 1919. Similarly, those industries that the war brought west, like the giant Skinner and Eddy shipyard that covered twenty-seven acres along Seattle's waterfront, capitalized on the region's unique blend of resources and facilities and did not build into the future beyond the war.

Here and there, an occasional major business arrived that did not fit the general pattern. Of these, the most exceptional was surely the motion picture industry. The earliest moviemakers had based their operations primarily in the Northeast; but they soon trekked west, lured by an appealing climate that provided year-round filming, a varied terrain for scene shooting, and, at least in some cases, a long distance from Thomas Edison and his suits against them for

The "back ranch" of Universal Studios, Universal City, California, where many Westerns were filmed. Courtesy of The Museum of Modern Art.

infringing on his patents. By 1912, the Los Angeles area was home to the nation's largest concentration of motion picture companies, the biggest cluster of "studios" being in the formerly quiet and unincorporated hamlet of Hollywood.

Moviemaking came into its prime during the 1920s. By now, the industry clearly ranked as one of California's greatest, spending over $150 million per year and employing, at full- and part-time, one hundred thousand people by 1929. The largest studios grew into major enterprises, many of them giant mergers of smaller companies, such as Metro-Goldwyn-Mayer, formed in 1924. Warner Brothers contracted with 108 auxiliary firms. However, "Hollywood" did much more than fuel the 1920s growth of southern California: the town and the area came also to symbolize the great American dream factory, a Babylon where beautiful people sinned and sensationalized to the titillation of the nation and the world.

In more prosaic terms, though, the West's evolving economy seemed less striking for what it had—unstable extractive industries—than for what it lacked—the lucrative, "value-added" manufacturing of finished products. Even despite its remarkably rapid development, the West still found itself gripped, like the Old South, in a colonial relationship to the urban-industrial Northeast and upper Midwest, to whom it shipped its harvests of natural wealth and from whom it purchased its manufactured wares. With the full sanction of the Interstate Commerce Commission, a highly discriminatory "basing point" system of product prices and railroad rates perpetuated this economic colonialism by forcing westerners to pay shipping rates from eastern manufacturing points, even if the tonnages in question actually originated from nearby sources.

Strikingly, the far western states held only 5 percent of U.S. manufacturing industry in 1914, generating a mere $80 million worth of manufactured goods. America's two dominant industries, steel and automobiles, did little more than market in the West. The major auto makers, led by Ford, General Motors, and Chrysler, did build some final assembly plants in California, as did tire maker B. F. Goodrich, in the 1920s; but these plants were actually small satellites of those in Detroit and simply served the local market. Steel, that most basic of manufactures, reached westward to include Pueblo's Colorado Fuel and Iron Company. CF&I employed fifteen thousand workers from New Mexico to Wyoming, stood as Colorado's largest industry, and became part of the Rockefeller empire. But, producing 7 percent of U.S. steel rails, it represented in truth only a pale reflection of the industry's centers of operation in Pennsylvania and the Great Lakes states.

Thus, as it entered into the Great Depression in 1930, the West seemed outwardly to be prospering as a cornucopia of wealth for the nation and the world. The region was actually very vulnerable, however, because of overproduction and low prices, inability to control the marketing of its products, the absence of more stable, higher-wage manufacturing industry, and its naked reliance on eastern banking and finance. Regional financial leaders like Jesse Jones of Houston, Marriner Eccles of Utah, and the remarkable A. P. Giannini of San Francisco—who was busily building his Bank of Italy (renamed the Bank of America in 1930) into a branch empire that by 1929 controlled 40 percent of California's bank capital—chafed at the West's subservience to eastern finance. In the decade ahead, they would find ways, with federal assistance, to free themselves from it.

The growth of an extractive economy found ready reflection in the growth of troubled labor relations. The years leading up to World War I witnessed a turbulent increase in union activity, which climaxed in a wave of union repression during the war and then receded in a long era of union setbacks during the conservative 1920s. The West's earliest labor organizations had tended to be, like those to the east, broadly inclusive of all workers, as well as politically active and ideological. This was true of the early miners' and railroad unions and of the various groups that appeared in San Francisco, the hub of frontier labor activity.

The Knights of Labor, which flourished nationally for a time, swept the West during the 1880s, organizing thousands of railroad workers and triumphing in a wave of strikes in 1885. But the Knights folded in 1886 when the Gould system defeated them in a series of encounters that ended in violence, as at Fort Worth and at Parsons, Kansas. Another attempt at broad industrial unionism came west with Eugene V. Debs's American Railway Union, which also failed after federal troops helped suppress a giant 1894 strike. Such failures led leaders of the highly skilled, or craft, unions to adopt a different strategy: to avoid the pitfalls of trying to gather all the workers, skilled or unskilled, in an entire industry or even the entire country and to concentrate instead on organizing simply the skilled workers in specific trades and on seeking "bread-and-butter" gains like higher wages and better hours. These were the goals of the American Federation of Labor, founded as a nationwide organization of craft unions under the direction of Samuel Gompers in 1886.

Craft unions, some affiliated with the AF of L and some

not, sprouted up across the West during the late nineteenth and early twentieth centuries. The numerous railroad workers now gathered into sixteen "railroad brotherhoods," which were organized by craft, such as the Firemen and Enginemen, Porters and Conductors. Their numbers and cohesive organizations brought them success and made them in the eyes of many the "aristocrats of labor," especially after the federal Adamson Act of 1916 granted them the coveted eight-hour day. By 1919, the rail brotherhoods numbered 1.8 million members, many of them in the West.

In maritime transportation, the International Longshoremen's Association, formed on the Great Lakes during the late 1870s, opened a Pacific Coast Division in 1912. The ILA waxed powerful on the West Coast, particularly in the strong ethnic-union cities of San Francisco and Seattle. The Oil and Gas Well Workers, an AF of L affiliate, moved quickly to California after its creation in 1899 and then on to Texas after a 12 percent wage cut at Spindletop. In 1918, the southwestern petroleum laborers formed a more powerful union, the International Organization of Oil Field, Gas Well and Refinery Workers, which numbered thirty thousand members within a year.

Other craft unions expanded westward, but in truth the AF of L brand of conservative and elitist unionism did not play well with the workers in the largest western industries. Among the hundreds of thousands of lumber, mining, and farm workers, for instance, laborers were often scattered and isolated, illiterate and divided into mutually hostile ethnic groups. Many of them, severely underpaid and pitilessly exploited, were thus in a hostile and radical mood. To these workers, conservative bread-and-butter craft unions made less sense than did broad and inclusive unions like the old Knights of Labor, which gathered in all workers, or at least all those in a given industry, and which pursued sweeping political as well as economic goals.

Such a union was the Western Federation of Miners, founded in 1893. The WFM frankly disavowed craft unionism in favor of industrywide organization. During the 1890s,

it clashed repeatedly with the mine owners, most spectacularly in Idaho and Colorado; but the union did win some
notable bread-and-butter victories too, particularly eight-
hour workday laws beginning in Utah in 1896. By 1907
it registered forty-four thousand members. But the WFM
moved steadily in a class-conscious and socialist direction. In
1905, colorful "Big Bill" Haywood and other WFM leaders
played key roles at the Chicago convention that founded the
Industrial Workers of the World.

As historian James Green comments, the IWW, whose
members became known as "Wobblies," "abandoned job
consciousness for class consciousness." Moving in the opposite direction from the AF of L, it aimed to create "one big
union," nationwide, which gathered in all workers, regardless of skill or lack thereof, and which aimed to take direct
political and physical action to reform society. Some IWW
leaders were outspoken socialists or "syndicalists," who advocated that organized workers should take over and operate
industries. They appealed not just to skilled craftsmen but
also to the anonymous and impoverished armies of lumber
and mining workers, many of them alienated immigrants,
and even to the thousands of "harvest stiffs" who worked
wretchedly in the fields of large western farms. Although
the IWW also organized major strikes back East, its fulcrum
lay in the West. Everywhere it went, dissension quickly followed.

Radical unionism spread rapidly throughout the region
during the years before the war, intermingling with a rising
socialist movement. As it did, a series of angry incidents
aroused public indignation. The efforts of the IWW's Agricultural Workers Organization to unionize farmhands led to
bitter confrontations with farm owners. In East Texas, black
and white lumberjacks and millhands, organized in IWW
locals, fought the efforts of the Southern Lumber Operators to destroy their unions. In 1910, a tremendous bomb
blast devastated the headquarters of the outspokenly antiunion *Los Angeles Times*, killing twenty-one people. When
two unionists, John and James McNamara, admitted their

guilt after first pleading innocence, the whole western labor movement felt the reverberations. In Utah, Wobbly songwriter Joe Hill became a martyr in 1915, after he was executed for murder following a trial that smacked of bias. Similarly, labor radical Tom Mooney went to prison for life on controversial charges of murder stemming from the bombing of a San Francisco parade that killed ten in 1916.

The most tragic episode of all grew out of a strike in 1913 by the United Mine Workers against the Rockefeller-owned Colorado Fuel and Iron Company. In April 1914, militiamen killed eighteen people, including twelve women and children, at the town of Ludlow. In the following weeks, a total of seventy-four died in sporadic warfare between management-militia and labor before federal intervention finally brought an uneasy peace. The "Ludlow Massacre" caused even partisan businessmen to wince and prompted John D. Rockefeller, Jr., to rethink the way his family did business.

As the United States entered the war in 1917, it seemed to many that a domestic war threatened between heavy-handed corporations and radical unions. Many of the labor radicals opposed the war as a capitalist conspiracy; and as we shall see in the following chapter, they fell victims to their business-patriotic enemies during the war and its aftermath. As a result, organized labor entered the 1920s badly weakened. The IWW collapsed; and the Mine, Mill and Smelter Workers, heir to the old WFM, joined many other unions in losing their coveted closed shop agreements and in having open shop (nonunion) contracts forced on them. Even in the union citadel of San Francisco, the once powerful Building and Trades Council lost out to businessmen who installed the open shop. Texas and California unionists watched impotently as big farmers imported seventy thousand Mexicans a year to work their fields. Having lost to their business-conservative foes, laborites could only watch and wait for a better day.

Thus, for workers as for farmers and businessmen, the great economic surge of the postfrontier era ended as it had begun, in uncertainty and depression. Beginning in the wake of the worst depression the nation had ever seen, the Panic of 1893, the unprecedented prosperity of the early twentieth century—fueled in large part by the last great opening of the West's bounty—crashed to earth in an even worse depression in 1930. Westerners, like other Americans, now found themselves forced to think about their economy, and their land itself, in a new way.

Chapter Two

Politics of the Postfrontier
Era, 1900-1930

The turbulence that characterized the western economic order during the first three decades of the century found ready reflection in regional government and politics. A mood of optimistic reformism highlighted the years from 1900 through 1916, a period often referred to as the Progressive Era. Then, during and immediately after America's involvement in World War I, supernationalists and conservatives rose to the forefront, smashing the power of the reformers and truly devastating that of the more militant antiwar socialists and radicals, whose fortunes had likewise been on the rise before the war. The country and much of the region remained in a rightist mood during the 1920s; but political unrest continued to dominate the troubled interior reaches of the West, where farmers and ranchers faced severe economic problems. In each of these phases of postfrontier political development, the West clearly rode on national currents of events. But the region also exhibited strong tendencies that set it off from the rest of the nation. Both before 1917 and after, many eastern observers viewed the now closed frontier beyond the humid plains as a land of extremists bent on overthrowing the established American order. They were partly right, perhaps, but mostly wrong; for in politics as in economics, the West was in fact moving toward, not away from, the national mainstream.

THE PROGRESSIVE ERA OUT WEST

The reformers of the early years of the twentieth century who referred to themselves as "progressives" are difficult to define as a group. They were a diverse lot, with a great diversity of concerns. Far from being radicals of the Left, most of them came from the broad American middle class. And most of them shared a highly moralistic and optimistic outlook and a determination that they, the stable mortar of American society, would not stand passively by while the newly emerging capitalists of industry and commerce ground them down into a propertyless "proletariate," as Karl Marx and other socialists had prophesied.

Thus, in large part, they turned to political reform to maintain and advance their station in society. The progressives adopted new ideas and strategies that set the stage for political debate that has endured to the present day. Turning away from the American tradition of close limitation on the power of government, they sought to build the authority of the state so that it could effectively regulate the giant corporations and other interests they saw preying on society. Witnessing the power the "interests" had over Congress, legislatures, and other public bodies, the progressives sought to remedy the situation by direct democracy, placing political power squarely in the hands of the people, whom they implicitly trusted to do right. In this fashion, they worked a basic shift in the course of American political thought, joining Alexander Hamilton's traditionally conservative belief in a strong central government with Thomas Jefferson's traditionally liberal belief in human rights, producing a melding of ideology that stressed progress, moralism, and democracy.

Gaining momentum quickly after 1900, progressivism reached into every sector of American life, into every corner of the nation, and into every level of government—local, state, and federal. Two popular presidents, the Republican Theodore Roosevelt and the Democrat Woodrow Wilson, led the cause of national reform. In the West, progressivism thrived to a greater extent than it did nationwide, drawing on

A pro-Nonpartisan League cartoon, published in the *Nonpartisan Leader* at the height of the League's controversiality in 1919. Courtesy of the State Historical Society of North Dakota.

the vital frontier heritage of popular democracy and resentment against exploitative eastern corporations. In the more commercially oriented coastal states, the western progressives were, not surprisingly, very middle-class in orientation. Naturally enough, in the interior West, the progressives drew much more strongly on the predominant agricultural population and on the still smoldering legacy of 1890s populism, the agrarian radicalism that had so frightened the East a decade earlier with its demands for an inflated currency and tough federal controls over unrestrained corporations.

As historians Arthur Link and Richard McCormick comment in *Progressivism*:

> Perhaps the most distinctive aspect of western progressivism was its passion for the more democratic, anti-institutional political reforms, such as the initiative, the referendum, and the recall, and a form of the direct primary which allowed voters to cross party lines. Not every western state adopted these measures, but they were more common there than anywhere else in the nation.*

*The initiative allows voters to enact laws directly by ballot, and the referendum to repeal them by ballot. These measures were pioneered by South Dakota in 1898. The recall allows voters directly to remove public officials from office. Each of these measures represents a form of direct democracy, permitting the electorate to bypass unresponsive legislatures. The direct primary allows the voters to nominate their parties' candidates by ballot, thus bypassing party conventions and bosses.

Western progressives tended to be more militant than eastern progressives and more determined to curb the powers of eastern corporations and to regulate eastern-based railroads.

Typically, progressivism surfaced initially in urban politics, as a reform reaction to the corrupt alliances that had developed between "machine" politicians and businesses with contracts for city services. These alliances resulted in graft and gross inefficiencies, and western progressives joined their counterparts across the land in attacking them. In both Los Angeles and Seattle, where a fruitful embrace of local politicos and saloon-prostitution interests afflicted the cities like a parasite, reformers recalled their derelict mayors and amended city charters to install businesslike governments during 1909–10. Los Angeles and Seattle, and many other cities, were following the example of Galveston, Texas, where a deadly hurricane and tidal wave had swept away six thousand lives in 1900. The disaster had exposed the inadequacies of Galveston's government system and had caused the citizens to replace it with a pathbreaking "city commission" administration, which simply applied the methods of business to government.

Two major western cities, Denver and San Francisco, emerged as notable national leaders in urban reform. Chafing at years of municipal corruption and ballot box stuffing, a fascinating group of Denver progressives overthrew the entrenched machine rule and established a reform mayoralty. They were led by wealthy Josephine Roche, editor George Creel of the *Denver Post*, and crusading Judge Ben Lindsey, a pioneer in juvenile court reform. Creel and Lindsey went on to become nationally prominent progressive figures.

The working-class city of San Francisco presented one of the nation's leading examples of urban reform. Through a complex system of bribes and kickbacks, clever boss Abraham Ruef had secured, three times, the election of Eugene Schmitz as mayor, and thereby presided over a vast empire of public pillage. After the earthquake of 1906 exposed to view the resulting inefficiencies, a well-to-do alliance of reformers, led by millionaire Rudolph Spreckels and editor Fremont Older, pressed the crusade that ended up placing Ruef in prison and launching a statewide progressive movement.

The two Pacific commonwealths of California and Oregon led the West as laboratories of statewide political reform. It was at the state level, where powerful corporate interests could dominate legislatures, governors, and courts alike, that the progressives had their greatest impact. Along with Governor Robert La Follette's Wisconsin, the strongly middle-class, Yankee state of Oregon set the pace for all others in pioneering reform.

Designed and pressed forward by the remarkable William S. U'Ren, the famous "Oregon System" opened the door of direct democracy with enactment of the initiative and referendum in 1902, followed by the direct primary and a clever system of forcing members of the legislature to commit themselves to voting for candidates for the U.S. Senate that the voters had already approved. When Oregon's Jonathan Bourne went to the Senate by this process in 1907, he could well boast that he was the first U.S. senator actually elected by the people.* A series of far-reaching social and political reforms soon followed, including the establishment of maximum working hours and minimum wages for women, the banning of free railroad passes by which the roads often "influenced" politicians, and the creation of an Industrial Accident Commission.

Led by brilliant and caustic Hiram Johnson, who had served as chief prosecutor in the trial of Ruef, the California progressives resembled their Oregon counterparts in their

*In 1913, the Seventeenth Amendment to the U.S. Constitution finally ended the often abused system of electing U.S. senators by the state legislatures and made their election by direct vote of the people the law of the land.

middle-class origins and their commitment to direct democracy. Drawing on well-organized Lincoln-Roosevelt Republican clubs and a new direct primary law, Johnson won first the Republican nomination and then the governorship in 1910 on the "promise to kick the Southern Pacific Railroad out of politics." Johnson's administration enacted a sweeping reform program like that in Oregon, a program that so impressed Theodore Roosevelt that he applauded it as the "greatest advance ever made by any state for the benefit of its people." The California progressives carried their distrust of the established political parties so far that, in 1913, they secured a state law permitting candidates for office to "cross-file," or run on more than one party ticket without even identifying their party affiliation. In this and other ways, the progressives, like the earlier Populists, disrupted party organizations and elevated personalities over party, prompting a perplexed Woodrow Wilson to comment: "I can't, for the life of me, in this place be certain that I can tell a Democrat from a Republican."

Throughout the West, every state produced some variation on these progressive themes. Kansas, which had earlier produced the nation's first antitrust statute and a virulent Populist movement, enacted a full panoply of progressive legislation, most notably a Blue Sky Law of 1914 that represented a major step forward in state regulation of corporate stock issues. Edward Hoch and Walter Stubbs provided effective leadership as reform governors, and the "insurgent" Republican Joseph Bristow replaced the "machine" incumbent in the U.S. Senate.

Similarly in Nebraska, railroad "machine" rule sagged markedly after 1901, and bipartisan progressives carried through their reform program during legislative sessions from 1907 through 1911, with major emphases on a tough railroad commission and the direct primary. In South Dakota, the effective, Theodore Roosevelt–style GOP governor Peter Norbeck persuaded the legislature to enact such sweeping measures as state-funded hail insurance and farm credits and a state-owned coal mine and cement plant. Popular reform governors became the order of the day, men such as John Burke in North Dakota, Ernest Lister in Washington, "Honest John" Shafroth in Colorado, and Thomas Campbell in Texas, whose administrations built on earlier, far-reaching Populist measures to enact tough-minded tax and insurance reforms.

The progressive tide swept even into states, such as Wyoming and Utah, that seemed safely under entrenched conservative rule. Millionaire stockman and Republican Senator Francis Warren, who freely used his influence to advance the career of his son-in-law General John J. "Black Jack" Pershing, presided over a machine that, generally speaking, ran Wyoming for the thirty years prior to his death in 1929. But even at that, the reformers had their day, beginning with an anti-gambling statute in 1902 and culminating with the progressive administration of Warren's enemy Governor Joseph Carey from 1911 to 1915. In Utah, a similarly conservative Republican machine, this one in league with the Mormon hierarchy and presided over by dour LDS apostle and Senator Reed Smoot (1903–33), held sway. This dominance was, however, far from complete. Liberals turned to enigmatic spokesmen like mine owner and Senator Thomas Kearns, owner of the *Salt Lake Tribune*, and Democrat Simon Bamberger, who won election to the statehouse in 1916 and sponsored a belated reform program.

Blending with an advocacy of statehood, progressivism also had a considerable impact on the remaining territorial governments in the Southwest. In the Oklahoma and Indian territories, colorful Democrat "Alfalfa Bill" Murray, who specialized in forging Indian-white political alliances, presided over the constitutional convention that paved the way to welding together the two halves of what became the state of Oklahoma in 1907. For the next fifty years, southern-style Democrats would run Oklahoma, just as they would neighboring Texas. In copperplated Arizona Territory, Roosevelt-appointed governors Alexander Brodie and Joseph Kibbey began disturbing the established order; but the main issue here and in neighboring New Mexico was the quest for statehood.

A combination of factors—such as the Southwest's "Wild West" image, eastern distaste for western Populism, and eastern concern about how mining millionaires seemed able to buy themselves seats in the U.S. Senate—obstructed the admission of these final two contiguous territories as states. As the *New York Evening Post* remarked: "We don't want any more states until we can civilize Kansas." An effort to join the neighboring southwestern territories into one state failed in 1905, mainly due to the refusal of Anglo-dominated Arizona to be joined with Hispanic New Mexico.

Finally, in 1910 Congress voted to admit the two as separate states. Two years later, after Arizona mollified President William Taft by removing its drastic constitutional provision allowing voter recall of judges, the two desert territories became the forty-seventh and forty-eighth stars in the flag. (Arizona readopted the recall provision after gaining admission.) In both of the new states, progressive personalities loomed large. Arizona's first state governor was George W. P. Hunt, a genuine friend of labor and foe of King Copper who would serve seven terms between 1912 and 1934, gaining him the sobriquet "George VII." In New Mexico, Democrat William McDonald became the first state governor; and the frail and wealthy Bronson Cutting, a New England transplant known as "El Don," fragmented party lines by cultivating and brokering the Hispanic vote in pursuit of reform causes.

Two primary manifestations of progressivism, the campaigns for prohibition and women's suffrage, had a heavy impact on the West. The epicenter of American prohibitionism seemed to lie on the fundamentalist Great Plains. Spearheaded by the Women's Christian Temperance Union and the predominantly female Anti-Saloon League, the prohibitionists won victory after hard-fought victory during the prewar years, often with local option and countywide triumphs preceding statewide success. By 1905, two of the

In this 1901 cartoon, both Carry Nation and the beleaguered bartender use the Bible as a weapon in prohibitionist warfare. Courtesy of the Kansas State Historical Society.

The Freethought Ideal.
SUPPLEMENT.

| VOL. VII. | OTTAWA, KANSAS, MARCH 1, E. M., 301—1901. | NO. 16. |

War Between Rum and Religion.
The Bible the Saloon Keeper's Shield & Shelter.

"Lay on McDuff, and damned be him who first cries 'Hold enough.'"—Shakespeare.

"This army of the Home Defenders declares its intent in its name. We are the fathers and mothers who, as God's host, have come to the help of the Lord against the mighty and we are here to withstand all the 'fiery darts of the wicked' with the shield of faith. We demand defense and will have it. No whisky, no tobacco or profanity shall defile our hearthstones. No man or woman who uses any of these defilements shall have or need ask to serve us. We will be your brother to help you to cleanse yourself from the filthiness of the flesh, but you need our assistance. We cannot use you in our business until you clean up. We are going to place before the people men and women who must be examples of virtue and strength, who shall serve us to reward good and punish evil. 'Happy is that people whose God is the Lord, yea, happy is that people in such a case. Kansas shall be free and we will set her on a hill that her light may go to every dark corner of the earth. Come with us and we will do the good, for the Lord hath spoken good concerning such a people."—Carrie Nation."

four states to have completely banned alcoholic beverages were in the West: North Dakota and Kansas. The Sunflower State seemed, indeed, to be the mecca of the "drys." It had approved prohibition in a constitutional amendment back in 1880; and it gave the movement perhaps its most unforgettable character in Carry Nation, whose hatchet-wielding attacks on saloons caught the country's imagination. Buoyed by the moralistic tide of progressivism, prohibition swept across the land. During the decade following 1908, for example, it emerged as the most hotly contested political issue in Texas, splitting the dominant Democratic Party into warring halves. By 1919, all of the western states except

California had gone dry; in 1920 the entire nation followed suit when the eighteenth Amendment became the law of the land.

Far more important to the future was the progressive campaign to grant women the vote, a campaign in which the Rocky Mountain states conspicuously led the nation. By the turn of the century, Wyoming, Utah, Colorado, and Idaho had all passed legislation enfranchising women. The explanation for women's first achieving their goal of suffrage in the West involves a complex combination of factors, including a desire on the part of policy makers to advertise the region favorably to potential settlers and to increase the voting power of "respectable" society against ethnic minorities, and perhaps also an attitude that old conventions were less relevant to the "new country."

Even before 1900, women were participating freely in many western elections. In Colorado they appeared in the legislature and in North Dakota in statewide offices by the mid-1890s. However, the big victories of winning the ballot in general elections came only with the tidal wave of moral-democratic reform during the Progressive Era. By 1918, all the western states except North Dakota, Nebraska, Texas, and New Mexico had granted the ballot to women. Indeed, until New York joined the fold in 1917, only states in the West had conferred this key right of citizenship on women. All American women followed their western sisters in gaining the vote with passage of the Nineteenth Amendment to the Constitution in 1920.

Naturally, the West also pioneered in women's occupation of high political offices. In 1907, eleven years before she could vote, Kate Barnard, commissioner of Charities and Corrections, was accurately termed "the most consummate politician in Oklahoma." Jeannette Rankin of Montana became America's first congresswoman in 1917, Nellie Tayloe Ross of Wyoming and Miriam "Ma" Ferguson of Texas the first female state governors in 1925, and Bertha Landes of Seattle the first woman mayor of a sizable American city in 1926. In 1933, North Dakota legislator Minnie Davenport

Craig gained the speakership of the state house of representatives. These were achievements of which the region could be justifiably proud.

On the stage of national politics, the progressive generation of westerners also had a major impact. In the main, they supported such vaunted reform legislation as the Hepburn Act of 1906 regulating railroads, the Pure Food and Drug Act of 1906, and the 1909 campaign to lower the protective tariff. A number of the younger western progressives, characterized by a fierce independence, a suspicion of corporate and governmental bigness, and an outspoken opposition to foreign involvement, would occupy positions of federal power even into the 1940s. Among the most prominent of them were Republican Senators Hiram Johnson of California and William E. Borah of Idaho, two influential isolationists whose years extended into World War II; Democratic Senators Thomas Walsh and Burton K. Wheeler of Montana, who led the investigations that uncovered the crimes of the Harding administration; Edward Costigan, the perennial Colorado crusader and foe of the ranching and mining barons; Congressman and later Senator George Norris of Nebraska, a revered leader of the reform bloc in the House of Representatives and later father of the Tennessee Valley Authority; William Allen White, the influential editor of the *Emporia Gazette* of Kansas; and Colonel Edward House, the wealthy gray eminence of Texas politics and later of the Wilson administration.

In its regional voting behavior, the new West proved less predictable than its older counterparts, the Democratic South and the Republic Northeast and Midwest. In 1904, it voted overwhelmingly for the reelection of the progressive Republican president, Theodore Roosevelt, who played heavily on his ranching days in North Dakota: only Texas cast its ballots for the Democrats. The region again went Republican for William Howard Taft, Roosevelt's handpicked successor in 1908, with only five western states remaining loyal to the perennial prairie reformer William Jennings Bryan of Nebraska, who was making his third and final

Theodore Roosevelt at Glenwood Springs, Colorado. Courtesy of The Denver Public Library, Western History Department.

run for the presidency. In the complex campaign of 1912, which pitted two great reformers, the Democrat Woodrow Wilson and the independent Progressive Party candidate Theodore Roosevelt, against the conservative Republican Taft, the West demonstrated its strong ties to progressivism. Only Utah voted for Taft, with California, Washington, and South Dakota opting for Roosevelt and all the other states of the region for Wilson. In 1916, the West joined the South to reelect the reformist and presumably antiwar Wilson to a second term. Wilson swept the entire region, except for Oregon and South Dakota, and in the end narrowly won the crucial votes of California after his GOP opponent unwisely seemed to have snubbed the state's Republican leader, Hiram Johnson.

In the final analysis, one must admit that the progressives fell far short of many of their goals. Some of their reforms, such as railroad regulation, proved ineffective or counterproductive. Their emphasis on direct democracy often required far too much of the voters. Oregonians, for instance, had to consider sixty constitutional amendments between 1902 and 1914, and the notorious Oregon "bedquilt ballot" of 1912 listed 136 candidates and thirty-seven measures to consider. More serious, the middle-class progressives usually overlooked the concerns of groups below their station in life. Like their Old South kin, Texas and Oklahoma progressives worked actively to disfranchise the Negro, whereas the erratic Idaho Democratic leader Fred Dubois split his party by attempting to deny the vote to Mormons. California progressives, largely as a concession to their labor allies, led the successful effort to secure a law in 1913 that made it impossible for Japanese to own land. Indeed, one of the most sordid episodes of the entire era occurred at Brownsville, Texas, in 1906. Following a ten-minute shoot-out there involving black troops, President Roosevelt discharged all 167 black soldiers in the three companies involved, without any proof as to which of them were or were not involved.

In their efforts to build the regulatory powers of government and to curb the abuses of exploitative corporations, however, the progressives definitely set the stage for future political debate. And in their concerns with the conservation of natural resources for future generations, they changed the West forever.

THE WEST AND THE NATION—
THE CONSERVATION MOVEMENT

The origins of conservation predate the Progressive Era; but the moralistic reformism of the period brought this movement, like a number of others, to a crest. Even as early as 1872, an alliance of farsighted citizens and railroad promoters orchestrated the creation in Wyoming Territory of the giant Yellowstone National Park, preserving for the edification of future generations some of the world's most spectacular wonderlands. This concept, a triumph of concern for posterity over selfish development, set a new precedent

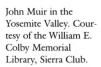

John Muir in the
Yosemite Valley. Cour-
tesy of the William E.
Colby Memorial
Library, Sierra Club.

for the nation and the world; and more national parks, like
California's majestic Yosemite, were established in time.

The related but far larger issue of reserving the nation's
remaining landed heritage—the great preponderance of it
in the West—for the use and sustenance of future generations developed apace during the 1880s and 1890s. Moralistic advocates like Director John Wesley Powell of the U.S.
Geological Survey and John Muir, the Scottish immigrant
and naturalist whose spiritualistic belief in the importance
of wilderness to man was reminiscent of the ideas of Ralph
Waldo Emerson and Henry David Thoreau, crusaded for an
end to the reckless alienation of western lands. The apos-

67

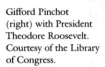

Gifford Pinchot
(right) with President
Theodore Roosevelt.
Courtesy of the Library
of Congress.

tolic Muir played a key role in both the establishment of
Yosemite National Park and in the founding of the Sierra
Club in 1892. Increasingly, conservation advocates found
public opinion favoring their cause. In 1891, the Harrison
administration won from Congress the repeal of the mischievous preemption laws and of the Timber Culture Act, along
with the little-noticed authorization to withdraw from entry
publicly owned woodlands into "forest reservations." President Benjamin Harrison set aside thirteen million acres in
fifteen such reserves; the administration of President Grover
Cleveland added twenty-one million acres more, and that of
William McKinley another seven million. Although some of
this land eventually reverted to entry, a significant precedent
was thus established.

On these foundations, the crusading conservationist President Theodore Roosevelt, himself an avid hunter and camper, built an empire of federal lands in the West. One of Roosevelt's closest friends and associates was Gifford Pinchot, who headed the small Forestry Division in the large U.S. Department of Agriculture. Joseph Petulla correctly draws a sharp distinction between "resource conservationists" like Roosevelt and Pinchot and "nature preservationists" like Muir. Whereas both groups valued wilderness in and for itself, and both were genuine conservationists, they differed sharply otherwise. Purists like Muir believed the public lands should remain pristine and inviolate, as eternal havens for humans and animals. They looked toward the activist "environmentalists" of modern times. Pragmatists like Pinchot, on the other hand, preferred words like *scientific management* and *multiple use*. They advocated putting the lands to useful production but administering them wisely in the public interest.

In 1905, the crafty bureaucrat Pinchot maneuvered the transfer of the forest reserves from the sleepy Interior Department to his province in Agriculture, where he developed the U.S. Forest Service into a truly dedicated organization to administer them. Meanwhile, his friend the president was far surpassing his predecessors in setting aside forestlands. During his terms in office, Roosevelt removed more than 100 million acres from the public domain, creating 118 reserves, so that by 1909 the national forests numbered 159 and covered 151 million regal acres. His land withdrawals also established five new national parks, sixteen national monuments, fifty-one wildlife sanctuaries, and fifty million acres of coal lands. Roosevelt's successors continued the withdrawals, increasing especially Uncle Sam's reserves of coal and oil lands and water power sites. At the same time, the federal government began imposing regulations on, and fees for, cattlemen's usage of public lands for grazing.

All of this represented a far-reaching revolution in federal land policy, a turning away from wholesale giveaways or cheap sales of the public domain and a turning toward the policy of husbanding fragile resources. Westerners, who liked most of Roosevelt's policies, generally detested the conservation moves in which he took such pride. To them the lockups meant a denial of opportunity and aggravating fees and regulations. To small-time lumbermen and cattle-men, the new system seemed only to favor the big operators who could buy their own lands and easily pay access fees to the public domain. Controversy flared all across the West, most pointedly at a large and angry Denver Public Lands Convention in 1907, and even burst into national politics.

In 1910, President Taft ignited a political fire storm when he fired Pinchot from his position as chief of the Forest Service for his persistent accusations that Secretary of the Interior Richard Ballinger, a Washingtonian, was undermin-ing conservation policy by improperly opening certain of the reserved western lands. Although Ballinger was even-tually exonerated, national progressive opinion forced him to resign and heavily favored Pinchot. Ballinger represented western opinion faithfully, however, in his questioning of the legality of some of the reserves and in his belief that such government policies favored large corporations over the common folk.

Another controversy, of less national importance than the spectacular Ballinger-Pinchot affair, better illustrated the contradictory strains within the conservation movement. This episode involved the campaign of the San Francisco community to secure federal approval of a plan to dam and flood the lovely Hetch Hetchy Valley, two hundred miles to the east in Yosemite National Park. The resulting con-troversy became heated and prolonged. Arguing that this desecration of such a choice locale amounted to nothing but "ravaging commercialism," the aging Muir and his preser-vationist allies opposed the plan. Pinchot, and for a time Roosevelt, endorsed the idea as a practical and efficient uti-lization of natural resources. Finally, the developers won, gaining approval of the project in 1914, with final comple-tion years later.

The same basic divisions characterized the campaigns to

create more national parks and monuments that, with the rapidly increasing numbers of cars and highway miles, might serve more and more millions of Americans as playgrounds and spiritual oases. In addition to the established preserves of Yellowstone and Yosemite, more of the West's most impressive scenery now came under federal preservation, including Washington's awesome Mount Rainier and Olympic national parks in 1899 and 1938, respectively; the lovely crests of the continental divide in Montana's Glacier and Wyoming's Grand Teton national parks in 1910 and 1929; Colorado's popular Rocky Mountain National Park in 1915; and the stupendous expanses of Arizona's Grand Canyon (1919) and Utah's Zion and Bryce Canyon national parks (1919, 1928).

Dozens of other sites, many of them historical monuments like Wyoming's Fort Laramie and New Mexico's Fort Union, joined the family of federally funded and maintained facilities during these years. For a long time, the national parks seemed poor and neglected stepchildren of Uncle Sam. The U.S. Army had charge of some, like Yellowstone, and struggled to stave off poachers and looters. Finally, in 1916, Congress created the National Park Service. Under the capable leadership of its first director, Stephen Mather, and his equally able assistant, Horace Albright, the Park Service began the long task of caring for these treasure lands and of making them accessible to the people of America.

At first glance, it might seem obvious that the multipurpose-use advocates like Pinchot prevailed with the creation of national forests, to which users had access by paying fees, whereas the preservationists won their share with the national parks, kept under lock and key in pristine condition forever. In truth, things were much more complicated than that. Preservationists could easily become pawns of private interests. Many Californians believed that the Pacific Gas and Electric Company financed Muir's crusade against Hetch Hetchy, in order to forestall public hydroelectric power. On the other hand, resource conservationists were also open to charges of aiding big developers by serving to crowd out smaller ones.

All things considered, the resource conservationists came out well ahead of their preservationist critics. By the 1920s, the preservationists were wringing their hands at the flooding of humanity into their precious parks and were betraying their essential elitism by castigating the poorer folk who camped in the parks as "sagebrushers" that cluttered up the pristine wilderness. Nothing more graphically revealed the triumph of developers than the passage in 1920 of the federal Water Power Act, which created the Federal Power Commission and turned over choice, publicly owned hydroelectric sites to private promoters at highly favorable long-term lease rates.

The conservationists, in sum, contributed much to future generations by leading the charge to reverse the discredited and bankrupt policy of land giveaways. But, as can be seen in their arguments over preservation versus multiple use and in their problem of frequently playing into the hands of the very promoters they supposedly most feared, they also bequeathed knotty problems about public lands. For both good and bad, they created the "Uncle Sam's West" that is so much a part of the region's profile today.

WORLD WAR I—THE TRIUMPH
OF THE CONSERVATIVES

Though it is true that a mood of prosperous confidence undergirded the progressive years prior to America's entry into World War I in 1917, it is also true that these years witnessed a rising tension between the left and the right. Western conservatives, often representing entrenched wealth and corporate interests, had not really retreated far in the face of progressive reform; indeed, they accepted and even advocated much of it. And when their interests or traditional ideology faced real threats, such powerful guardians of the right as Senators W. A. Clark of Montana, Francis Warren of Wyoming, Joseph Weldon Bailey of Texas, or Albert Fall of

New Mexico were quite capable of mounting more than an adequate defense. The ire of the conservatives focused less on the moderate progressives than on the rising voices of the far left, voices that cried out against corporate exploitation and trumpeted labor militance and the socialist demand for nationalizing industry.

A series of sensationalized acts of violence involving the far left captured western attention during the prewar years: the bombing of the *Los Angeles Times* by labor radicals in 1910, the atrocious Ludlow Massacre in 1914, the sentencing of laborite Tom Mooney for a California bombing in 1916, the growth of the militant Industrial Workers of the World, with its flamboyant campaigns for socialism and free speech (see above, pp. 51–52). The West certainly had no regional monopoly on militance of left or right, but its prevalence of exploitative industries and angrily organized workers caused it to reverberate with political tension to a greater extent than did the nation at large. These reverberations, already mounting before the war, rose to a climactic crescendo with its onslaught.

Two prairie states, Oklahoma and North Dakota, epitomized the rise of prewar radicalism of the left. In both states, heavily indebted farmers lashed out at the corporate-railroad alliances that they viewed as oppressing them. This time, they turned more directly to outright socialism than they had during the Populist 1890s. As in Texas, farm tenancy in Oklahoma exceeded 50 percent; and among these desperate farmers, socialist organizers like Oscar Ameringer made spectacular headway. In 1912, the Socialist party's presidential candidate, Eugene Debs, captured 16 percent of the Oklahoma vote; in 1914, Socialists elected five state representatives, and their gubernatorial candidate took 21 percent of the ballots cast.

Agrarian anger in North Dakota took aim at the "Old Gang" led by the infamous "Big Alex" McKenzie, who presided over a powerful machine advancing the interests of St. Paul-Minneapolis-based railroads and grain trusts. Even after the gang was routed in 1906, the same corporate domi-

A. C. Townley addressing a Minnesota rally in 1917. Courtesy of the State Historical Society of North Dakota.

nation continued. In 1915, a crafty politico who had failed at farming, Arthur Townley, organized the statewide Nonpartisan League, and within a year he had thirty thousand signed-up members. With flamboyant leaders like William Lemke and Lynn Frazier, the NPL aroused enormous controversy by pressing an avowedly socialistic program, featuring a state-owned bank, grain elevators and mills and state-sponsored farm insurance. League leaders outspokenly opposed American entry into the war, and the league's enemies on the Right denounced it as a purveyor of atheism, anarchism, and free love. Nonetheless, by boring into the dominant Republican party, the league swept the 1918 election and enacted much of its program the next year. Meanwhile, it lapped into neighboring Minnesota, Canada, and the wheat regions of the Northwest. At its zenith, it claimed 250,000 members in thirteen states, and many more sympathizers in addition. It seemed, like the IWW, to be sweeping the land with its gospel of antiwar socialism.

America's entry into World War I in April 1917, on

the side of the "Allies" (Great Britain, France, and Russia) and against the German-Austro-Hungarian alliance, brought with it considerable controversy. The great majority of westerners, like most Americans, joined in the upwelling of nationalism and supported the war with gusto. Most westerners viewed the German cause with distaste, among other reasons because of German meddling in revolutionary Mexico. After the colorful Pancho Villa led a raid into New Mexico killing seventeen Americans in 1916, President Wilson ordered a six-thousand-man army under General John J. Pershing into Mexico on a two-year retaliatory expedition that ended in frustration.

However, many westerners, located far away from the strongly Anglophilic East Coast centers of national power, opposed intervention in the war. It was no mere coincidence that many of these opponents of the war were socialists, who saw it as a capitalist war and a poor man's fight. Millions of them, especially in the plains states, were Germans who naturally felt strong ties to the Fatherland; millions more were Scandinavians who came from a tradition of socialism and neutrality; and countless more were Irish, who naturally opposed any alliance with the despised British. Hence, anti-involvement sentiment flared throughout the West long before actual entry in the war in 1917.

Long loyal to his home state of Nebraska's large German population, Secretary of State William Jennings Bryan resigned in 1915, no longer able to support President Wilson's harsh stand toward Germany, and assumed a leadership role in the nationwide peace movement. When Wilson persisted in defending the right of Americans to travel on the ships of belligerent nations, Senator Thomas Gore of Oklahoma and Representative Jeff McLemore of Texas, another state with a large German element, led the unsuccessful effort to counter Wilson. The North Dakota congressional delegation, representing thousands of Germans and Scandinavians, voted unanimously against going to war.

Some of the harshest antiwar spokesmen, especially leaders of the Industrial Workers of the World and the Nonpartisan League, continued to hold forth even after war was declared. Joined by some locals of the American Federation of Labor, the western-based IWW called out fifty thousand lumber workers on strike in August 1917. Although the AF of L unions returned to work under a hostile public reaction, the Wobblies stayed out, some of their spokesmen even calling for outright sabotage of the war effort. Prompted by IWW and other militants, a remarkable group of Oklahoma sharecroppers—poor whites, blacks, and Indians—founded secret societies in the valley of the South Canadian River to oppose the draft, destroying bridges, pipelines, and other property to vent their wrath. Theirs became known as the "Green Corn Rebellion," supposedly from the rumor that they would live on that diet while marching on Washington.

The opponents of war brought down on their heads a violent storm of right-wing, patriotic reaction. For the war not only reversed the progressivism of the preceding years but also fanned the most virulent outbreak of intolerance in American history. The Communist takeover of Russia in the fall of 1917 added fuel to the fire, raising the specter of a worldwide Red revolution. To be opposed to the war, to be a German-American, or even simply to be a nonconformist, invited harassment or worse.

Louise Olivereau, a Colorado radical, received a forty-five-year prison sentence for "speaking against American involvement in the war"; and a Los Angeles minister got six months for stating that he preferred the ideals of the Communists to those of the Merchants and Manufacturers' Association. In Oklahoma, where the Green Corn rebels faced a rough repression, a German Mennonite preacher was hanged twice until he fainted, simply because of who and what he was. Hundreds of pacifistic Mennonites and Hutterites fled the West for Canada. In Montana, a Miles City mob beat NPL fieldman Mickey McGlynn senseless in the basement of the Elks Club, and unidentified vigilantes lynched IWW organizer Frank Little from a Butte trestle. At Bisbee, Arizona, two thousand vigilantes illegally rounded up nearly twelve hundred IWWs and other miners and "deported" them by train, dumping them in the New Mexico desert.

Federal, state, and local governments not only tolerated such activity but often took the lead in it. In association with the federal government, each state created a Council of Defense to coordinate and press the war effort. Twenty-four states, most of them western, enacted "criminal syndicalism" laws that made it illegal to obstruct war production, the draft, or recruitment of the military or even to criticize the government or its policies. For instance, engulfed by anti-German hysteria, the Texas Council of Defense recommended banning German, indeed all foreign languages, from usage in the state. In early 1918, the legislature enacted the sweeping House Bill 15, which in effect outlawed dissent and mandated that ten minutes of each school day be devoted to the teaching of patriotism.

Similar events occurred, to a greater or lesser extent, throughout the region. Montana passed a similarly sweeping state Sedition Act that became the model for the notorious federal Sedition Act of 1918, usually considered the most flagrant violation of civil liberties in American history. The University of Nebraska Board of Regents devoted two weeks to an investigation of pro-German activities and eventually forced two faculty to resign. A terrible Houston riot in August of 1917 involving black troops resulted in the deaths of seventeen people. Later in the year, in the largest murder trial in U.S. history, thirteen of the blacks were consigned to death and forty-one to life imprisonment; eventually, six more were executed and twelve more given sentences of life imprisonment in one of the most severe instances of execution ever seen in this country.

The main fury of the superpatriots descended on leftist organizations like the Nonpartisan League, which touring patriots like Theodore Roosevelt effectively denounced as "Bolshevistic," and especially on the Industrial Workers of the World. Government-sponsored orators, along with the media, characterized the IWW as "Imperial Wilhelm's Warriors." The *Tulsa World* counseled: "Strangle the I.W.W.'s, kill 'em just like you would any other kind of snake. . . . It is not time to waste money on trials and contrivances like that." In September 1917, agents of the U.S. Department of Justice systematically raided IWW offices all across the West, arresting 160 of the Wobblies—including prominent leaders like "Big Bill" Haywood and Elizabeth Gurley Flynn—on the charges of violating federal Sedition and Espionage acts. More than one hundred of the arrested IWW members were eventually convicted, receiving sentences of up to twenty years. To counter the IWW appeal in the Northwest forest, the government joined forces with industry to create a non-striking union, the Loyal Legion of Loggers and Lumbermen, and even tried using the Army to cut timber.

Nor did the campaign against the antiwar left end with the abrupt close of the war in November 1918. To the contrary, America's near-hysterical fear that communism was spreading out of revolutionary Russia—now compounded by a postwar wave of strikes—fanned the flames of what by 1919 was becoming known as the "Red Scare." Some of the big postwar strikes were genuinely frightening. In February 1919, the workers of Seattle staged a "general strike," with unions shutting down the entire city in support of their beleaguered brethren in the shipyards. The Seattle general strike ended peaceably after four days, with demagogic Mayor Ole Hanson leading the counterattack that falsely portrayed the strike as the beginning of a real revolution.

The ugly postwar mood erupted in many forms, many of them involving mobs and vigilantes. A severe race riot racked Tulsa in May 1921, resulting in eighty people killed; another hit Longview, Texas, the following month. On Armistice Day of 1919, a pitched battle erupted in the town of Centralia, Washington, between parading veterans and a group of IWW members. Four of the paraders and two Wobblies died in the fray. Later, vigilantes seized another of the Wobblies from jail, castrated him, and hanged him.

All across the West, the radical organizations fell back under the tide of conservative reaction. In North Dakota, the Nonpartisan League lost its hegemony in the election

Blacks arrested during the Tulsa race riot of 1921. Courtesy of the Rudia Halliburton, Jr., Collection, University Archives, John Vaughan Library, Northeastern State University, Tahlequah, Oklahoma.

of 1920; and in 1921, in the first recall election of state officials in U.S. history, Lynn Frazier was removed as governor and William Lemke as attorney general. The IWW too faced continuing persecution: 31 Wobblies went to prison in Idaho and 164 in California between 1919 and 1924. Neither the NPL nor the IWW would ever again regain its prewar strength. The Socialists faced a similar decline. In Oklahoma, which had been the leading Socialist state of the Union before the war, the party could muster only fourteen regular members by 1924. Socialism, in fact, took its steepest postwar falls in the West; its national concentrations of influence now lay mainly in the East and Midwest.

Clearly, in the region as in the nation, the years of war and postwar reaction, 1917–20, marked a sharp departure from the prewar mood of tolerant optimism and progressive reform. Nationalistic and probusiness conservatives now held sway, smashing the radicals of the left and forcing the progressives onto the defensive. It seemed symbolic that western progressives like Senators Borah and Johnson were also isolationists who led the successful fight to block American membership in President Wilson's League of Nations, the symbol of world progressivism. The West entered the 1920s

—the decade that, witnessing the rapid spread of cars, electricity, movies, and radio, might well be termed the first of modern times—in an insular and intolerant mood.

THE TUMULTUOUS TWENTIES

American historians have frequently stressed two themes as characterizing the hectic decade of the 1920s: the conservative Republican dominance of the period, epitomized by the administrations of Presidents Warren Harding, Calvin Coolidge, and Herbert Hoover, and the nasty mood of intolerance and nativism that surrounded the first half of the decade. The West reflected both themes, more of the latter and less of the former, since whereas some parts of the region shared fully in the vaunted Republican prosperity of 1922–29, other parts—mainly those dominated by depressed agriculture—did not.

The nation and the region remained in a negative and intolerant frame of mind after war's end for several reasons. The war, which had been sold as a great crusade, ended abruptly and on a sour note, leaving a bitter residue of antiforeign and antileftist sentiment. Hard-pressed by the postwar farm depression, the countryside witnessed a loss of population to mushrooming cities and the triumph of the worldly ways of the city over traditional values. Even the great crusade for prohibition seemed now to have resulted only in a nationwide debauch of lawbreaking drunkenness. Rum roads crossed both the northern and southern borders of the West by the hundreds, radiating throughout the interior. Farmers jokingly spoke of grain yields in terms of gallons rather than bushels to the acre. "Bootleggers," the roar of whose engines on backroads and through fields became a familiar western lullaby, marketed such choice delicacies as Colorado's famed "Leadville Moon[shine]" at ten dollars per five gallons.

During the 1920s, the West fully shared in an important new national trend: the flight of unemployed farm workers and other rural folk to the cities, a trend that has persisted ever since. Urban Texas grew by a remarkable 58 percent during the decade. Urban southern California witnessed a mighty invasion, especially from the Midwest, heavily composed of retirees heading westward with their savings in search of the good life. Louis Adamic referred to them as "tired and retired people mostly from the Middle West"; and H. L. Mencken quipped that California was being populated by "middlebrow middlewesterners." Los Angeles soon had the distinction of holding the highest percentage of population over age forty-five of any of the country's ten largest cities.

These immigrants, joined by others from the rural West itself, changed the socioeconomic caste of Los Angeles, and of other western cities as well. In contrast to labor-liberal-antiprohibition San Francisco, which was the traditional urban hub of California, Los Angeles was conservative, fundamentalist, antilabor, and dry. A similar contrast appeared between conservative Portland and liberal Seattle to the north. In *The Pacific Slope*, historian Earl Pomeroy describes the resulting milieu of the 1920s Far West as "political fundamentalism," a direct blend of rightist politics and revivalistic "Old Time Religion" that portended what the nation would witness again sixty years later. Radio personalities like Aimee Semple McPherson and the Reverend "Fighting Bob" Shuler in Los Angeles became the order of the day, mixing personalized religion, politics, melodrama, and down-home music.

Easily the worst manifestation of postwar reaction was the rebirth, and the extension beyond the Old South, of the Ku Klux Klan. The reborn KKK resembled the original southern Reconstruction-era version with its persecution of blacks and with its hoods, fiery crosses, sloganeering, and brutality. But this reborn Klan was truly national in its sweep, and its enemies now numbered all "un-Americans"—Catholics, Jews, and foreigners of all sorts, as well as blacks. The entire West, especially the southern plains, experienced an eruption of KKK activity during the five years following the war. Led by Denver physician John Galen Locke, the Colorado

Klan grew to such dimensions that it could boast of its role in the election of a governor, a U.S. senator, and the mayor and chief of police of Denver. Reflecting the trend in many states, the Colorado Klan faded rapidly by 1925, with the easing of postwar tensions and the unearthing of KKK frauds and crime, in this case Locke's jailing for income tax fraud and contempt of court. Despite Oregon's earlier progressive reputation, that state—with a very small Catholic population—in 1922 elected a pro-KKK governor and enacted by initiative a law that forced all children to attend public schools, clearly taking aim at closing parochial schools. Fortunately, the law never took effect; the U.S. Supreme Court struck it down in 1925.

The western states bordering the Old South saw the worst of Klan behavior. Venerable Kansas progressive William Allen White ran for governor on an anti-KKK ticket in 1924, and lost. Klan activity rose to frightful proportions in Oklahoma, but in 1922 anti-KKK candidate John Walton rode a wave of backlash into the governor's chair. Walton's erratic behavior, however, culminating in his attempt to place the whole state under martial law, led to his impeachment and removal from office. In 1926, an equally eccentric prohibitionist and pro-Klan candidate, Henry Johnston, won election. Incredibly, three years later he also was evicted from office. Texas too emerged as a center of Klan activity, with at least eighty thousand active members and more than fifty reported "acts of terrorism" in 1920–21. In the town of Lorena, a gunfight between KKK paraders and a sheriff's posse ended with ten people wounded. By 1922, Dallas dentist Hiram Evans had become the "Imperial Wizard" of the entire national organization; and in Earle Mayfield, Texas had a U.S. senator who openly supported the Klan.

Here too the KKK issue badly disrupted state politics. In 1924, Miriam "Ma" Ferguson won the governorship in an anti-KKK campaign. Her husband, "Farmer Jim," had been impeached and removed from the statehouse seven years earlier and could not legally hold office again; so now Ma was running for vindication, promising "two governors for the price of one." Irregularities, especially in awarding highway contracts and in mass-pardoning criminals, again erupted, as they had in the first Ferguson administration; and Ma lost reelection in 1926. But "Fergusonism" would continue to enliven and complicate Texas politics for years to come.

The sour mind-set of the early, "tribal twenties" faded appreciably in the prosperous glow of the middle and later decade, although Catholic presidential candidate Al Smith, traveling by train in 1928, viewed crosses burning in the Oklahoma countryside. And in 1930, the *Denver Post* could still exude a common western bias: "New York has been a cess pool into which immigrant trash has been dumped for so long that it can scarcely be considered American any more." As this virulence of the far right abated, the political mood of the nation mellowed into a more traditional sort of conservatism. Speaking generally, the West mirrored this Republican trend. The Harding landslide of 1920, which buried the Democratic party of ailing Woodrow Wilson, carried every western state except Texas into the Republican column; and there most of them firmly remained throughout the decade.

Actually, however, western politics of the 1920s were far more complex than these simple presidential election victories might indicate. Strong progressive groups, composed heavily of distressed farmers and beleaguered union workers, remained active after 1919 throughout the West, especially the rural West. Yet they were fractionated between Democrats, Republicans, and independents and thus had trouble organizing; and they could not buck the national conservative Republican tide. The two states of Idaho and Nevada well illustrated the situation.

Conservative Republicans deftly outfought both the Idaho Democratic party, which remained debilitated after the now defunct Nonpartisan League had captured it, and a strong Progressive party, whose leaders would not and could not join up with the Democrats. Independent GOP Senator William Borah simply went his own independent way, ignoring party lines while winning plaudits as a leading figure in foreign policy circles. Similarly in Nevada, banker-boss George Wingfield maintained the hegemony of conservative Republicanism by playing Democrats and independent Republicans against one another, balancing Republican Tasker Oddie in one Senate seat with crafty Democrat Key Pittman in the other.

Western progressives in both major parties, especially those from the depressed interior states, did manage to score some victories during the inhospitable 1920s. Agitated by what they viewed as an overweening commitment to corporate business and an indifference to agriculture by conservative Republican administrations in Washington, prairie senators like Arthur Capper of Kansas, George Norris of Nebraska, and John Kendrick of Wyoming formed a formidable "Farm Bloc" of western and southern lawmakers. Dubbed the "Sons of the Wild Jackass" by an unfriendly press, they scored some notable victories, such as federal regulation of stockyards and grain exchanges, and created a powerful agricultural congressional bloc which would wield great strength for more than half a century to come. At the same time, western reform governors like Democrat Pat Neff in Texas and Republican Joseph Dixon in Montana attempted to carry on the prewar style of progressivism, albeit with limited success. The West led the country during these years in developing state-based old-age pension plans, with Nevada and Montana enacting the first in 1923; and five of the six states that ratified the ill-fated constitutional amendment to outlaw child labor also lay in the region.

However, the regional elections of 1924 and 1928 graphically demonstrated the weaknesses of Democrats and of progressives in both parties. Western and southern Democrats fought hard in 1924 to get the presidential nomination for the capable dry-progressive William McAdoo, President Wilson's son-in-law, who was now a resident of California. After failing at a marathon national convention that deadlocked over interregional squabbling, the western Democrats found little appeasement in their party's throwing them a sop—the vice-presidential nomination of Nebraska Governor Charles Bryan, the brother of William Jennings Bryan. A new Progressive party entered the field in 1924, running an attractive ticket of the venerable crusader Robert La Follette for president and the fast-rising Montana Senator B. K. Wheeler for his running mate; and this campaign drew off massive western support that might have gone to the Democrats. In the seventeen western states, La Follette garnered twice as many votes as did the Democratic candidate, John W. Davis, and in California four times as many. Only Oklahoma and Texas hung on in the Democratic column, as Republican incumbent President Calvin Coolidge swept all of America except the South, winning a landslide reelection.

The Republicans did even better in 1928, the zenith year of prosperity and conservative satisfaction. At their national convention in Houston, the Democrats by now had quieted the infighting of four years before and were under safe eastern-conservative control. They nominated for president the governor of New York, Al Smith, an eastern urbanite and a dripping "wet" who in the words of the *Pocatello* (Idaho) *Tribune* spoke "a different language." The result this time was an even greater Republican sweep than that of 1924; Herbert Hoover, a self-made man who could legitimately call himself a westerner, having spent part of his youth in Oregon and graduated from Stanford, took every state in the West.

Thus during the middle and late 1920s, the tempestuous West quieted down and joined more fully in the national mood of Coolidge prosperity and conservatism. Republican conservatives like Congressman Willis Hawley of Oregon and Senator Reed Smoot of Utah, cosponsors of the disastrously protectionist Hawley-Smoot Tariff of 1930, typified the probusiness, stand-pat profile of the era. So did the conservative western governors of the time, men like Friend Richardson of California, Roland Hartley of Washington, Billy Adams of Colorado, and Richard Dillon of New Mexico. Like the legislators with whom they worked, these executives sought not adventure and reform. They were satisfied with the system and worked simply for businesslike government, balanced budgets, and reduced taxes. To their astonishment, however, the apparent tranquillity of the time, and the conservative mood accompanying it, would soon vanish with the onset of the Great Depression in 1929–30.

Chapter Three

Depression, New Deal, and War, 1930-1945

During the period from 1930 through 1945, the West passed through a time of tumult and sweeping change, prompted first by the worst depression the world had ever seen, then by a massive federal effort to cope with the problems caused by the depression, and finally by American involvement in the Second World War. In essence, the New Deal and the war effort combined to produce the same result: a revolutionary new federal role in the West. This new federal role involved unprecedented expenditures, on everything from old-age pensions to mighty dams; and these expenditures, which would prove to be ongoing, served to underwrite a new prosperity and stability for the region. Viewed from the brief perspective of a half-century, therefore, these years represent a historic turning point of equal importance to the general closing of the frontier. The Great Depression brought about the crisis of that old, exploitative economic order that was based on the unrestricted taking of the West's bounty; and the New Deal and World War II signaled the beginning of the new order, in which we still live today. Henceforth, for good or bad, the sustaining and regulating hand of the federal government would be the foremost influence in the region, whereas the grip of the old corporate empire builders—such as railroads and lumber and mining barons—steadily weakened.

THE GREAT DEPRESSION

The great crisis of American capitalism began with the legendary Wall Street panic of autumn 1929. Optimists like President Herbert Hoover predicted a quick recovery, but instead the U.S. economy fell into a steep and steady decline. Things grew progressively worse from 1930 to 1933 with factory closures, mass unemployment, and the spreading of depression around the globe. At the heart of the national problem lay the ailment that had been afflicting the West in particular for over a decade, even as most of the nation had prospered: an overheated and unregulated economy that was producing more than the market could absorb, leading to rock-bottom prices and eventual shutdowns, bankruptcies, and unemployment.

The West, whose agricultural subregions had experienced little of the vaunted 1920s prosperity, was hit by this newest and worst of depressions considerably later than were the older regions to the east. Locked factory gates and breadlines came early to those industrial heartlands. It took longer for the ripple effects to reach the remote West, whose raw wealth fueled the mills and factories "back East." By 1931, however, the West was suffering the full brunt of the disaster, as already low product prices fell catastrophically lower and as demand in some cases all but disappeared.

In the Pacific Northwest, lumbermen marketed in 1933 only about one-third the product that they had shipped in the boom year of 1926. Salmon packers saw their sales dwindle by 120 million pounds from 1929 to 1932; and in the same period, Idaho's silver mines fell in production from $39 million to $9 million. Farm prices, seriously depressed since the close of World War I, now simply collapsed as consumers tightened their belts. Cotton sagged to a miserable three cents per pound by late 1932, and wheat fell to eighteen cents per bushel in Nebraska and twelve cents in Montana —the lowest prices since the reign of Queen Elizabeth I in the sixteenth century. Western cattlemen faced the ruinously low price of $4.14 a hundredweight.

In the Southwest, the flooding of oil from the East Texas and other newly opened fields into an already saturated market brought ridiculously low prices, as everyone drilled and refined at capacity to gain at least some profit. As prices fell below a dime per barrel, service stations hawked free chickens to lure in customers. Oilmen even pleaded for a federal takeover of the industry in order to save it. In the absence of federal action, Texas Governor Ross Sterling, one of the founders of Humble Oil (today's Exxon), and Oklahoma Governor "Alfalfa Bill" Murray both sent in the state militia to enforce well closures in an effort to deal with overproduction and waste.

Some areas, however, fared better than others. The coastal states, with their more balanced economies, generally did better than the interior states, with their highly vulnerable farms, ranches, and mines. But everywhere, the signs of hardship multiplied as people sought desperately to cope. Hopeless drifters, varying in age from young boys to old men, languished in "Hoovervilles" in every major city and "rode the rails" incessantly, as if mindlessly pursuing lost dreams of frontiering. Some communities dealt kindly with the down-and-out. In Texas, where folks even took to eating armadillos ("Hoover Hogs"), the city of Midland permitted transients to garden on unused public land. Oklahoma City was more typical, though, in arresting the derelicts and hustling them out of town.

In Sweetwater County, Wyoming, unemployed coal miners simply helped themselves to company veins, and juries refused to convict them. Similarly, New Mexico rustlers became so brazen in their search for food that cattlemen openly threatened to wreak vigilante justice on them. Unemployed Idahoans turned to arson in the dry forests to gain work at fire fighting. Few were so vulnerable or so threatened as the elderly. The Townsend movement, a visionary and unworkable old-age pension scheme calling for monthly payments of two hundred dollars to all elderly citizens, to be funded by a national sales tax, arose in California and spread like wildfire throughout the country. By September 1934, the

A "Hooverville" in Seattle in the 1930s. Courtesy of the Special Collections Division, University of Washington Libraries, photo by Lee, negative no. 20702.

Townsend organization boasted twelve hundred local clubs, most of them in the West, and the elderly were clearly becoming political. Most ominous of all, banks began failing in frighteningly large numbers, as anxious depositors withdrew their money. In October 1932, Nevada's governor declared a "bank holiday," which halted all withdrawals, and other state executives soon followed suit. It began to seem that the capitalist system itself might soon collapse.

The world of western agriculture, which was still very much the region's economic mainstay, seemed turned upside down. When their markets collapsed, Washington apple growers turned to the clever expedient of simply selling large cratefuls to unemployed men for $1.75. These men then sold the fruit on the street for five cents apiece, and thus the apple peddler became a fixture of the depression throughout the country. Communists and other radicals successfully organized the desperately poor fieldworkers of California into the

Cannery and Agricultural Workers Industrial Union, setting off a wave of strikes at Hayward, Vacaville, and elsewhere from 1932 to 1934. The growers formed vigilante outfits to counter them, and Governor Frank Merriam sent in the National Guard to restore order. Across the plains, agrarian radicalism flamed once more. Angry Nebraska farmers, carrying signs that read "Be Pickets or Peasants," halted a train in 1932 and removed its cargo of cattle in a symbolic attempt to withhold produce and raise prices. The Farm Holiday Association, dedicated to stopping the eviction of farmers from their land by mortgage foreclosure and to withholding crops from market, swelled rapidly in number. One of its Nebraska leaders announced that "200,000 of us are coming to Lincoln and we'll tear that new State Capitol Building to pieces."

At the heart of their woes lay not only collapsing prices but also the most graphic environmental disaster in American history, the droughts and "Dust Bowl" epoch of 1931–37. This cycle of drought was worse than anything anyone could remember. At Vinita, Oklahoma, the temperature surpassed 100 degrees for thirty-five consecutive days in mid-1934; on the thirty-sixth day, it reached 117 degrees. That summer, the Sooner State harvested only 3 percent of its wheat crop. The year 1936 proved to be the hottest, driest, and coldest in North Dakota's history. Annual precipitation fell to a mere 8.8 inches. As the incessant heat baked the earth, the eternal plains winds fanned up massive clouds of dust from farmlands that had for years been intensively pulverized. Thus would nature punish the environmental sins of the pioneers.

The "dusters" swept the full expanse of the Great Plains, but the central and southern areas were hardest hit. One great storm, that of May 11, 1934, carried away an estimated three hundred thousand tons of Great Plains topsoil. Yellowish dust from South Dakota, Nebraska, and Kansas darkened the skies over Cleveland, fell on Washington, D.C., reddened the snow of Boston, even created a haze over ships three hundred miles beyond the Atlantic coast. Terrified plains dwellers taped their windows in a losing struggle

A dust storm approaching Stratford, Texas, April 14, 1935. Courtesy of the Prints and Photographs Collection, Barker Texas History Center, University of Texas at Austin.

to seal out the dust and turned on their lights at midday. Some nearly suffocated, and many contracted dust pneumonia. Rare snowfalls blended with blowing dust to form a messy "snirt."

As usual, a variety of pests accompanied the drought. Locusts actually worsened it by devouring stubble in the grainfields. Swarming in vast clouds, the grasshoppers plugged car radiators, ate clothes on the line, and even stalled trains when their mashed bodies turned to pulp on the tracks. One huge swarm, descending on Killdeer, North Dakota, filled the streets of the town to a depth of four inches. Only with the breaking of the drought and the development of the insecticide DDT at the close of the "dirty thirties" would the pestilence abate.

Natural calamities, plummeting farm prices, and—as we shall see—government policies that paid landowners to remove ground from production combined to drive small farmers, especially tenant farmers, from the countryside. Perhaps a half million of them, ranging from "Dokies" in the North to "Okies" in the South, fled from the devastated Great Plains. Over half of them headed for the promised land of California, in a sort of forlorn aftershock of the passed frontier. John Steinbeck told their story movingly in *The Grapes of Wrath* (1939). Heading off in their rattling jalopies to new states that did not want them, they became the most famous victims of the Great Depression, symbols of a land of lost opportunity. Actually, most of the Okies came not from the dust-blown lands of western Oklahoma but rather from the heavily populated and poverty-stricken cottonlands of the state's southeast quadrant.

Not everyone suffered in the depression. Many westerners came through it comfortably enough. Some even profited, especially those who had sufficient capital or credit to buy up failed farms and other property at bargain rates. But poverty did spread to unprecedentedly large numbers of people; and as it did, local and state governments quickly proved themselves inadequate to deal with the problems. City and county governments relied on property taxes for revenue, and these were drying up with the faltering economy. So they simply did what little they could, improvising along the way. Dallas, for instance, granted reliefers not money but food, which could not be spent on booze and frivolity. In Wyoming, school districts cut back to six-month terms; in Idaho and South Dakota, towns went back to the old practice of boarding teachers; and by 1933, some Oklahoma and New Mexico communities simply closed their schools for lack of revenue. The state governments did little better. They too relied on dwindling property taxes, which the public wanted reduced. Therefore, although a number of them began experimenting with new income and sales taxes, most simply slashed expenditures and did very little to assist their impoverished people.

Under the leadership of Republican President Herbert Hoover, the federal government also moved slowly and conservatively in dealing with the depression. Hoover firmly believed that government intrusion into economic and personal affairs must be kept in close check. Thus his administration made only limited efforts to deal with the deepening crisis. For instance, Hoover utilized the Federal Farm Board to provide loans to agricultural cooperatives in order to assist them in storing surplus crops to keep them off the glutted markets. He also prevailed on Congress to create a Reconstruction Finance Corporation to make emergency loans to threatened corporations and later to the states for use in relief. But he steadfastly refused to move the federal government directly into relief for the unemployed or for farmers, or even to deal with the menacing oil problem.

This cautious conservatism led Hoover and the Republicans to overwhelming defeat in the crisis election of 1932. Even though Hoover had swept the nation and the region in 1928, four years later he lost every western state to his Democratic foe, Franklin D. Roosevelt, who seemed to promise a much larger federal role in coping with the depression. All across the West, 1932 witnessed a political revolution, as conservative Republican incumbents who had been comfortably ensconced for years gave way to untried Democrats. In Utah, even the mighty Republican strongman Reed Smoot lost out to little-known college professor Elbert Thomas. In the three Northwest states, where Hoover had carried every county but one in 1928, he carried only two in 1932.

THE NEW DEAL AND THE WEST

Few knew what to expect of the new Democratic president, Franklin Roosevelt, or of the many unseasoned Democrats who followed him into Congress and the state governments. The masses of voters clearly demanded federal action, however, and Roosevelt and the Democrats gave it to them. The Democrats' hectic program of unprecedented federal expenditures and regulation quickly became known as the "New Deal." During the period from 1933 to 1939, the New Deal produced the most sweeping wave of governmental reform in U.S. history. The president and his program would soon enjoy their greatest popularity in the South and the West, precisely those regions that so desperately sought to escape, with federal assistance, their "colonial" subservience to the East.

In the spring of 1933, the Roosevelt administration and a

friendly Congress launched a barrage of relief, reform, and recovery efforts of dizzying complexity. Historians have perhaps been most accurate in describing this early New Deal as a "broker state," which simply attempted to find out what each major economic group most wanted and then sought to give it to them. For instance, the West's preeminent economic interest was agriculture. For years, agrarian spokesmen had been pleading for direct federal aid to depressed farmers and ranchers. Now, the experimentally inclined New Dealers gave it to them by adopting the so-called domestic allotment plan, as articulated by M. L. Wilson of Montana and other westerners, with congressional enactment of the landmark Agricultural Adjustment Act of May 1933.

This revolutionary legislation aimed to reduce the crippling commodity surpluses and thereby to raise farm prices to the same level of "parity" with general prices that had existed in the good years before World War I. To accomplish this, the law created an Agricultural Adjustment Administration (AAA), which granted direct benefit payments to farmers who voluntarily reduced their acreages. In dramatic fashion, the federal government thus began a new policy of direct subsidies to farmers. Even in a thinly populated state like Wilson's Montana, these AAA benefits soon totalled $10 million yearly, providing a badly needed flow of cash through rural economies. The policy established by the AAA would prove enduringly vital to the western region. When the U.S. Supreme Court invalidated the law, the administration simply continued the policy with other means and agencies.

The New Deal created a number of other programs to promote the recovery of agriculture, including several aimed at refinancing farm mortgages at low rates of interest in order to halt the deadly spread of foreclosures. In 1935 came two new agencies that would work mighty changes on the West: the Rural Electrification Administration, which promoted the building of electrical lines to remote locations through a program of low-interest loans, and the Soil Conservation Service, which began restoring eroded lands with the reseed-

95

ing of native grasses and other conservation efforts. The REA brought the wonders of modern life to the rural West years before such advances would have arrived via the marketplace. Along with other federal conservation efforts, the SCS began the long task of restoring the ravaged land. A major part of this endeavor was the creation of forested "shelterbelts" to abate the Great Plains dust storms. To the surprise of many doubters, this program proved successful; and by 1940, more than forty million trees grew along twenty-five hundred miles of handsome shelterbelts. Quite convincingly, *Fortune* magazine speculated in 1935: "It is conceivable that when the history of our generation comes to be written in the perspective of a hundred years the saving of the broken lands will stand out as the great and most enduring achievement of the time."

Western ranchers got their New Deal bonanza with a federal program of purchasing surplus livestock and with enactment in 1934 of the Taylor Grazing Act. This epochal measure opened the federally owned rangelands, almost all of them in the West, on a regularized basis to grazing leases by stockmen under a tightly controlled system of permits and fees like those administered by the Forest Service in the national forests. By the close of the New Deal, more than eleven million livestock were feeding on over 140 million federally owned acres. Despite frequent grumbling about controls and fee rates, and about how the new policy favored larger over smaller operators, the West generally welcomed the new, scientific system of range management.

In a true sense, the Taylor Grazing Act signaled the federal government's admission of the frontier's closing. Henceforth, western lands must be husbanded, not given away; all unreserved federal lands would be closed to entry, thereby ending the age-old policy of homesteading and cheap sales. Stockmen, miners, and lumbermen could access these lands in the future only on the government's terms. In February 1935, President Roosevelt formalized the new policy by closing the public domain forevermore to settlement. Later that spring, by proclamation, he withdrew the remaining

165.7 million acres of public domain, which were set aside for grazing and other classified usages. This change of course in public policy marked one of the most important and far-reaching governmental actions in American history, one that would go far toward fashioning the modern West.

Crusty Secretary of the Interior Harold Ickes, a wily and stubborn bureaucrat, came to wield an awesome power over the West, not only because he controlled the vast grazing lands but also because he commanded the Bureau of Reclamation and the Public Works Administration, which the New Deal had formed to build dams and other large projects. Often working together, the PWA and the Reclamation Bureau, and also the Army Engineers, initiated an enormous dam-building campaign throughout the arid West during the New Deal, dams that provided not only irrigation to farmers but also cheap electric power, flood control, and jobs for the unemployed. During these years, therefore, the Bureau of Reclamation began in earnest its momentous shift toward erecting huge, multipurpose dams, thereby becoming the key federal agency in the entire West.

The first of the great multipurpose dams was Boulder (Hoover) Dam on the lower Colorado River, begun in 1931 and completed in 1935 to supply large volumes of water and electricity, mainly to southern California. To build it, the Reclamation Bureau contracted with the so-called Six Companies, not one of which was big enough individually to raise the necessary capital. Among the group were such future western giants as the W. A. Bechtel Company, Morrison-Knudsen of Boise, Utah Construction, and Henry J. Kaiser. The hard-driving contractors finished two years ahead of schedule, at the cost of 110 lives lost in temperatures ranging up to 140 degrees. They had found a new western bonanza in big-time federal contracts—and had laid the foundation of an enormous nexus of big contractors, big government, and big regional politicians that would go far toward determining the future of the new West.

All across the arid West, monumental dams arose to symbolize the New Deal's role in building up the regional economy: Mansfield Dam on Texas's Colorado River, which boosted the careers of young Congressman Lyndon Johnson and of the soon-to-be-mighty construction firm of Brown and Root; the Colorado–Big Thompson Project, which diverted waters eastward under the continental divide through a thirteen-mile tunnel; Conchas Dam and the Tucumcari Project in New Mexico; the Gila Project in Arizona; the Provo River Project in Utah; and giant, earth-filled Fort Peck Dam on the Upper Missouri River in Montana. By late 1936, the Reclamation Bureau had nineteen major western dams under construction. In addition, this agency and others built scores of smaller, earthen dams to serve various localities.

The Pacific states benefited enormously. In California, the Bureau of Reclamation took over from the state government the building of the far-flung Central Valley Project, whose mighty dams like Shasta and whose miles of canals would in the years ahead make that state America's agricultural leader. Along the large and swift-flowing Columbia River, the Army Engineers erected Bonneville Dam, and the Reclamation Bureau built awesome Grand Coulee Dam, the "biggest thing on earth," which irrigated more land and generated more power than all the dams of the Tennessee Valley Authority combined. To distribute and market the electricity from these Columbia dams, the government created the Bonneville Power Administration, which in effect began supplying the Northwest with federally subsidized cheap power.

The great New Deal dams meant more than jobs and subsidies. They epitomized the new Uncle Sam's West. In these years of national need and national and regional pride, few criticized the projects or even pointed out the incongruity that one federal agency was spending millions to bring new western lands into agricultural production while another one (the AAA) was spending millions to take other western lands out of production.

The West's other extractive industries also joined in the federal largesse. A major thrust of the early New Deal came with creation of the National Recovery Administration, a new federal agency that collaborated with leaders in every major industry to enact "codes of fair competition" aimed at cutting back ruinous competition and low prices. The NRA program ran counter to traditional antitrust policy and was soon scuttled by the U.S. Supreme Court, but in the short run it had a sizable impact on the region. For instance, it seemed likely for a time to restructure the lumber industry, which had been depressed for most of a decade. The NRA's lumber code of 1934, fashioned by David Mason and other industry leaders, achieved some measure of stability and served to spread throughout the West the ideas of conservation and sustained-yield forestry. But the NRA code never really worked. Too many lumbermen were able to evade it, and accusations that the largest corporate leaders worked to draft the codes in their own interest proved largely to be true.

The NRA codes worked little better in the besieged oil industry, which was flooded by "hot oil" (that is, oil produced in violation of state efforts to prorate or limit production) from the East Texas and other new fields out West. By the spring of 1933, East Texas oil sold for four cents per barrel. The NRA code began the key federal rescue effort to cut back such squandering; and with the Connally Act of 1935, Congress effectively forbade the shipment of "hot oil" in interstate commerce. Under the iron hand of Interior Secretary Ickes, this time wearing the hat of U.S. Petroleum Administrator, the federal government thus baled out the threatened oil industry by doing what businessmen and the states could not do for themselves, limiting production on a national scale. Soon, the price was back to one dollar per barrel and climbing.

The New Deal came to the rescue of another depressed western industry in similar fashion with the Silver Purchase Act of 1934. Pressed through Congress by a determined phalanx of senators from the seven lightly populated silver states of the West, this measure mandated the Treasury Department to purchase silver either until silver reached a price of

$1.29 an ounce or until it amounted to one-fourth of the federal monetary reserve. The law was a neo-Populist measure, echoing the western silver inflationism of the 1890s. But, since most silver derived as a by-product of copper and lead mines, the act really amounted to a hefty subsidy of the whole western mining industry and thus had a major regional impact. Historian Richard Lowitt is correct in noting that the miners resembled the oilmen in extracting aid from Uncle Sam strictly on their own terms under the New Deal.

Other western constituencies received specific programs too. Arguably, some of them, like those Indian tribes that questioned the Wheeler-Howard Indian Reorganization Act of 1934 (see chapter 4), had little voice in what they got. But most resembled the farmers, oilmen, and miners in getting some approximation of what they wanted. For instance, organized labor: first with the NRA and then more emphatically with the National Labor Relations Act of 1935, the government moved to guarantee and oversee the rights of labor unions to bargain collectively. All across the West, old unions reorganized and new ones emerged to win collective bargaining agreements and better wages and hours.

Throughout the Mountain West, the Mine, Mill and Smelter Workers regained the closed shop in a series of generally nonviolent strikes. On the West and Gulf coasts, another established union, the International Longshoremen's Association, led by the gaunt and radical Australian Harry Bridges, struck from Houston to San Diego to Seattle in 1934, closing down the Pacific ports for ninety-eight days. The Houston strike was grave enough to be termed a "waterfront reign of terror." At San Francisco, the labor offensive expanded into a three-day general strike that shocked the nation. Police and national guardsmen drove back the strikers with machine guns, but labor won important concessions nonetheless. Conspicuous among the rising new unions was the Teamsters, which won favorable contracts from regional shippers in the fast-rising trucking industry. Even in the fantasyland of Hollywood, activists like Groucho Marx, Boris Karloff, and newcomer Ronald Reagan estab-

The 1934 labor dem-
onstration in San
Francisco. Courtesy of
The Bancroft Library,
University of California
at Berkeley.

lished a closed shop system under the Screen Actors Guild.
With New Deal encouragement, the economic and political
power of organized labor rose to unprecedented heights.

To the masses of westerners, as to all Americans, the most
visible and important New Deal programs were those that
provided public "relief" to the unemployed and dependent.
In 1933, the Roosevelt administration broke sharply from
the cautious Hoover policy and created the Federal Emergency Relief Administration, which granted federal relief
funds directly to the states. They in turn had to match them
with their own funds and administer them to the needy. The
search for relief matching monies in a time of depression
led many of the western states to institute new income taxes
or, as with Colorado and Wyoming in 1935, to enact new

sales taxes. The states frequently bungled their relief operations, leading to charges of sloppiness, "boondoggling," and
political manipulation.

Consequently, in 1935 the federal government took another giant step with the creation of the famous Works
Progress Administration (WPA), which now bypassed the
states and placed the unemployed directly on federal work
relief. Thousands of WPA workers found federal employment doing everything from building airports to working in
women's sewing circles to painting murals in public buildings. Many western counties built their modern systems of
graveled rural roads with federal WPA dollars; and many a
western town received federally built schools, courthouses,
and sewage systems via the WPA, which they could not
otherwise have afforded for years to come.

The year 1935 marked a second major surge of New Deal
reform. In addition to the WPA, an additional keystone of
this "Second New Deal" emerged with congressional passage of the far-reaching Social Security Act, which created
the federal retirement-pension system still in effect today and
which also initiated a federal-state unemployment compensation program and authorized federal grants to the states
to assist them in caring for the disabled and other "unem-
ployables." Thus began the system of federally assisted state
welfare programs for the indigent poor that to this day, in
the West and elsewhere, differ markedly in what they cost
and what they provide.

The New Deal also developed other relief programs, targeted at specific groups. For instance, the WPA's National
Youth Administration gave high school and college students
part-time employment to keep them in school and out of
the job market. The WPA's Federal Arts Project offered sustenance to such major western artists as Jackson Pollock,
and the Federal Writers' Project similarly employed authors
of the caliber of Arizona's Ross Santee and Idaho's Vardis
Fisher. Of special importance to the West was the popular
Civilian Conservation Corps, which took single young men
off the streets and out of job competition with husbands and

fathers and put them to work on public lands. The "CCC boys" labored to eradicate the white pine blister rust fungus in North Idaho, planted wheatgrass on eroded rangelands in the Dakotas, built thousands of miles of mountain trails, and in many other ways helped to restore and preserve the western landscape.

Politically, the New Deal swept the West, knocking down conservative and Republican establishments of the 1920s and initiating the greatest period of liberal and Democratic domination of government the region has ever seen. Roosevelt's personal popularity, and the popularity of his programs, are attested by the fact that, after carrying every western state in 1932, he repeated that achievement in the election of 1936. In his 1940 reelection campaign, Roosevelt carried all the western states except Colorado and the North Dakota–Kansas tier; and in 1944 he won all but the same group with Wyoming added. Riding the tide of Democratic popularity, westerners occupied posts of key congressional leadership. The gruff John Nance Garner of Texas gave up the position of speaker of the House of Representatives to become Roosevelt's vice-president during 1933–41; and in turn, the astute and honorable Sam Rayburn, a key Texas New Deal congressman, captured the speakership in 1940. Nevada's hard-living Key Pittman chaired the influential Senate Foreign Relations Committee, and tough Burton K. Wheeler of Montana headed the Senate Interstate Commerce Committee.

The New Deal tide carried many new personalities into state politics, including several cranks and radicals of the far left and far right. In Kansas, for instance, John "Goat Gland" Brinkley, a "medical authority" whose main claim to fame was his theory of restoring male fertility by goat gland transplants, made two unsuccessful but well-supported runs for governor. In North Dakota, flamboyant Governor William Langer made national headlines by enforcing a moratorium on the hated farm mortgage foreclosures and employing the National Guard to halt sheriffs' sales that defied his order. After the state supreme court removed him

Governor William H. "Alfalfa Bill" Murray of Oklahoma. Courtesy of the Western History Collections, University of Oklahoma Library.

from office for political corruption, Langer won an acquittal and was reelected as governor and eventually as U.S. senator. Socialist novelist Upton Sinclair won the Democratic gubernatorial nomination but lost a heated election campaign in 1934 on a radical platform to "End Poverty in California," and the leftist Washington Commonwealth Federation for a time played a dominant role in the Democratic party of that state. In Colorado, a mob of angry relief workers occupied the state capitol in 1935, holding it long enough to convene a Communist party meeting inside.

In general, though, the political eccentrics of the 1930s were more colorful than truly dangerous. Oklahoma Governor "Alfalfa Bill" Murray gained a good deal of nationwide notoriety for his homespun ways, his battles with the legislature, and his frequent use of the National Guard for dubious purposes. Murray frequently wore dirty socks and no shoes. When his enemies threatened impeachment, he retorted that it would "be like a bunch of jack-rabbits tryin' to get a wild cat out of a hole." Despite his anticapitalist rhetoric, however, Murray proved in practice to be rather conservative and eventually opposed the New Deal. Jim Ferguson maneuvered his wife Miriam back into the Texas governorship in 1932, promising to "be on hand picking up chips and bringing in water for mama." But although the Fergusons once again raised controversy, they aroused less of it than before. "Ma" declined to run again in 1934; and the governorship passed to James Allred, who is still remembered as "Texas's last liberal governor." In 1938, the Lone Star governorship went to yet another flamboyant soul, W. Lee "Pappy" O'Daniel, a shrewd chap who had risen to fame with a radio show complete with country music from the "Light Crust Doughboys," lots of homilies, and the byword "Please pass the biscuits, Pappy." Like Murray, O'Daniel posed as the common man's friend but proved in practice to be a reliably conservative defender of established economic interests.

In truth, the western state governments varied widely in their responses to the deluge of New Deal programs. Some governors were avowed conservatives, unfriendly to the Roosevelt endeavors, men such as Charles Martin in Oregon, Clarence Martin in Washington, "Sunny Jim" Rolph and Frank Merriam in California, and "Big Ed" Johnson in Colorado. Others were genuine liberals of varying degrees, friendly to the New Deal, most notably Culbert Olson in California, Payne Ratner in Kansas, Ernest Marland in Oklahoma, Charles Bryan in Nebraska, and Herbert Maw in Utah. Most were essentially pragmatists, like Republican Alf Landon of Kansas, who cooperated with Washington most of the time, deftly applying federal funds to help balance state budgets. Likable and popular, Landon gained the Republican presidential nomination in 1936, only to be buried in the Roosevelt landslide.

All the state governments wrestled with the knotty problems of raising new revenues to match federal relief expenditures, coping with the fast-growing federal bureaucracy, and dividing the political plums that came with the New

Deal programs. Efforts by local politicos to control relief jobs in their own interest caused Roosevelt's relief director, Harry Hopkins, to seize control of all such funds in Murray's Oklahoma and Langer's North Dakota. Hopkins also faced constant struggles over relief in other states, such as Texas and Colorado. Forced to institute new taxes, some state political leaders went down to defeat. This happened to Idaho's colorful Governor "Cowboy Ben" Ross, who grudgingly sponsored a sales tax in 1935 and then suffered defeat, along with the tax on a referendum, the next year in a U.S. Senate race. Relief dollars and other forms of political patronage had much to do with directing progressive support away from the Republicans and toward the Democrats. As in New Mexico, where the Hispanic Democrat Dennis Chávez replaced Republican Bronson Cutting as senator and as the state's key power broker after Cutting's death in 1935, the Democratic party now burgeoned as the party both of the masses and of liberal leadership.

Beyond dispute, the New Deal had a great influence on the West, both in the short term with relief and recovery measures and in the longer term with enduring reforms and capital investments. As a region, the West gained far more in federal expenditures per capita than did the nation at large. The three leading states, of all the forty-eight, in New Deal dollars expended per capita were Nevada ($1,130), Montana ($710), and Wyoming ($626). Compared to per capita investments in eastern-urban states such as Rhode Island ($167) and New Jersey ($177), these amounts indicate the extent to which the West monetarily benefited from the New Deal. The thinly populated West gained such windfalls in federal spending because of its low land-person ratio, its large acreages of federally owned land, its low incomes matched by high unemployment, and its large dam projects.

It is hardly surprising that such rewards paid off handsomely in political popularity for Roosevelt and for Democrats in the West. However, even though the New Deal did fashion long-term Democratic majorities throughout much of the region, the huge vote majorities for the New

Deal soon began eroding as traditional western distrust of Uncle Sam combined with rising anger at a burgeoning and bothersome bureaucracy. Thus, as the New Deal played out in the late 1930s, the western attitude toward it shifted, in James Patterson's words, from enthusiasm "to grudging acceptance, then to suspicion." Just as they had a half-century before, and as they would a half-century later, westerners, more than most Americans, enjoyed their cake of federal subsidy even as they relished the pleasure of complaining about it. As the cartoon philosopher "Mr. Dooley" observed: "On the one hand we extend our lips for a benevolent kiss; on the other hand, we feel a compulsion to kick these meddlers in the arse."

Complaints aside, no one could truthfully deny that the New Deal had gone far toward lifting the region from the grip of depression or that it had introduced a new era in federal governance of the West. In this sense, the New Deal's impact on the West was truly revolutionary. Whereas in 1930 most westerners who sought any governmental assistance at all looked for it in places like Pierre, Santa Fe, or Boise, by 1940 they looked primarily eastward to Washington, D.C.

THE IMPACT OF WORLD WAR II

The New Deal years of the 1930s wrought enormous changes throughout the West, but the frenetic period of World War II wrought even greater ones. By the fall of 1939, German aggression in Europe and Japanese aggression in Asia had wrapped the globe in an even more terrible war than that of twenty years before. The United States had begun gearing up for war well before the Japanese attack on Pearl Harbor pushed it into the fray in December 1941, and it remained at war until Japan's final defeat in August 1945. The mighty war effort transformed all regions of the country, but none so much as the still wide-open West. Millions flocked to the region's new military installations and wartime production plants, which were geared primarily to the war in the Pacific. Every facet of the western economy and social order changed under the sweeping forces of this greatest of all national crusades in American history.

Every western state claimed at least one sizable military installation, some old and some new, by 1942; but in some states, the military invasion was simply overwhelming. During the two decades between the world wars, an important wing of the U.S. Navy had been moved from the Atlantic to the Pacific harbors of San Francisco Bay, San Diego, and Los Angeles–Long Beach, slanting urban California, in Roger Lotchin's phrase, "toward a kind of military welfarism." These great naval bases, along with the giant Marine Corps training ground of Camp Pendleton and such army centers as Fort Ord, Travis Army Air Corps Base, and the western headquarters at San Francisco's Presidio, made much of California seem like one big armed camp.

Washington boasted the huge naval shipyards at Bremerton, where the crippled Pacific Fleet retired for repairs after the Pearl Harbor attack. Among Utah's ten major installations were the Hill and Wendover air bases, Dugway Proving Ground, and the sprawling Ogden Arsenal. Colorado Springs emerged as a major military center with both the Ent air base and Camp Carson's thirty-seven thousand army trainees. Kansas doted on General Dwight Eisenhower, commander of Allied armies in Europe, who told his home folks in 1945, "The proudest thing I can claim is that I'm from Abilene." But it also had two of the army's largest bases with Fort Leavenworth and Fort Riley and many smaller ones, which included, with the state's inviting flatlands, a number of Army Air Corps training locations.

Texas, nurturing its hybrid southern-western military traditions, probably surpassed all other states in its dedication to the war effort. The Lone Star State laid claim to the chief naval commander in the Pacific, Admiral Chester Nimitz; to the most decorated war hero in U.S. history, Audie Murphy; to Oveta Culp Hobby, commander of the Women's Army Corps; and to Eisenhower as well, since he was born there. Texas A&M produced more army officers during the war than did West Point. The Third and Fourth armies were both based at San Antonio, which was also home to Kelly, Brooks, and Lackland air bases and to Randolph Field, the "West Point of the air." Altogether, Texas counted forty flying fields, including Carswell Field at Fort Worth, the national headquarters of the Army Air Corps training command.

More than 8,000,000 people moved to the lands west of the Mississippi during the ten years after 1940, with 3,500,000 moving to California alone, which surged to a population of 10,586,000 by midcentury. Booming wartime industry accounted for even more of this remarkable flood of immigration than did the military. Industrialists received huge federal contracts, often funded by loans from the powerful Reconstruction Finance Corporation, directed by the authoritarian Jesse ("Jesus") Jones of Houston, and from the RFC's subsidiary Defense Plant Corporation.

The state of California received roughly $35 billion in federal expenditures during the war, fully 10 percent of the national total. Two great military industries propelled the boom in California (and its two neighbors to the north): aircraft production and shipbuilding. Southern California rapidly emerged as America's foremost center of airplane manufacturing, with the firms of Ryan and Convair at San Diego, Douglas at Santa Monica and other locations, and Lockheed, Hughes, Northrop, and North American in the Los Angeles Basin. More than 300,000 workers found aircraft industry jobs in California during the war. Similarly, the immense Boeing plants spreading across greater Seattle employed 40,000, building first the workhorse B-17 "Flying Fortress" bombers and then the majestic B-29 "Superfortresses." In the interior, Boeing also constructed bombers at Wichita; and Fort Worth, along with nearby Garland and Grand Prairie, likewise developed as a leading center of the new aviation industry.

Even more dramatic in its impact was the mushrooming shipbuilding industry. During the war, Uncle Sam spent $4.7 billion on West Coast shipyards, by 1943 employing 280,000 just in greater Los Angeles and in the San Francisco Bay area, which was the foremost shipbuilding locale

Kaiser's Oregon shipyards at night during World War II. Courtesy of The Bancroft Library, University of California at Berkeley.

in the country. Towering over this industry, and others related to it, stood the remarkable Henry J. Kaiser, the most powerful westerner of his time. Imposing, hard driving, and intelligent, Kaiser had made his mark during the preceding decade, most notably as a big-time dam builder. Dubbed "Sir Launchalot" by the press, Kaiser boasted a shipyard empire that reached the length of the West Coast. Combined, his yards produced a new ship every ten hours at their peak. By war's end, the Kaiser enterprises had produced fully one-third of all U.S. wartime shipping. Near all of his major installations, Kaiser erected company hospital-clinics, which set new standards in affordable medical care for his workers.

The manufacture of weaponry took on other forms at other locations. At Denver's big Rocky Mountain Arsenal, for example, Remington Rand employed up to 20,000 workers fabricating poison gas and ammunition. Even submarine chasers were built at Denver, then shipped by rail for assembly on the coast, stunning more than one onlooker who suddenly witnessed ship towers coming around a railroad bend high in the mountains.

In addition to defense industries, the war also boomed the West's basic extractive industries, and added some new ones as well. Mining and petroleum extraction surged to capacity, and the large majority of U.S. domestic oil now came from the West. As Nazi submarines wrought havoc on vulnerable coastwise Atlantic oil tankers in 1942, the government funded the "Big Inch" pipeline to carry Texas oil the 1,254 miles to Pennsylvania. An important new petrochemical industry arose as a result of the Japanese conquest of natural rubber sources in Southeast Asia. American scientists quickly perfected processes of manufacturing synthetic rubber for tires and hoses vital to war making. With funding from the RFC and its Rubber Reserve Corporation, $325 million worth of petrochemical-synthetic rubber plants sprouted along Houston's busy and polluted ship channel, forming a manufacturing complex that would grow mightily in the years after the war. The Rubber Reserve Corporation also subsidized a major Goodyear works at Phoenix and invested more than $59 million in synthetic rubber plants in the Los Angeles Basin, incidentally contributing to a problem that first appeared during the war years, "smog."

For lumbermen also, the war brought increased product demands; but their share of national production actually shrank to less than 38 percent by 1945, since railroad bottlenecks and higher freight rates obstructed access to eastern markets. For farmers and ranchers, on the other hand, booming wartime markets brought high prices and prosperity. After Pearl Harbor, the federal government began mass-purchasing foodstuffs for the military and for its allies. By 1943, it was buying up 80 percent of all lower-grade beef, 35 percent of lamb and mutton, and 50 percent of canned fruit and vegetables. Rationing was introduced for civilians; and with a government guarantee of 90 percent of parity, prices shot upward. These bonanza prices, plus abundant rainfall throughout most of the West during the war years, meant welcome profits for those farmers and ranchers who had survived the lean times of the 1920s and 1930s.

Profits and inflation made it easy to pay off debts and to acquire the new trucks, tractors, and harvesters that farmers needed to work larger acreages. As low-paid farm workers fled the countryside to seek higher-paying jobs in defense plants, machines suddenly seemed everywhere to be replacing manpower in agriculture. Sheep ranchers, who were already in difficulty as synthetic fibers threatened the wool market and as tender, grain-fed beef supplanted mutton, now found it nearly impossible to hire hands. So, many simply converted to the less labor-intensive business of raising cattle. Western farm and rural populations visibly dwindled, but few worried amid such undreamed-of good times. Mechanized farmers, incredibly, raised 50 percent more crops per year during World War II than they had during World War I, only a quarter-century earlier. Particularly in the Southwest, growers of fruit, vegetables, and sugar beets, who still required armies of field hands, had to import them, primarily from Mexico. Under a series of *bracero* agreements between the United States and Mexico, 219,000 Mexican workers were brought northward from 1942 to 1947.

New basic industries emerged among the old, such as the largest tin smelter on earth at Texas City, or the giant, federally funded Basic Magnesium plant near Las Vegas, valued at $150 million and drawing on the cheap power from Boulder Dam. Cheap, federally subsidized electricity also drew an important new metal industry to the Northwest, aluminum. The progressive Roosevelt administration was eager not only to foster the growth of this lightweight, electricity-intensive metal near West Coast aircraft plants and shipyards but also to undercut the eastern Alcoa aluminum monopoly. Hence, RFC loans supported the building of nine new western plants, including the five that Henry J. Kaiser erected at Spokane and other Northwest locations. This federally nurtured industry took firm root; by the mid-1950s, Kaiser Aluminum commanded 25 percent of U.S. output, a classic example of federal assistance to the West in breaking the bonds of economic colonialism.

Symbolically most important of all, the war brought with it a major westward extension of the steel industry. The eastern captains of big steel—anxious to maintain their sway under the so-called Pittsburgh-plus system, which charged eastern rates plus transportation from Pittsburgh, no matter where the steel might actually be manufactured—vigorously opposed any competition from the West. As in the case of aluminum, however, Roosevelt listened to the logic of making steel in proximity to burgeoning western markets, as well as to the pleas of his western supporters. At Provo, Utah, the RFC's Defense Plant Corporation poured more than $200 million into the Geneva Steel Works, built by Utah Construction and operated by the western subsidiary of U.S. Steel.

The Geneva Steel Works rose to become the largest steel facility west of the Mississippi; but even more frightening to the eastern establishment was Kaiser's bid to build a large plant at Fontana, east of Los Angeles. At first stymied, Kaiser eventually won—with the support of his California banking ally A. P. Giannini and Jesse Jones of the RFC—a $150 million government loan to construct the Fontana facility, which utilized coal from Utah and iron ore from the Mojave Desert. Big steel had come to stay. Even though U.S. Steel closed the Geneva Works after the war, it reopened in 1948; and a Federal Trade Commission investigation after the war forced the end of the hated basing-point price system. Eastern industrialists watched these developments with dismay. *Fortune* magazine observed that Kaiser had simply "backed a truck up to the mint." As for Kaiser, he saw all of this as a triumph for "the independent industrialization of the West." And Giannini purred: "The West has all the money to finance whatever it wants to; we no longer have to go to New York for financing, and we're not at its mercy."

In yet another way, the federal government fostered western development by its expenditures on military science.

A. P. Giannini, 1935. Courtesy of The Huntington Library, San Marino, California.

Like their counterparts around the country, major western universities contracted with federal agencies, particularly the new Office of Scientific Research and Development (OSRD), to research a host of military questions. Scientists at the University of Washington Applied Physics Lab performed torpedo research; those at Rice Institute investigated nuclear processes; and researchers at the University of Texas, the University of New Mexico, and the California Institute of Technology performed rocketry experiments. Ernest Lawrence's Radiation Laboratory at the University of California at Berkeley, which first developed the cyclotron, emerged as a world leader in nuclear research, attracting the talents of great scientists like J. Robert Oppenheimer and Glenn Seaborg. At Hanford, Washington, the OSRD built the world's largest plutonium plant, employing nearly twenty thousand workers to supply the materials for the first atomic bomb. At the isolated and secret Los Alamos Laboratory in New Mexico, a team of the world's foremost scientists, led by

Oppenheimer and including Edward Teller and Leo Szilard, brought to success the Manhattan Project, detonating the first atomic bomb. With the explosion of July 16, 1945—"the day the sun rose twice"—the nuclear age was born at Alamogordo, and the world changed forever.

Whether lured west by science, the military, or industry, the wartime immigrants represented the greatest inflow of humanity in the region's history. Denver grew by 20 percent during the war, attracting 100,000 new residents; and Tucson nearly doubled, from 48,000 to over 90,000. With its dam, its magnesium plant, a cluster of military installations, and the beginnings of its modern gambling-entertainment business, Las Vegas tripled in population from 8,422 in 1940 to 24,624 in 1950. Yet even the precipitous growth of these interior cities was dwarfed by what happened to their sisters on the Pacific Coast.

Already a major city by 1940, Portland almost doubled in size during the war, attracting 160,000 new citizens for a swollen total population of 359,000. One hundred thousand more newcomers poured into its suburbs. The larger city of Seattle grew from a population of 368,000 in 1940 to 530,000 by 1944. Incredibly, San Diego increased by 147 percent between 1941 and 1945, from a civilian-military populace of 202,000 in 1940 to 510,000 in 1944. More than 500,000 newcomers invaded the Los Angeles Basin during the war, and even more descended on the cities around San Francisco Bay. As Gerald Nash demonstrates, the mushrooming little cities of the East Bay represented the most spectacular boomtowns in the country. Vallejo grew to over 100,000, an increase of more than 500 percent. Between 1940 and 1943, Richmond saw its quiet populace of 23,642 surge to a turbulent 150,000.

The boom brought to the West an unprecedented prosperity but also an unprecedented chaos of social problems: traffic jams that lasted for hours, endless lines of shoppers with their ration books, and sharp increases in crime, venereal diseases, juvenile delinquency of unsupervised adolescents, and divorce rates. Racial tensions mounted apace as, for the first time, western cities drew large black populations. Seattle, for instance, saw its black populace expand from under 4,000 to nearly 30,000 from 1940 to 1945. Spanish-speaking Americans also suffered the pangs of wartime discrimination. More than 220,000 Mexican Americans inhabited the big East Los Angeles barrio as the war began, most of them in dire poverty. Although seventeen Hispanic Americans earned Medals of Honor, most of their white fellow citizens disparaged them, angered especially at the Mexican youths who dressed flashily in "zoot suits," formed "pachuco" gangs, and baited servicemen. In mid-1943, thousands of uniformed servicemen roamed through the East Los Angeles barrio on several nights in succession, searching out and beating the zoot-suiters.

One western minority, the Japanese Americans, found themselves the target of one of the most shameful persecutions in the nation's history. Almost all of the 118,000 Japanese Americans lived in the Far West, 100,000 of them in California. The fact that they were singled out for exceptional treatment, compared to German or Italian Americans, is attributable partly to the genuine fear of invasion following Pearl Harbor, partly to racism, and partly to the national rage at Japanese triumphs and atrocities in the Pacific in early 1942. On the night of January 24, 1942, a lone weather balloon drifting over Los Angeles set off an air-raid scare, complete with blazing antiaircraft guns, two deaths from heart attacks, and three people killed and dozens injured in the ensuing melee. Actually, Japan lacked the ability to attack the Pacific Coast with any real strength, although it did attack and occupy, for a time, islands in the Aleutian group off Alaska. Its only strikes on the West Coast were two submarine shellings, near Santa Barbara in February and near the mouth of the Columbia in June 1942.

California Governor Culbert Olson and Attorney General Earl Warren championed the popular demand that since the Japanese Americans posed a direct threat to national security, they must be rounded up and interred. General John DeWitt, who headed the Western Defense Command,

Evacuation of Japanese Americans at Bainbridge Island, Washington, in March 1942. Courtesy of the *Seattle Post-Intelligencer*.

agreed, even though the *Nisei* (American-born Japanese Americans) were U.S. citizens: "A Jap's a Jap. . . . It makes no difference if he is an American citizen." Despite its liberal reputation, the Roosevelt administration concurred and in February 1942 authorized the army to begin relocating "dangerous" residents of "war zones." The War Relocation Authority moved the Japanese Americans to a number of Relocation Centers in remote interior locations. Some of the barbed wire–enclosed compounds were quite large; Heart Mountain, in northern Wyoming, housed nearly eleven thousand Japanese Americans by late 1942.

For the victims, it was a bitter experience. Many suffered mistreatment and the loss of all their property. Ironically, thousands of young Japanese American men served with distinction in the armed forces. Their 442nd Regimental Combat Team earned a Medal of Honor, 52 Distinguished Service Crosses, and 560 Silver Stars and came to rank as the most decorated army unit of the war. In early 1944 the WRA began disbanding the camps, and the unfortunate victims filtered back to communities that still distrusted them. Most of them passed back into the American mainstream, and their fellow citizens soon came to realize the tragic wrong that had been done to their loyal neighbors.

Aside from this episode and the brief, post–Pearl Harbor alarm that caused it, the war years were generally a time of patriotic national unity and of conservative resurgence. The New Deal gave way to the war effort; and agencies long popular in the West, like the Work Projects Administration and the Civilian Conservation Corps, folded their tents. Liberals, anxious to press on with the reforms of the 1930s, now found themselves on the defensive. FDR's favorite New Deal congressman, Lyndon Johnson of Texas, lost a special Senate election to the conservative "Pappy" O'Daniel in 1941; and in Nebraska, the venerable progressive Republican Senator George Norris went down to defeat at the hands of archconservative Kenneth Wherry in 1942.

A mood of consensus and conservatism blanketed the western state governments in wartime. Governor John Moses of North Dakota typified his regional counterparts as he cashed in on the wartime agricultural prosperity to eliminate debts and garner surpluses while keeping taxes down. New Mexico Governor J. J. Dempsey and Arizona Governor Sidney Osborn were similarly unflinching conservatives. Conservatives also firmly recaptured Texas, where popular Governor Coke Stevenson succeeded O'Daniel and where the openly anti-Roosevelt, anti-Truman "Texas Regulars" dominated the Democratic Party. More moderate state executives, such as Ralph Carr in Colorado and Arthur Langlie in Washington, hewed to the middle of the road, avoiding controversy and partisanship. The classic rendering of this form of politics appeared in California, where progressive Republican Earl Warren defeated the embattled liberal Democrat Culbert Olson for the governorship in 1942. Taking advantage of the state's peculiar primary system, which permitted candidates to cross-file in both major parties, Warren so soothed the electorate that in 1946 he won the nominations of both parties, coasting to a landslide victory.

Amid the rejoicing over war's end in August 1945, amid such a mood of nonpartisanship and patriotism, few paused to reflect on the enormous changes that the war, and the preceding depression and New Deal, had wrought on the nation and the region. The brief fifteen years between 1930 and 1945 had been the most hectic in the history of the West, witnessing unprecedented economic and environmental disasters, the massive new federal presence introduced by the New Deal and the war, and of course the socioeconomic transformations of 1941–45. Although these years did not literally end the old colonial domination of the West by the East, they certainly began its demise and laid the foundations of a new era, one in which Uncle Sam would loom much larger than eastern corporations over the western horizon and one that would continue unabated into the late twentieth century.

Chapter Four

Social Patterns in the
Modern West

When former California resident John Steinbeck
swung his camper through the West while preparing to write *Travels with Charley* in 1960, he
was, again and again, surprised to discover how much social
patterns in the region had changed since the days of his
youth on the West Coast. The changes that Steinbeck, and
many other observers, noted were manifold; but most striking were the region's rapid urbanization, its diverse blend
of ethnic groups, and the fast-changing roles of gender and
family. For change, more than continuity, has been and still
is the hallmark of western society in the twentieth century.
Even when the region followed national patterns, it likewise diverged from those patterns in important ways. And,
as always, intraregional patterns often contrasted in marked
ways from those broader trends characterizing the West as
a whole. Thus, the timeworn stereotype of the West as the
hallowed preserve of ruggedly independent Marlboro Men
bore little resemblance to the real West of modernity, a land
of flux and striking cosmopolitan diversity.

THE URBAN WEST

In the popular imagination, the West is firmly ensconced as
a rural land of cowboys and Indians, mainly devoid of settle-

ment. Yet, the most significant fact of its social development has been its hectic and continuing urbanization. Perhaps the most graphic irony of its past and present is that the American West is an urban region, more urban than the country as a whole, even though vast, unpopulated expanses separate its sprawling metropolitan areas. Texas historian Walter Prescott Webb accurately depicted the region in the 1950s as a near-desert whose civilization was rooted in a scattering of "urban oases."

This pattern of lone cities isolated amid thin rural populations was less clear in 1900 than it is today. At the dawn of the century, about 25 percent of all westerners lived in urban areas (then defined as incorporated towns and cities of at least twenty-five hundred inhabitants), a percentage considerably below the national average. The nation as a whole gained an urban majority in the 1920s, but the West did not cross that threshold until the 1930s. In the ensuing fifty years, however, millions flocked to western cities, especially those of the Sunbelt stretching from Houston in an arc to Sacramento. By 1980, the West stood as the most citified of American regions —80.4 percent urban, compared to a national average of 73.7 percent. California, the most populous state with more than 23,660,000 inhabitants, led all other states with its 91 percent urbanization. Among the seventeen western states, only North and South Dakota had more rural than urban residents. Reflecting the drastic urban imbalance of the western demographic profile, though, are the region's ratios of people per square mile. Texas, for example, about 80 percent urban in 1980, had only about 54 people per square mile. Even more striking, both Nevada and New York were 85 percent urban; but each square mile of Nevada averaged 7 people, whereas each in crowded New York averaged 371. Of all the western states, only California with 151 residents per square mile surpassed the national average of 64.

A bird's-eye view of the West in 1900 would have clearly revealed that most of the West's major cities lay along the region's eastern and western borders, with Denver and Salt Lake City as atypical cities of the arid interior. Eighty years

Population of Major Western Cities

City	1900	1910	1920	1930	1940	1950	1960	1970	1980
Albuquerque	6,238	11,020	15,157	26,570	35,449	96,815	201,189	244,501	332,239
Billings	3,221	10,031	15,100	16,380	23,261	31,834	52,851	61,581	66,842
Boise	5,957	17,358	21,393	21,544	26,130	34,393	34,481	74,990	102,160
Cheyenne	14,087	11,320	13,829	17,361	22,474	31,935	43,505	41,254	47,283
Colorado Springs	21,085	29,078	30,105	33,237	36,789	45,472	70,194	135,517	214,821
Dallas	42,638	92,104	158,976	260,475	294,734	434,462	679,684	844,401	904,078
Denver	133,859	213,381	256,491	287,861	322,412	415,786	493,887	514,678	492,365
El Paso	15,906	39,279	77,560	102,421	96,810	130,485	276,687	322,261	425,259
Fargo	9,589	14,331	21,961	28,619	32,580	38,256	46,662	53,365	61,383
Fort Worth	26,688	73,312	106,482	163,447	177,662	278,778	356,268	393,455	385,164
Houston	44,633	78,800	138,276	292,352	384,514	596,163	938,219	1,233,535	1,595,138
Kansas City, KS	51,418	82,331	101,177	121,857	121,458	129,553	121,901	168,213	161,087
Las Vegas	—	—	2,304	5,165	8,422	24,624	64,405	125,787	164,674
Los Angeles	102,479	319,198	576,673	1,238,048	1,504,277	1,970,358	2,479,015	2,811,801	2,968,579
Oakland	66,960	150,174	216,261	284,063	302,163	384,575	367,548	361,561	339,337
Oklahoma City	10,037	64,205	91,295	185,389	204,424	243,504	324,253	368,164	403,484
Omaha	102,555	124,096	191,601	214,006	223,844	251,117	301,598	346,929	313,939
Phoenix	5,544	11,134	29,053	48,118	65,414	106,818	439,170	584,303	789,704
Portland	90,426	207,214	258,288	301,815	305,394	373,628	372,676	379,967	366,383
Salt Lake City	53,531	92,777	118,110	140,267	149,934	182,121	189,454	175,885	163,034
San Antonio	53,321	96,614	161,379	231,542	253,854	408,442	587,718	654,153	786,023
San Diego	17,700	39,578	74,361	147,995	203,341	334,387	573,224	697,471	875,538
San Francisco	342,782	416,912	506,676	634,394	634,536	775,357	740,316	715,674	678,974
San Jose	21,500	28,946	39,642	57,651	68,457	95,280	204,196	459,913	629,531
Seattle	80,671	237,194	315,312	365,583	368,303	467,591	557,087	530,831	493,846
Sioux Falls	10,266	14,094	25,202	33,362	40,832	52,696	65,466	72,488	81,343
Spokane	36,848	104,402	104,437	115,514	122,001	161,721	181,608	170,516	171,300
Tucson	7,531	13,193	20,292	32,506	35,752	45,454	212,892	262,933	330,537
Tulsa	1,390	18,182	72,075	141,258	142,157	182,740	261,685	330,350	360,919
Wichita	24,671	52,450	72,217	111,110	114,966	168,279	254,698	276,554	279,835

Source: 1980 Census of Population, Bureau of Census (corrected). Includes largest city of each western state (urban centers, not Standard Metropolitan Statistical Areas).

later, a similar perspective would disclose a like pattern, but with a major difference—a string of burgeoning new metropolitan areas stretching across the Southwest from Texas to California. These urban giants along the West's peripheries held most of the region's people and most of its action in 1900; almost all of the western plains, Rocky Mountain, and intermountain subregions consisted of placid, more traditional societies based on farms and small towns and cities.

When the new century began, San Francisco stood as the largest and most significant of western cities. It had been so since the 1850s and would remain so until Los Angeles surpassed it around 1920. With its long tradition of economic, social, and cultural leadership, metropolitan San Francisco (population 1,576,000)* remains to this day a key western city, a leader especially in commerce, banking, and culture. But, a peninsular city nearly surrounded by water, "Baghdad by the Bay" long ago reached its physical limits, as did many other core cities in America, forcing floods of newcomers to settle in adjacent cities that soon came to be known as "suburbs"—such as San Mateo and San Jose to the south or industrial Oakland on the "east bay." For millions of visitors, San Francisco, with its grand old central core, its rich ethnic heritage, and its picturesque cable cars, embodies an earlier West that now draws on global cosmopolitan influences to form one of America's most vibrant and fascinating cities.

*This figure, and subsequent ones, represent what the U.S. Bureau of the Census refers to as "Metropolitan Statistical Areas" or "Primary Metropolitan Statistical Areas"—that is, urban-area populations—as of 1985. In contrast, the population in 1985 of San Francisco proper was only 679,000, whereas that of the entire "Bay Area" (a "Consolidated Metropolitan Statistical Area") was 5,809,000.

Los Angeles, San Francisco's more dynamic rival to the south, grew steadily to become the West's greatest metropolis. Little more than a sleepy pueblo before 1880, it surged ahead during the next two decades, largely because two railroads linked it to the East and to northern California. Over the next half-century, its population nearly doubled every decade until it became the first western city to boast a million inhabitants. A number of factors—appealing climate, broad stretches of open land in the surrounding basin, excellent transportation systems, and booming oil, motion picture, and other industries—combined to lure hundreds of thousands of newcomers to the "Lotus Land" of Los Angeles and its suburbs.

123

The growth patterns and spatial designs of this "Fragmented Metropolis," as Robert Fogelson aptly termed Los Angeles, provided a paradigm for other urban areas of the Southwest. Whereas older, nineteenth-century cities like San Francisco, Portland, Denver, and Salt Lake City developed traditional core areas, from which suburbs later radiated outward, Los Angeles pioneered a new, more distinctly western urban landscape, featuring a minimal core city with only a weak centripetal force and a maximal centrifugal pull of people, businesses, and whole "downtown" sections to peripheral suburbs: "seven suburbs in search of a city," as one wit put it. Thus, for better and worse, Los Angeles (8,109,000) provided the model for the rapid-growth, low-density, sprawling format that has come to characterize the typical metropolitan areas of the modern West.

Other western cities followed various paths to the present. Until 1900 Portland, by its natural control of the Columbia River trade corridor to the interior Northwest, remained that region's chief urban center. But during the dynamic decade following 1900, the natural seaport of Seattle nearly tripled from 80,000 to 237,000 population, largely because of the Alaska gold rush and new rail connections to the East and steamship ties to the Orient. The great military-industrial booms of World War II sent Seattle, especially, on another dramatic growth sprint. Conservative and slower-growing Portland (1,147,000) thus lost its regional hegemony to bustling Seattle (1,724,000) as the century evolved.

On the east-central rim of the West, the traditional gateway cities of Omaha (612,000) and Kansas City (Missouri-Kansas, 1,494,000) grew rapidly in the early century, as did the transportation and agricultural-processing industries on which they were based; but after 1930, they leveled off for similar reasons. Of the two, Omaha seemed more sluggish and tied to the old order of railroads and packing plants, Kansas City more up-to-date and commercial, as symbolized by its creation of America's first planned shopping center, Country Club Plaza, in 1923. Meanwhile, Wichita (435,000) grew rapidly, not only as an oil and wheat-milling center but also as a hub of aircraft manufacturing.

Denver and Salt Lake City likewise entered the twentieth century as notable western urban areas. Already the greatest of the West's interior cities by 1900, the "Mile High City" of Denver (1,614,000) continued to forge ahead because of its central location and fair mountain climate, its regional leadership in securing federal offices and employment, and its rising status as a western hub of natural resources and energy industries. Across the Rockies, Salt Lake City (1,025,000) expanded at a similar though lesser rate, not only as the core of Mormondom but also as a crossroads center of communications and transportation industries.

The most spectacular urban growth in the modern West, however, occurred in the southwestern Sunbelt, the zone extending from those borderland southern-western cities of Tulsa, Oklahoma City, Dallas, and Houston to southern California. In 1900, only Los Angeles among these isolated cities could boast as many as 100,000 citizens, with old San Antonio next at 53,000. By 1940 oil and commerce, primarily, had pushed several of these urban areas past the 200,000 mark: Los Angeles, San Diego, Houston, Dallas, San Antonio, and Oklahoma City. Then, the unprecedented surges of World War II and after changed everything. By 1985, metropolitan San Diego stood at 2,133,000, San Antonio at 1,236,000, Oklahoma City at 976,000, and Tulsa at 733,000. Even more spectacular were the small cities that mushroomed into large ones. Only a small city of 35,000 in 1940, Albuquerque soared to 201,000 in 1960 and to 464,000 by 1985. During the same period, El Paso rose from 97,000 to 277,000 to 545,000; Tucson grew from 36,000 to 212,000 to 586,000.

The rival Texas metropolitan areas of Houston and Dallas–Fort Worth and the aptly named Phoenix, Arizona, trailed only Los Angeles as western wonder-growth areas. With a population of less than 50,000 in 1900, the man-made seaport and oil mecca of Houston surged to nearly 600,000 by 1950 and to 3,222,000 by 1985, ranking this

"Baghdad on the Bayou" as America's fourth-largest city, second only to Los Angeles in the West. Somewhat smaller than its rival to the south, but with a more diversified financial-commercial economy, metro Dallas counted 2,312,000 inhabitants by 1985; its more "western" sister-city of Fort Worth numbered 1,200,000. And then there was Phoenix, a quiet desert town of 65,000 in 1940, which grew into a metropolis of 439,000 by 1960 and then into a megametropolis of 1,847,000 by 1985.

A scanning of census profiles at twenty-year intervals offers an interesting vantage of the West's place in urban America. In 1900 only San Francisco, and in 1940 and 1960 only Los Angeles, among western cities ranked among the nation's very largest. But in 1980, five of the country's ten largest cities were located in the Sunbelt Southwest: Los Angeles, Houston, Dallas, San Diego, and Phoenix. Among the nation's greatest urban concentrations, or "Consolidated Metropolitan Statistical Areas," the West demonstrably held four: the Los Angeles Basin (12,738,000), the San Francisco Bay area (5,809,000), greater Houston (3,623,000), and greater Dallas–Fort Worth (3,512,000). Not only was the West an urban region, its cities stood at the forefront among all cities in the nation.

PATTERNS OF URBAN, SUBURBAN, AND RURAL DEMOGRAPHY

Statistics detailing urban growth reveal a good deal about the region, but they do not tell the full story. One must also consider the *patterns* of this urbanization. Why did these cities grow so rapidly and attract the diverse populations that they did? How did the older rural areas and newer suburbs fit into the picture? Clearly, the most widespread urban growth in the recent West occurred in the region's two imperial and most populous states, California and Texas (population, 14,227,600), which in 1987 ranked first and third in the nation.

During the past half-century, the conurbanizations of these two megastates rested on the building of empires both within and beyond the states' borders. Just as old San Francisco had staked out much of Nevada and Oregon as its domain, so did the new Los Angeles Basin and Bay Area metropolitan centers embrace hinterlands that reached to some extent into all the states bordering California. And just as California cast out a wide network of sociocultural influence based on industry, finance, and the electronic media, so too did Texas, whose sway reached especially into the realms of finance, petroleum, and country music. These new axes of urban empire ran not only east-west, as in olden days, but also south-north. So the California arc ran north to Washington, as well as east to Nevada; and the Texas orbit embraced not only "Poor New Mexico, so far from Heaven, so close to Texas," but also Oklahoma and Arkansas.

Other megatrends also loomed especially large in creating the new western metropolitan order. Surely, one of the most significant has been government spending, especially for military-aerospace purposes. From greater Seattle's Boeing aircraft plants to San Diego's giant naval facilities to Houston's Johnson Space Center to Omaha's Strategic Air Command headquarters to Colorado Springs' Air Force Academy, Uncle Sam's monetary presence in the urban West is ubiquitous, so omnipresent as to be nearly unnoticeable, like the forest and the trees. As one commentator noted in the late 1960s, federal defense spending, with its armies of government and private sector employees and retirees, may have been the "single most important economic and demographic factor in the history of the West during the past two decades."

Closely related to federal spending has been the high-tech industrial revolution described below. All of the West's major metropolitan centers have their featured high-tech loops and clusters of "industrial parks." The south Bay Area's Silicon Valley is most famous; but the Los Angeles Basin has its Orange County complex, Dallas its bustling northern, high-tech suburbs of Plano and Richardson and its Interstate Loop 635, San Antonio its Loop 410, Tulsa its world-leading data-processing facilities, Phoenix its space-age complexes led by Motorola, Sperry Flight Systems, Honeywell Information Systems, Goodyear Aerospace, AiResearch, and Western Electric.

Particularly along the West Coast and the southern rim, international trade has also contributed heavily to the rise of western cities. The rapidly expanding American commerce with East Asia impacts the West especially, of course. The awesome cluster of Japanese, Korean, and other Asian banks near Pershing Square in Los Angeles symbolizes this influence. So do the literally hundreds of Japanese plants in the three coastal states, such as the Toyota–General Motors joint venture in California, and the major inland intrusions too, like the Hitachi semiconductor plants in Dallas and the disk-drive production facilities in Oklahoma.

Equally important, the U.S.-Mexican border looks more and more like a conduit than a real boundary, with ever more American plants on Mexican soil and ever more hectic exchange of products and workers all the way from San Diego–Tijuana on the west to the many Texas-Mexican border cities on the east. Also international is the oil labyrinth, which brought such prosperity to the petroleum capitals of Houston, Dallas, Midland-Odessa, Tulsa, and Oklahoma City in the 1970s and such devastation in the 1980s. Aside from Houston, no city rode this roller coaster so spectacularly as did Denver. The city attracted thirteen hundred oil and energy industries during the boom times; but its "Oil Patch," like similar districts in Calgary, Casper, and other petroleum centers, now yawns with unfinished buildings and abandoned offices.

Yet another social magnet of the urban Sunbelt, frequently overlooked, is the prosperity-born lure of tourism, leisure, and retirement. The postwar influx of tourists, retirees, and wintertime "snowbirds" dwarfed the earlier migrations. They now came, with their hefty savings and conservative politics, to large meccas like San Diego and Las

Vegas and to smaller ones like Carmel, California, and St. George, Utah. Retirees truly transformed Arizona. Del Webb, a western genius at laying out planned communities, led the way with his classic Sun City retirement complex near Phoenix; and many more developments followed, with their handsome pools, well-manicured golf courses, desert flora, and such appealing names as Carefree and Leisure World.

As for the westering immigrants themselves, they were much too diverse and numerous to categorize simply. During the first two decades of the century, before the imposition of laws that nearly halted foreign immigration, a broad stream of multiethnic immigration, mostly European, flowed westward, joined by an oft-noted flow of respectable New Englanders and other northeasterners. Then, during the 1920s, midwesterners and southerners seemed more prevalent, tincturing western towns and cities with their conservative moralism and their racial and social prejudices. French commentator André Siegfried noted that in the West of the 1920s he found "the same bias, the same fears, and the same religious intolerance" that he had encountered in Appalachia and in Tennessee at the Scopes Trial. These newcomers, comfortably adhering to Protestant fundamentalism, ethnocentrism, and prohibition, conflicted with their more tolerant and worldly predecessors, who had come in frontier and postfrontier times.

The tide of immigration ebbed during the 1920s and 1930s and then swelled again to flood stage during World War II and its aftermath. These new westerners represented all walks of American life and all regions of the nation and world, as cosmopolitan as, and far more numerous than, the gold rushers of a century earlier. During the late 1960s and the 1970s, with yet a new surge of westering, this time mostly to the Sunbelt, the mix again shifted: fewer blue-collar and more white-collar workers, more retirees, and many more non-Anglos, headed for the core central cities.

The booming migration of Hispanics, blacks, Asians, and Indians to western cities had truly profound results. Even the oldest of the region's nonwhite groups, the Indians, were evenly divided between reservations and cities by the 1980s. By 1980, seventeen metropolitan areas of the region hosted at least one hundred thousand Hispanics, whereas only seven metropolitan areas in the rest of the country could make that claim. Like their sisters across the nation, the major cities of the West tended more and more to be white on their peripheries and racially mixed in their cores. Thus Los Angeles, the Ellis Island of modern America, became populated increasingly by Mexicans, Asians, and blacks in its downtown. By the 1980s, Los Angeles County was home to one million blacks and well over two million Mexican Americans—the largest gathering of Mexicans outside Mexico. It also held the largest aggregation of Japanese outside Japan and the greatest number of Koreans outside Korea. Indeed, greater Los Angeles no longer had a white majority, or any other majority.

Whereas the pouring of these variegated populations into the West's cities marks the dominant trend of modern times, it is hardly the whole demographic story. Midsized western cities like Boise, Billings, and Santa Fe are as different from the megalopolises of Houston and Seattle as they are from such smaller cities as Grand Island, Nebraska, or Elko, Nevada. Even the mushrooming, lily-white suburbs of the major cities, which are so often stereotyped as all alike, are in fact different in many ways.

These suburbs of western cities evolved according to environment and circumstance. Thus the small and attractive cities flanking Los Angeles, such as Pasadena, Anaheim, and Newport Beach, nestled amid orange groves and along beaches, saw much of their individual identities pulled away from them as the dividing open spaces were rapidly filled during the great post-1940 building boom. The fine old Pacific Electric interurban rail lines, with their memorable "big red cars," gave way to freeways that bound the suburbs together. And though Los Angeles eventually did develop a skyline, its central business district never dominated such sizable suburbs as Orange County to the south, which by the 1980s could boast of being "the state's third-largest downtown area." Even by the 1950s, it was clear that no core district could dominate a "sixty-mile metroplex radiating in each direction." By the 1980s, more than thirteen million people lived in the two-hundred-mile corridor stretching from Santa Barbara to San Diego, an urban-suburban concentration that promised to become the nation's largest by the year 2000.

Geography and an earlier ascent to metropolitan status made for a considerably different pattern in old San Francisco, where the core city on the peninsula packed in so tightly that developers even filled in much of the bay shore to gain more space. South Bay settlements, led by San Jose, grew slowly; and the expanses of water meant fixed distances between San Francisco and the railroad-industrial cities on the East Bay. Construction of the Bay Bridge in 1936 and the magnificent Golden Gate Bridge in 1937 and adoption of the Bay Area Rapid Transit (BART) rail system in 1962 —the only system of its kind in the region—provided networking, but not really the sort of suburban homogeny seen in Los Angeles. Even in the late twentieth century, therefore, the city by the bay retains more of its oldtime charm than does its southern rival, a contrast of modern dynamism and traditional regality that has often served as a bone of contention between the two imperial cities.

Like San Francisco, the great cities of the northern West tended, even with the proliferation of suburbs, to maintain their core hegemony and to build new skyscraper complexes in the central city. Seattle, for instance, sustained an overwhelming population-economic-social dominance over the metropolitan corridor spreading north to Everett and south to Olympia. Similarly, the big business blocks around Temple Square in Salt Lake City anchored that city's hold over the urban corridor stretching from Utah Lake and Provo-Orem on the south to Ogden and the north shore of the Great Salt Lake. Denver's spectacularly high rising buildings of the central city, which in the 1970s local folks dubbed the "nesting ground of the forty-story crane," likewise symbolized its role not only as state capital but also as metropolitan capital of the "front" reaching from Littleton and Englewood north nearly to Boulder.

The Sunbelt boomtowns also had their central city renaissances and their soaring new skyscrapers, like the beautiful glass "Texas sandstone" structures of Dallas. But they tended much more toward the Los Angeles style: mushrooming suburbs surrounding less-hearty central districts —seemingly an architectural expression of their southern-based individualism and conservative rejection of any form of discipline. This certainly seemed the mode in Tulsa, and even more in Phoenix, where affluent and well-manicured suburbs like Glendale, Scottsdale, Mesa, and Tempe outweighed a relatively anemic downtown. Even with their awe-inspiring new central business blocks, Houston and Dallas were most notable for their suburban sprawl. Houston annexed its suburban areas so vigorously that it became, in one description, a "557-square-mile monster"; but its central core could still be depicted as "twenty-seven significant buildings surrounded by trivia," and it held out against integrated urban planning until 1982. By the 1970s, the Dallas–Fort Worth "metroplex" stood as America's largest in physical size, stretching sixty miles from end to end, and as its eighth- or ninth-largest concentration of population. But most of its growth—25 percent during the frenzied 1970s—took place in the maze of suburbs that stretched in all directions, most notably in the thirty-three miles lying between the two core cities.

Regardless of location, metropolitan westerners, like other Americans, took avidly to the suburbs if they could afford to, fleeing from the jammed and smog-bound central cities in search of peace and quiet. In the process, they left less desirable areas unoccupied and erected their ring roads, sprawling neighborhoods, and ever larger shopping malls along coveted waterways and high foothills. More often than their eastern counterparts, western cities like Houston and Oklahoma City moved to annex these "crabgrass frontiers"; but annexation did not really change the cities' suburban nature. Indeed, the West did much to fashion the American ideal of the good life in suburbia, complete with broad lawns, split-level ranch-style homes, and barbeques on the patio—all as set forth in *Sunset* magazine. The West indisputably had the land to support such life-styles, but some wondered whether it would forever have either the water or the economic dynamism to do so.

Whereas the West became increasingly urban during the twentieth century, much of its landmass remained overwhelmingly rural, particularly the most desolate reaches of the Southwest and the Great Basin and the broad expanses of the northern plains and Rockies. Cold, windblown, and semiarid North and South Dakota remain more than 50 percent rural to this day; Idaho and Montana are little more than half urban. Even in the predominantly rural Dakotas, the rural share of the populace is failing to keep pace with the slowly growing urban communities. In contrast to western Canada, the U.S. plains and Rockies have failed to nurture the rise of large cities and instead have remained hinterlands to metropolitan areas lying far to the east and west. In the five-state region from Idaho to the Dakotas, there is only one city of more than one hundred thousand residents, Boise. This major subregion of the West remains an agrarian-rural outback, a part of what regionalist Joel Garreau calls the "Empty Quarter." Dwindling or static small towns serve an eroding farm population; and small cities like Rapid City, Great Falls, and Cheyenne serve as distribution centers for huge surrounding areas.

Still, the long-term decline in rural population, so evident in this subregion, has leveled off considerably in the last several years, in part because of the oft-remarked discomforts of modern city living. During the 1970s, the percentage of rural growth in Texas matched the percentage of its city growth; and in California, a rural expansion of 13 percent was fully two-thirds of the 19 percent urban growth rate. But still, the West of the 1980s presents itself as an optical illusion—the most urban part of the United States, yet the preserve also of seemingly endless and nearly unpopulated mountains, plains, and deserts. In its southwestern quadrant, the West offers visitors the most vibrant of American cities. In its "Old West" northeastern quadrant, it offers tourists "the last of what is best."

ETHNIC DIVERSITY IN THE MODERN WEST

Whereas the West grew consistently more urban in the twentieth century, the ethnic makeup of its population became not more uniform but, if anything, more diverse than it had been during the previous century. The most important ethnic groups of frontier times—the Irish, Cornish, Greeks, and Italians of the rail and mining towns; the Basques of the Great Basin; the Germans and Scandinavians of the agricultural plains—still make their presence felt in the modern West. But generally, with each passing decade, at least in most of the region, the bonds of tradition and ethnic loyalty have weakened, and these European Americans have increasingly passed into the national mainstream. In contrast, the non-European nationality and ethnic groups of the West, primarily Hispanics, blacks, and Asians, in addition to Indians, have held much more strongly to their separate identities. These groupings have given the region the leavening of social diversity that makes it such a cosmopolitan place today.

The new century brought drastic changes for the Native Americans of the West, and many of these changes stemmed from their relationship with a paternalistic federal government. In 1887, Congress enacted the most sweeping legislation in history related to Indians, the Dawes Severalty Act, which set out to force the assimilation of Native Americans into the mainstream of national life. The product of well-meaning religious and political reformers, mainly in the East, and of avaricious western pioneers, the Dawes Act embodied the central strain of contemporary thinking about Indians and their role in American society. By this time, most Americans believed that Indians could not and should not remain isolated on reservations, removed from white society: assimilation, not separation, must be the goal if they were to survive and sustain themselves. And the best way to achieve this end must be to make them farmers, with their own parcels of land.

The Dawes Act stipulated that each head of an Indian household would be allotted 160 acres (80 acres for single adults and 40 acres for minors), or 320 acres if the land was suitable only for grazing. These Indian lands would be held in trust for twenty-five years to protect the recipients from alienation, and the Indians would become U.S. citizens on first receiving their allotments. (Later, the Burke Act of 1906 would delay citizenship until the end of the trust period.) To the glee of western speculators, once the reservation lands had been divided among qualified Indian recipients, the remainder would be sold. Unfortunately, indeed tragically, the dreams of the reformers were seldom realized. Inheritance problems, pressing financial needs, varying kinds of familial and individual incompetences, and greedy and corrupt officials usually forestalled wise and fair-minded implementation of the allotment program. Sadly, after lands in excess of allotments were sold, the total of 138 million acres held by Indians in 1887 had dwindled to 52 million by 1934.

In the words of historian Francis Paul Prucha, the goal of the Dawes Act—to turn individual Indians into farmers and stockmen—"failed miserably." Often, white authorities overseeing the reservation programs proved to be either impotent or oblivious to diverse Indian traditions and to the physical conditions Indians faced in taking up allotments. No matter how one considers the Dawes Act and its implementation, Prucha adds, the results were "disappointing and damaging." Ironically, in fact, after the implementation process began, less Indian land was being cultivated than before the program.

By the late 1920s, therefore, bureaucrats had clearly failed to turn Indians into agriculturists. According to critics, most notably those preparing the Meriam Report (*The Problem of Indian Administration*, 1928), reservations were in a deplorable state; and giant infusions of funding would be necessary to bring economic conditions, health care, and schools up to acceptable levels. Although the authors of this influential study did not advocate rescinding previous policies, other more outspoken opponents of the assimilation-allotment policy, particularly John Collier, did indeed call for wholesale change.

No other person of the twentieth century wielded more influence over the planning and implementation of Indian policy than did John Collier. Already convinced that Indians needed a "new deal" before he was named commissioner of Indian affairs by President Franklin Roosevelt in 1933, he immediately set out to redirect the policies of the previous half-century. Albeit in compromised form, his ideas took shape in the pathbreaking Indian Reorganization (Wheeler-Howard) Act of 1934. Sometimes called a Magna Charta for Indians, the IRA stopped the allotment process and returned surplus lands to Indians instead of continuing their sale to whites. Furthermore, the act encouraged a revitalization of tribal unity by urging the tribes to draft and adopt constitutions allowing more political self-control. Other provisions supported economic and cultural developments among the many Indian groups.

Collier strongly supported the IRA, despite the compromises it contained. Like an itinerant evangelist bent on converting Indian and non-Indian alike, he traveled the country spreading the gospel that Indians must plan and direct more of their own affairs. But not all took up his message; in fact, nearly 30 percent of all the tribes—including the largest tribe, the Navahos—rejected the invitation to write new constitutions. Yet even without unanimous support, even without effecting the revolution he hoped for, Collier still ushered in a new era in Indian-white relations, one that, though often challenged and sometimes redirected, in many respects endures today.

Within a decade after Collier's resignation in 1945, however, governmental attitude shifted once again, this time in a direction that aimed to undo much of what he had attempted to accomplish during the 1930s and early 1940s. Taking up where the earlier allotment strategy had been heading before the New Deal and the IRA, Indian Commissioners Dillon Myer and Glenn Emmons began to implement "withdrawal programming," better known as "termination." As a new assault on tribalism, termination meant an end to government responsibility for tribes and an assimilation of all Indians into American society; in addition, Indians would lose their lands and other resources, for which individually they would receive compensation. Using a variety of means to overcome their opponents, Emmons and like-minded congressmen and other bureaucrats during the Eisenhower administration succeeded in terminating the Klamaths of Oregon and several smaller groups in Oklahoma and Utah, as well as the Menominees of Wisconsin. Under termination, these reservation lands were sold, the earnings given to former tribal members, and federal responsibilities transferred to the states or taken over by private corporations or other groups.

Few if any positive effects resulted from the termination program. In fact, opponents and critics tried to blunt its impact even before it was implemented; discontent with and fear of its negative influences soon led policy makers to move in other directions. Before the termination impulse was spent, however, it also served to encourage the relocation of increasing numbers of Indians to cities. Here too the goal was assimilation, the shedding of unique Indian traditions for the blandness of the American melting pot. Again, the results discredited the assimilationists. Nearly one-third of the thirty-five thousand Indians resettled in cities during the Eisenhower years returned to the reservations, and many others suffered from the serious socioeconomic and psychological dislocations of living in the "concrete prairies" so different from their rural homelands.

The hectic 1960s were a watershed for western Indians, just as these years were for so many other segments of American society. Spurred by an increased public sympathy for minority groups, a rising pan-Indian spirit, and a general discontent with traditional American society, policy makers now paid greater heed to Indian demands for more self-determination in ruling their own lives and in controlling

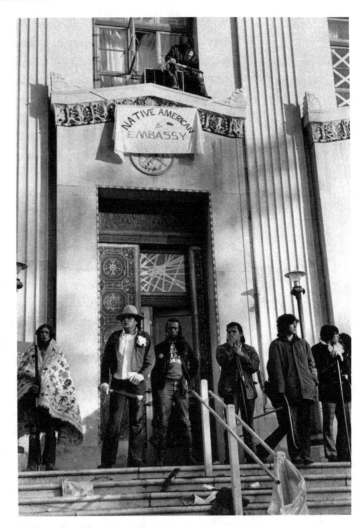

Native American demonstrators guard the door to the Bureau of Indian Affairs building in Washington, D.C., during the occupation of November 1972. Courtesy of the Bettmann Archive.

government actions that affected them. Since that time Indians have been granted a much larger role in determining economic, educational, and health-care policies that originate in Washington, D.C., and in regional offices of the Bureau of Indian Affairs. In addition, the past two decades have witnessed an impressive increase in tribalism and tribal self-determination, in part because of the federal Indian Claims Commission rulings and a succession of other court decisions and congressional enactments. Thus, the pendulum swung back again toward the policies of the Collier era and away from the assimilationism of the Dawes Act and termination.

As ethnologists remind us, however, government policy toward Indians is only one part of the story, for Indians were never merely passive recipients of the decisions. Reacting first to the Collier reforms and then to the threats of termination, western Indians organized themselves to make their voices heard. Beginning with the National Congress of American Indians in 1944, and then in 1961 with the National Indian Youth Council and in 1968 with the most radical of the Native American groups, the American Indian Movement (AIM), these organizations became more and more influential. Usually they operated within normal civic channels; but sometimes they directly defied white society, as with the controversial "fish-ins" in the Pacific Northwest, the seizure of Alcatraz island by militants in 1969, or the occupation and sacking of BIA offices in 1972. In the most publicized of such protests, AIM-led militants in 1973 invaded Wounded Knee, South Dakota, site of a notorious military massacre of the Sioux back in 1890. Under the radical leadership of Russell Means and Dennis Banks, the AIM rebels held the village as a gesture of their hatred of the BIA and their demand for self-determination.

Meanwhile, less sensational events and trends signaled a rising self-consciousness among all Indian groups. In the cultural sphere, such Indian writers as N. Scott Momaday, Leslie Silko, James Welch, and Louise Erdrich produced nationally recognized novels about Indian life; new Native American newspapers and newsletters began publication; and numerous new Indian schools and colleges appeared, including Navajo Community College in Tsaile Lake, Arizona. In addition, Indian leaders like the Navajo Peter MacDonald drew on their training and experience to encourage economic development and new job opportunities in cities and on the reservations. Others supported pan-Indian organizations to advocate Red Power or to secure their lands and rights in the courts, as happened with the return of the Blue Lake area in New Mexico to the Taos Indians in 1970.

This notable resurgence of confidence among Indians, these impressive cultural achievements, and the promising economic developments must not, however, mask the large problems confronting Indians in the American West. Unemployment, alcoholism, school dropouts, and disease and other health problems all afflict Indians far more severely than they do the general population. And even with increasing help from government and private sources and with encouraging successes at economic development, most reservation and nonreservation Indians still face a bleak future. Admitting the diversity of Indian experiences, which includes the oil wealth of the Osages, one must yet conclude that the tragic history of Native Americans in the West casts a long shadow into their future.

The classic push-and-pull factors common to all transnational migrations, as well as a long series of jarring socioeconomic shifts in North America, shaped the history of a second ethnic group in the modern West: Hispanics. Millions of Mexicans fled their depressed and disrupted homeland, heading north in search of jobs, tranquility, and security. For some immigrants, their dreams came to fruition, but for others they turned to nightmares. The disruptive effects of world wars, depressions, and social upheavals on both sides of the border made the symbiotic relationship of Mexicans and Anglo-Americans a complex and troubled one.

The half-century that followed the tumultuous 1840s—the decade during which the United States annexed first Texas and then the entire Southwest in the Treaty of Guadalupe Hidalgo, thus absorbing all of northern Mexico—brought large and traumatic changes to the Hispanic residents of the transferred territories. With the exception of some *ricos* in New Mexico, most of them lost their lands and other possessions, as well as their political power. During the decades following the gold rush, Anglos who flooded the area pushed their predecessors aside until most of these Spanish-named Americans retained little of their former sociocultural status. More changes, most of them unpleasant, awaited them in the new century.

Between 1910 and 1917, as the disastrous Mexican Revolution disrupted the country's social order, thousands of immigrants streamed northward. Some were doctors, lawyers, and other professionals who could easily return when the revolution subsided; but the more numerous *pobres,* fleeing conscription and the terror of all-out civil war, hoped to find jobs to support their families, which usually remained behind. Even as the revolution played out, American demands for cheap labor in factories and on farms increased due to the economic frenzy of World War I and the boom times of the 1920s. So the Mexicans kept coming. Even though they often experienced ruthless discrimination in employment, in living conditions, and in social situations, most stayed, because no matter how unfavorable their status, it seemed better here than back home.

The depression of the 1930s ushered in even more unsettling times. Smarting under the new pressures of socioeconomic failure, Americans lashed out at the Mexicans, accusing them of worsening the situation and demanding that they be returned to "where they came from." Under heavy pressure from American laborers, government officials, and other groups, hundreds of thousands of Mexicans and Mexican Americans, perhaps as many as half a million, were repatriated to Mexico in the early 1930s. At the outbreak of World War II, therefore, Spanish-speaking Americans were probably at the nadir of their existence in the United States.

World War II, however, brought changes that would gradually alter the lives of American Hispanics. In the first place, many Hispanics served in the armed forces and returned determined to better their living conditions and those of their people. Thousands of Hispanic veterans took advantage of the GI Bill to get college educations and to apply their educations toward improving life in Chicano communities. Of the approximate 2.7 million Chicanos in the United States at the outbreak of war, between four hundred thousand and five hundred thousand went to war. In Los Angeles, Mexicans made up 10 percent of the city's population but suffered 20 percent of its war casualties.

Yet opportunities arose with the demand for unskilled labor as wartime industries and agriculture rapidly expanded in the early 1940s. To meet this demand, government officials turned to Mexican workers, especially after Japanese field workers disappeared into internment camps. Under concerted pressure from U.S. authorities, the Mexican government reluctantly entered into the *bracero* (strong-armed worker) program that provided for the importation of thousands of unskilled laborers. Between 1942 and 1947, more than 220,000 braceros moved north to meet this demand. Despite the frequent abuses they suffered, hundreds of thousands of Mexican workers kept coming, toiling for wages much higher than those available south of the border. The bracero program continued to expand because it provided a low-priced and stable source of labor. By 1949 bracero contracts totaled one hundred thousand, and that number more than quadrupled between 1956 and 1959. But growing dissatisfaction of the Mexican government, of American labor unions, and of the braceros themselves, combined with increasing mechanization on the farms, gradually undermined the bracero program, until it was ended in December 1964.

Meanwhile, the flood of undocumented workers crossing the border rose dramatically. By the mid-1970s, unofficial figures estimated the annual number of crossings at approximately nine hundred thousand, perhaps 90 percent of them Mexicans. The Immigration and Naturalization Service tried various procedures to stem the tide, but with little success; and the perplexing and intertwined problems of uncontrolled, illegal immigration and the American market for low-paid factory and farm workers continued unabated into the 1980s.

The expanding Hispanic population of the West, in the meantime, grew steadily more cohesive and vocal. Gradually, as Chicano communities and urban *barrios* gained in numbers and strength, they began to organize and to resist mistreatment. By 1930 more than half of the Chicano population, American-born as well as immigrant, lived in urban areas, constituting better than half of El Paso, almost half of San Antonio, and about 20 percent of Los Angeles. These urban concentrations greatly encouraged a mounting sense of self-identity among Spanish-speaking peoples. Such organizations as the *mutalistas* (mutual aid societies), LULAC (League of United Latin American Citizens, 1927), El Congreso de los Pueblos de Habla Español (Conference of Spanish-speaking Peoples, 1938), and the American GI Forum (1948) helped to unite Chicanos and to crystallize their reactions to the racism, prejudice, and injustices they often encountered.

Not surprisingly, the rising Chicano consciousness fueled an increased activism among Hispanic workers. During the early years of the century, and then more heatedly in the 1930s, Hispanic laborers played central roles in walkouts, strikes, and other agitations among agricultural workers in the Southwest. They particularly combatted wage discrimination, job displacements, and union biases. Even as Mexican Americans gained an increasing share of skilled and professional jobs after World War II, however, they remained heavily overrepresented among the downtrodden farm and unskilled factory workers. For instance, five times as many Mexican-American women as those from other ethnic groups worked at farm labor.

These earlier evidences of growing Hispanic consciousness and strength seemed feeble gestures compared to the dramatic occurrences of the 1960s and thereafter. Like several other minority groups in this period, Mexican Americans came suddenly of age as a forceful and outspoken segment of western American society. The most significant embodiment of this new assertiveness was the rising prominence of several Chicano spokesmen, the most notable of whom was César Chávez, the dynamic leader of the United Farm Workers movement. A skilled and indefatigable labor organizer with growing support from a variety of religious and other groups, Chávez participated in or engineered a series of strikes and boycotts on behalf of agricultural workers against the California growers. Greatly successful, these strikes and boycotts in the 1960s and 1970s forced the giant grape and lettuce agribusinesses to raise wages of field workers, provide more fringe benefits, and recognize the workers' unions. Through these efforts, Chávez effectively called attention to the plight of Chicano farm workers and galvanized the support of many Americans for his activities.

Other Chicano movements aimed in different directions. The fiery Reies Tijerina (El Tigre) led a series of confrontations in New Mexico with local and governmental agencies in the late 1960s in an attempt to dramatize the loss of Hispanic lands to Anglos and to the government; but his militancy, though expressing the dilemmas of many northern New Mexicans, alienated moderate and conservative Hispanics and narrowed his support. Meanwhile, Denverite Rodolfo "Corky" Gonzales took a different tack through his community-based Crusade for Justice, which attempted to speak especially for Chicano youth in urban barrios. Symbolizing still another approach was José Angel Gutiérrez, whose La Raza Unida party and astute political activities in Crystal City, Texas, illustrated what diligent grass-roots organization could achieve politically for Mexican Americans.

Less dramatic but equally notable were Chicano advancements in the realms of education and culture. Frequently barred from adequate schooling in the early decades of the twentieth century, Mexican Americans made giant strides after the 1950s in obtaining better educations for their children, especially in California and in previously segregated areas of Texas. Symbolic of these advances were the bilingual education programs established in many areas of the region, frequently over the opposition of Anglos who argued that they were unnecessary and too expensive. At the same time, numerous colleges and universities in the West began offering courses in Chicano history and culture, and some even established Chicano Studies programs. Concurrently, the appearance of wall murals and graffiti art, new magazines, and novels gave display and voice to Chicano cultural stirrings. Journals like *Aztlán* and the works of such writers as Rudolfo Anaya, Tomás Rivera, and Ron Arias signaled an emerging and broadly based Chicano culture and literature.

Despite these advances, several very large problems remain. Millions of Chicanos continue to crowd into barrios like East Los Angeles, where unemployment, crime, and illiteracy rates are high and where wage and educational levels are low. And though Spanish-speaking Americans could flex their political muscles if they were to unite, they have seldom done so in concerted political campaigns. Thousands of young Hispanics are still dropping out of school, and too few are entering the ranks of college-educated professionals. Only by dealing with these vexatious problems will Chicanos be able to structure their own communities and find their proper place within the larger host society. If this does not happen and if illegal immigration continues unabated —reversing, it is said, the results of the Mexican War—the fate of America's Hispanic citizens, of their newly arriving *compadres,* and of all other Americans as well is surely to be troubled.

Like the Hispanics, western blacks also immigrated in large numbers to the region and experienced intransigent poverty. As the new century began, approximately 766,000 blacks lived in the West, nearly all of them in the region's eastern borderland areas of Texas (621,000), Oklahoma (55,000), and Kansas (52,000). Most of them had moved there either as slaves before the Civil War or as poor farmers and laborers afterward, and most remained in rural areas. With the exception of the large East Texas contingent, the experiences of blacks in the twentieth-century West would differ dramatically from those of their pioneer-era predecessors and from those of other minority groups as well.

The trickle of black immigration westward at the turn of the century turned gradually into a flow and then into a flood, with few headed toward the region's northern reaches and most toward the southern. Although Arizona, Nevada, Oklahoma, Colorado, and Washington have experienced large growth rates in their black populations over the past several decades, the imperial states of California and Texas are by far the greatest growth areas. Indeed by 1980, of the roughly 4.3 million western blacks, more than three-fourths lived in these two states: 1.8 million in California and 1.7 million in Texas. Texas historically had a large black community; California's black population—like that of the rest of the region—boomed especially during and after World War II.

The main spurs to westward black migration in the early twentieth century were the wish to escape the South and its racial confines, the desire to secure better jobs, and the hope that discrimination would be less marked in the West. As one of these blacks put it, he was going west "to make more and easier money"; and as another dubiously concluded after reaching the West Coast, "there is no antagonism against the race." The great demands for unskilled and domestic workers during World War I and the California boom of the 1920s intensified these draws. Interestingly, although the largest gathering of western blacks congregated in Los Angeles, they experienced little blatant discrimination before 1920; but the tide began to turn with the arrival of so many midwestern and southern whites in the following decade. One cynic reflected these changing attitudes when he referred to the black nightclubs in the Central Avenue area as such dens of iniquity that they would make "Sodom look like a Sunday School picnic."

World War II brought the major turning point in black immigration to California and the West. The number of blacks in that state jumped from 124,000 in 1940 to 462,000 in 1950, 884,000 in 1960, and 1,400,000 in 1970. Thousands of blacks moved into the Central Avenue and Watts areas of Los Angeles and into large sectors of Oakland, Berkeley, and Richmond on the east side of San Francisco Bay, drawn by the allure of high wages and the hope of escaping the discrimination they had previously known. Many of them indeed found the good jobs they sought, but most also encountered the noxious racism they had hoped to avoid.

The two decades following the war brought both progress and disappointments to the blacks of the Far West. In Los Angeles County, for example, the black population spiraled from 25,000 before the war to 650,000 in 1965; but the new arrivals were usually confronted with segregated housing and abysmal public transportation. Moreover, few of them could aspire to leadership in labor unions, which remained in the hands of whites with seniority. Although Californians, like other Americans, struggled with the civil rights issue and enacted laws that forbade discriminatory practices in housing, rentals, real estate, and the courts, racist practices prevailed in day-to-day life. Then in 1964, California Proposition Fourteen, an act allowing homeowners to choose to whom they might sell, passed by a two-to-one margin, seemingly undoing previous civil rights legislation. Even though declared unconstitutional in the U.S. Supreme Court, this "right-to-sell" legislation reflected the nationwide white backlash and fear of neighborhood integration so prevalent in the white America of the time.

Sparked by the nationwide militancy of the 1960s, black discontent in California ignited in the unfortunate Watts riot in Los Angeles, August 11–16, 1965. Fueled by blacks' long-held grievances against whites, especially by their discontent with housing and police practices, the Watts conflict exploded after a white policeman arrested a black man for drunken driving; it soon mushroomed into a full-scale battle. In this most violent and destructive racial disturbance in the history of the West, thirty-four people died, most of them black, more than one thousand were injured, hundreds of buildings were destroyed, and $40 million was lost in property damage. The Watts riot clearly demonstrated that western cities, like others across the land, seethed with racial discontent.

The history of western blacks in Texas took a different path. At the century's beginning, most Texas blacks lived in the rural reaches of the state's humid eastern sector. After 1940, hundreds of thousands more immigrated, joining in the great Texas urban boom. By 1960, nearly four out of five of them lived in cities. Unlike their California counterparts, Texas blacks carried the added burden of long-established southern patterns of segregation. Even after the U.S. Supreme Court disallowed segregation in public schools in 1954, for instance, white Texans resisted compliance, allowing only about one-fourth of the state's black students into formerly all-white schools in 1963. Gradually, however, the nationwide crusade for integration opened these schools, like others, to all children, regardless of race.

Although Texas ranked among the top states in the size of its black populace, it avoided much of the racial violence and turmoil of the postwar era. Some argued that white domination kept a tight lid on racial disruption, but others asserted that the state's unique patterns of settlement and society made the difference. Although white leaders were slow in allowing full black political participation and educational opportunity, black middle and professional classes grew in Dallas and other cities, particularly in Houston, which boasted of more millionaire blacks than could be found in any other U.S. city. In Texas, many upwardly mobile blacks remained in their own urban areas instead of departing to the white suburbs; and more than in most cities, they were able to live in one-family housing rather than in crowded apartment and tenement complexes. Revealingly, Texas experienced no major race riot in the 1960s to match those that ripped through Detroit, Newark, Washington, D.C., or Los Angeles.

By the 1960s, western blacks were gaining national prestige in political endeavors. Augustus Hawkins, a California assemblyman from Los Angeles from 1935 to 1962, became the state's first black congressman in the latter year. During the following decade, Ronald Dellums and Yvonne Braithwaite Burke joined him in the U.S. Congress. Then Tom Bradley became mayor of Los Angeles, Wilson Riles state superintendent of education, and flamboyant Willie Brown Speaker of the state assembly. Black political leadership came more slowly to Texas; but Barbara Jordan of Houston, a distinguished state senator, moved on to Congress, where she served with similar distinction. Meanwhile, radical black leaders from the West like Eldridge Cleaver, Bobby Seale,

Congresswoman
Barbara Jordan of
Texas. Courtesy of the
Prints and Photographs
Collection, Barker
Texas History Center,
University of Texas at
Austin.

and Huey Newton of the Black Panthers and Communist
Angela Davis evoked storms of national controversy.

By the 1980s, western blacks could count both victories
and persistent problems. For the most part, the outright segregation of earlier decades had ended; but blacks still ranked
among the poorer westerners, with higher rates of unemployment, crime, and school dropouts and with lower rates
of income and advanced education. Although they increasingly joined in the broadening economic expansion of the
postwar era, they still lagged depressingly behind most other
westerners in achieving economic and social equality.

Whereas Native Americans are the oldest western ethnics,
Hispanics the most numerous, and blacks among the most
recent, Asians are the most variegated. The major groups of
western Asians—Chinese, Japanese, Filipinos, and Indochi-
nese—all had common experiences in the West, but each

also has its distinct history. Overall, the Chinese constituted the largest Asian group in the early-twentieth-century West, despite the negative impact of the Exclusion Act of 1882, which ended Chinese immigration and helped to drive down their numbers from 107,000 in 1890 to a low point of 62,000 in 1920. At first, a majority of the American Chinese resided on the West coast, nearly half of them in California as recently as 1940. They moved increasingly to cities, where 91 percent of them lived at the latter date. Working primarily as farm laborers and in service industries, they also ran small businesses, particularly restaurants, laundries, and "mom-and-pop" grocery stores.

During the Second World War, many young Chinese men joined the armed services while others worked in war-related industries. Concurrently, the earlier exclusion acts were repealed; and for the first time in many decades, Chinese immigration rates climbed in the 1950s, augmented by refugees from the Communist revolution after 1949. In the following decades, economic conditions for the Chinese of the West brightened considerably, with the percentage of Chinese men going into the professions larger than that of any other minority. In fact, by 1970 more than 25 percent of Chinese men had completed four or more years of college, the highest mark of any ethnic group in the United States.

Along with these changes in economic and educational status came other social transformations. As a result of further eliminations of immigration restrictions, more Chinese women emigrated, from Taiwan and elsewhere, so that by the 1960s male and female numbers in Chinese communities were nearly balanced. And larger numbers of Chinese Americans gravitated eastward, especially to New York, though the largest concentrations remained in the Pacific Rim cities of San Francisco, Los Angeles, and Seattle. As it had since the 1850s, San Francisco remained America's most Chinese city. More than 8 percent of all American Chinese lived there, in and out of Chinatown, their many shops and restaurants and nineteen Chinese newspapers a tribute to ethnic cohesiveness. Reforms of the postwar years, especially those legislated during the 1960s, brought an end to most of the "yellow peril" burdens of earlier decades; and the Chinese thus proved able to pass more directly into the American mainstream without losing their distinctive ethnic identity.

The Japanese tasted the same bittersweet fruit as did the Chinese in the early decades of this century. First sought as low-paid, unskilled laborers after the Chinese had been excluded, the Japanese in America swelled in numbers from 24,000 in 1900 to 72,000 in 1910 and on to 139,000 in 1930, before anti-Japanese restrictions began to take their toll. Although the infamous San Francisco School Board crisis of 1906–7 pointed up anti-Japanese hostility on the West Coast, pressing labor needs outweighed blatant racism and kept the doors open to Japanese workers. But the Immigration Act of 1924, a measure that Japan considered a rude slap in the face, effectively shut down Japanese entry for the next twenty-eight years. Even prior to these times, exclusionist state laws had kept most Japanese from owning land. In these cases, California farmers, alarmed at the alacrity with which the Japanese worked their property and succeeded financially, lobbied to keep the Japanese defined as aliens and thereby unable to buy land. To counter this opposition, some Japanese placed their land in the hands of their American-born children (who were citizens by birth) or formed ethnic cooperatives.

The Japanese-American war of 1941–45, as described above, brought terrible dislocations to the Japanese of the West, most notably the forced removal of thousands to desolate internment camps and the consequent loss of property. After the war, many Japanese hesitated to return to the coast, hearing of such warnings as the one in a small-town Oregon newspaper headline: "So sorry please, Japanese not wanted in Hood River." Nevertheless, within a decade, most of the Japanese internees had returned to the Pacific states, finding that the intervening years had leavened the region with millions of newcomers from all parts of the nation and world.

In the 1940s and 1950s, a series of court decisions lessened discrimination against the Japanese, and once again they demonstrated their will and ability to adapt to a social system that often treated them ambivalently. By 1950 nearly half of the 168,000 mainland Japanese had returned to the West Coast, and a decade later nearly 157,000 lived in California alone. Thousands of war brides and other immigrants added to the Japanese population in the West, whereas improved relations between the United States and Japan, the stability of Japanese families, and Japanese devotion to hard work and American mores all forced Americans to revise negative attitudes. Few if any western ethnic groups have demonstrated such remarkable ability to balance the maintenance of tradition with successful accommodation to the host society.

The pattern of Filipino experience in the West paralleled and departed from those of the Asians. In the early years of the century, a scattering of young males came to Hawaii and the West Coast as itinerant students and field workers. Later, after World War II and the granting of Philippine independence by the United States in 1946, immigration restrictions were lifted, and thousands of young Filipino males flocked to California farmlands, where they joined Hispanics as the backbone of the state's agricultural work force. The simple demography of their situation meant that western Filipinos lacked the rooted family and community life that brought stability to the Chinese and Japanese. This situation changed, however, with the easing of job discrimination and the mounting immigration of Filipino professionals, especially to Hawaii and California. Between 1966 and 1976, 276,000 of them came to the United States, swelling their national totals to about 500,000 by the early 1980s. Females and children constituted a large share of this new immigration, suggesting that Filipino life in the West might now more closely approximate that of most other Americans.

The Asians arriving most recently in the West are those from Indochina—the Vietnamese, Cambodians, Laotians, and smaller groups like the Hmong. Before the fall of the U.S.-backed South Vietnamese government in April 1975, only 20,000 Vietnamese, and far fewer Cambodians and

Laotians, had immigrated to America. But the collapse of the Saigon government opened the door for nearly 170,000 refugees in the next few years, almost 90 percent of whom were Vietnamese and most of whom came to the West. Most of these unfortunate immigrants came by way of refugee camps and the sponsorship of religious or civic groups and naturally gravitated to low-paying service jobs such as waiting tables and cleaning hotel rooms. Although friction sometimes erupted, as when Texas Gulf Coast fishermen lashed out at their new competition from these people, the Southeast Asian immigrants seemed to adjust rapidly to their new surroundings in such western areas as Washington, California, Texas, Oklahoma, and New Mexico, particularly considering the traumatic experiences they had undergone so recently. Their appearance was but one more indication of the rapid and remarkable pluralization of western society.

MEN, WOMEN, AND FAMILIES
IN THE MODERN WEST

Whether defined as nuclear or extended, families are, of course, a central strand of the western experience, but generalizing about them is difficult. Scholarly research into this aspect of the modern West's history is only just beginning; so, at this point, one must rely on scattered statistics, vignettes of individual men, women, and children, and the general experiences of Americans in order to gather insights and to draw a few conclusions.

Male experiences in the West are clothed in paradox. Although popular imagery, especially that of the Old West, portrays men as cowboys, adventurers, and other giants in a wide-open landscape, the reality has been a male existence that was less and less rural, more and more urban-industrial. Similarly, most historical writing about western men, like that about all American men, has focused on their public rather than on their private or personal lives. But the rising interest in women's history and social history has forced scholars to examine the "missing man," to ask new questions about men's roles as fathers, sons, and workers in addition to their roles as leaders and public citizens.

For the most part, men's experiences in the new West followed national patterns. At the turn of the century, American husband-fathers were expected to be masculine protector-breadwinners, a long-rooted tradition. In their work outside the home, the "men's sphere," they were also to be energetic examples of ambition and activism for their children and others. This ideal of the "Victorian patriarch" continued well past 1900, but new socioeconomic shifts slowly began to change the roles of husbands and fathers. Suburbanization and other factors widened the chasm between home and workplace, reducing the time men spent with their families. At that same time, the woman's suffrage campaign and the emergence of the "New Woman" by the 1920s added further challenges to the traditional images of middle-class manliness.

Yet generally speaking, the two decades after 1930 did not bring dramatic alterations in men's roles. Instead, the hard challenges of the times reinforced traditional male and female expectations. Even when unprecedented numbers of women took jobs outside the home during the war, they usually did not expect or demand enduring changes in their traditional roles as mothers and housekeepers. In fact, the postwar boom brought with it a corresponding marriage boom and "baby boom." But change was in the air. Growing numbers of fathers found their wives employed outside the home and their children in need of additional guidance. With these changes came calls for partnership and role sharing in marriages of the 1950s and early 1960s.

The mid-1960s brought the greatest challenges of this century to fatherhood and families. Many women demanded liberation from what they considered their second-class status; and the most militant among them advocated the destruction, or at least the radical reorientation, of traditional social structures, including the family itself. Concurrently, many young people, especially on college campuses, rallied

Japanese "picture brides" arrive at the San Francisco pier, 1919, already married to men they have never met. Courtesy of the Department of Special Collections, University Research Library, UCLA.

to transform society and the family into more democratic and less patriarchal structures.

Despite the many myths to the contrary, western men generally fit national patterns quite closely, but certain regional divergences from the norm stand out. In the first place, the region has always demonstrated larger ratios of men to women than the nation at large. In 1900, men in the West outnumbered women by a ratio of 54 to 46, in contrast to a national ratio of 51 to 49. Forty years later, for every 51 men in the West there were 49 women, whereas the national figure had closed to 50.2 to 49.8. By 1980, western women finally outnumbered men, but the ratio of 49.3 men to 50.7 women still remained ahead of the national ratio of 48.6 men to 51.4 women. Indeed, the census of 1980 revealed that the only states in the Union besides Alaska and Hawaii that had a preponderance of males were all in the West: North Dakota, Wyoming, and Nevada. In two other western states, Montana and Idaho, the genders were virtually balanced.

Early in the century, western Asian and Hispanic men greatly outnumbered females, causing real difficulty for

155

those wishing to marry within their own groups. In 1900, for example, Chinese men outnumbered women 19 to 1, and still by 3 to 1 forty years later. Not until 1980 did the numbers finally balance. The Japanese faced the same problem. At the century's turn, 83 of each 100 of them were male; and four decades later, men made up 54 percent of the Japanese populace. By 1970, the percentages had switched, with women totaling 54 percent of the Japanese population. Filipinos faced the same problems. Not until after World War II did sufficient numbers of Filipino women, some as wives and some as marriageable young women, arrive for Filipino men looking for mates within their own ethnic heritage. Clearly, racial attitudes and immigration restrictions worked strongly against the establishment of Asian families and social stability.

Similarly, Hispanic men, entering the United States as migratory field hands, usually either were single or were family breadwinners who came alone. Thus, until after midcentury when the pattern shifted toward family immigration, they found themselves socially isolated. For Indian families, the modern West was equally traumatic. Pressured by assimilationist policy, Indian men could no longer follow the familiar ways of hunting and fishing; neither they nor their wives and families could find social stability based on an alien system of agriculture. All sorts of western men, therefore, coped with unsettling circumstances in the modern West, circumstances at least as challenging as those that had confronted their pioneer forefathers.

Western women resembled their male counterparts by generally participating in national trends. Indisputably, however, an impressive number of western women gained renown throughout the country for their outstanding contributions to specific endeavors. For example, whereas famous leaders like Susan B. Anthony, Elizabeth Cady Stanton, Anna Howard Shaw, and Carrie Chapman Catt led the national fight for suffrage, the westerners led in real gains. The most influential of the western generals was Abigail Scott Duniway, Oregon's doughty "rebel for rights" who traveled throughout the Far West speaking for suffrage and organizing activist groups. Flinty May Arkwright Hutton of Idaho likewise stumped for suffrage while also supporting loggers and other workers. And Nevadan Anne Martin led the suffrage campaign in her state and twice ran unsuccessfully for the U.S. Senate. With the adoption of the Nineteenth Amendment in 1920, making woman's suffrage a reality, western women could and did congratulate themselves on their leadership role in this effort.

Another exceptional western woman, Jeannette Rankin of Montana, broke tradition in 1917 by becoming the first American congresswoman. A pacifist and feminist, she was retired by her constituents after she voted against U.S. entry into World War I; but back in office in 1941, she cast the lone vote against war with Japan after Pearl Harbor, another act that assured voter rejection back home. For the rest of her long life, Rankin remained an ardent advocate of feminism and pacifism, surviving long enough to lead in opposition to the war in Vietnam.

Subsequently, several western women rose to high political office. Perhaps the most controversial was Miriam Amanda "Ma" Ferguson, who was twice elected governor of Texas during the 1920s and 1930s after her impeached husband no longer qualified for the office. In some ways corrupt, in others sincerely dedicated to their depressed supporters, the Fergusons were too opportunistic, anti-intellectual, and demagogic to leave a positive legacy. Nellie Tayloe Ross of Wyoming likewise succeeded her husband as governor in the 1920s and served satisfactorily. President Franklin Roosevelt later appointed her director of the U.S. Mint in 1933, a position she held for two decades.

In more recent times, women have become far more prevalent in high political offices throughout the region. Oregon's Maurine Neuberger replaced her deceased husband as a Democratic U.S. senator in 1960, and longtime Congresswoman Edith Green became a leader in the areas of educational and social welfare legislation. Nancy Kassebaum, daughter of the venerable presidential candidate Alf

Landon, won and rewon a U.S. Senate position from Kansas; and congressional posts went to a number of influential western women, including two black Democrats, Barbara Jordan of Texas and Yvonne Braithwaite Burke of California, and also presidential aspirant Patricia Schroeder of Colorado. The controversial Dixy Lee Ray, a noted physicist, served as governor of Washington for one hectic term, and Kay Orr was elected governor of Nebraska in 1986. Likewise, several of the West's largest cities elected female mayors after 1970, among them Dianne Feinstein of San Francisco, Patience Sewell Latting of Oklahoma City, Kathy Whitmire of Houston, and Annette Strauss of Dallas.

Much more diverse and basic were the myriads of contributions that women made to modern western society and culture at local levels. As they had in the pioneer era, women usually played the central roles in establishing and maintaining the region's hundreds of thousands of schools and churches. More often than not, women constituted a majority of teachers in schools and Sunday schools, though men usually occupied the administrative and leadership positions. Through wide assortments of literary and social clubs, women sponsored and sustained the dramatic, musical, sociocultural, and service activities that enlivened just about every western town and city. As much as men, therefore, women formed and sustained western society and culture.

The achievements of the region's well-known women writers, such as Willa Cather and Leslie Silko, will be delineated in the following chapter. But it is worth noting here how the writings of modern western women have deepened our understanding of their West, and of the West in general: the Texas of young Katherine Anne Porter, the Dakota of Louise Erdrich, the California of Mary Austin, and the urban West of Joan Didion. Yet a new dimension of the woman's literary West is now coming into focus with the publication of a rich variety of collections of the personal letters, diaries, memoirs, and oral histories of western women. Such books as Joanna Stratton's *Pioneer Women* (1981), Elizabeth

Hampsten's *Read This Only to Yourself* (1982), and Ann Marie Low's *Dust Bowl Diary* (1984) add revealing vistas of western social and cultural life, particularly from the perspective of rural women.

Despite all these public contributions, it remains true of western women, as of all American women, that the majority are primarily involved in homemaking and wage-earning employment. In work activities, as in most other facets of everyday life, women of the West seem very much in the national mainstream and therefore should be viewed in a nationwide context. One must realize, first of all, that whereas in 1900 less than one in five American women were employed outside the home, by 1980 more than half of all married women—and 60 percent of all mothers—had wage-earning jobs. In less than a century's time, a majority of America's women had joined the work force, a development, as will be seen, of dramatic consequences for American families.

Women wage earners increased rapidly in number during the first two decades of the twentieth century, mostly as low-paid clerical workers, stenographers and typists, dressmakers, housekeepers, and maids. Generally speaking, women gravitated toward certain livelihoods according to their ethnic and social backgrounds: Irish and other working-class women toward jobs as maids and dressmakers, Hispanic women toward field work, Asian women toward both field and domestic work, plains farmwives toward a variety of home and field tasks in partnerships with their husbands, and so forth.

World War I offered new employment possibilities for western women when they took jobs in a variety of factories and war-related industries. Although men were not always receptive to working alongside women, gender-specific divisions of labor were often easier for men to accept. From Idaho, one source reported: "Women are being employed in considerable numbers in the lumber mills. . . . They wear overalls, do a man's work and receive a man's wages." Laboring in the lumber mills, the Idaho women were helping to prepare "white and yellow pine for airplane use." Many other women, then and later, carried more and more of the burden of farm work. In spite of the threat some men felt from working side by side with females, women proved their ability to serve well and dependably in these new occupations.

Most of these jobs returned to males, however, with war's end; and in the West, the depressed economy of the 1920s and 1930s offered few opportunities for working women. The percentages of female laborers grew slowly, and those who held jobs often faced criticism from onlookers who wanted the positions saved for men. Exemplifying this viewpoint was a Kansan who wrote to President Roosevelt denouncing working wives as "thieving parasites of the business world." Another kind of problem emerged in San Antonio. There, as a recent study of women workers in that city concludes, race and class prejudice enlarged the difficulties of black and Hispanic females looking for work, as "the caste structure of the 1930s interacted with local economic conditions to the benefit of Anglo workers." In general terms, opportunities for women had so stalemated by 1940 that the percentage of working women stood at the same level as it had in 1910.

Then came the Second World War, a watershed in the history of American women. Overnight, Rosie the Riveter became a reality in the nation's burgeoning wartime industries. Between 1940 and 1945, the numbers of employed women rose more than 50 percent, and particularly conspicuous in this expanding work force were married women over the age of thirty-five. Thousands of women found work in aircraft factories, shipyards, and other war-related plants. In San Francisco alone, the female labor force grew from 138,000 to 275,000. Yet other sources indicate that western women may have been generally more open than others to change. A scholar who has carefully studied the results of a Roper Survey interviewing twenty-eight hundred American women in 1943 (three hundred of whom lived in Rocky Mountain and Pacific Coast states) concluded that western women embraced change more readily than did females in

Women at work in a California Goodyear plant during World War II. Courtesy of The Huntington Library, San Marino, California.

other regions. Better educated, more optimistic, and less tied to traditional religious beliefs, western women in the 1940s accepted more liberal, pacesetting views of life and society, just as western women had earlier pioneered in campaigns for woman's suffrage and coeducation.

These boom conditions and the resultant changes were not, however, without their problems. Some men, jarred by unwanted and threatening female competition, harassed women workers; nor could women count on equal pay for equal work. In addition, trying to balance home responsibilities with full-time jobs often resulted in absenteeism and other difficulties. Despite all that, most women enjoyed working, appreciating especially the additional income that was needed to meet soaring wartime expenses. When the war ended, four of five women workers wanted to remain on their jobs, even though they were usually the first to be laid off. But in the postwar expansion, many were soon rehired.

For example, twice as many California women had jobs in 1949 as in 1940.

Still, sharp increases in the numbers of gainfully employed women did not bring an immediate revolution in women's status. Historian William Chafe notes in *The American Woman* that "unprecedented numbers of females joined the labor force, substantially altering the existing distribution of economic roles"; but "only minimal progress was made in the areas of greatest concern to women's rights advocates—professional employment, child-care centers, and a uniform wage scale." Instead, during the two decades after the war, Americans seemed afflicted by a "cultural schizophrenia" in regard to women's roles. This bifurcated outlook accepted the growing numbers of women working outside the home but at the same time expected them to hold to the traditional roles of wife and mother, to the "cult of domesticity" inherited from the nineteenth century. Caught between such earlier ideals of womanhood and the pressures of the workplace, women suffered mounting pressures, evidenced in soaring divorce rates and addictions to tranquilizers and alcohol.

The frenetic 1960s marked another dividing point, comparable to World War II, in the definition of women's roles as more women joined the ranks of wage earners. Between 1960 and 1980, the number of female laborers nearly doubled. Yet, equality of pay and opportunity still failed to follow. In 1985, women's pay averaged fifty-five to fifty-seven cents for each dollar paid to men, and relatively few women moved as rapidly as did men up the administrative ranks. Unhappily, the problems related to familial restructuring also continued. By the 1980s, nearly 50 percent of all marriages were ending in divorce. Obviously, family organization had faced jarring transitions: by 1980, only 15 percent of American families consisted of a working man and a woman who remained at home with the children; thirty years earlier, 70 percent of American families had conformed to this traditional pattern.

Across the West, all of these changes and all of these advances and concomitant problems in women's evolving status in society found ample reflection, especially in the Sunbelt boom and bust of the 1970s and 1980s. The nationwide crusade for an Equal Rights Amendment to ban federal and state discrimination against women, which began so optimistically in 1971 and eventually failed by 1982, offers some gauge of regional participation in this national sociological phenomenon. Thirty-five of the fifty states ratified this controversial measure so vital to the feminist cause, three short of the required three-fourths majority. Among the seventeen western states, however, all but four ratified, a margin of more than 75 percent. Reflecting a national trend of northern acceptance and southern hesitance, all the states of the northern West ratified. Among the states of the southern West, conservative Oklahoma voted no; and so did the desert commonwealths of Utah, Nevada, and Arizona, where the entrenched Mormon church worked vociferously against the amendment. Thus did the ERA campaign seem to symbolize the status of western women: advancing more rapidly than their national peers in a fast-changing society, except in the region's dry and conservative core.

Like their parents, western children and adolescents faced experiences that usually followed but sometimes departed from national norms. Historian Robert Wiebe has characterized the half-century of American history from 1870 to 1920 as a "search for order." This quest for stable patterns in economic, political, and cultural affairs was also evident in American families. By the opening decades of the new century, families were bent on a new, systematic approach to their institution based on two central tenets of the Progressive Era: efficiency and moral order. Advocating an "intense family life," parents tried to keep their children and teens at home longer instead of allowing them to venture into the world at as early an age as was common in the preceding century. Also, since the birth rate had been cut nearly in half between 1800 and 1900, fathers and mothers could devote more time and energy to each child in the perilous journey from childhood to young adulthood.

By the early 1900s, parents were receiving help from several institutions in child rearing and acculturation, including public schools, which by then grouped students by age, and such civically inclined youth organizations as the YMCA, YWCA, 4-H, Boy Scouts, Girl Scouts, and Campfire Girls. Along with families, these institutions served as agents of moral and social order for children and adolescents. The noted Denver juvenile judge, Ben Lindsey, further embodied these progressive persuasions when he urged courts to consider juveniles not as adults but as teenagers deserving of special understanding and consideration. His decisions to separate young offenders from older, chronic criminals in jails and prisons became models for reformers throughout the country.

By the 1920s, new behavioral patterns were beginning to emerge among American youth. As contemporary novelists Ernest Hemingway and John Dos Passos observed, the experiences and disillusionments of World War I catapulted young men out of a protected and idealistic adolescence and into a grim new world for which they were ill prepared. But one can make too much of the 1920s as a watershed for American youth. As historian Paula Fass notes, the changes were in tone, in degree, and in mood. The 1920s brought no generational revolution, in spite of the frequent association of the decade with "flaming youth." A development of the time that did signal future trends was the emergence of nursery schools and child-care centers, which allowed working mothers to leave their children in dependable hands.

Children and adolescents suffered deeply the pangs of the Great Depression. Western travelers of the 1930s, for example, commented on the shoeless children of the prairies, the pathetic waifs riding the rails, the hungry adolescents adrift in the cities. Although hundreds of thousands of regional families were either destitute or on relief, they got along by stretching every dime for necessities, which meant few extras for children. No one rendered a more moving portrayal of the anguish that the depression wrought on western families than did John Steinbeck in his classic *The Grapes of Wrath*. Unable to support their families, the men in the novel lose their self-esteem and soon withdraw, and the younger men abandon their families in hopes of saving themselves or of fighting the injustices that engulf them. Puzzled, depressed, and yet innocent, the children wonder at the disintegration of their once orderly existence. Only the heroines, Ma Joad and her daughter Rose of Sharon, are able to provide order for their families and their shattered community. Thus, Steinbeck implied, as the depression undermined traditional families only the warm humanism of the women provided hope for the present and future.

The World War II years were as fraught with familial tension and transformation as any of this century. Millions of men and women went off to war or to newly opened wartime jobs. Millions of children found themselves in hastily contrived day-care centers, or more or less on their own; and millions of adolescents found themselves pushed rapidly toward adulthood as they took over household work and assumed the duties of family members "off in the war." The adjacent war-industry cities of Portland, Oregon, and Vancouver, Washington, provide intriguing examples of communities trying to cope with these wartime impacts on families. In Portland, the Kaiser corporations supported a center for children aged eighteen months to six years which included a swimming pool, playrooms, and meals that women could take home to their families—all for seventy-five cents per family per day. In nearby Vancouver, industries, businesses, and community leaders joined to establish an extended school program designed to help working families. Including activities in sports, drama, and recreation, and directed by teachers, wives, and advanced students, the school taught more than three thousand students at a cost of a bit more than seven cents per child.

In most respects, wartime family and social problems and dislocations far outweighed the benefits of new employment and higher wages. With the mass immigration into West Coast cities came increased juvenile delinquency problems that neither families, schools, nor social service agencies could handle. For example, juvenile delinquency arrests

A day-care center for children of employees at the Kaiser shipbuilding plant in Portland, Oregon. Courtesy of The Bancroft Library.

doubled in Los Angeles between 1940 and 1943, and one southern California social worker once counted nearly fifty children in locked cars in a war-industry parking lot.

The wartime phenomenon of working mothers became institutionalized in the postwar era, helping to finance the great rush to suburbia and coinciding with the "baby boom" that refashioned American demography. By the mid-1950s, one in four women with young children was working outside the home, and a decade later the percentage had risen to nearly 40 percent. Whatever one concludes about the cause-effect relationship, families of the postwar generations clearly underwent dramatic changes as American society moved through the perils and pitfalls of urban-industrial transformation.

A vivid manifestation of these changes during the past two or three decades arose with the youth culture of the modern West. If New York's Greenwich Village symbolized

A Free Speech rally
at the University of
California at Berkeley,
October 2, 1964. Cour-
tesy of The Bancroft
Library.

a rebellious and bohemian American youth early in the twentieth century, San Francisco and the Bay Area became its
western counterpart in the postwar years. In the 1950s the
Beatniks and in the 1960s the Hippies and Flower Children
found the North Beach and Haight-Ashbury districts of San
Francisco a haven for their coffeehouse readings of the Eisenhower era and for their antiwar marches and "love-ins" of the
years that followed. Across the bay at the University of California campus at Berkeley, the Free Speech movement of the
mid-1960s, led by fiery student leaders like Mario Savio and
Bettina Aptheker, confirmed the suspicions of conservatives

that the largest and best university system in the country had lost control to what these critics considered know-nothing student radicals. To others, these events seemed but another manifestation of the liberal, tradition-breaking West, where new societies were again aborning.

By the 1980s, statistical indicators revealed that family and demographic profiles in the West differed in several respects from those of other regions of the country. In 1985, greater percentages of children under five resided in the Far West than in any of the other three general regions as defined —Midwest, Northeast, and South; the Far West similarly held the smallest percentage of persons sixty-five and older. Utah and Idaho, the states with the largest percentages of Mormon population, led the nation in percentages of children between five and seventeen. The census of 1980 further revealed that of the six states with the smallest average households (parents and children), five were in the West. Conversely, Utah was the only western state that ranked among the six states with the largest average households. In addition, if Alaska was included, all of the five states with the highest birth rates were western, but not one of the five states with the lowest rates of birth lay in the region.

Other findings of interest emerged from the census of 1980. Westerners seemed to marry more often, and to divorce more often, than did other Americans. Five of the six states with the highest marriage rates were western, and so were six of the ten states with the highest rates of divorce. Not one of the five states with the longest-lasting marriage averages was western, but all five with the briefest averages were. As in frontier times, westerners of the past two decades seemed to be more mobile and to experience more demographic shifts than other Americans. The impact of the large influx of immigrants from Mexico, from the Far East, and from other parts of the United States is also clear. In 1980, eight of the ten states with the highest percentages of non-native-born residents were western. These statistics seem clearly to indicate that the velocity of social change has been, and continues to be, greater in the West than in the nation at large. For children and for families, and for the region's minority peoples, the dislocations of these changes have been particularly disruptive.

If, more than a quarter-century after his earlier jaunt, John Steinbeck were once again to herd his sturdy camper through the West, he would encounter a region even more changed and diversified than the one he marveled at then. Likewise, if those who, nearly a century ago, dismissed the region as a languished frontier that simply took its cues from the East were to revisit it now, they also would have to concede that, at least to a considerable extent, the West has emerged during the last several decades as a vanguard of social change in the United States.

Chapter Five

Culture in the Modern West

T he developing culture of the modern West drew on the legacies of the nineteenth century and on new sources of influence as the twentieth century came of age. In the early years of the new century, western cultural spokesmen struggled to find regional voices that would help to break the colonial cultural bonds of prior times. Then, in the 1920s and 1930s, the West began to find its cultural identity in a rising chorus of regionalism. With the arrival of the post–World War II era, western historians, novelists, and painters took giant strides forward, so much so that it seemed the old colonial ties to eastern and European culture had, in some respects, been broken and the West had become a national pacesetter. In the areas of religion and education, the modern West simultaneously followed and broke with previous cultural patterns. Whereas much of the interior West seemed bound to tradition, California especially pioneered in new directions with its churches and its schools. Meanwhile, the popular culture of the region, particularly the evocation of a legendary "Wild West" of rodeos, dude ranches, and cinematic splendor, enjoyed a great vogue nationally and internationally. It would, however, be mistaken to conclude, as the twentieth century nears its end, that the West has evolved a unified, static regional culture. To the contrary, continuing change and subregional diversities mark the culture of the region. Although the most dynamic sectors of the West, notably California and Texas, have moved rapidly through colonial and postcolonial stages of maturation, other areas lag well behind. At the same time, intraregional rivalries have arisen to vie with the lingering tensions between West and East, all of which further complicate the situation.

HISTORIANS AND THE AMERICAN WEST

For nearly a century, the most influential thesis explaining the history of the West has been that which the noted Frederick Jackson Turner advanced in 1893 with his seminal essay "The Significance of the Frontier in American History." Addressing a meeting of the American Historical Association at the Columbian Exposition at Chicago, Turner asserted that the westering frontier did more than any other force to shape the American character. He urged his audience, and other students of American history, to trace the clear, formative lines between the frontier and the rise of democracy, individualism, and nationalism in the United States. For nearly forty subsequent years, a majority of American historians subscribed to the Turner thesis, emphasizing the actual movement of the frontier rather than the maturing institutions that first took root there.

In 1925, Turner published a second pathbreaking thesis, "The Significance of the Section in American History," in which he counseled scholars to study the key formative influence of sections, or regions, in American history. Contemporary historians, and more recent ones as well, paid less heed to Turner's sectional hypothesis than to his frontier thesis; but this regional theme merits much more scrutiny, since the West as region has long since replaced the West as frontier. In fixating on a limited view of Turner's frontier thesis, while largely overlooking his additional stress on regional developments, subsequent historians severely narrowed the master's imaginative hypotheses and bequeathed to later generations a "to-the-West" perspective without a balancing "in-the-West" point of view. Had the heirs of Turner followed both these routes to interpreting the past, our understanding of the totality of western history, especially of the modern period, might be far greater than it is.

Turner's successor at the University of Wisconsin, after he moved to Harvard in 1910, was Frederic Logan Paxson, who fleshed out and elaborated on the frontier interpretation in *The Last American Frontier* (1910) and in his Pulitzer Prize–winning *History of the American Frontier, 1763–1893* (1924). The frontier interpretation declined in vogue during the depression but then enjoyed a renaissance after World War II, in large part because of the influential writings of the able Ray Allen Billington, whose widely adopted text *Westward Expansion* (1947, 1982) served as a primer for two generations of students learning about the West. Billington demonstrated his admiration of Turner in his brilliant biography *Frederick Jackson Turner: Historian, Scholar, Teacher* (1973) and set forth an elaborate articulation of the frontier interpretation itself in his *America's Frontier Heritage* (1966).

As a graduate student of Turner's, Herbert Eugene Bolton became intrigued with frontier societies, but he went on to cast his historiographic net much wider than did most Turnerians, depicting what he called the "Epic of Greater America"—the impacts of Spanish and other European colonizers on the New World. Bolton focused especially on the "Borderlands" regions, where the expanding United States met the northern reaches of New Spain–Mexico, in a succession of romantic and dramatic historical narratives.

A new historical interpretation of the West began to surface in the 1920s. At the same time that western novelists, poets, and artists began participating in the regionalist movements sweeping the nation during the 1920s and 1930s, a few historians also turned to depicting the West as a separate, identifiable region. In his highly influential study *The Great Plains* (1931), Texas historian Walter Prescott Webb emphasized in evocative prose the shaping power of the southern plains, describing how the plains gradually laminated successive layers of varied societies and cultures into a new regional identity. Webb's stressing of the arid environment as the key influence on the formation of western society had, and continues to have, a great impact on the writing of regional history. At about the same time, Kansan James Malin urged students of the West, unfortunately too often in turgid prose and in privately printed volumes, to pay more heed to people/land relationships, to changes over time, and to humankind's enormous potential for innovation and experimentation. Like Webb, Malin fostered a new western regionalism by stressing the environment as a molding force of human and societal character.

In other writings, such as *Divided We Stand* (1937), Webb concluded that interregional conflict and exploitation characterized much of American history. Others agreed with this "plundered province" depiction of the West, particularly the noted journalist-historian Bernard DeVoto, who asserted in gripping prose that the American East held the West as a colonial hostage. Still other journalists, economists, and sociologists addressed different facets of the West-as-colony theme, arguing that the region must liberate itself from the grasp of alien economic and political interests. Although the "plundered province" view of the West as colony lost popularity as the region gained in population and economic strength after World War II, it still remains a strongly held belief among some westerners.

During the decades after 1950, the overwhelming emphasis on the frontier in western historiography faced serious and telling challenges. Such historians as Earl Pomeroy and William Goetzmann contended that western society and culture owed as much, or more, to eastern precedent as they did to the uniqueness of westering circumstances. The influential Pomeroy, and others as well, asked historians to take another look at the cultural baggage that pioneers had brought with them to the West—and also to turn much more of their attention to the evolving twentieth century. Turner, even though he lived into the early 1930s, was not much interested in writing about the first three decades of the new century, having already concluded that the 1890s marked the close of the frontier. So Pomeroy and Gerald Nash led the way in profiling the modern, postfrontier West, stressing such mainstream themes of U.S. historiography as economic and ethnic diversity and conflict, and urban growth and domination. By the 1970s, these new directions for study of the modern West seemed to have converted a growing number of historians in the field.

Behind this revisionist dialogue among historians loomed an even larger shadow over the depiction of the western past —the "Wild West" image of the frontier, which attracted not only the public at large but also many historians. This view of the subject deprecated social science tools for analyzing society, such as statistics and demography, which Turner himself had advocated. Instead the Wild West aficionados, like Civil War buffs, emphasized battles, bugles, and bullets and were more successful in conjuring up a mythical West for escapists than in advancing a real understanding of the place as it was and is. Their romantic glorification oversimplified a complex sociocultural experience and further limited scholarly study of the twentieth-century West.

WESTERN LITERATURE

In two ways, the 1890s were a turning point in western American literature. The popularity of the dime novel rapidly declined during that decade, and the genre of the cowboy novel soon arose to surpass it, reaching an apogee with the publication in 1902 of Owen Wister's *The Virginian*. The second major transition occurred as the local-color movement gradually subsided and as new, realistic writers such as Hamlin Garland, Frank Norris, and Jack London began publishing their best work. Over the next four decades, the West experienced a rich flowering of literary regionalism, particularly evident in the writings of such notable authors as Willa Cather and John Steinbeck. By the post–World War II era, westerners could be justifiably proud of the quality and variety of prose and poetry their writers were producing.

During the first three decades of this century, the popular

Jack London and his second wife, Charmian. Courtesy of The Huntington Library, San Marino, California.

novelists of the cattle country fashioned the fictional "Western," utilizing a triplex of action/adventure, conflicts between white and black hats, and the alluring landscape of a wild and free West. Authors such as B. M. Bower (the only woman who wrote Westerns early in the century), Frederick Faust (writing under the pen name of Max Brand, as well as more than fifteen other pseudonyms), and Clarence Mulford (who created Hopalong Cassidy) turned out dozens of Westerns by the 1930s; but Zane Grey led the pack. A former baseball star and dentist, Grey turned to writing frontier adventure stories early in the century. His novels *Heritage of the Desert* (1910) and *Riders of the Purple Sage* (1912) allowed him to put his brand on the Western. His larger-than-life characters, sentimental and romantic plots, and extraordinary descriptions of the western landscape appealed to millions of readers. Rarely a year went by between 1915 and 1925 without one of his novels topping the best-seller lists.

Although shorter, the careers of realists Garland, Norris, and London signaled the rise of a new kind of truly serious western literature. Having experienced firsthand the frustrations and injustices that midwestern farmers suffered at the end of the nineteenth century, Garland graphically presented their lives in such works as *Main-Travelled Roads* (1891) and *Rose of Dutcher's Coolly* (1895) and thereby became a literary spokesman for agrarian protest groups like the Populists. Garland also called for a new fidelity to factual fiction, a credo he called *veritism;* but after 1900, except for his revealing autobiography *A Son of the Middle Border* (1917), he abandoned his earlier realism to fashion numerous romantic novels about the West.

Norris's career, on the other hand, was tragically brief. After the publication of *McTeague* (1899), in which a coercive environment gradually destroys the life of an oafish dentist, Norris turned to the subject of farming and ranching communities of California at the mercy of monopolistic railroads, in *The Octopus* (1901). Unfortunately, Norris died from a ruptured appendix in 1902, before his career had come to full fruition. London's life was also brief, but he wrote fifty books and hundreds of stories and essays between 1898 and his death in 1916. His probing stories of Alaska, the Canadian Klondike, and California—in *The Call of the Wild* (1903), *White Fang* (1906), and *Martin Eden* (1909) —were memorable treatments of the molding, even abusive, power of the environment over animals and humans. Whereas *The Iron Heel* (1907) painted a depressing picture of frontier social conditions, his *Valley of the Moon* (1913) portrayed the idyllic life in London's beloved Sonoma Valley, a dreamlike agricultural setting to which he tried to flee for nourishment before his untimely death.

Although many western authors portrayed the West as an uncivilized frontier in need of taming, another group, particularly in the 1920s and 1930s, sought to depict the profound and moving relationships between the region and its culture. Whereas earlier local-color writers had stressed surface details of regional dialect, dress, and social customs, the new regionalists ventured further in focusing on the West's peculiar shaping of specific characters and cultural characteristics. For example, in *The Land of Little Rain* (1903) Mary Austin demonstrated how the desert climate and ter-

Willa Cather at work, circa 1900. Courtesy of the Willa Cather Pioneer Memorial Collection, Nebraska State Historical Society.

rain of southern California determined the flora and fauna, the occupational types, and the outlook of the residents. Such writers as Austin, and the editors of regional journals like *Frontier*, *Midland*, *Southwest Review*, and *Folk-Say*, advised authors to study and then depict subregions of the West in their prose and poetry.

Like the South, the West participated fully in the new wave of local and regional writing that swept over the country in the 1920s and then reached flood stage in the 1930s, spurred by such New Deal agencies as the Federal Writers' Project. Western and southern regionalists shared in the mood of discontent that gripped American intellectuals after World War I. But whereas writers like Ernest Hemingway, F. Scott Fitzgerald, and e. e. cummings went to Europe as expatriates, regionalists stayed home, arguing that an understanding of American society and culture was better attained by studying the many facets of the country firsthand than by denouncing it from abroad.

Nebraskan Willa Cather and Californian John Steinbeck were the most significant of these new western regionalists. The premier woman writer of the West, Cather was born in Virginia but was reared primarily in Red Cloud, Nebraska. She grew up in country rich with immigrant and farming traditions, which she worked into such notable regional novels as *O Pioneers!* (1913) and *My Ántonia* (1918). Cather was particularly adept at showing how plains experiences and traditions molded the minds and personalities of people, how the new environment redirected the outlooks of those who immigrated there. In numerous well-crafted short stories and in her southwestern novel *Death Comes for the Archbishop* (1927), Cather moved a giant step beyond the cursory descriptions of the late-nineteenth-century local colorists and demonstrated what redolent western literary regionalism might become in the hands of a talented artist.

At the other end of the West, John Steinbeck began his notable depictions of Pacific Coast life in the late 1920s. Just as Cather chronicled life-styles of midwestern and southwestern peoples, Steinbeck treated numerous California character types in such notable novels as *Tortilla Flat* (1935), *In Dubious Battle* (1936), and *Cannery Row* (1945). But it is for his Pulitzer Prize–winning novel *The Grapes of Wrath* (1939) that he is best known. This moving story of Okies and Arkies tractored off their land, their traumatic journey along Route 66, and their search for work in California deserves a ranking as perhaps the most memorable of all western novels. The only westerner to win the Nobel Prize for literature, Steinbeck was a penetrating observer of social conflict, a wise commentator on the search for community, and an especially apt depictor of the brotherhood of all peoples, as the startling end of *The Grapes of Wrath* so convincingly proves. Like the best of other American regional writers—for example, southerner William Faulkner and New Englander Robert Frost—Steinbeck utilized regional settings and characters to treat universal themes of human experience.

Other talented writers participated as well in the harvest of western regionalism. In the Pacific Northwest, H. L. Davis produced his memorable novel of pioneer Oregon, *Honey in the Horn* (1935), which won the Pulitzer Prize. Vardis Fisher carved out a niche with a series of stark, realistic novels of back-country Idaho and his panoramic historical-fictional treatment of the Mormons, *Children of God* (1939). What Davis and Fisher did for the Northwest, Paul Horgan, Harvey Fergusson, and Conrad Richter attempted for the Southwest. These three novelists, who spent many years in New Mexico, utilized the richly varied history of the region and of its Indian, Hispanic, and Anglo cultures to produce historical fiction with a notable multicultural flavor.

Although California poet Robinson Jeffers and Nevada novelist Walter Van Tilburg Clark are less often listed as regional writers, they too depicted the shaping power of western settings on character development and ideology. The finely and yet starkly etched poems of Jeffers, especially those dealing with California coastal settings, are remarkable illustrations of his understanding of the human, animal, and plant life springing out of these unique environments. Clark, on the other hand, in his pathbreaking novel about violence in a frontier town and its surroundings, *The Ox-Bow Incident* (1940), and later in *The Track of the Cat* (1949), challenged the trite and clichéd images of the West in popular fiction and instead filled his novels with carefully constructed metaphorical and symbolic characters and settings. Few, if any, other western writers surpass his talent at depicting the insights his characters gather from their western experiences.

After World War II, several new directions in western American literature became clear. For the third time in its history, the Bay Area of California emerged as the setting of an important western literary movement. Just as local-color writers of the late nineteenth century and novelists like Frank Norris had found San Francisco and its environs provocative settings for their fiction, so did a host of new writers in the 1940s, 1950s, and thereafter. After the war, the controversial "Beat" or "Beatnik" writers organized coteries in San Francisco and other California cities linking nation-wide to Denver, New York, and other sites. Such authors as Jack Kerouac in his novel *On the Road* (1957), Allen Ginsberg in his controversial collection *Howl and Other Poems* (1956), and Lawrence Ferlinghetti in his gathering of poems *A Coney Island of the Mind* (1958) became spokesmen for a western and national literary movement. These Beat writers, in their coffeehouse and public readings, railed against what they considered the smugness, materialism, and meaning-lessness of Eisenhower America. Although the Beats were sometimes depicted as cultural barbarians innocent of intel-lectual achievements, they did provide notable dissenting voices that were heard, if not heeded, in many parts of the urban West. And their experimental literary forms and social criticisms prefigured the works of later western countercul-tural writers, such as Ken Kesey and Gary Snyder.

More notable than the Beats as western writers were a group of historical and regional authors whose careers began in the 1930s and 1940s and flowered in the following de-cades. A. B. Guthrie, Jr., Montana's creator of masterful historical fiction, gained renown and several prizes for his novels *The Big Sky* (1947), *The Way West* (1949), and *These Thousand Hills* (1956). Midwesterner Wright Morris dealt movingly and probingly with the molding power of the high plains on human settlement and activity in such novels as *The World in the Attic* (1949), *The Works of Love* (1952), and *Cere-mony in Lone Tree* (1960). Texan Larry McMurtry empha-sized a strong sense of place and conflicts between an older, cowboy West and a new generation of oil-rich westerners in *Horseman, Pass By* (1961) and *The Last Picture Show* (1966). In McMurtry's novel *Lonesome Dove* (1985), which won the Pulitzer Prize, he presented the panorama of a nineteenth-century cattle drive crisscrossed with lively descriptions and character portraits. A fourth major historical-regional novelist, Frederick Manfred, developed a sure sense of setting in his novels about the twentieth-century rural Midwest, *The Golden Bowl* (1944) and *This Is the Year* (1947). This same feeling for place and historical tradition characterizes his Siouxland novels about the northern plains and Rockies, most notably *Lord Grizzly* (1954), *Riders of Judgment* (1957), and *Conquering Horse* (1959).

The most significant of the western historical-regional novelists, however, is Wallace Stegner. Reared on the tail ends of Canadian and American frontiers, Stegner drew on his own experiences, his immersion in western history, and his fertile imagination to produce such notable works as *The Big Rock Candy Mountain* (1943) and *Wolf Willow* (1962). Later, in the Pulitzer Prize–winning *Angle of Repose* (1971), a large novel embracing life in the nineteenth- and twentieth-century Wests, Stegner produced the best western novel of the past generation. Two more recent novels, *The Spectator Bird* (1976) and *Recapitulation* (1979), illustrate Stegner's deep understanding of a western past impinging on its present. In these works, as well as in his superb essays on conservation and western culture and in his biographies of John Wesley Powell (*Beyond the Hundredth Meridian*, 1954) and of Bernard DeVoto (*The Uneasy Chair*, 1974), Stegner has solidified his position as the leading man of western letters.

Alongside this persisting trend of historical-regional fiction lay several other strands of western literature. If Robinson Jeffers was *the* notable western poet of the first half of the twentieth century, more recently the works of William Stafford and Gary Snyder have gained a good deal of favorable and deserved attention. Something of a western Robert Frost, Stafford excels in treating people-land relationships and in probing the dutiful lessons one learns from tradition and personal experiences. More interested in showing what westerners can learn from nature, Indians, and the Far East, Snyder has experimented with several literary forms and themes to call readers to a new, more inward understanding of themselves. These two poets, and others such as Theodore Roethke and his student Richard Hugo, have won several recent major literary prizes, serving notice that western poets merit greater attention as major American writers.

Other writers utilized the stereotypes of the Wild West myth to provide humorous or serious satires of the region. During the depression, Nathanael West, an easterner living on the West Coast, portrayed Hollywood and modern California as havens for decadent waifs and grotesques in his novels *Miss Lonelyhearts* (1933) and *The Day of the Locust* (1939). His depiction of California and the modern West as nightmarish distortions of frontier opportunity and the American dream found a later reflection in Thomas Berger's *Little Big Man* (1964), a novel by a nonwesterner that depicts General Custer as a maniac and his Indian opponents as more civilized human beings than the pursuing white society. John Seelye's *The Kid* (1972), Max Evans's *The Rounders* (1960), and Robert Day's *The Last Cattle Drive* (1977), as well as several of McMurtry's recent novels, also illustrate this seriocomic strain in recent fiction of the West.

This style of tongue-in-cheek humor, often mixed with biting social criticism, likewise characterizes the novels of the Oregonian Ken Kesey. As one of the gurus of the countercultural groups that sprang up in the 1960s, Kesey lambasted the coercive and lobotomizing tendencies of a mindless and materialistic American society and government in his characterization of "the combine" in *One Flew Over the Cuckoo's Nest* (1962). Just as Kesey praised the western defiance and individualism of the two heroes in this novel, Randle P. McMurphy and Indian Chief Bromden, so did he celebrate the same human characteristics in the lives of a gyppo logger family in the more regionalistic novel *Sometimes a Great Notion* (1964).

For the first time, Indian and Hispanic authors have, over the past two decades, been turning out probing novels about the experiences of their peoples in the West. Describing a young Indian caught between native and Anglo worlds,

N. Scott Momaday (Kiowa) produced a memorable experimental novel, *House Made of Dawn* (1968), the first novel by an American Indian to win the Pulitzer Prize. A similar conflict lies at the center of *Ceremony* (1977) by Leslie Silko (Laguna Pueblo), another Native American novel set in the Southwest. James Welch (Blackfeet–Gros Ventre) won considerable acclaim for both his poetry and such commendable novels as *Winter in the Blood* (1974). The best of the Chicano writers is Rudolfo Anaya, whose first novel, *Bless Me, Ultima* (1972), was a moving portrayal of the identity crises and cultural conflicts besetting the life of a young Mexican American growing up in the Southwest. These recent Indian and Hispanic novelists have revealed the hidden worlds of minority experience that earlier writers such as Ole Rölvaag, William Saroyan, Robert Laxalt, and John Okada illuminated for Norwegians, Armenians, Basques, and Japanese. They have much to tell, especially that the American West is a more complex sociocultural region, with a richer variety of ethnic experiences, than most Americans have realized.

It must be noted, however, that most writers of Westerns deal not with these themes of cultural complexity but rather with predictable literary formulas. The literary progeny of Zane Grey—writers of popular Westerns such as Max Brand, Ernest Haycox, Luke Short, and Will Henry—turned out hundreds of formula novels about the Wild West that owed far more to timeworn plots than to the rich crop of regional literature coming to fruition during the past seventy years. Although each of these authors had his personal trademark—Brand's use of ancient myths, Haycox's utilization of "complex" characters and historical events, Short's violence and speedy narratives, and Henry's employment of real historical characters—these were minor differences within a distinct and consistent literary formula.

The best known of these "writers of the purple sage" was the most recent, Louis L'Amour. From *Hondo* (1952) through nearly ninety succeeding volumes (he preferred to call them "frontier novels"), L'Amour faithfully provided his readers with entertaining story lines combined with abundant historical and geographical information. Through his portrayal of several historical families in his multivolume Sackett series, he set down his personal interpretations of the European settling of successive American frontiers. More than any other writer of Westerns, L'Amour demonstrated the continuing hold that the mythic Old West has on Americans, and on other readers around the world.

Over the near century that has passed since the 1890s, therefore, western American literature has matured as a varied and often complex regional muse. Although some authors have continued to follow the familiar patterns and to use the stereotyped characters of the formula Western, the best have invoked the unique as well as universal experiences of the West to produce serious and probing commentaries on the life and culture of the region. In the works of Cather, Steinbeck, and Stegner, western writing rises to the lofty status of noteworthy American, as well as regional, fiction. The recent literary achievements of the northwesterner Ivan Doig, Californian Joan Didion, and North Dakotan Louise Erdrich (Chippewa) suggest that western novelists will continue their progress in producing literature of regional and national distinction. The West's rising literary sophistication has drawn more concentrated scholarly study as well. In 1965, the Western Literature Association was established with its journal, *Western American Literature*, evidence of and a force for advancing the maturing culture of the American West.

ART AND ARTISTS OF THE WEST

Whereas western literature moved rather quickly through colonial and regional stages into a postregional era, western artists marched more slowly toward cultural independence. Artists of the West, like the writers, tried to incorporate nonregional as well as regional influences into their works; but they were less successful, early on, in advancing new ideas or in producing works notably different from those of their predecessors or from those appearing in other American regions.

What might be termed the "classical" art of the West was romantic frontier art, already well established by the 1890s. To this day, it remains the most ubiquitous and popularly esteemed genre of the region, showing up, seemingly, in every home, tavern, motel, and drugstore from Houston to Seattle. This is the art of those giants of the Old West Charles M. Russell and Frederic Remington. Remington lived and worked until 1909, Russell until 1926; and both remained true to the romantic-primitivistic-frontier philosophy that had always been the keystone of their books, paintings, drawings, and sculpture. Their subject was always the untrammeled and unspoiled frontier: the virgin land, noble Indians, courageous soldiers, and heroic cowboys. They begot countless imitators, good ones and bad ones, who make better-than-ever incomes at numerous art auctions every year, testifying to the enduring mass appeal of this art form. It is an art form, however, born of the nineteenth, not the twentieth, century.

By the 1920s, though, new artists and new techniques began to appear, redirecting western creativity to some extent from its exclusive frontier focus. In one sense, this redirection resulted from the arrival of new artists with eastern and European backgrounds and training. In another, it resulted from the rise of a new regionalism, which reoriented art just as it did literature. Again like literature, western art emerged after World War II less tied to frontier and regional subjects, but also less tied to eastern influences, becoming more and more independent and experimental in form and content.

In the early 1900s, the new, eastern painters who took up western subjects gathered in Santa Fe and Taos, New Mexico, eventually establishing one of the most notable American art colonies of the twentieth century. At first, they followed in the footsteps of George Catlin, Albert Bierstadt, and Remington, all of whom had come west,

reacted positively to the scenes and peoples they encountered, and integrated these new subjects and experiences
into their already formulated ideas about art, culture, and
society. Attracted especially to the novel landscapes and the
bright and clear sunlight of the Southwest, and fascinated
with Indian and Hispanic cultures, such artists as Ernest L.
Blumenschein, Bert Geer Phillips, Oscar E. Berninghaus,
W. Herbert "Buck" Dunton, Victor Higgins, Walter Ufer,
and E. Martin Hennings began spending long months each
year near the stunning Sangre de Cristo Mountains of northern New Mexico. Soon, some relocated permanently to
Santa Fe and Taos. These painters, and others as formidable
as Marsden Hartley, Robert Henri, John Marin, and John
Sloan, produced superb artwork that married their training
in modernistic techniques and their experiences in Europe
and the East with their new discoveries of western scenes,
peoples, and events.

The earliest works of the Taos–Santa Fe painters reveal
the attempts of these outsiders to come to grips with new
colors, landscapes, and cultures. As Blumenschein wrote:
"No artist had ever recorded the New Mexico I was seeing. . . . The color, the effective character of the landscape,
the drama of the vast spaces, the superb beauty and serenity
of the hills, stirred me deeply." He captured these stirrings
in *Sangre de Cristo Mountains* (1925) and *Canyon Red and
Black* (1934). The evocative power of the new riot of colors
and rural landscapes also characterized Dunton's *Pastor de
Cabras* (ca. 1926) and Walter Ufer's *Where the Desert Meets
the Mountains* (pre-1922).

Equally apparent in the work of these painters is their fascination with Pueblo Indian and Hispanic cultures. In their
depictions of these cultures, the Taos–Santa Fe artists often
revealed as much about themselves as about Pueblo life, for
instance in such renderings as Joseph Henry Sharp's *Crucita,
A Taos Girl* and Phillips's *Song of the Aspen* (ca. 1926–28).
Gradually, however, as their enthusiastic reactions to the
physical appearances and novel dress of the Indians abated,
the artists treated their subjects less as nature's primitives and

Passing By, Ernest Martin Hennings (1924). Gift of the Henry W. Ranger Fund, National Academy of Design; photo courtesy of The Museum of Fine Arts, Houston.

more as real people, for example, E. Irving Couse's *The Pottery Decorator* and Hennings's *Passing By* (1924), which depicts three blanket-clad Indians riding near a richly foliaged cottonwood.

Although artists were slower to deal with Hispanic traditions, perhaps because Indian life seemed somehow more wonderfully strange, they eventually succeeded in capturing on canvas much of the Spanish presence in the Southwest. Sometimes they dealt with Spanish artisans and craftsmen, as Phillips did in *The Santero* (ca. 1930) and Blumenschein in *The Plasterer* (1921). On other occasions they emphasized dress and character types (Emil J. Bistram's *Comadre Rafaelita*, 1934), daily work activities (Hennings's *The Goat-*

187

herder, 1925), or Spanish architecture (Ufer's *Oferta para San Esquipula*, 1918). But perhaps richest of all were the depictions of Hispanic religious customs and traditions, which Willard Nash captured in *Penitentes* (ca. 1930) with his treatment of the unique Spanish religious group of northern New Mexico and which Barbara Latham rendered in her richly decorative and colorful portrait of a Hispanic cemetery in *Decoration Day* (ca. 1940).

Meanwhile, in the Midwest a different artistic tradition was arising. At the same time that historians Walter Prescott Webb and Bernard DeVoto were calling for a recognition of the West as region and that novelists Willa Cather and John Steinbeck were writing their best regional fiction, several artists in the Great Plains also succumbed to this new regionalism. Concurrently, a rising tide of government sponsorship and an enlarged interest in Far Eastern art and culture influenced other western artistic works produced in the 1930s and 1940s.

To many Americans, the rapid and sometimes searing changes of the interwar years seemed to confirm fears that a surging urban-industrial society was thrusting aside an older, rural America. Beginning in the 1920s, a new group of artists, best represented by Thomas Hart Benton of Missouri, Grant Wood of Iowa, and John Steuart Curry of Kansas, presented their conviction that the nation needed to preserve its local traditions and avoid giving way before the steamrollers of bureaucracy, materialism, and foreign influences. In their works, which began appearing in the late 1920s and early 1930s, these new regionalists, sometimes dubbed American Scene painters, attempted to recapture the power of local scenes and experiences that they feared faced extinction.

Their work has often gotten a bad press. Arguing that the American Scene regionalists were frequently chauvinistic and sentimental about local subjects, some critics dismissed their paintings as nostalgic longings for earlier and simpler times. Some works of Benton, Wood, and Curry indeed suffer from these limitations, but their paintings also testify to

Baptism in Kansas, John Steuart Curry (1928). Gift of Gertrude Vanderbilt Whitney; photo courtesy of the Whitney Museum of American Art.

the significance of regional art to a larger understanding of the varied aspects of national culture in the 1920s and 1930s. The work of John Steuart Curry is perhaps less known today than the expansive murals of Benton or the seriocomic portraits of Wood, but at its best Curry's art was highly evocative. For instance, *Baptism in Kansas* (1928), the compelling *Tornado Over Kansas* (1929), and his later plains landscapes all illustrate what one historian has called Curry's favorite theme: "the clash between ragged agricultural civilization in the wheat belt and the force of a capricious and often violent nature."

Beginning in the 1930s, the Pacific Northwest produced a triplex of important artists who, if not regionalists, at least shared several common interests. Both Mark Tobey and Morris Graves were intrigued with Far Eastern art and philosophy; Tobey betrayed his fascination for Oriental brushwork and calligraphy in his painting *Transit* (1948). After

189

living for a time in a Zen Buddhist monastery, Tobey returned to Seattle convinced that an artist must "know both worlds, East and West." In *Transit* and *Broadway* (1936), he employed a technique of "white writing"—a series of crisscrossing light lines on dark canvases—to suggest the complexities and numbing qualities of modern urban existence.

Clearly influenced by Tobey, Graves also studied Oriental culture in Japan. In a series of paintings of strange and mysterious birds—one art historian calls him "an Audubon of the psyche"—Graves suggested the enigmas of all life. In such works as *Blind Bird* (1940), *Bird in the Spirit* (1940–41), and *Ceremonial Bronze Taking the Form of a Bird* (1947), these birds became symbols of "rest from the phenomenon of the outer world." Another disciple of Tobey's, Kenneth Callahan, produced a series of paintings depicting the world as a "mass of humanity evolving into and out of nature." This perspective is particularly evident in *Revolving World* (1944), which pictures a group of people tossed about in an endless whirligig. Although the individual styles of these three artists differ a great deal, they share a common interest in Oriental culture, depict a complex and impersonal world, and draw heavily on the climate and terrain of the Pacific Northwest. To some observers, their similarities seem sufficiently marked for the triumvirate to be referred to as the "Northwest School of Painters."

The most durable line of influence between the modernist movement of art, which developed early in the twentieth century in New York, and western art was in the life and work of Georgia O'Keeffe. First as the protégé and then as the wife of noted photographer and sponsor of modern art Alfred Stieglitz, O'Keeffe attempted to render her highly personal images in eye-catching shapes and colors. Depicting flowers so enlarged that their parts covered entire canvases, she seemed to be experiencing, as one critic has written, "a private world in which natural forms were adopted or transformed to express a lyric vision, and real objects became the vehicles for a poetic fashion." After spending a few months of each year painting in Texas or New Mexico, she moved to the Southwest following World War II, after which her work included more of the artifacts, architecture, and color of New Mexico settings and landscapes. Always individualistic and independent, symbolizing for many "the new woman," O'Keeffe fused modernistic techniques and western objects, scenes, and hues in such works as *Ranchos Church #1* (1929), *Cow's Skull—Red, White and Blue* (1931), *From the Faraway Nearby* (1937), and *Red Hills and Bones* (1941). No painter better illustrates than Georgia O'Keeffe that some facets of western American culture are best viewed as kaleidoscopic blends of national and regional ideas and experiences.

As with so many aspects of American society, World War II redirected cultural trends of the prewar decades and set in motion others that would hold sway in the postwar years. Indeed, the deaths of Grant Wood and John Steuart Curry, symbols of the American Scene regionalism of the 1930s, signaled the end of an era. As the great war ended, cultural pressures were no longer inward but outward, away from regionalism and toward a new internationalism. Artists in the American West now found themselves at work primarily in national-international contexts that drew them out of their more localized emphases and toward more expansive world views. If the archetypal western painter of the 1930s was a regionalist dealing with his own locale and declaring his independence from New York art circles, the typical western artists of the postwar decades were of two sorts: abstract expressionists with little sense of place, and those who were tied to locale but whose art was nonetheless experimental. In both instances, these new artists were *in* the West but not necessarily *of* it.

In the postwar era, abstractionist art became increasingly popular throughout the country. As an integral part of the modernist movement in art and culture, abstractionism, particularly abstract expressionism, characterized artists who emphasized color, form, and shape almost to the exclusion of patterns in the natural world. Rather than utilizing figures or objects, abstract expressionists created new forms and designs that derived from subjective reality and broke from previous realistic patterns. These revisionist tendencies found full expression in the work of Jackson Pollock, a Wyoming native who spent his early years in the West and studied with the well-known regionalist Thomas Hart Benton. Pollock's interest in Indian art, especially in the emotion-releasing work of Navajo medicine men in preparing sand paintings, led to his own famous practice of drip painting, which tellingly illustrated the free-form nature of so many abstractionists. A major center of the abstract expressionist movement was the Bay Area California School of Fine Arts, where David Park, Elmer Bischoff, and Richard Diebenkorn, as students and teachers, became vanguards of the new movement. Within a decade, however, these painters were moving in new directions, bearing out the interpretation of western art as usually fast-moving and sometimes chaotic.

Alongside the free-wheeling, controversial, and seemingly undisciplined work of the abstract expressionists grew up a welter of other styles that also reflected the increasing cultural pluralism of region and nation. The same yeasty culture of California that spawned the Beat writers, the later Hippies, and a gamut of improvisational music groups also nurtured groups of painters variously known as Pop artists, Conceptualists, and Photo Realists. Pop artists like Wayne Thiebaud, William T. Wiley, and Robert Arneson employed all sorts of artifacts from popular culture and the mass media for their artwork, which they argued ought to be for all "folks" and not just for the elite and erudite. Reflecting the performance orientation of the 1960s and 1970s counterculture in California, the Conceptualists strove to remove the barrier between art and life by staging "events" or "happenings" that were central to their artistic vision. Television press conferences and exhibits at familiar urban sites became integral parts of Conceptualist art, actions that naysayers dismissed as stunts or exhibitionism rather than art. One "happening," Christo's *Running Fence* (1976) of more than two million square yards of nylon fence stretching across nearly twenty-five miles of northern California, was but the most notorious of many such stagings.

To the initiated, the works of the Photo Realists seemed more serious than those of the Pop artists and Conceptualists, yet also more like photographs than paintings. Such artists as Robert Bechtle, Richard McLean, and Ralph Goings urged other painters to reassert the importance of the object in their "sharp-focus" realism. Photorealistic renderings of such commonplace subjects as pickups, western highways, fast-food restaurants, and skyscrapers emphasize the two-dimensional reality of the photograph and the importance of the everyday life of ordinary people. If the "Dude Ranch Dada" of the Pop artists and the "happenings" of the Conceptualists illustrated how far experimentation might go in the modern art of the West, the works of Photo Realists epitomized a more conservative bent that became pronounced in the 1970s and 1980s.

The coexistence of these varied and startingly different new art forms alongside the traditional art of the Remington-Russell mode and the numerous works of Indians and various ethnic groups offers an illustration of the mosaical quality of culture in the region. Especially in major cities along the southern and far western expanses of the region, impressive new museums and art galleries offer ever greater varieties of first-rate western art, a testament to the maturation of this facet of western culture since the colonialist-regionalist decades prior to World War II.

RELIGION IN THE MODERN WEST

During roughly the first half of the twentieth century, the same issues and controversies that united and divided churchgoers in the United States also characterized religion in the West. The religious censuses taken during these years revealed that denominational loyalties in the region closely followed national patterns. In the ensuing decades, however, a number of indicators—changes over time in mainline Protestant and Catholic churches, developments within the various western sects, and the growing strength of new religious bodies—indicated that religious experiences in the region no longer so closely coincided with those in the nation at large.

Many historians of American religion speak of a consensus that united the nation's Protestants during the more than half-century from the Civil War into the 1920s. Although disturbing issues like Darwinism, Social Darwinism, and "higher criticism" of the Bible shook Protestant churches during these decades, and sometimes caused interdenominational squabbles, religious liberals and conservatives usually did little more than jab verbally at one another. Protestant anxieties mounted, though, as more and more Catholic immigrants entered the country, as the various sects argued more heatedly about evolution and such conservative strictures as *The Fundamentals* (1909–14), and as the worldly cities outpaced the more pious countryside. During the hectic 1920s, the harmony of earlier days gave way to a factionalism between liberal "modernists" and conservative "fundamentalists" that, in the words of one historian, "marked the passing of the Protestant hegemony in the United States."

Several of the changes and controversies that undermined the national Protestant consensus were evident in the West; some, in fact, emerged there in exaggerated form. For example, the rapidly urbanizing West Coast struck observers with its amazing growth, its "glacial dullness," its seeming reincarnation of a puritanical "Iowa on the loose." To the insightful journalist Carey McWilliams, Los Angeles seemed "a center of Comstockism and Fundamentalism." The Protestant crusade against religious modernism took its nastiest turn with the previously described rise and fall of the Ku Klux Klan, which momentarily turned even progressive Oregon onto a course of intolerance and persecution.

Although Protestant growth and influence in the West came largely through denominations such as the Methodists, Baptists, Lutherans, and Presbyterians, a small group of outspoken ministers were often leaders of this fundamentalist vanguard. One of the most outspoken in his opposition to liberalism and in his conviction that Christ, the Bible, and Protestant Christianity were *the* solutions to the nation's problems was Mark Matthews, pastor of Seattle's First Presbyterian Church from 1901 until his death in 1940. Even though he was rabidly conservative in theology, Matthews was also a social reformer who launched several crusades to "clean up the city." By both attacking the special interests that he saw dominating the poor and urging his flock to fight the devil, whom he saw at work all around him, Matthews built his congregation into the world's largest Presbyterian Church.

Meanwhile in Texas, the Reverend J. Frank Norris, minister of the First Baptist Church of Fort Worth for more than four decades, similarly slashed at modernists, evolutionists, Catholics, and city officials, all of whom he depicted as undermining Christian tradition and standards of decency. The "Texas Tornado," as Norris was called, parted company even with the conservative Texas Baptist Convention to set up his own Bible seminary; and he delighted his followers with a series of thundering debates with the famed agnostic Clarence Darrow. He preached every Sunday morning to crowds as large as five thousand, who reveled in his harpooning of the city's "fat cats" and of the liberal ministers who opposed him.

Perhaps the most famous leader of the fundamentalist crusade that swept the nation, especially the South and West, in the 1920s was the Nebraska layman William Jennings Bryan. A genial and beloved man and a seasoned political veteran, the "Great Commoner" was nonetheless a rigid fundamentalist who died suddenly after exhausting and embarrassing himself attacking evolutionism in the Scopes Trial of 1925. Less lovable than Bryan, and bearing fewer redeeming features, were two politically potent preachers of the time, Gerald P. Winrod and Robert P. "Fighting Bob" Shuler.

Winrod, a hard-shelled Kansas Baptist, riveted the attention and loyalty of hundreds of thousands with his radio sermons and his writings in his *Defender Magazine* during the 1920s and 1930s. He lashed out at evolutionists, modernists, and Jews, even going so far as to praise the Hitler

regime in Germany. After he lost badly in a primary campaign for the U.S. Senate, a campaign based on racism and
intolerance, his national following rapidly dwindled. More
of a traditional minister, "Fighting Bob" Shuler built up a
powerful regional following based on his Methodist minis-
try in Los Angeles during the 1920s. Carried far and wide
by radio, his fiery sermons denounced the saloon, political
corruption, Catholics, evolutionists, and worldly ministers.
In his prime, he wielded such influence that critic Edmund
Wilson convincingly called him "the real boss of Los Angeles."

Probably the most striking, and most misunderstood, of
the western Protestant leaders was one of Shuler's favorite
targets, Aimee Semple McPherson, whom unsympathetic re-
porters and historians too often treat as a fraudulent Pied
Piper leading thousands of southern Californians into yet
another weird cult. Arriving in Los Angeles in 1918, a poor

196

widow with little education, the striking "Sister Aimee" displayed rare abilities at working hard, organizing pageantry, and gaining recognition. At her Four Square Gospel Church, which emphasized Christ as Savior, the role of the Holy Spirit, physical healing, and the Second Coming, she appealed dramatically to the rootless new immigrants to California with stagings that featured her wearing lavish clothing or pitchforking the devil. Despite her dubious personal life, which included a "kidnapping" in 1926 that may well have been a love tryst, and her garish showmanship and squabbles, she extended her empire and held her loyal followers for nearly two decades by offering them orthodox Christianity as well as spectacles. She accomplished a good deal and deserves a better reputation than she got. As Carey McWilliams concluded: "Mrs. McPherson was a more sympathetic character than her critics or enemies."

While these polemical leaders captured most of the attention, the majority of the Protestant congregations worshipped and grew quietly. So did those of the Roman Catholic church. The religious census of 1906 revealed the Catholics to be the largest church-attending population in about two-thirds of the western states and territories. In six of these seventeen states, they made up more than 50 percent of the religiously affiliated. Heavy concentrations of Catholics lay along the northern tier of western states from the Dakotas to Washington and along the southern rim from Texas to California, where there were large gatherings of Irish, Germans, Italians, Hispanics, and other immigrant groups that held fast to their church traditions.

In only two states of the early-twentieth-century West, Kansas and Oklahoma, did Methodists outnumber Catholics; but in about half of the other states, they placed second behind Catholics. In Texas the Baptists led all other denominations; and in many other states, they rivaled the Presbyterians as the next largest Protestant grouping behind the Methodists. In the center of the West, the Mormons made up a large and growing segment of the population in Idaho, Arizona, Nevada, and Wyoming, constituting 80 percent of

the churchgoers in Utah. These profiles of religious affiliation did not change much until World War II and after, when
massive immigration and drastic liturgical and other changes
began to shift the denominational demography of the West.

In the first decades of the new century, Catholics held
strong in areas formerly Mexican, in areas retaining mining
populations, and in the northern plains, with its heavy European immigrant population. Generally speaking, Catholics
in the West, as in the East, adhered well to their traditions
in the growing urban areas. But in the rural regions, they
suffered the same "leakage" from the faith that they had in
the previous century, despite the heroic efforts of prelates
like Father (later Bishop) Edwin Vincent O'Hara. Attacks
by the Ku Klux Klan and by rabid fundamentalist groups
and the closing of large-scale immigration made the 1920s
and 1930s a hard time for western Catholics. Still, continued
population flows to the West from the Northeast and from
Mexico augmented church membership. The elevation of
San Antonio (1926), Los Angeles (1936), Denver (1941),
and Omaha (1945) to archdioceses symbolized this growth.
In addition, missionaries and other church workers continued their labor on Indian reservations, where they won
far more converts than did even their closest rivals among
the Protestants.

By midcentury, Catholics retained their numerical su-
periority in the West, in much the same subregions that
they had earlier; but their lead over their nearest Protestant
rivals was falling, and they made up a smaller percentage
of churchgoers than they had earlier in the century. More
than ever, western Catholics were urban dwellers; and many
remote rural areas found themselves without priests. In the
generation following the mid-1960s, church growth stalled
nationwide, indeed declined in some locales. With fewer
young women and men joining religious orders, hundreds
of Catholic schools, and some colleges, had to close. At the
same time, what historian John Tracy Ellis terms "a per-
vading spirit of unrest" covered Catholics in the nation and
region, resulting from the liberalizing church reforms of the

Vatican II Council of the early 1960s. Conflicts not unlike those that had earlier afflicted the Protestants raged between liberals and conservatives, such as controversial Cardinal James Francis McIntyre of Los Angeles, over matters of church policy and liturgy.

Although these trends seemed to bode a gloomy future, western Catholics also found brighter prospects, such as the naming of the first cardinals from the region, McIntyre of Los Angeles and Aloisius Muench of Fargo, both in the 1950s. Western Catholics had long lamented their relative lack of political power beyond the local level; but like their counterparts across the land, they gloried in the presidential triumph of John F. Kennedy in 1960, which seemed to symbolize their rise to parity with Protestants. In truth, Catholics of the region could point to many signs of vitality: the past achievements of selfless humanitarians like Katharine Drexel, who applied her immense inheritance of wealth to a lifetime of helping Indians and blacks; Father Edward Joseph Flanagan, whose famous Boys' Town near Omaha became "the most famous haven for homeless, delinquent, and destitute boys in the world"; or such forward-looking leaders as Bishops Charles Buswell of Pueblo and Victor Reed of Oklahoma City–Tulsa.

By the 1980s, Catholic strength in the West seemed to have reached a plateau. Whereas Roman Catholics constituted 21 percent of the population of the United States, they totalled about 16 percent of the inhabitants of the seventeen western states. Only New Mexico with 34 percent and North Dakota with 27 percent of their populations Catholic ranked significantly above the national average; at the other extreme, only 5 percent of either Oklahoma or Utah were. Only the swelling tide of Mexican immigrants to the Southwest served to offset a generally level or falling Catholic population in the region. However, statistics tell little of Catholic vitality and involvement in the West. The church has become increasingly active in a broad range of reform causes, from providing refuge for Latin American refugees to supporting César Chávez's labor campaigns

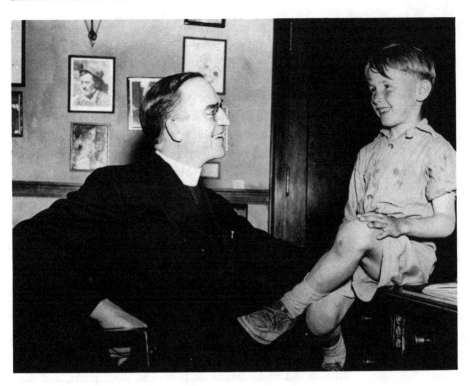

Father Edward Joseph
Flanagan and friend.
Courtesy of Father
Flanagan's Boys' Home.

and the controversial Seattle bishop Raymond Hunthausen's pronouncements against the arms race.

Jewish experiences in the modern West differed markedly from those of Christians. Although more than two million Jews joined in the great Euro-American immigration between 1880 and 1920, few made their way to the West, the great majority remaining in the cities of the Northeast. In 1920, no Jewish community made up so much as 5 percent of any major western city, but over the next four decades Jewish numbers greatly increased, particularly on the West Coast. Despite the barbs of anti-Semitic groups like the KKK, western Jews rose to positions of political as well as business influence. For instance, Jews dominated much of the Hollywood scene and rose to high political offices in the region, as in the cases of Governors Moses Alexander in Idaho, Simon Bamberger in Utah, and Neil Goldschmidt in Oregon.

In the climate of nationalism and consensus of World

War II and after, Jews in the West, and in all regions of the United States, prospered and moved fully into the American mainstream. Ideological differences abated; and even within the faith, reform and conservative congregations came together in mergers. Refugees from Nazi persecution in the 1930s and 1940s swelled an already sizable Jewish enclave in San Francisco. But the largest of all western Jewish congregations grew up in Los Angeles, a community that numbered 225,000 by 1948, the fourth largest in the United States. Three decades later, the Jewish populace of Los Angeles had surged to nearly a half-million, ranking it second to New York City in size in the country. Meanwhile, Jewish congregations clustered across the region, from the sizable gatherings and synagogues of Dallas and Phoenix to the small Sephardic groups in the Pacific Northwest, reflecting the considerable diversity of American Judaism—from the older, established German-Jewish families to the newer descendants of East European refugees of the Nazi Holocaust. But the late 1980s still found perhaps as many as three-fourths of all western Jews residing in urban California.

Whereas the numbers of many established Protestant and Catholic churches leveled off or declined after midcentury, some church memberships continued to climb, particularly the western-based Mormons and conservative and evangelical Protestant groups. All too often, students of American religion forget the Mormons after the close of the nineteenth century. But the Church of Jesus Christ of Latter-day Saints (LDS), as the religion is formally known, has continued to grow rapidly in numbers and influence in this century; and as a result, it has become an increasingly recognized national and international religious body.

Even after making allowance for the persistence of pioneer characteristics and after revising the ultraconservative and all-American stereotypes of the Mormons, one must admit that the Saints have changed much since their arrival in the Salt Lake Valley nearly 150 years ago. In fact, when church President Wilford Woodruff issued his landmark manifesto of 1890 officially ending polygamy, he symbolically ushered in a new era, even though ensuing events proved that some Saints and many other Americans were not prepared to end their differences over the controversial issue of plural marriages. For example, when LDS authority Brigham Roberts was elected to Congress in 1898, he was denied his seat on the grounds that he was a practicing polygamist. The issue surfaced again four years later when another LDS leader, Reed Smoot, was elected to the U.S. Senate. Smoot, who was not a polygamist, withstood the attacks and entered the Senate—despite the comment of one critic that he was "a polygamist who doesn't polyg." The Senate's acceptance of Smoot seemed to signal something of a semiofficial acceptance of Mormonism. Meanwhile, the church tried to prevent polygamous unions, excommunicating members who refused to follow its directives, but failed to achieve complete success.

Even as the church worked at resolving the old issue of polygamy, it consolidated and expanded its growing empire in the United States and overseas. LDS membership numbered something over two hundred thousand in 1900, more than one and a half million in 1960, three million in 1970, and approached four million by the late 1980s. More than twenty thousand missionaries, mostly males on two-year assignments, carried forward this expansionist work of spreading Mormonism around the world. In addition to their astronomical rate of growth, the Mormons also gained more acceptance from other Americans, for instance with the appointments of such Saints as Ezra Taft Benson (later president of the church) and David Kennedy to presidential cabinet positions.

In contrast to other frontier-born religious bodies, the Mormon church has become a truly international organization, rivaled perhaps only by the Pentecostals in the growth of American-sponsored missionary activity in Central and South America. The church's emphases on traditional lifestyles, the family, church attendance, and local communities, as well as its conservative politics, are reminders of its close affinities to evangelical Protestantism. But the high Mormon birth rate—more than twice the national average—the unique church welfare system, the devotion to non-Biblical teachings of Mormon prophets, and the Mormon church's huge portfolio of investments all point up as well its important differences from Pentecostal, Holiness, and fundamentalist groups. In sum, the Mormons remain one of America's most distinct religious groups. Headquartered at the crossroads of the region, Salt Lake City, they represent one of America's most dynamic and fastest-growing churches.

Even before the sociocultural turbulence of World War II, winds of change began gusting through the western religious order, winds that would disrupt existing patterns and bring new and sometimes exotic religions onto the scene. Most noticeable among the Protestant denominations was the lessening dominance of such established churches as the Methodists, Presbyterians, and Congregationalists and the corresponding rise of fundamentalist-evangelical groups.

As more and more southerners moved west, the Southern Baptists, largest and most powerful of the fundamentalist denominations, burgeoned from Texas to California, and beyond the Southwest as well. Newer evangelical groups also grew rapidly. Most of them were little known, even though some had arisen in the region. Organized in Texas in 1908, the Church of the Nazarene brought together several former Methodist and Holiness associations from around the country; and what became known as the Assemblies of God Church, now the largest of the Pentecostal organizations, had its origins in Kansas, California, and Arkansas and spun off as a denomination in 1914. These older and newer evangelical groups, which *Life* magazine aptly called the "Third Force of Christendom," expanded spectacularly in the postwar era; by the 1980s, they constituted a sociocultural-political force of great importance.

At the same time, another arm of *Life*'s "Third Force" mushroomed in size and influence, the nondenominational evangelical ministries. Baptist minister Charles Fuller began his "Old Fashioned Revival Hour" in the 1920s, and by the end of the next decade the radio program "played on more stations than any other single-release prime-time broadcast." Under his direction, the Fuller Theological Seminary arose in California, an institution many consider the most notable evangelical graduate seminary in the United States. In 1949, the famous touring evangelist Billy Graham made his first headline splash with a Los Angeles tent revival; and at about the same time, Bill Bright was busy organizing his Campus Crusade for Christ, now based near San Bernardino, which eventually sent collegians two by two across the country and abroad converting college students to evangelical Christianity.

In a more controversial vein, Oral Roberts, first a Pentecostal revivalist and faith healer and later a member of the Methodist church, established his headquarters in Tulsa and gradually built a large university and medical complex. Many other evangelists based themselves in California, including Robert Schuller, whose TV "Hour of Power" originated from his spectacular Crystal Cathedral in Garden Grove. By the 1980s, California and the Southeast ranked as the two prime national centers for a new coterie of radio and television evangelists heard across the country and around the world.

Throughout the twentieth century, the Far West has also attracted what some consider a strange assortment of cranks, fanatics, and cults. Even before Sister Aimee began gathering her flocks to Los Angeles, Katherine Tingley, known as the "Purple Mother," organized a theosophical society in 1897 on scenic Point Loma in San Diego that drew hundreds of settlers and thousands of dollars before it folded in the 1930s. Similarly, followers of New Thought and other metaphysical and religious groups found the positive thinking identified with early-twentieth-century California much to their liking. In the 1930s, the I Am cult, which featured a strange mixture of incredible and bizarre beliefs, won the loyalty of many Californians. Later, and much more tragically, hundreds flocked to the Reverend Jim Jones of the People's Temple, whose strange teachings eventually led his congregation to abandon San Francisco for Jonestown, Guyana, where nearly all perished in a mass suicide in 1978.

By the 1980s, therefore, the American West, especially the Southwest, hosted a variegated assortment of religions. Ranging from the traditional Protestant and Catholic churches to the fast-growing evangelical-fundamentalist congregations and on to exotic fringe groups of every conceivable persuasion and life-style, this diversity of religions convinced many observers that parts of the new West were indeed seedbeds of novel religious culture. Nothing better illustrates the modern West's evolution from a colonial region—looking elsewhere for its cultural cues—into a pace-making, trendsetting, postregional culture than does California, with its diverse, chaotic, always invigorating panoply of religious denominations, associations, sects, and cults.

EDUCATION IN THE WEST

Whereas slightly more than half of all westerners in the twentieth century have claimed church membership, a much larger majority have attended schools. Indeed, no social experience involved more westerners than did attendance of elementary and secondary schools, colleges, and universities. Thus schooling lies at the center of western culture and is pivotal to an understanding of that culture.

As the new century opened, westerners shared fully in the American tradition of schooling. Every western state except Texas received a federal bequest of public lands—section sixteen of every township, under the Land Ordinance of 1785—to support a system of public schools. And in this region, as in its older counterparts, one-room schools, featuring the stalwart schoolmarm and schoolmaster and rote learning from McGuffey readers, were a major part of the rural life of a majority of people. John Swett, state superintendent of schools in California, stated well the inherited American commitment to public schools: "The wealth of the state must educate the children of the state."

Similarly, the frontier West quickly sprouted private, usually religiously affiliated, colleges. More reliant on public spending than the older and wealthier regions, however, the West naturally gravitated less to private institutions of higher learning than did, say, New England, and leaned more to public institutions. Here too federal support proved vital. Under the famed Morrill Act of 1862, all states received endowments of public land to support "land-grant colleges," colleges that would provide practical and basic education to the masses at feasible cost. With this and other federal and state support, all the western commonwealths established college-university systems. In many of them, such as Kansas, Texas, and Washington, land-grant or "A&M" campuses developed, usually in farm country, independent of more comprehensive universities, often also flanked by "normal" teachers colleges and "tech" or mining schools. Some others, like Nebraska, Arizona, and California, merged the land-grant college and the comprehensive university function into one institution, often revealing their ideologies in such decisions. For instance, conservative and rancher-dominated Wyoming opted for one central, cost-effective campus, whereas the more populist-progressive Montana, where mining laborers and small farmers prevailed, established a multiunit system of smaller but more accessible campuses.

In all fields of education—elementary, secondary, and postsecondary—major structural and ideological changes impacted the West after the turn of the century. Most of the states and territories of the region already had viable elementary school systems by 1900, but the idea of high schools was a recent innovation. Over the next three decades, however, following a national trend, secondary schools emerged all across the region, especially in booming urban areas. In fact, the West forged ahead of most other regions in the quickness with which it established public high schools. Fast-growing California set the pace for the region, experimenting even before 1920 with "junior highs," which established school units of six years, three and three, and with junior colleges. Generally speaking, the most remarkable innovations in western

The North School, Fremont, Nebraska, 1904. Courtesy of the Nebraska State Historical Society.

education occurred in those parts of the region undergoing the most rapid and thorough sociocultural changes.

Equally important in shaping educational practices in the early-twentieth-century West were a number of new ideas influencing educators throughout the country. In the decades surrounding 1900, psychologists, educators, philosophers, and other theorists argued for new approaches in educating children, insisting that new scientific studies proved that traditional modes of schooling retarded rather than encouraged learning. The most influential of these idea merchants, John Dewey of Columbia University, stressed that children learned by doing, that education should prepare children to live in a democratic society rather than simply to pass rote-memorization examinations. Dewey's philosophy of Progressive Education stimulated a national revolution in the educational fields. Throughout the West, his ideas were quickly embraced and put to work. Although rural school districts usually resisted change, urban educators continued to embrace Progressive Education well into the 1950s. In California, for example, one of Dewey's disciples, vivacious and dynamic Helen Heffernan, enthusiastically preached the doctrine for all of her nearly forty-year stint as state director of elementary education.

A parallel transformation shifted the roles of parents, local communities, teachers, and school administrators in the educational process. In the early years of western schooling, parents, teachers, and local officials followed the time-honored precedent of centering as much control as possible in the family and community. But by the early years of the new century, school administrators, reflecting a national "search for order," strove increasingly to take the schools and their curricula "out of politics," which meant wresting control from parents and politicians and putting it in the hands of educational professionals. Western schools clearly displayed the resulting trend toward specialization and bureaucratization by the 1920s.

These changes brought a fair measure of trauma to the nation and region. Although reformers and advocates of more and better public schools accomplished, at least statistically, much of what they called for, they usually limited their perspective to their own moral, religious, and racial values and evinced little interest in or sensitivity toward the children of families whose ethnicity, class, or moral principles differed from theirs. For instance, in 1906 the San Francisco Board of Education ordered the segregation of Japanese children into a separate school, triggering an angry response from Japan and prompting President Theodore Roosevelt to convince the "infernal fools in California" to rescind their order. As noted earlier, Oregonians betrayed their nativistic anti-Catholicism with a compulsory school attendance law in 1923 aimed at destroying parochial schools. In East Texas, where one-third of the population was black, nearly all the high schools in 1929 were white-only.

If questions of race, class, and religion plagued schooling efforts, so did issues of financial support. Like other Americans, westerners were usually as verbal as ambitious politicians in their vocal support of public education but equally reluctant to back up their rhetoric with hard cash. By long tradition, most western states relied primarily on local property taxes to support their elementary and secondary schools. Oregon was typical in that such school support represented the biggest tax demand by far on local property owners. Especially in rural areas and especially in hard times like the Great Depression, this reliance could prove woefully inadequate. So, particularly during the prosperous years after World War II, state after state turned to statewide "equalization" tax funds to provide school funding assistance to localities. As early as 1948, the progressive state of Washington secured more than 70 percent of its public school revenues from statewide sources.

In all of these matters, westerners generally followed quite closely nationwide educational trends, but such conformity can easily be exaggerated. For in other ways, westerners pioneered educational changes or sharply redirected national trends to fit regional circumstances. No other part of the West even approached California in the breaking of new ground in education. In its early implementation of high schools, junior highs, and junior colleges and in its advocacy of progressive education, California leaped ahead of the region, indeed ahead of most of the nation. Its remarkable willingness to experiment and innovate seemed a reflection of its race toward urbanization in the prior century.

Most noteworthy is the state's system of colleges and universities. Of humble nineteenth-century origins, higher education in California did not grow rapidly until this century. Yet today its state system usually ranks as the best in the United States, and the strongest units in the system generally rank among the best universities in the world. In the Master Plan of 1960, the state formalized a three-tiered program that had been evolving during the previous decades. At the apex of the system stood the campuses of the University of California, most notably the most prestigious units at Berkeley, Los Angeles, Davis, Santa Barbara, and San Diego (La Jolla). Only the top 10 percent or so of California's high school graduates were eligible to enroll in these universities, which provided most of the system's doctoral, advanced professional, and research programs.

The second of the system's three tiers consisted of the nineteen campuses of the California State University and College System. Here, the top one-third of the state's high school graduates could access strong programs at reasonable costs, at such campuses as those at San Diego, San Jose, and Fresno. By the late 1970s, this system awarded more than one-half of the undergraduate and one-third of the master's degrees conferred in the state each year. The third component of the system was the junior or community colleges. First established in the early years of the century, junior colleges expanded rapidly, especially during the prosperous 1960s, until by the 1980s they numbered nearly one hundred. Initially conceived as two-year, postsecondary institutions, they also came to assume the bulk of the state's vocational and technical training programs. Until recently, the California community colleges, which form the nation's largest system, did not charge tuition, thus providing unprecedented opportunity to the state's citizenry, regardless of income.

With all its strengths, higher education in California also suffered chronic problems, which found reflection elsewhere. As happened heatedly in both Texas and Washington, conservative superpatriots attempted to purge liberal or dissenting professors, most dramatically during the Berkeley loyalty-oath controversy of the 1950s discussed below. Student protests against the impersonality of the great "multiversities" and against the Vietnam War and other issues polarized many campuses, with Berkeley again leading the way with its dramatic "Free Speech Movement" of 1964. And as in most states, the problem of too many campuses, battles over funding, and struggles between various localities surrounding the campuses seemed to haunt every legislative session.

California's problems and achievements typified, in magnified image, those of the region at large. The state's premier private colleges and universities, such as Stanford, Mills College, the Claremont group, and the California Institute of Technology, had their counterparts in other states: Rice University in Texas, Colorado College, Reed College in Oregon, Whitman College in Washington. Still, in the West, public institutions dominated higher education more than did public institutions in regions to the east. Every western state could claim at least one respectable state university; and the Universities of Texas at Austin and Washington at Seattle ranked among the best in the nation. Others, such as the Universities of Colorado and Arizona, could also make considerable claims of excellence. Meanwhile, expanding cities fueled the rise of new campuses with large enrollments, like Portland State and Arizona State universities and the University of Nevada at Las Vegas.

Unfortunately, excellence in some western state systems of higher education contrasts with perennial problems in others. In the Dakotas, Oklahoma, Montana, Kansas, and Oregon, for example, multiunit systems have been underfunded in comparison with neighboring states, a situation that now hampers these states in their efforts to compete for high-tech industries. Even the Universities of Texas and Wyoming, which built dramatically when oil revenues flowed in, experienced much harder times when these revenues dried up in the 1980s. Still other problems afflicted the slower-growing states of the interior West: a hesitation to invest heavily in educating young people who seemed likely to migrate elsewhere; a reluctance in Idaho, New Mexico, and Oklahoma to hire outsiders who seemed less likely to adhere to local precedents; even a doubt in some mountain and plains states about accepting the federal funding that became so abundant in the 1960s, for fear of the bureaucratic red tape that accompanied it.

Generally speaking, the most perplexing puzzles in western education involved the region's growing racial and ethnic minorities. Some westerners attempted to achieve genuine equity in education, whereas others showed little commitment to this idealistic goal. But whether one assessed the education of Indian, black, or Hispanic children, the results were usually the same: the educational experiences of these children were measurably inferior to those of whites. Sometimes these inequalities resulted from blatant racism; in other instances, right-minded and progressive planners were unable to organize schools and curricula that met the particular needs of minorities.

Schooling of Indian children in the modern West exemplifies these problems. Both the federal government and missionaries had established boarding schools by 1900, but most of these failed to provide significant numbers of Indian children with an effective combination of a solid academic training and a curriculum design balanced between Indian and white sociocultural contexts. In 1928, the landmark Meriam Report denounced schools for Indians as substandard and likely to remain so unless salaries for teachers and living conditions for students were sharply improved. When reformer John Collier became the new chief of the Bureau of Indian Affairs under the New Deal, he featured the improvement of schools as a keystone of his "new deal" for Indians. The results included more day schools and Indian teachers on the reservations and a greater emphasis on bilingual texts and adult education.

These changes improved things, but at midcentury only six thousand spaces existed for the thirty thousand or so school-aged Indian children in the Southwest. The government did step up funding for new schools and for the improvement of those in existence. Increasingly, however, the trend was toward enrolling Indian children in public schools, encouraging their "mainstreaming," or acculturation, into the dominant society. By the 1980s, larger numbers of Indian youth attended public schools and colleges than ever before, but dropout rates were depressingly high, a result primarily of cultural barriers. Tribal leaders and educationists worked ever more intensely to break those barriers, by improving schools and building community colleges on the reservations and by assisting Indians to complete their degrees in public institutions.

The same pattern of ongoing problems and limited successes characterized the educational picture for western blacks. Revealingly, the pathbreaking Supreme Court decision disallowing segregated schools, *Brown* v. *Board of Education of Topeka* (1954), and the first major confrontation that resulted from it, in Little Rock, Arkansas, in 1957, both arose not in the Deep South but on the western fringe of the South. Most western subregions that had maintained segregated schools bowed to integration within a few years after 1954, although East Texas and other intransigent areas held out longer. Before court-ordered integration, these segregated schools were nearly always inferior to those for whites. Indeed, segregationist states commonly provided only 75 percent as much financial support for black students as they did for whites. Of course, integration alone did not end the problems. As the Los Angeles–Watts riot of 1965 and the numerous battles over forced busing and racial balancing revealed, westerners, like other white Americans, fought school reform measures when they thought that their children would be disadvantaged or threatened. Thus, although segregated schools passed into history, contention and difficulties continued, with black children concentrated in sub-par, central-city schools and the children of affluent whites either in private schools or in sheltered suburban schools.

Possibly even greater challenges confronted those who worked to achieve educational equity for the children of Spanish-speaking homes, especially in the Sunbelt Southwest. Added to issues of race and class, in this case, was the problem of structuring curricula in a second language. During the 1960s and 1970s, southwestern schools made great strides in working bilingual strategies into the curriculum; and in the case of *Lau* v. *Nichols* (1974), the Supreme Court mandated that schools provide special assistance to non-English-speaking students. But in the 1980s, as an accompaniment of the new conservatism, bilingualism rapidly lost favor. Only in major Hispanic population centers like Los Angeles, Tucson, Albuquerque, El Paso, and San Antonio did dual-language instruction seem safely entrenched.

Clearly, as long as schooling remains inextricably tied to shifting sociocultural realities and sentiments, then educators, students, parents, and all citizens of the West will continue to face the dilemma of providing quality education for everyone in a context of cultural diversity.

During the years following the yeasty 1960s, westerners shared fully in the American debate about schools. Even while priding themselves on their presumably high rates of literacy and their well-funded and elaborate school systems, Americans fretted about growing signs of trouble: a rising tide of functional illiteracy and mathematical incompetence, charges that American schools were too soft and undemanding compared to those abroad, clear indications that low salaries were undermining the teaching profession. With the economic downturn of the 1980s, westerners came more and more to realize that education was the key to their social, cultural, and economic future—just as, in truth, it always had been.

IN SEARCH OF A REGIONAL CULTURE

The American West did not spawn a separate, unified regional culture during the twentieth century, but it did experience sporadic flowerings of regionalism, particularly during the years before 1940. Moreover, especially since the 1960s, subregions of the West have produced variations of regional culture that differ from both national and regional trends. Of the several barriers to a truly uniform regional culture, three seem especially noteworthy: the varieties of terrain and cultural landscape within the region, the rapidity of demographic change, and the stereotyping of the region as a "Wild West."

From the flat wheat fields of North Dakota to the burgeoning cities and gigantic farms of California, from the sprawling ranches and mushrooming cities of Texas to the green and brown expanses of the Pacific Northwest, the West encompasses a remarkable variety of physical and cultural landscapes. For instance, the wet and fertile areas bounding the eastern and western rims of the West contrast sharply with the high and dry terrains of its interior heartland. Paradoxically, California, the most populous state in the West and in the nation, is also the richest agriculturally. Most states of the region, in fact, are geographically and culturally divided into contrasting halves. This is true of the entire tier along the 98th meridian, for instance the oft-noted "East River–West River" division along the Missouri River in South Dakota. Both Oregon and Washington are humid and liberal on the west side, dry and conservative on the east. The Tehachapi Mountains divide northern from southern California, a division that finds political and cultural expression in a liberal north and a more conservative south.

The rhythms of agricultural life that shape the society and culture of the Great Plains tier of states are far less central to New Mexico, Arizona, and Nevada. Nor is the dominating urbanization of California and the Sunbelt characteristic of the sparsely populated interior West, except for the Rocky Mountain "front" areas flanking Denver and Salt Lake City. Generally speaking, the most notable cultural achievements have occurred in the cities; but also noteworthy are the literary and artistic colonies of Taos–Santa Fe, New Mexico, Carmel, California, and Paradise Valley in Montana. In cultural oases such as these, spectacular surrounding landscapes truly symbolize the environmental barriers to a unified western culture.

At the same time, recurring floods of newcomers pouring into the West in this century redirected, again and again, sociocultural patterns that themselves had been in place less than a generation or two. As noted in chapter four, these successive tides of immigration, especially during the past half-century, bent and frayed western institutions and mores that had never had time to become deeply rooted. Indeed, no other American region in this century has experienced such a continual buffeting of demographic change as has the West. Equally upsetting, these sweeping movements of humanity came in the context of a world-wrenching depression, two world wars, and two subsequent wars in East Asia, and with a procession of federal expenditures that periodically engulfed cities like Seattle, San Diego, Phoenix, Albuquerque, and Denver with new armies of primarily or secondarily paid government employees. This too disrupted the evolution of a true western culture. As Patricia Nelson Limerick writes, "It is a disturbing element of continuity in Western history that we have not ceased to be strangers."

And then there is the delimiting and mischievous problem of the Wild West syndrome. The stereotype of the region as an open, untamed, and masculine frontier, already formed in the Buffalo Bill touring shows and in the art and fiction of nearly a century ago, waxed unabated in the popular culture of the new century. To mass consumers of pulp fiction and cinema and television in this country and abroad, the monolithic image of the West as a static and wild frontier—not as a vital part of a changing nation and world—seemed as constant as the land itself. The mythmaking frontiering of Louis L'Amour, John Ford, and John Wayne still, unfortunately, does more to shape thinking about the West than do the notable achievements of a Willa Cather or a Wallace Stegner. Symbolic of this situation is the fact that within an hour's drive of Hollywood's film sets lies the greatest aggregation in the West of the forces shaping the modern region.

But despite all this culturally disruptive diversity and change, centripetal forces of unity and cohesion are at work. Especially in the first half of this century, most westerners, in one fashion or another, sensed and disliked their cultural subservience to the East. So, in a true sense, western regionalists like Walter Prescott Webb, Bernard DeVoto, Vardis Fisher, and John Steuart Curry did speak for their contemporaries. The regional experiences that they rendered were demonstrably "western." Sometimes reacting negatively to economic colonialism, sometimes powered positively by regional assertiveness, sometimes even buoyed by federal support of the region and themselves, these culture makers carried the West in the 1930s and 1940s, to the highest crest of regional identity that it has ever known.

Eddies of this high tide of western regionalism swirled

past the World War II years. Interest in western historical subjects remained high, an interest demonstrated by the historical novels of A. B. Guthrie, Jr., Frederick Manfred, and Frank Waters and by the paintings of Peter Hurd and Alexandre Hogue, among others. But the social and cultural changes that began in the early 1940s brought more transitions than continuities, powering the West into a postregional era characterized by new relationships with the nation at large and by novel intraregional diversities.

In admittedly brief perspective, the post–World War II West seems to have become culturally both core and periphery. Just as Americans pledge their allegiance to state and nation under the federal system, so do modern westerners find themselves following contrary tracks of cultural influence. During the postfrontier era of the early twentieth century, the West stood undeniably on the periphery of an eastern-based core culture; but during the 1940s and 1950s, the tides of cultural influence became more complex. Today, strong cultural currents, for instance in publishing and classical music, continue to flow primarily westward out of Atlantic centers like Boston and New York. But others, such as one or two other major publishers and the electronic media, flow eastward from California, emanating from the West. For example, recent literary developments in California and Texas have fathered western and national trends, and the Far West has also pioneered in pacesetting religions and in educational developments for the nation.

Indeed, California and the southwestern Sunbelt have become as culturally alive as any area of the United States since the 1960s, even though other, more secluded stretches of the West clearly remain under the lion's paw of outside cultural influences. Thus, residents of the less populous West could now complain about the nuisance of other westerners, in addition to that of the easterners of old. Oregonians, Coloradans, and Utahns grumbled about "Californication," the inundation of Californians and their suburban ways. Arizonans groused that living next to California along the Colorado River was like trying to sleep next to a restless elephant.

When Oklahomans joked about "Baja Oklahoma" south of the Red River and when New Mexicans threatened to fence out the imperious Texans from the area that the latter called "Lapland"—that is, where Texas laps into New Mexico—their humor betrayed a certain resentment. Put another way, cultural currents rising in the region now flowed as strongly as those coursing in from the outside.

Although these shifting allegiances and influences raised obstacles to the West's forming a unified regional culture, were there not at least some cultural characteristics that still appeared particularly western? Many westerners, as well as tourists and outside observers, seemed to think so. They cited the region's size, space, openness, and newness as qualities essentially different from those of other U.S. regions. The rolling grain fields of the plains, the Big Sky country of the Rockies, and the arid expanses of the Great Basin and the Columbia Plateau repeatedly awed travelers, as did the remarkable distances between cities and the sense of pristine newness that seemed to characterize everything except the older Indian and Hispanic cultures. And as numerous polls showed, westerners traveled more than other Americans and thought nothing of taking weekend car trips that would have struck Bostonians and New Yorkers as the experience of a lifetime.

Taken together, although such characteristics have not produced a unified or unique culture, they have given the West a special aura and flavor. Equally clear is that the very expansiveness and openness of the region, and the mobility and adaptability of its people, promise more change than continuity for the future. The regional chauvinist hoping to champion a more unique western culture faces a difficulty akin to the man attempting to trap the reflection of the moon: just as he thinks he has finally trapped his quarry, it moves off again beyond his grasp.

Chapter Six

The Modern Western Economy

In terms that economists sometimes use, the hectic years of the New Deal and World War II might be described as the period of "takeoff" in the evolution of the western regional economy. The sudden infusion of federal spending during these years did not end in 1945 but instead continued in other forms, leading to the gradual demise throughout most of the region of the West's old "colonial" subservience to the East and its rise to a position of national economic equality. The West's older extractive industries, based on the harvesting of its natural resources, crested during the prosperous 1950s and 1960s; then, generally speaking, they began to decline, some of them seemingly never to rise again. Meanwhile, new electronic, aerospace, "high-technology," and "service" industries—attracted and nurtured by federal expenditures—sprang up in profusion, particularly in the Sunbelt of the Southwest and California. Thus contrary trends, of extractive industries in climax and decline and high-tech and service industries on the rise, sharply define the development of the modern western economy.

UNCLE SAM'S WEST

With the end of the war in 1945, many feared and predicted that the nation would abruptly fall back into an economic depression. To the contrary, the postwar years witnessed instead the greatest sustained prosperity that any nation has ever seen, and the West shared fully in that prosperity. During the fifteen years after war's end, the population of the entire region beyond the Mississippi grew from thirty-two million to forty-five million people. All subregions of the West shared in this growth, but very unevenly. None could match the incredible boom in Arizona and southern California, as mobile Americans headed for the hot, dry climates now made livable by air conditioning. Arizona's population grew by a remarkable 163 percent during these fifteen years, and California surged from a populace of nine million to one of nineteen million. By 1962, California had surpassed New York to become the most populous American state; and architect Frank Lloyd Wright quipped that all of the country seemed tilted westward, so that everything not nailed down was sliding toward California.

Beyond dispute, the federal government played a major part in the West's takeoff and in its escape from its colonial past. The U.S. government was rapidly emerging by this time not only as the region's chief landlord but also as its chief financier. In the eight states of the sparsely populated Great Basin and Rocky Mountains, Uncle Sam now owned more than half the land, from a low of 30 percent in Montana to a high of 86 percent in Nevada. By 1958, in the eleven states of the Far West, federal expenditures exceeded tax revenues in all but three. To a large extent, the federal government both subsidized the West's developing economy and, through custodial agencies like the Bureau of Land Management (newly created in 1946) and the U.S. Forest Service, managed its resources. Such reliance, as we shall see, bred more antagonism than affection. But when confronted with criticisms of such federal subsidies, western spokesmen often replied that since the centers of national

Area of States and Federally Owned Lands

State	Total (1,000 acres)	Owned by Federal Government[1] Acres (1,000s)	Percent
Nevada	70,264	59,996	85.4
Idaho	52,933	33,747	63.8
Utah	52,697	32,334	61.4
Wyoming	62,343	31,387	50.3
Oregon	61,599	30,110	48.9
California	100,207	48,009	47.9
Arizona	72,688	32,107	44.2
Colorado	66,486	24,165	36.3
New Mexico	77,766	26,474	34.0
Washington	42,694	13,123	30.7
Montana	93,271	27,617	29.6
South Dakota	48,882	3,169	6.5
North Dakota	44,452	2,365	5.3
Oklahoma	44,088	1,656	3.8
Texas	168,218	3,825	2.3
Nebraska	49,032	717	1.5
Kansas	52,511	725	1.4

1. Excludes trust properties.

Source: U.S. Bureau of the Census, *Statistical Abstract of the United States* (Washington, D.C.: Government Printing Office, 1984).

wealth still remained primarily in the East, the expenditures were appropriate. A new regionalism was evolving.

Federal funding and influence poured into the region through a myriad of channels, varying in form from Social Security pensions to airport subsidies. Among the greatest of these fiscal conduits were defense expenditures, fueled by the mounting tensions of the Cold War. In the early 1960s, the *Los Angeles Times* reckoned that fully one-third of the employees in the area depended directly or indirectly on the defense industry for employment. By that date, the West Coast was garnering nearly half of all Defense Department research and development contracts. Military installations, many of them evolving from World War II bases, grew up in every state, from Grand Forks Air Force Base in North Dakota to the giant Strategic Air Command headquarters at Offutt Air Force Base near Omaha to the army's Fort Sill, Oklahoma, and Fort Bliss at El Paso to the marines' Camp Pendleton, California. In addition to its U.S. Navy facilities, San Diego claimed in 1959 that 78 percent of its manufacturing employment related to defense industries. And San Antonio, with its four air force bases and the army's sprawling Fort Sam Houston, epitomized the metropolis built on the military— "the army's mother-in-law," as some wags called it.

Uncle Sam became a major presence in every western state, but in some his role was overwhelming. In Washington, that presence manifested itself not only in military bases like Fort Lewis and the Bremerton Naval Yards but also in the nuclear complex at Hanford, one of the world's largest concentrations of reactors, and in the cheap, federally subsidized electricity marketed through the Bonneville Power Administration, which attracted and held a major national share of the energy-intensive aluminum industry. Federal contracts to Boeing Aircraft in Seattle transformed the Washington economy, generating seventy-three thousand jobs in 1958, at the peak of the company's construction of the still used B-52 bombers. Washington passed through cycles of boom and bust as defense and commercial contracts came and went, for example in the early 1980s, when the state had the third-highest unemployment rates in the country; but aerospace now meant more to Washingtonians than did even their traditional lumber business.

The aerospace industry counted heavily elsewhere too, for example with Lockheed, Douglas, and others in Los Angeles, Hughes Aircraft and Learjet in Tucson, and North American, General Dynamics, and LTV in Dallas–Fort Worth. Wichita, where Boeing also moved in force, became the nation's leader in manufacturing private and commuter planes, housing plants of the Learjet, Beach, Cessna, and Gates companies. Houston's acquisition of the munificent Johnson Space Center allowed it to boast that its name was the first word spoken by man from the moon.

Three other western states also offer graphic examples of the rising federal presence in the region. Utah ranked among the top states by the 1960s in the percentage of its work force directly employed by Uncle Sam, nearly 11 percent. With fourteen thousand civilian workers, Hill Air Force Base near Ogden stood as the largest employer in the state; and other federal operations bases, like the big Internal Revenue Service Center at Ogden, also loomed large. Big defense contractors like Morton Thiokol, which doubled Brigham City's six thousand populace after 1956, brought in federal dollars secondarily through purchases rather than direct employment.

To humorist Tom Lehrer, New Mexico in the 1950s seemed the province of the Atomic Energy Commission:

> Down the trail you'll find me lopin'
> Where the spaces are wide open,
> In the land of the old AEC.
> Where the scenery's attractive
> And the air is radioactive,
> Oh, the Wild West is where I wanna be!

Alamogordo grew by 220 percent during that decade, due primarily to missile research at Holloman Air Force Base; and Roswell surged to a population of nearly forty thousand, becoming the state's third-largest city, due in large part to Walker Air Force Base. Booming Albuquerque got federal fiscal transfusions not only from Kirtland Air Force Base, the nation's primary center of nuclear air weaponry, but also from Sandia Laboratories, the AEC's main military-industrial design complex. With seven thousand employees, Sandia ranked as the state's largest employer by 1960. The AEC also bankrolled the isolated "federal company town" of Los Alamos, its prime nuclear research site, which with a populace of thirteen thousand at the peak of the Cold War constituted one of America's most imposing and peculiar gatherings of expert scientists. In the 1980s, New Mexico garnered a sizable share of Strategic Defense Initiative ("Star Wars") funding and could boast more Ph.D.'s per capita than any other state.

Centrally located and naturally enticing, Colorado likewise attracted more than its share of defense expenditures. Colorado Springs got the $200 million Air Force Academy, completed in 1958; the army's Fort Kit Carson; and in 1966, the awesome, $150 million Combat Operations Center of the North American Air Defense Command, the "bomb-proof" electronic hub of nuclear air defense imbedded in Cheyenne Mountain. Boulder acquired the primary installations of the National Center for Atmospheric Research and of the National Bureau of Standards. Much of the fuel firing Denver's big postwar takeoff was federal, such as the Denver Mint, the U.S. Customs House, the Fitzsimmons Hospital, the AEC's Rocky Flats plutonium site, the Denver Arms Plants that evolved into the massive Denver Federal Center, and big contracts to defense newcomer Martin Marietta. After the Soviet Union detonated its first atomic bomb in 1949, frightened federal policy makers considered making Denver, safely insulated in interior America, an alternate capital to Washington, D.C. With more than thirty-three thousand federal employees by 1980, more than any other city except Washington, D.C., Denver ranked as the West's greatest federal nerve center.

Every western state exhibited some variation of these themes. The plains states had more to do with agriculturally

Department of Defense Contract Awards and Estimated Annual Payrolls

State	Contract awards [1] ($ million)		Estimated annual payroll [2] ($ million)	
	1963	1983	1963	1983
Total U.S.	28,108	118,744	12,809	50,458
Arizona	286	1,360	130	652
California	5,836	26,387	1,746	8,269
Colorado	444	1,007	243	947
Idaho	9	49	30	125
Kansas	332	1,575	180	568
Montana	79	117	54	93
Nebraska	33	163	114	356
Nevada	13	159	52	242
New Mexico	62	463	163	547
North Dakota	65	137	57	225
Oklahoma	111	612	308	1,076
Oregon	42	181	46	97
South Dakota	81	42	41	131
Texas	1,203	8,229	1,112	3,619
Utah	428	722	142	605
Washington	1,041	3,986	335	1,573
Wyoming	125	39	24	83

1. Military awards for supplies, services, and construction.

2. Covers active-duty military and direct-hire civilian personnel, including Army Corps of Engineers.

Source: U. S. Bureau of the Census, *Statistical Abstract of the United States* (Washington, D.C.: Government Printing Office, 1966, 1984).

oriented agencies like the Soil Conservation Service and the Commodity Credit Corporation, the Great Basin–Rocky Mountain states more with land stewardship agencies like the Bureau of Land Management and the U.S. Forest Service. More than other American regions, the West, especially its federally owned midsection, chafed at the burgeoning numbers of new federal regulatory agencies, which grew from a total of ten in 1940 to more than fifty by 1980. Some of these newer agencies, like the postwar Atomic Energy Commission (1946), the Environmental Protection Agency (1970), and the cabinet-level Department of Energy (1977), wielded greater authority over the West than over other regions. As a result, the West grew proportionately more restive with their rules and regulations.

Arguably, the federal government had its greatest impact on the postwar West through its sponsorship of reclamation. Two powerful federal agencies, each with its coteries of regional business, agricultural, and state and municipal affiliates, poured billions into "harnessing" the precious waterways of the arid West, damming, diverting, and sometimes depleting them to draw hydroelectricity and water, to slake the thirst of mushrooming cities and parched croplands. The Army Corps of Engineers focused its efforts primarily on flood control and the development of navigable waterways, which usually drew its activities to the lower and larger reaches of the major rivers; but its aggressive rivalry with the Bureau of Reclamation also led it, with the passing years, far from its initial fields of endeavor. On a larger scale, the Bureau of Reclamation in the Department of Interior moved increasingly toward large "multiple use" projects that would deliver subsidized water as well as cheap electricity to farms and cities. Through its hegemony over the West's key resource, water, the Bureau of Reclamation emerged after the war as the primary engine of federal priming of the regional economy, and thus also as the lodestone of regional-federal politics. Bureau directors like Michael Straus and Floyd Dominy became vital power brokers in western politics through their alliances with regional congressmen and senators.

Every major river of the West came, to a greater or lesser extent, under the control of the dam builders and water pumpers. Along the central continental divide, the Colorado–Big Thompson Project diverted precious Colorado River water under the mountains to the South Platte; the Frying Pan–Arkansas Project made a similar west-east penetration of the divide; and so did the San Juan–Chama Project, diverting Colorado waters to the Rio Grande. In New Mexico, the Elephant Butte Dam on the Rio Grande formed the state's most important body of water. On the Red River boundary between Oklahoma and Texas, Lake Texoma ranked second in size only to Lake Mead among southwestern water masses. Under the tutelage of Oklahoma's strongman-senator Robert Kerr, Congress poured $1.2 billion into the Arkansas River Navigation and Flood Control Project, forming a 446-mile navigable channel all the way from the river's confluence with the Mississippi to the "seaport" of Tulsa. This venture, costing more than the St. Lawrence Seaway and the Panama Canal combined, struck many as a quintessential pork barrel.

All across the western expanses of the southern and central plains, postwar reclamation transformed the agricultural economy, bringing a new diversification of crops and a new stability. The North and South Platte area of Wyoming-Colorado-Nebraska became one of the heaviest irrigated locales in the country. Not all irrigation drew from stream diversion; much also derived from the pumping of groundwater. Reaching from South Dakota to the South Texas plains, the Ogallala Aquifer is the world's greatest underground reserve of freshwater. With the development of mobile, center-pivot sprinkler systems, the wealth of its waters turned the plains into what Donald Green has called "the land of the underground rain." Here as elsewhere, however, the pumping of groundwater raised serious concerns. By 1980, the Ogallala water table was falling several feet a year in some locales, which threatened its exhaustion by the year 2020 and the devolution of much of the southern plains into saline deserts.

During and immediately after the war, much discussion centered on the idea of extending the model of the New Deal's Tennessee Valley Authority—with its network of federally built and operated dams and its concept of holistic river basin development—to other major river basins across the land. Two prime contenders for such strategy were the West's two greatest rivers, the Columbia and the Missouri. In the end, neither basin came under a TVA-style system; but compromise approaches led to the damming of each of them anyway. On the mighty Columbia, the Army Engineers continued to develop the lower river, with new dams like The Dalles and John Day. The Bonneville Power Administration, which lacked the far-reaching authority of the TVA, marketed cheap, federally supported hydroelectric power to private and public customers in the region. And the Bureau of Reclamation carried forward its damming program upstream. Eventually, thirty big dams held back the waters of the Columbia system: older ones like Bonneville and Grand Coulee on the main river and newer ones like Libby on the Kootenai, Lower Granite and Little Goose on the lower Snake, and the ill-fated Teton Dam on the upper Snake, whose earthen walls crumbled in 1976, flooding a broad stretch of southeastern Idaho.

A proposed Missouri Valley Authority stirred up considerable controversy across the north-central plains region during the war. In the end it failed, in large part because the rival federal agencies, threatened by such a powerful newcomer, came up with a compromise solution to forestall it. In the so-called Pick-Sloan Plan, the Army Engineers agreed to confine their efforts downstream, the Bureau of Reclamation upstream. One cynical observer came near the mark in terming it "a shameless, loveless shotgun wedding." But the dam building still proceeded, with Canyon Ferry joining the older Fort Peck Dam on the mainstream of the upper Missouri, Yellowtail Dam on the Bighorn fork of the Yellowstone, and two massive new projects on the central Missouri, the Garrison Diversion in North Dakota and the Oahe in South Dakota. Both of these latter developments remain uncompleted, surrounded by controversy about their environmental, monetary, and human costs—the Garrison Project decimated the Fort Berthold Indian Reservation, and tribal chairman George Gillette openly sobbed as he deeded away his people's lands—and about the wisdom of flooding river bottomlands only to divert water and reclaim lands elsewhere. So the mighty Missouri no longer runs free. Yet, ironically, its great Yellowstone tributary is now the West's only major river whose mainstream remains undammed.

Nowhere did reclamation count so heavily as on the lower Colorado River, which crosses the parched and picturesque canyonlands of the Southwest. The completion of Hoover Dam proved to be only a first step in harnessing the Colorado, and the big postwar booms in California and Arizona greatly whetted appetites for its diverted waters for farm and city. A long scramble resulted, as upstream states contended with those below for their entitlements even at the cost of lobbying in ludicrously inefficient projects, as Arizona quarreled with imperial California, and as Mexico reacted angrily to being left with only a trickle of brackish water emptying into the Gulf of California. Finally, after a long succession of congressional acts and elaborate court suits, well depicted by historian Norris Hundley, came a decisive Supreme Court decision in 1963 and the monumental Colorado River Basin Project Act of 1968, an omnibus of many plans and projects and the most expensive congressional commitment in history, all of which brought rewards to Arizona and an epochal "dividing of the waters" and development strategy.

Meanwhile, even as the squabbling continued, so did the damming of the upper river. The developers, politicians, and bureaucrats met opposition from a rising environmentalist movement (see below, pp. 284–86) when they attempted to flood Dinosaur National Monument at Echo

Park on the Green River and even the Grand Canyon itself. But they did get mighty Glen Canyon Dam, whose huge Lake Powell rivaled Lake Mead in its storage of a two-year river flow, and a number of others including Navajo and Flaming Gorge dams. Powerful congressmen like Colorado's Wayne Aspinall, working with the Bureau of Reclamation, were able to secure ample federal funding for massive irrigation projects, even in high and dry environments where their cost-effectiveness was minimal.

So the upstream states got their share of the beleaguered Colorado's bounty, and so did metropolitan southern California and the agribusinessmen of the Imperial and Coachella valleys and especially those of the sprawling Central Valley, the most elaborately irrigated area on earth. Utah mapped strategy for its Central Utah Project, the price of which quadrupled over first estimates; and Arizona got its colossal Central Arizona Project. As it began sluicing water eastward through its three-hundred-mile cement waterway toward Phoenix and Tucson in 1985, the CAP's cost had far surpassed $2 billion; and its mighty subsidization of scarce desert water allowed Arizona consumers, overwhelmingly urban, not rural, the nice luxury of the eighth-highest per capita rates of water use in the country.

By most material standards, the Bureau of Reclamation, the Army Engineers, and other public and private sponsors of irrigation could claim incredible victories in the triumph of technology and planning over the deserts. By 1982, irrigated lands in the United States totaled 49 million acres; 41.3 million of those acres lay in the seventeen western states, with California leading all states. The bureau itself could, by 1980, boast of over nine million acres under irrigation on nearly 150,000 farms and could well present itself as the most vital sponsor of western growth.

But there was a darker side to this rise of what the historian Donald Worster aptly calls the western "hydraulic society." As Marc Reisner comments: "The point is that despite heroic efforts and many billions of dollars, all we have managed to do in the arid West is turn a Missouri-size section

Irrigated Farm Acreage

	1950	1964	1982
Total U.S.	25,787,455	37,056,083	49,002,433
Arizona	963,560	1,125,376	1,097,825
California	6,438,324	7,598,698	8,460,508
Colorado	2,872,348	2,690,018	3,200,942
Idaho	2,137,237	2,801,500	3,450,443
Kansas	138,686	1,004,210	2,675,167
Montana	1,716,792	1,893,360	2,023,003
Nebraska	876,259	2,169,317	6,039,292
Nevada	727,498	824,511	829,761
New Mexico	655,287	812,723	807,206
North Dakota	35,294	50,548	162,643
Oklahoma	34,071	302,081	492,077
Oregon	1,306,810	1,607,659	1,807,882
South Dakota	78,069	130,050	376,447
Texas	3,131,534	6,384,963	5,575,553
Utah	1,137,995	1,092,270	1,082,328
Washington	589,035	1,149,842	1,638,470
Wyoming	1,431,767	1,571,192	1,564,576

Source: U.S. Bureau of the Census, *U.S. Census of Agriculture* (Washington, D.C.: Government Printing Office, 1952, 1964, 1982).

green—and that conversion has been wrought mainly with nonrenewable ground-water." In 1982 the Bureau of Reclamation finally dropped even the pretense of enforcing the unit size limit—160 acres—for receiving subsidized irrigation waters. In an age of growing crop surpluses, it seemed ever more incongruous to supply big agribusinesses with expensively diverted waters for which Uncle Sam bore 90 percent of the costs. And then there was the host of environmental problems: depleted rivers, falling water tables, accumulations of salt and selenium that threatened the future of lands and their wildlife, reckless assumptions about growth that even envisioned hauling waters hundreds or thousands of miles from the basins of the Klamath, Columbia, or Yukon to that of the Colorado or directly to southern California. No one could say, yet, whether Americans had conquered the desert or whether the desert would return to conquer them.

THE MODERN TRANSPORTATION NEXUS

As the years accumulated after 1945, the trends in western transportation that had first appeared during the 1920s became ever more pronounced: declining railroads and public transportation, accompanied by frenetic expansion in the use of motor vehicles, highways, and aviation. Out West, where the ratios between people and square miles tilted strongly toward the latter, these trends bore an even greater significance than they did for the nation as a whole.

Following the boom times of World War II, American railroads fell on hard times, unable to compete with everyman's obsession with bigger and better cars, cars that were propelled by cheap gasoline and traveled on publicly built and maintained roads. Rail passenger traffic fell by one-half between 1949 and 1967; and even passenger-friendly roads like the Santa Fe cut back their services until, eventually, only selected routes had any passenger service at all, via federally sponsored Amtrak.

Meanwhile, the railroads concentrated on their most advantageous business, hauling bulk freight, via ever larger diesel freight engines. But with highly paid union workers and the rising competition of big trucks and of barges, which traveled on federally constructed channels and which, like trucks, were for the most part unregulated, the heavily regulated railroads lost more and more of their freight business too. However, through forfeiting the unprofitable passenger business, the railroads have subsequently won back much of the bulk traffic, which now constitutes 90 percent of their trade. More than three times more fuel-efficient than trucks, diesel trains have increasingly specialized in hauling truck trailers "piggyback" over long distances, in carrying new cars and trucks to market in giant racks, and in packing all sorts of heavy products and bulky raw materials across the land, often in machine-moveable containers. Long "unit trains" carry western coal to midwestern and Pacific Coast electrification plants.

Still, total trackage continued to decline as the roads closed unprofitable rural spur lines and as the number of independent railroads steadily shrank in number. By the mid-1980s, only seven major railroads were left, carrying between them 85 percent of the total tonnage hauled by significant lines. Of these six, four served the West: Burlington Northern (the merged Burlington, Northern Pacific, and Great Northern), Pac Rail (the merged Union Pacific and Missouri Pacific), and the Santa Fe and Southern Pacific systems. The "deregulation" of railroads seemed sure to bring even more mergers, probably between the remaining eastern and western systems, into three or four regional monopolies. Thus, all across the rural West, the weed-grown humps of abandoned railroad beds, standing beside modern paved highways, symbolized the lost dream of public transportation and the lost investment in nineteenth-century subsidies to western railroads. This was a waste that, it seemed likely, the nation would some day regret.

As rails declined, highways proliferated. Fueled by cheap, imported oil and bankrolled by the great postwar prosperity, America's love affair with the automobile now entered its

Railroad Mileage

	1946	1965	1985
Total U.S.	237,699	224,863	159,360
Arizona	2,165	2,070	1,757
California	7,583	8,113	6,438
Colorado	4,928	4,115	3,388
Idaho	3,114	3,074	2,180
Kansas	8,701	8,254	7,509
Montana	5,185	5,079	3,326
Nebraska	5,898	5,630	4,597
Nevada	1,822	1,635	1,451
New Mexico	2,584	2,286	2,062
North Dakota	5,269	5,264	4,579
Oklahoma	6,052	5,736	3,289
Oregon	3,600	3,466	2,889
South Dakota	3,995	3,907	1,953
Texas	16,386	15,354	12,853
Utah	1,924	1,811	1,493
Washington	6,013	5,911	3,927
Wyoming	1,983	1,947	1,993

Source: Association of American Railroads, *Railroad Mileage by States* (Washington, D.C.: Assoc. of American Railroads, 1948, 1966, 1986).

climactic phase. Cars and trucks grew larger, more opulent, and with big V-8 engines, faster and more powerful; more important, their ownership became more widespread than ever. In many respects, the wide-open West with its mobile populace seemed to pace the nation in advancing the automobile culture, as it had earlier in the 1920s. By 1960, as cars approached their zenith in size, gaudiness, and fuel inefficiency, Los Angeles County counted more cars than did all but seven states of the Union, and it was estimated that half of the core city's surface area was devoted to their passage, parking, and maintenance.

Bigger and more numerous motor vehicles required bigger and better highways. The new highways resembled their predecessors of the 1920s and 1930s about as much as those early paved roads had resembled frontier trails. Using massive earth-moving equipment, the new road builders frequently abandoned the narrow confines of traditional, water-level routes and moved huge amounts of fill to create broader and steeper grades. California led the other states with its Collier-Burns Act of 1947, which projected a $2.4 billion, fourteen-thousand-mile system of modern highways, featuring three hundred miles of urban freeways. These frenetic California freeways became the marvel and the consternation of the country, and they continued to grow at a geometric rate.

In 1956, the federal government made its greatest of all commitments to the automobile mode of travel with the enactment of the Federal-Aid (or Interstate) Highway Act. This monumental program envisioned a forty-one-thousand-mile network of limited-access multilane interstate highways linking all the major cities in the land and freeways belting and crossing the large urban areas. The interstate highways program was funded through a Highway Trust Fund, derived from federal taxes on users, with the "feds" paying 90 percent and the individual states the rest. The program several-times-over exceeded its original cost estimate of $27 billion, requiring large transfusions of federal tax dollars; and in the big and underpopulated states of the interior

West, the federal government has paid up to 95 percent of the bill. These colossal spans of concrete and asphalt, both interstate and other improved highways, became one of the wonders of the postwar world: foreign visitors frequently listed the two greatest marvels of America as being its super-highways and the cornucopias of its supermarkets. And the highway system continues to evolve. A melancholy moment came in 1984 when the last few miles of America's most cele-brated old highway—Route 66, Steinbeck's "mother road" joining Chicago to Los Angeles—was bypassed by the inter-state near Williams, Arizona.

As had happened before the war, the commercial airplane expanded in usage alongside the automobile. By the late 1950s, commercial jet liners, most of them manufactured in the West, began to displace the older propeller craft. Air travel and air freight became more and more a common prac-tice; and with federal subsidies, large, new airports became key landmarks in all cities. The West has some of the largest: Los Angeles International, Denver's crossroads Stapleton International, and the world's physically biggest, Dallas–Fort Worth International. The region has been served by a number of the biggest air carriers, including major national ones like United and American and large regional ones that became national and international like Northwest Orient and Texas International. As was the case with the railroads, the vaunted, post-1978 federal "deregulation" of airlines, along with market forces, is leading to a steady attrition of familiar regional airlines. Dallas-based Braniff went bankrupt in 1982 (although it was later revived); Denver-based Fron-tier followed in 1986. Others are being absorbed by larger lines, such as Western Airlines, which passed into the maw of Delta in 1987.

The new mobility, especially that of the automobile, brought countless social, economic, and cultural changes to nation and region. Core downtown areas gradually eroded as car-based shopping malls drew away their customers. Com-mercial "strips," featuring obtrusive signs and car-based busi-nesses like drive-in restaurants and service stations, developed along the approaches to cities of all sizes. Billboards cluttered the handsome vistas of western highways. As the old city-center hotels dwindled and closed, new motels with center courts and swimming pools replaced the old "motor courts" of prewar times along the strips peripheral to cities. The motels often played up Old West connotations with ranch-style decor and names like "Trail's End" or "Thunderbird."

The cresting automobile age transformed western tourism and made it into a major pillar of the regional economy. Before the 1950s, tourists in autos still seemed pioneers, crossing the mountains and plains with considerable discomfort and inconvenience. Later, traveling swiftly in comfortable cars, they seemed ubiquitous. By 1950, nearly two-thirds of all Americans took vacations, and four-fifths of them went by car. They came to the West's expansive beaches, its publicly maintained mountains and forests, and its growing numbers of national parks and monuments. By the 1970s, the National Park Service maintained more than 30 million acres in over 280 different units—many of them new western locales designated after the war, such as Arizona's Petrified Forest, South Dakota's Badlands, Washington's North Cascades, and Utah's Canyonlands, Capitol Reef, and Arches national parks.

They also came to see the new Sunbelt cities and to enjoy the many specialized tourist centers funded by private capital, such as Walt Disney's multi-million-dollar "Disneyland," which opened in Orange County, California, in the mid-1950s, or such popular ski resorts as Colorado's pathbreaking Aspen and Vail, Utah's Alta, Snowbird, and Sundance, and Idaho's Sun Valley. In some western states, tourism came to rank third or even second in income production, behind agriculture and various extractive industries, generating considerable cash flows although not many high-paying jobs. By 1949, it ranked number two in southern California, surpassed only by aircraft production, bringing in three million tourists and $457 million in income annually.

The importance of tourism varied considerably by state

and region, from less in the plains states to greater in the Rockies and on the West Coast. In one state, Nevada, tourism became the mainstay of a peculiar economy. Nevada re-instituted legalized gambling in 1931, and six years later the Reno-based gaming business began its great takeoff when Harold Smith and his father launched "Harold's Club," with a mighty ad campaign and an atmosphere of clean, open family fun. Other major operators, like William Harrah, also flourished at Reno and Lake Tahoe; but then, after the war, Las Vegas, situated adjacent to southern California, began its rapid ascent to become America's number-one gambling and nightclub mecca, "tinseltown."

The gangland murder of mobster Bugsy Siegel, who had organized Las Vegas's first great casino, the Flamingo, led the state to initiate a program of gambling regulation. But though these efforts kept the gamblers reasonably straight-forward, they did not prohibit organized crime from taking over much of the business. Nor could they blunt the criticisms that Nevada had twice the national average of suicides, the worst rates of alcoholism in the country, and an open and thriving community of prostitutes. Defenders of Nevada's unique statewide system of gambling point out that Las Vegas has been America's fastest-growing city of less than 500,000 population, with a populace rising from just 20,000 after the war to over 475,000 by 1980; that in percentage terms, Nevada was the nation's fastest-growing state; and that over half the state's jobs derived from gaming and related businesses. Along with federal expenditures, gambling lifted Nevada from a somnolent desert backland to a thriving fun capital. But the price paid was distressingly high.

EXTRACTIVE INDUSTRIES—CLIMAX AND DECLINE

Despite the considerable westward march of industry during World War II, the region entered the postwar era still heavily reliant on its traditional extractive industries, especially the key ones—agriculture, mining, lumber, and petroleum. These industries had fallen on hard times during the 1920s and 1930s, had been propped up by New Deal relief and recovery programs, and then had thrived on the boom markets of wartime. Now they entered their supreme period of development. Generally speaking, these resource industries surged forward with the postwar boom into the 1950s, enjoyed an uneven prosperity through the continuing growth cycles of the 1960s, then fell on hard times after 1970. In all cases, new technologies and booming domestic and foreign markets stepped up production during the quarter-century after the war. But dwindling resources, increasing foreign competition, and faltering markets caused the extractive industries of the West to decline beginning in 1969–71, the pivotal time when American dominance of the world economy began visibly to erode.

Western farmers and ranchers entered the new era on a wave of prosperity that carried well into the 1950s, but in truth they continued to face the same problems of postfrontier agriculture that had surfaced back in the 1920s: fewer and fewer producers yielding greater and greater surpluses of commodities. Their situation was not unique; western farmers simply found themselves caught up in national and global trends. Between 1935 and 1980, the total number of farms and ranches in the United States fell from 6,814,000 to 2,428,000, the farm population from 32,161,000 to 6,051,000, the farm populace as a percentage of the total population from 25.3 percent to less than 3 percent.

Behind these lifeless numbers worked a continuing revolution in agriculture. As farm-ranch units diminished in number, they grew ever larger in acreage and became more highly capitalized, mechanized, and reliant on high technology. These "factories in the field" bore little resemblance to yesterday's homesteads, with their expensive and ever more sophisticated machines: giant, four-wheel-drive tractors costing more than $100,000, self-propelled wheat combines with thirty-foot headers that self-leveled on hillsides, sixteen-row corn planters, four-row cotton pickers, even mechanical fruit and tomato pickers. Synthetic chemical fertiliz-

239

Fritz Fredrick in his wheat field in Grant County, North Dakota, July 1936, indicating how tall his wheat would have been with normal rainfall. Courtesy of the Library of Congress.

ers, like anhydrous ammonia and natural gas–based nitrates, vastly enriched crop yields; and so did environmentally dangerous chemical herbicides and pesticides. The use of chemical fertilizers increased sixfold in applications between the 1940s and 1980s, pesticides twelvefold. Such intensive applications of chemicals, new machine technologies, and new plant and animal varieties that had been developed through selective breeding and genetic engineering made the modern farm wondrously productive. But they also made it dangerously reliant on petrochemicals that alter the soil, degrade the environment, and encourage insect adaptations, and on fossil fuels and fertilizers that can sometimes soar in price and drive marginal farmers toward bankruptcy.

Even expanding markets at home and abroad could not absorb the bounties of these harvests; and so the nation again faced the problem of the prewar years, huge commodity surpluses and low prices. Uncle Sam continued to provide the same sorts of assistance to agriculture as were first used dur-

Fritz Fredrick in his wheat field in Grant County, North Dakota, July 1977. Courtesy of Bill Ganzel, *Dust Bowl Descent*.

ing the New Deal: payments to farmers who took lands out of production, as with the Eisenhower administration's unpopular Soil Bank program of 1956, and various kinds of price-support systems that involved federal loans to farmers using their stored crops as collateral. By the late 1950s, with surplus crops overflowing federal warehouses even as the farm population dwindled away, more and more Americans began to question such elaborate and expensive systems of federal subsidy.

The "farm problem" seemed suddenly to vanish in the early 1970s, when the Soviet Union, mass-purchasing American grains, stimulated a rapid rise in prices by removing the surpluses. "It's just a helluva great year," commented a South Dakota farmer in 1973. Farmers had forty-four million more acres in crop in 1975 than they had had three years earlier. Following the advice of their bankers, they bet on future prosperity, indebting themselves to purchase land and equipment. By the later 1970s, however, with contracting markets, the surpluses and depressed prices were back;

and, with inflation and high interest rates compounding the problem, another wave of farm failures swept the hinterlands. As in the 1890s and the 1920s and 1930s, another wrenching cycle of agricultural attrition characterized the 1980s. Clearly, the traditional "family farm," a major pillar of the western tradition, was passing from the scene, giving way to small "hobby farms" on one end and to large, vertically integrated corporate farms, or "agribusinesses," on the other. Incredibly, by the mid 1980s, America's two hundred thousand largest agricultural units yielded almost two-thirds of its farm-ranch production.

Across the mosaic of its subregions, the West exhibited patterns of both diversity and conformity in its evolving agricultural profile: diversity in the humidlands along its eastern and western peripheries and in the irrigated oases of the Southwest and a conformity toward cereal grains and beef cattle in the nonirrigated drylands of its interior. The region's two imperial states, California and Texas, best exhibited the rich diversities and broad margins of western agriculture.

California has been, since the 1930s, America's leading agricultural state. It contains, mainly in the broad Central and Imperial valleys, fully one-fourth of all the nation's irrigated lands; and its agricultural marketing centers, such as Fresno, Bakersfield, and Sacramento, are among the world's greatest. Probably no place on earth is such an agricultural cornucopia. Except for tobacco, California grows every temperate-subtropical crop—more than three hundred different commodities. It raises one-third of the nation's citrus fruits, second only to Florida; it is second only to Texas in cotton harvests; and in verdant valleys like the Napa, Sonoma, and Salinas it yields over 80 percent of American wines, a $4.5 billion industry by 1985. California's farms are true agribusinesses—highly specialized, heavily reliant on government-subsidized water, and organized as steeply capitalized corporations. Fifteen percent of them produce over 70 percent of the state's farm income.

Texas rivals California as a mighty agricultural producer,

with its farm economy more evenly divided between crops and livestock. Cotton is, and long has been, its chief crop; the state's 1984 yield of more than four million bales was one-third greater than that of its nearest competitor. Its gulf shorelands are America's prime rice-growing region, its lower Rio Grande Valley a major national source of citrus fruits and vegetables, and its poultry farms and sheep ranches among the nation's greatest. However, as in the past, cattle still dominate the Texas farm economy. With over fourteen million head in the mid-1980s, Texas runs over twice as many cattle as the next leading state, Nebraska. And increasingly, it does more than raise cattle. By tax adjustments, the use of new computerized technologies, and other strategies, it surpassed Iowa in 1971 in numbers of feedlots, concentrated especially in the Panhandle area, and thus increasingly rivaled the Midwest in cattle finishing.

The West's eastern zone, that is, the Great Plains region, forms an increasingly variegated agricultural province. The traditional cornbelt-cattle-and-hog-feeding nexus laps into the eastern South Dakota, Nebraska, and Kansas area; the nation's wheat-growing heartland spreads across its center; and rangeland pastures blanket its high and dry western reaches. In these high plains states, agriculture still remains supreme, as it has since first settlement, setting the economic, social, and political cadence of the region. The two Dakotas have the highest percentages of total population reliant on agriculture of any states in the Union. In Nebraska, it is estimated that four of every five people rely on agriculture, directly or indirectly, for their income. Year in and year out, Kansas far and away leads the nation in wheat raising, with North Dakota second. Oklahoma is a leading producer of both wheat and beef; but in the marginal terrain of South Dakota, cattle prevail, with range operations in the dry western portion and feedlots in the wet eastern area.

Across the semiarid reaches of the interior West, this same pattern emerges: wheat and other cereal grains in the arable areas and cow-calf cattle ranching in the larger but more marginal expanses suitable only for pasture. Such is the case

243

in the eastern plains–mountain foothills areas of Colorado and Montana and in the dry interior areas of Washington and Oregon. Cattle predominate, on the other hand, in the high and cold benchlands of Wyoming; a variety of reclamation crops such as sugar beets and potatoes lead agricultural production on Idaho's Snake River plain; and cotton, fruit, and vegetables are prevailing crops along Arizona's irrigated river bottoms. The old pattern of shipping western cattle to midwestern feeders for market continues but has given way somewhat to western finishers, like those in the Texas Panhandle, the Central Valley, or the mammoth Monfort feedlots at Greeley, Colorado, which feed not only corn but also grains and sugar beet pulp. Meanwhile, the sheep industry has steadily declined, the victim not only of declining wool markets but also of federal constraints on the poisoning of predators like wolves and coyotes.

So western agriculture looks less and less like it used to— the socioeconomic foundation of the region—and more and more like a business, still predominant in much of the West but employing ever fewer people, either directly or in related businesses. As in most other facets of the American economy, smaller operators have fallen by the wayside, and larger "agribusinesses" continue to grow. Meanwhile, that other traditional pillar of the western economy, metal mining, fell even more spectacularly than did agriculture.

The postwar years saw an intensification of the same trends in metal mining that had surfaced earlier in the century: copper dominating precious metals, open-pit mines displacing deep shafts, powerful new technologies—such as giant shovels that take ten tons of ore at a time—replacing old methods. Major gold and silver mines were few and far between; the Homestake in South Dakota dominated western gold, and the Sunshine and Bunker Hill and Sullivan complexes in northern Idaho dominated silver and lead. For the most part, precious metals derived from small mining outfits and as by-products of big copper mines. Only one major new metal came to western prominence after the war: uranium for nuclear energy, which was mined heavily in New Mexico and Utah. Modern-day prospectors, armed with Geiger counters, filed more than three hundred thousand claims in four Utah counties alone by 1959; and Charlie Steen, a nineteenth-century-style plunger, made it big with his Mi Vida Mine at Moab. Salt Lake City became the Wall Street of uranium stocks.

Economists of the postwar era spoke of a "copper belt" running north from Arizona and New Mexico through Nevada and Utah to Montana. As in most American industries by this time, a handful of large corporations dominated the mining of the red metal and of its lesser precious and base metal by-products: ASARCO, formerly American Smelting and Refining; Phelps Dodge, based primarily in Arizona; Kennecott, with its largest operations in Utah; and Anaconda, now diversified from its old Montana matrix. By the 1970s, Arizona yielded more than 50 percent of U.S. copper output and had twenty thousand workers employed in the industry. The great majority of American reserves lay within a 150-mile radius of Tucson, making Arizona by far the epicenter of western metal mining. Utah, with Kennecott's cavernous Bingham Canyon mine, ranked second; and Montana, where Anaconda opened a pit in the center of Butte, came in third.

Western copper-based mining crumbled during the 1970s and then crashed in the 1980s. A flood of cheap copper imports from South America and Africa, high labor costs, toughening environmental protection laws, and the loss of their communication markets to satellites and fiber-optic wire combined to undercut the region's miners. The coup de grâce came during the 1970s when booming oil-energy conglomerates set out to buy up the devalued western metal companies. Sohio acquired Kennecott, Arco got Anaconda, Gulf Resources and Chemical bought Idaho's Bunker Hill works, and so forth. The oilmen dreamed of new riches in integrated resource conglomerates, but by the 1980s they faced only tightening markets and big losses. So in the early 1980s came the great unloading. Arco closed down its western Montana mines; Sohio-Kennecott shut down Bingham

Canyon; Gulf closed its Coeur d'Alene mines; and AMAX terminated most of its molybdenum operation at Leadville, Colorado. The independent mining firms also weakened badly: Phelps Dodge closed many of its Arizona properties, and ASARCO banked the fires of its giant, arsenic-belching smelter at Tacoma.

Clearly, this oldest of western industries has fallen for good. Low-cost southern-hemisphere mines command the markets of the world; Chilean miners earn only one-tenth of those in America; and flooded mines are in effect lost forever. The mining of precious and base metals will continue in the West and even surge, as it did in the late 1980s, but only on a reduced basis at places like Bingham Canyon or Butte and at smaller, shorter-term mines that use nonunion labor. Never again will metal mining buttress the economies of entire subregions of the West as it did from 1850 until 1980.

Like mining, the lumber industry boomed during the quarter-century following the war, then fell on hard times. Lumber markets surged with the big postwar building boom; and the western industry grew into a true "wood products" enterprise, as by-products like particleboard, pulp paper, and formaldehyde were gathered from lumber wastes formerly discarded. Heavy trucks and portable power saws allowed efficient logging in the remote backcountry, spearheading a technological revolution in lumbering that nowadays equips modern mills with computerized scanning saws that selectively cut logs according to their individual configurations and with chipping headsaws that can process entire logs into cut boards and usable particulates in one operation.

During the boom years from the mid-1940s through the 1960s, smaller "peckerwood" outfits joined in the prosperity with bigger operators like Weyerhaeuser, Boise Cascade, Georgia Pacific, Crown Zellerbach, and Champion International; but in this industry, as in others, capital-intensive new technologies inevitably fostered the giants. The clear-cutting of large swaths of timberland, fifty to one hundred acres at the least, became the common mode of operations, after

A mature forest near Willow Creek, Idaho, after it had been clear-cut in the early 1930s. Courtesy of the National Agricultural Library Special Collections, Forest Service Photo Collection, Beltsville, Maryland.

which the ground was burned and replanted. The sustained-yield philosophy, by which timberlands were nurtured as perennial croplands, was clearly the order of the day; but only the large firms could truly afford it. By the late 1960s, nonetheless, even the largest and most progressive firms found themselves in a quandry, cutting more from their own lands than replanting could replace. Even in the magnificent Douglas fir forests of southwestern Oregon, America's greatest remaining stands of "old growth" timber eroded rapidly. This meant, of course, an ever greater reliance on timber sales from the national forests. With the Multiple Use–Sustained Yield Act of 1960, Congress ordered the U.S. Forest Service to allow only as much cutting as could be replenished by reforestation.

The onset of hard times in the wood products industry coincided with the downturn in mining. With the tight-money crisis of the early 1970s and the collapse of the building boom, lumber markets contracted sharply. A mounting environmentalist movement criticized clear-cutting, cheap timber sales, and backcountry road construction on public lands; and the National Environmental Policy Act of 1969, which required environmental-impact statements, made new developments more difficult and costly. Cheap imports, especially from British Columbia, flooded the American market; and customers like Japan chose to purchase logs rather than expensive, American-planed lumber. On top of it all, this increasingly automated industry began shifting its main centers of operation away from the Pacific Northwest and toward the Southeast, with its fast-growing forests and cheaper labor. So, by the early 1980s, this industry too lay in the throes of severe depression, with hopes for only limited recovery. In Oregon, the nation's leading lumber state, fully one-fourth of the wood products work force was unemployed; and Georgia Pacific had moved its corporate headquarters from Portland to Atlanta.

In part, the trends in western petroleum reflected those in mining and lumber. The unparalleled prosperity of postwar America was based, in considerable part, on cheap fuels and energy; and much of this cheap energy flowed from western oil and gas fields. Admittedly, the United States came to rely ever more heavily on imported oil, especially from the Persian Gulf and Venezuela, and became a net importer in 1947. But as late as 1954, imports accounted for only 17 percent of U.S. consumption. Most of the oil and gasoline that powered the great American dream machine came from home, 78 percent of it from four states: Texas, which reigned supreme, Oklahoma, California, and Louisiana.

For nearly thirty years after the end of World War II, even with the low prices of cheap imports, the oil industry garnered enormous profits. By the mid-1950s, eight of America's twenty-six largest companies were in petroleum. To some extent, these profits flowed directly from the structures of political preference carefully assembled by southwestern politicians, most notably the artificially high 27.5 percent oil depletion allowance, which was not lowered until

1976. They also flowed from new technologies that paralleled those in other industries, such as deep drilling, computerized refineries, and the flooding of old oil fields with water and solvents to recover hitherto unreachable deposits. The tapping of lucrative offshore oil fields from large stationary platforms became feasible after the war. Following a marathon political duel between advocates of federal ownership of offshore lands and those of state ownership, the Eisenhower administration and Congress handed the states and their oil industry allies a major victory with the Submerged Lands Act of 1953. Offshore oil drilling has, in the intervening three decades, contributed much to the oil revenues of Texas and California, and has also fueled the flames of environmentalist protests.

California's offshore fields, like the one that contaminated the Santa Barbara Channel with leakage in 1969, combine with older ones in the Los Angeles Basin, at Elk Hills, and elsewhere to keep California among the top-producing states, the domicile of Atlantic Richfield and other major companies. But oil does not dominate the industrial giant of California as it does the big petroleum states to the east. Texas still reigns supreme in petroleum, even though its production peaked in 1972 at 1.3 billion barrels and dropped below 1 billion by the 1980s. Drawing on both offshore and onshore wells, Houston is America's oil capital and is the center as well of such affiliated industries as the manufacture of oil field and refinery equipment and the petrochemical industries, whose "spaghetti bowl" of pipeline linkages intertwine the Houston ship channel. Dallas too is a major petroleum finance capital; and the industry spreads across much of North and West Texas, most notably to the massive installations and office complexes at Midland-Odessa in the Permian Basin. Natural gas became a major energy industry in its own right in northern and western Texas and throughout the interior West, a preferred form of cheap and clean fuel marketed both by regional utilities and by giant conglomerates like Texas-based Tenneco.

Just as corporate giants like Humble (Exxon), Gulf, and

Texaco grew up in Texas, so did others like Phillips, Kerr-McGee, and Continental Oil (Conoco) in Oklahoma. Tulsa and Oklahoma City rank as oil capitals alongside their Texas sister cities; and by the 1970s, all but five of Oklahoma's seventy-seven counties contained producing oil and gas wells. By that time, however, most of these fields were in decline, and 60 percent of the state's oil came from "secondary recovery methods." Older fields predominated too in Kansas; and older and newer ones in Wyoming supported thirteen thousand oil and gas jobs, propping up a sagging agricultural economy and making Casper a thriving mini-Tulsa. Newer technologies, meanwhile, brought in deeper and more difficult deposits, like the Williston Basin of Montana and North Dakota, which came in during the 1950s and boomed the regional economic center of Billings.

The fossil fuels economy experienced mighty convolutions beginning in the early 1970s similar to those experienced by the West's other extractive industries, but with a different twist. Following the Arab-Israeli War of 1973, the Middle East–based Organization of Petroleum Exporting Countries (OPEC) embargoed oil exports to the industrial nations, sharply driving up prices and setting off economic shock waves around the world. In the United States, the immediate result was mushrooming prices for gasoline and oil, long lines at gas pumps, and huge windfall profits for energy companies and for those states that benefited from taxing them. Suddenly, it seemed that Texas—where in the later 1970s petroleum still employed over three hundred thousand people and provided 20 percent of the tax income—and other western energy states might now rise up as matured colonies that would rule the old metropolitan regions to the east.

The soaring price of imported oil not only set off a mighty surge of exploration across the West but also stimulated the precipitous development of other fossil fuels. It now appeared that the great deposits of oil shale—the fossil fuel kerogen imbedded in limestone—that lay across much of western Colorado and neighboring areas of Utah and

Wyoming might become cost-effective to mine as oil prices continued to rise. The shale had to be heated to nine hundred degrees Fahrenheit for release; and it required massive excavations, water diversions, and waste rock dumpage. Leading the pack of developers, Exxon projected a thirty-year, $500 million program to erect 150 plants across the Colorado western slope.

A similar, far grander bonanza seemed to lay in the West's most abundant fossil fuel, coal. This prosaic fuel, first developed by railroads and other frontier users, had long ago lost most of its markets to cleaner and higher-BTU oil and natural gas. The heartland of American production still lay in Appalachia and southern Illinois. Even before the 1973–74 crisis, however, western coal had been making a comeback. Like metals, the lower-grade western coal could be strip-mined with giant shovels and either burned to generate electricity at the mine mouth or hauled to urban plants in long unit trains. Unlike the eastern mines, those in the West employed only limited work forces, mainly teamsters and operating engineers. Symbolically, for the first time in U.S. history, in 1970 the West could boast the nation's largest coal mine, Utah Construction's Navajo Mine near Farmington, New Mexico.

The Farmington–Four Corners complex of coal-fired plants was soon generating twenty-two hundred megawatts of electricity, carried by high-tension wires mainly to southern California and emitting so much steam and pollution as to become for space travelers the most visible human activity on earth. Other plants, like the large one at Lynndyl, sprouted across central and southwest Utah, to the distress of environmentalists worried about air pollution and the nearby scenic parklands.

In the meantime, coal developers turned their attention to the nation's greatest coal reserves, which underlay the arid plains of eastern Montana and Wyoming and western North Dakota. Major energy companies moved in to develop pit mines and some mine-mouth plants, such as the large ones at Colstrip, Montana. Rock Springs, Wyoming, which mushroomed from a population of eleven thousand in 1970 to twenty-six thousand in 1980, and its cross-state sister Gillette became bywords for rampant growth and social dislocation. While the Bureau of Reclamation and its corporate affiliates talked of making the northern plains into a "national sacrifice area," mining out its coal and diverting its fragile rivers to get the nation through the energy squeeze, Montana and Wyoming, along with other western states like New Mexico, enacted tough new environmental and coal severance tax laws to protect and enhance themselves. In 1981, the U.S. Supreme Court upheld the legality of Montana's sky-high 30 percent coal severance tax, even as an Ohio congressman protested: "Montana and Wyoming have become a domestic OPEC, earning millions of dollars at the expense of the other states."

Thus did the big 1970s energy boom seem about to transform the interior West, to reverse its national role from the oppressed to the oppressor. In the end, however, it did not happen; and the reason lay, once again, in global economic forces. Artificially high prices stimulated intensive exploration and output of fuels, as well as energy conservation, around the world, so that by the mid-1980s the world was awash in an oil glut, and prices were plummeting. In 1986, oil fell well below twenty dollars per barrel. The big energy states like Texas, Oklahoma, and Wyoming, which had ridden the roller coaster upward in the 1970s, now rode it downward in the 1980s, with shutdowns, layoffs, and big state deficits. Exxon closed its western Colorado shale oil prospect, and the mining of coal dwindled on the northern plains and elsewhere. Economists predicted that the energy glut would endure well into the 1990s, meaning long-term depression for much of the West.

So in this instance, as in so many others, the region paid the price for its heavy reliance on extractive industries, with alternating cycles of boom and bust. The fossil-fuel industries will probably rise again, but probably not soon. For the other extractive industries—agriculture, lumber, and metal mining—the longer-term prospect is gloomier. As the economist Peter Drucker comments, the world economy is glutted with natural products and it seems likely to remain that way. Even that traditionally greatest of American exports, agriculture, faces a bleak future: it is estimated that within a few years only Japan and the Soviet Union, among all the major nations, will not be food exporters. Therefore, except for the wild card of its abundant but currently depressed energy reserves, the future of the West seems to lie not so much in its traditional extractive industries as in other, newer sectors of its economy.

THE NEW ECONOMIC ORDER

The newer economic mainstays of the western economy, which have arisen mainly since 1945, are multifold and not easily summarized. Forty-five years ago, the economic future of the region was thought to lie in the move westward of the traditional eastern-midwestern manufacturing industries. Yet the end of the discriminatory "basing point" pricing system after the war did not lead to a major western steel industry. The major centers of U.S. steel production remained in the Midwest and the South; and the western outposts of big steel in Colorado, Utah, and California did not flourish. Symbolically, the old Geneva Steel Works in Utah closed in the mid-1980s, reopening with a small work force and reduced productivity, a victim, like much of the U.S. industry, of foreign competition. Nor did that other most basic of American industries, automobile manufacturing, move west. Even the indomitable Henry J. Kaiser failed when he tried during the 1950s to rival Detroit with his Kaiser-Frazier cars. For the most part, basic U.S. industries like steel, automobiles, rubber, and machine tools remained firmly based in the Northeast–Middle Atlantic–Upper Midwest heartland, with satellite or assembly divisions in the major western market areas of California and Texas, for example, the large USX automated steel fabrication works in Houston.

Instead of basic manufacturing, two new forms of mass employment served to restructure the western economy after

World War II: "service" industries and "high technology" corporations. The growing service professions that have provided such an increasing proportion of U.S. employment since 1945 are, in large part, a direct result and reflection of postwar prosperity, for they serve to meet the limitless needs and desires of an affluent public. The term *service* embraces an impossibly diverse range of industries, from rich and influential banking, insurance, legal, and health professions to automotive and restaurant services, to barbers and hairdressers, to an endless variety of main street shops.

In the rising importance of its service industries, the West simply reflects a national trend. It has, for instance, about its proportionate share of America's seventeen million administrative and clerical workers, almost two million health professionals, and seven hundred thousand lawyers. A look at any of the West's major cities quickly reveals, however, just how important these industries are to the area economies. Houston's 154-acre Texas Medical Center is one of the world's greatest and is a major component in the city's financial structure. Dallas's two hundred insurance companies and its banking headquarters, including three of Texas's five largest, serve to make it Houston's rival for statewide economic dominance. San Francisco's thriving financial district, which includes the headquarters for such major concerns as Bank of America and Wells Fargo, has been a significant factor in that city's continuing vitality, even as it lost much of its seaport trade to the containerized facilities at Oakland. Yet, even at that, Los Angeles surpassed San Francisco in 1965 to become the West's key financial-banking center. Nor do the biggest cities have all the financial action. South Dakota astounded the American banking world in 1981 by offering New York's Citibank such an attractive support package that the state lured the credit card headquarters away to Sioux Falls.

What came to be known, by the 1970s, as the West's "high-tech" revolution actually began during and immediately after the war. The new, postwar electronics industry, which evolved into a higher, computer-oriented phase beginning in the 1960s, was a national and global phenomenon; but its center of gravity lay in the West. Why did these "sunrise industries" gravitate so heavily westward? In large part it was because they were directly interconnected with the western-based defense-aerospace industries and with the accompanying defense-research dollars for universities and private sector investigators that the federal government channeled westward during and after the war. Also, these new corporations, with their affluent, white-collar work forces, favored the sunny life-style of the Southwest, as well as the nonunion atmosphere there.

For example, the end of the old order in Arizona began in the late 1940s with the arrival of electronics giant Motorola in Phoenix, attracted in part by a new state right-to-work law (that is, a law that bans compulsory union membership). Arizona's probusiness, easy-taxation climate soon attracted many more new businesses, including electronics-aerospace firms such as Sperry-Rand, Hughes Aircraft, General Electric, and Honeywell and others like Greyhound bus lines, Ramada Inns, and the Del Webb retirement meccas. As a result, Arizona rapidly broke away from its sleepy borderlands past and away from its traditional economic reliance on the "3C's"—copper, cattle, and cotton—to become a heartland of the new corporate West. By the 1980s, nearly 40 percent of the Arizona economy related to high-tech industries, and Phoenix's Valley of the Sun ranked third behind metropolitan San Francisco and Boston as national high-tech centers. The state's population mushroomed to 3.1 million by 1984, a better than fourfold growth since 1945. One-fifth of these Arizonans lived in fast-rising Tucson, and over half of them in greater Phoenix, which grew by 30 percent during the 1970s to advance from America's twentieth-largest to its ninth-largest city (twenty-sixth-largest in general metropolitan area).

The real nationwide pacesetter of the new high-tech-computer revolution was "Silicon Valley," south of San Francisco and centered in Santa Clara County and San Jose. Like its cross-continent rival complex, Route 128-Cambridge in

Massachusetts, the Silicon Valley grouping of high-tech industries developed from fertile business-defense-research collaboration between a major university, Stanford, and a host of nearby aerospace-electronic companies. By the 1970s, the South Bay area manifested all the signs of the new high-tech era: big-name outfits like IBM, Apple, and National Semiconductor, thousands of new high-paying "Yuppie" jobs, well-manicured industrial parks, posh new suburbs with skyrocketing housing prices, an embargo on labor unions, and a genuine population explosion. Santa Clara County grew from a population of 290,547 in 1950 to nearly 1,300,000 in 1980; San Jose increased from a mere 95,280 in 1950 to become a major western city of over 600,000 by 1980. As *Fortune* magazine put it, one twenty-five-mile stretch of Santa Clara County housed "the densest concentration of innovative industry that exists anywhere in the world."

Silicon Valley soon had rivals all across the region and nation. In wealthy and conservative Orange County, south of Los Angeles, a sunny and probusiness climate attracted large clusters of high-tech and aerospace companies, making it for a time the nation's fastest-growing county, with seven hundred thousand newcomers in the 1960s and five hundred thousand more in the 1970s. Greater Salt Lake City grew by 38 percent during the 1970s, in large part because of new plants built by Rockwell International, Sperry Univac, and Litton. In Oregon, even without California-style investments in higher education, Tektronix became Portland's largest employer. In Idaho, Boise became the northern intermountain area's most impressive boom city, growing by 54.2 percent during the heady 1970s. A main reason was a new Hewlett-Packard plant directly employing twenty-eight hundred people. Similarly, the new "sunrise industries" figured largely enough in the big Denver boom to make the city, in the words of Neal Peirce and Jerry Hagstrom, "the most important scientific-technical center between Boston and California."

The interior Southwest garnered much of the action in

the age of the microchip. With fast-rising firms like Lear-jet, Hughes Tool, and IBM, Tucson grew by 26 percent during the 1970s; Albuquerque, with Honeywell, Sperry Flight Systems, and others, increased 34.5 percent. Tulsa, a data processing and telecommunications center, had by 1981 the lowest unemployment percentages of any major U.S. city. Working aggressively to move away from a dangerously heavy reliance on oil and agriculture, Texas came to rival California in its funding of universities and other strategies to lure in high-tech industries.

Building on the wealth of scientific talent at the University of Texas, Austin spawned its own "Little Silicon Valley," with Texas Instruments and Motorola, among others. The city grew by more than one-third during the hectic 1970s. Nearby San Antonio, with its dynamic Hispanic Mayor Henry Cisneros promoting development, sprouted a growing ring of high-tech businesses around its Loop 410. With big aerospace firms like LTV to build on, Dallas–Fort Worth emerged as a national leader in computer-high-tech industry. Two of its giant figures on the national stage were Erik Jonsson, the founder of Texas Instruments who went on to serve as mayor of the city, and headline-grabbing H. Ross Perot, the builder of Electronic Data Systems. High-tech industries, especially as applied to petroleum-petrochemical, medical, and steel industries, had much to do with the great Houston boom of the 1970s, a decade that added 906,000 newcomers to the metropolitan area. This chaotic and uncontrolled growth prompted the 1981 election of planning advocate Kathy Whitmire as mayor and the enactment a year later of the city's first land-use law.

As the West, especially the Southwest, rocketed upward in economic activity and in population growth because of the twin booms in energy and high-technology industries during the 1970s, the so-called Sunbelt, running from Florida to California, was commonly seen as the future seat of American empire. *Business Week* declared in 1975 that the flow of investment capital and of people to the Sunbelt threatened to collapse the older, industrial heartland of the northeastern quadrant of the United States—the so-called Rustbelt or Frostbelt—and launch a "second war between the states." World historian Paul Johnson wrote in *Modern Times* (1983): "The shift of America's center of gravity, both demographic and economic, from the North-East to the South-West was one of the most important changes of modern times."

The futuristic prophecies of a "Sunbelt revolution," which would be based on high-priced energy and on what John Naisbitt called the "sunrise industries of the new information age," carried the day for a time. After all, between 1970 and 1974 the South and West, combined, accounted for over 90 percent of the nation's metropolitan growth. During the thirty-four years prior to 1974, the metropolitan growth of these combined regions was fifty-two million, whereas that of the rest of the country was only thirty-five million. If, today, the area enclosed by a circle with a sixty-mile radius centered on Los Angeles were to become a separate nation, it would be the fourteenth wealthiest on earth.

Yet, by the mid-1980s, these prophecies seemed less than prophetic. The energy boom had turned to bust; and while the western energy states fell into depression the Frostbelt enjoyed a renaissance. In fact, business indicators revealed that many new industries preferred the Northeast-style climate of high taxes–high services to the Southwest style of lower taxes–lesser services. Nor did the new high-tech industries prove to be quite the panacea predicted. Contrary to many projections, by 1986 the United States had become a net *importer* of high-technology products, especially from Asia, and the bloom was off in Silicon Valley. High-technology industries, along with energy and certain other natural products industries, are indeed the way of the future for the West. But these industries, alone or combined, cannot immunize the region from national and global economic trends and competition.

Although a focus on the West's primary extractive industries, its new high-technology, service, and tourist industries, and its multitude of federal installations explains the main forces of its modern economy, other factors figure in the equation. In a lightly populated state like Montana, for instance, where agriculture remains the dominant industry, more people find employment in service to state and local governments than on all farms and ranches. As in all regions of America, smaller "main street" firms are giving way to nationwide chain stores and conglomerate corporations. A fair number of these familiar super-service corporations arose in the West, organizations as diverse as the J. C. Penney chain of stores, the first of which appeared in 1902 in tiny Kemmerer, Wyoming; the giant Tandy Corporation, whose familiar Radio Shacks first surfaced in Fort Worth; and Ray Kroc's ubiquitous McDonald's restaurants, which first erected their golden arches in California and Arizona in the mid-1950s.

Nor should one forget the importance of export trade to the West. Houston is the third-largest port in the United States, second only to New York and New Orleans, and is among the world's greatest oil depots; and the major Pacific ports are thriving centers of exports and imports to and from the nations of the Pacific Rim. Much of this ocean commerce, as can readily be seen at the docks of San Pedro, Long Beach, Oakland, or Puget Sound, is by now highly automated and computerized "container" transport. As economist Richard Carlson notes, the West is the "free-trade heart of the United States": it both imports and exports, on average, more than the rest of the nation. These imports and exports, of everything from the most mundane raw materials to the most sophisticated computerized equipment, increasingly engage the region with the rest of the world and make the West the most favorably inclined of all American regions to policies of free trade.

And then, finally, there is the continuing role of organized labor in the western economy. American labor unions entered the postwar era on a wave of militant strikes that arose, primarily, from severe inflation. In fact, the 1945–46 strikes took more workers off the job than had the strikes of 1919–20, following the previous war. Then, riding upward on the great wave of 1950s and 1960s prosperity, organized labor entered its greatest age of affluence and political influence, capped by the merger in 1955 of the American Federation of Labor with the Congress of Industrial Organizations. Union membership rose, nationally, from 17.5 million in 1956 to 19.4 million in 1970, largely because of the organization of the legions of new public and service sector workers. But even in those growth years, the percentage of unionized workers relative to the total work force declined from 33 to 27 percent. This percentage decline reflected trends that increasingly continue to spell trouble for organized labor. As the older, blue-collar manufacturing industries atrophied, so too did union membership. At the same time, the unions had a hard time recruiting in the newer white-collar, service, and high-tech industries, succeeding to some extent with public sector and service workers but generally failing in the highly paid high-tech work force.

The West exemplified these national trends, in an exaggerated manner. The region's most entrenched and powerful unions were concentrated in its extractive, transportation, and exporting industries; all flourished for a time after the war and then went into steep declines. After years of fighting to save the obsolescent jobs of locomotive firemen, the long-powerful Railroad Brotherhoods watched thousands of their members head down the road as passenger and other lines were closed. Similarly, the automation and containerization of dock facilities spelled "technological unemployment" for the International Longshoremen's Association, whose membership dwindled to a mere 116,000 by 1983. Automated mills and the exporting of jobs overseas and to the nonunion South undermined the International Woodworkers of America; and the tough and radical old Mine, Mill and Smelter Workers Union lost the last of its dwindling membership to the United Steelworkers in 1967. Although it seemed outwardly that César Chávez's militant United Farm Workers was winning the long struggle to bring effective organization to the exploited Hispanic field workers of the Southwest during the 1970s, the corporate owners simply countered, in fact, by using ever more complex harvesting machines, such as walnut and grape pickers, to trim their labor forces.

As the unions rooted in the West's troubled extractive industries lost membership, those based in the service and government sectors rapidly expanded. By the 1980s, the West's largest and most economically powerful unions included more than 400,000 members of the National Education Association, more than 300,000 members of the United Food and Commercial Workers, more than 150,000 members of the International Association of Machinists and Aerospace Workers, 150,000 members of the Service Employees International Union, 250,000 members of the American Federation of State, County and Municipal Employees of America, and more than 500,000 members of the International Brotherhood of Teamsters. The Teamsters became an especially potent force in the truck-intensive West, with their ability to win victories by closing down transportation and with their propensity to diversify into other fields of work. A key architect of this union's spectacular growth was boss Dave Beck of Seattle, whose minions did not hesitate to use force to "perfect their organization" and who, like his successor Jimmy Hoffa, ended up in prison.

More significant for the region than this shift in types of prevalent unions was the trend toward new industries that either broke the unions or bypassed them altogether. Unlike the older industrial heartlands of the Midwest and Northeast, the western Sunbelt favored "right-to-work" laws that made union organization more difficult and that served, as in Texas and Arizona, to help draw the new white-collar industries. In 1970s Arizona, for instance, only 18 percent of the work force belonged to unions. In addition, companies exported jobs to affiliates in Mexico and the Pacific Rim nations and thereby completely circumvented unions and higher-priced American labor. In the Arizona-Mexican cities of Nogales, U.S.-built components were transferred across the border for cheap labor-fabrication and then were brought back duty-free as completed products.

Thus the western economic profile of the late 1980s

looked drastically different from that of 1945. The rising federal role as regional financier-resource manager, which had begun so abruptly in 1933–45, was heightened, expanded, and institutionalized over the years. Such established trends as the general decline of extractive industries and the rising importance of tourism and of high-tech and service industries seem likely to project far into the future. But despite the declines, traditional mainstays such as agriculture, mining, lumber, and petroleum remain vital to the region and its future; and at some point the energy industries, and perhaps others, will rise again.

The severe economic downturn of the 1980s brought home to the West a central fact of life, one that the provincial and insular frontier thesis of Turner and his disciples had masked. The emergence of a world marketplace for resources and labor, the spread of American capital and technologies around the planet, and the huge glut of natural products all combined to weaken the American world role and to remind us that the United States always has been and is now more than ever fully integrated into a world system. Since the West is America's key supplier of natural products, it has suffered this depression more severely than have its sister regions.

As oil prices fell below $18 per barrel, copper below 60¢ per pound, Douglas fir below $1.33 per thousand board feet, and Nebraska farmland below $445 per acre, the vulnerability of the region—particularly of those parts with undiversified economies still overwhelmingly reliant on farming, oil, and other extractive industries—was everywhere to be seen. For the first time in modern history, personal incomes in the region grew more slowly than they did in the rest of the nation. And so, from the depressed 1890s to the uncertain 1980s, some trends seemed constant. The West still rose and fell, to a considerable extent, with its extractive industries. The new service and high-tech industries indeed held the key to much of the future; but even in these "sunrise industries," which now seemed less promising than before, the West still relied overwhelmingly, as it always had, on the sustaining hand of federal subsidy and regulation. Only those subsectors of the region that could diversify their economies to escape such heavy reliance on glutted natural products industries, or that could muster new technologies to market their products more competitively, seemed likely to prosper in the near future.

Chapter Seven   # Politics of the Modern Era, 1945-1987

T he sweeping socioeconomic transformations of the postwar decades brought with them similarly sweeping changes in the western political order. In the region generally, and more particularly in the mosaic of its subregions and states, the old patterns of the postfrontier era crumbled; and the West moved ever more directly into the national mainstream. Undercut by the great federal activism of the New Deal and the Second World War, the nexus of economic colonialism gradually eroded; as it did, the West rose up to play a larger and larger role in the political life of the nation. Seldom, however, did the West appear to behave politically as a truly uniform region, because in truth it was not. Yet, because of its heavy federal reliance, especially for water development and defense-aerospace funding, and because of its continuing role as the supplier of most of the nation's energy, mineral, and food resources, the West did have common concerns; and these found ample reflection in politics at home and in Washington, D.C. In its voting preferences, the region displayed the same range of liberal-conservative and Democratic-Republican variation as did the country at large. But from the limited vantage of the later 1980s, the West seemed, like the South, to have moved markedly toward a preference for conservatives of both parties, in part as a reaction against the liberalism of the entrenched northeastern "establishment." As America at large more and more embraced certain traditionally western political traits—for instance, direct participatory democracy and the disregarding of party lines—it seemed safe to say that the West had more than achieved parity with the older regions of the country. In some respects, it had become a political pacesetter for the entire country.

THE WEST IN NATIONAL POLITICS, 1945–72

During the quarter-century from the close of the war through the financial crises of 1969–71, the United States experienced a prosperity and world economic hegemony un-paralleled in history. These years saw the West participate more fully than ever before in the political life of the nation. New forms of mass transportation, such as jet aviation, and new forms of mass communication, such as television, broke down the old barriers of regional separation and brought even the distant Far West into direct and continuous contact with the eastern centers of governmental and business influence.

With each passing decade, the West shed more of the sub-regional political traditions of its frontier heritage. In the Southwest, this meant a diminution of the one-party loyalty to the Democrats that migrants from the Old South had brought west with them. On the northern Great Plains, similarly, it meant an ever-so-gradual erosion of the ties to the Republican party that earlier pioneers had brought with them from New England and the Midwest. But these traditions did not disappear altogether, as is witnessed in Kansas's age-old loyalty to Republicanism or Texas's to the Democratic party, which has only very recently faded. In truth, this region—like all the others—and each of its subregions evolved its own pattern of political cultures within a broader context of national mainstreaming.

America entered the new Atomic Age at war's end in a mood of reaction. The liberalism of the New Deal era seemed everywhere to retreat before an advancing conservatism stemming from the Cold War with Communist Russia, an unrest with wartime governmental controls, and an anger at runaway inflation and the postwar wave of strikes. The West reflected these themes. Yet, as in the past, the region continued to show a pattern, in contrast with the traditionally GOP (Republican) upper Midwest or the Democratic South, of balance, swaying back and forth in response to countervailing liberal-conservative and Democratic-Republican political currents. Thus this new region seemed less predictable and more of a national weather vane than did its older and more tradition-bound sisters to the east.

For instance, after the Republicans swept most of the West in the midterm elections of 1946, the Democrats rallied in the 1948 presidential election. With farmers fearful that the Republicans might end New Deal federal farm price supports, the West went for the underdog, incumbent Democratic President Harry Truman. All but five of the seventeen western states, those five being the North Dakota–Kansas tier plus Oregon, went Democratic. And so it was that the West joined with the Democratic South in pulling off the most celebrated upset election in U.S. history. The 1948 returns also revealed just how strongly the advanced liberalism of the New Deal era still influenced this region that had benefited so immensely from federal largesse. The far leftist Progressive party of 1948, running Henry Wallace for president and colorful Senator Glen Taylor of Idaho for vice-president, had by far its greatest success rates in the West. Seven of its top eight statewide voting percentages registered in the region.

Generally speaking, though, the West followed the national postwar trend to the right. The anti-Communist frenzy that became labeled "McCarthyism," after the Wisconsin senator who was its main proponent, erupted throughout the region, especially in the form of Red hunts and demands for loyalty oaths from teachers and public employees. When the California Board of Regents ordered the dismissal of thirty-two professors at the Berkeley campus who refused to take loyalty oaths, the issue disrupted not only higher education but also the politics of an entire state until its supreme court invalidated the oath and ordered the faculty reinstated two years later in 1952.

Red hunters in Texas could find only one Communist among the state's sixty thousand schoolteachers, but this fact did not dampen the suspicions of the true believers. In Hollywood, the U.S. House of Representatives' Un-American Activities Committee in 1947 launched a widely heralded search for Communists in the film industry which eventually shattered a number of prominent careers, most of them unfairly. Several national leaders of the rightist, anti-Communist crusade emerged from the West, including Congressman Martin Dies from Texas, Senators Karl Mundt from South Dakota, Kenneth Wherry from Nebraska, Zales Ecton from Montana, Herman Welker from Idaho, and Pat McCarran from Nevada, and a young California congressman named Richard Nixon, who won a U.S. Senate seat in 1950 by labeling his opponent, Senator Helen Gahagan Douglas, the "pink lady" and who won a national following by ferreting out supposed Communists and "fellow travelers" from the federal government.

As the nation learned by the early 1950s to live with the tensions of the Cold War and nuclear weapons, its political mood shifted to a more complacent, middle-of-the-road conservatism, well reflected by the personality and the administration of President Dwight Eisenhower (1953–61). Eisenhower hailed from Abilene, Kansas, and would in fact prove to be the first of four (out of a total seven) presidents of the next thirty-five years to come from the West. However, his ties to his home state were more emotional than firm, and he brought no "Kansas gang" with him to Washington. Westerners did play key roles in his administration, though. Controversial Richard Nixon was "Ike's" vice-president, equally controversial Ezra Taft Benson of Utah his secretary of agriculture, Oregon's Douglas "Giveaway" McKay his secretary of the interior, and wealthy Oveta Culp Hobby of Houston his secretary of health, education and welfare. Westerners wielded even more influence in Congress, where a pair of savvy Texas Democrats, Sam Rayburn as speaker of the House of Representatives and Lyndon Johnson as majority leader of the Senate, worked smoothly with the Republican administration to advance the interests of their state and region.

Such was Eisenhower's personal popularity that he carried every western state in both of his presidential campaigns, 1952 and 1956; but beneath the surface calm, several political controversies marked the region's evolving federal relationship. As noted earlier, the Eisenhower administration's surrender of offshore oil lands to the states pleased the Southwest but seemed a handout to big business in the eyes of progressive critics. The big dam-building campaign struck many sparks, as in the environmentalists' successful effort to stop the damming of Echo Park, Utah, and in Idaho's Hell's Canyon controversy, which ended with private industry rather than the federal government damming this spectacular Snake River canyon. Most controversial of all out West was the similarly conservative effort of Agriculture Secretary Benson to roll back farm price supports toward market levels. The Agriculture Acts of 1954 and 1956 did cut federal price supports; but mounting surpluses still plagued the government, and political anger in the farm regions did likewise. In the final analysis, Republican control of the federal government seemed little different to the region from the previous Democratic control.

In a cyclical swing typical of U.S. history, the pendulum of national politics began to move leftward and toward the Democrats in the late 1950s. The midterm elections of 1958 vastly enlarged the margins of Democratic control of Congress; and in the West, as elsewhere, liberal candidates generally carried the day. Keynoting this trend in the West was the hard-fought gubernatorial election in California, where Democrat Edmund "Pat" Brown defeated conservative Republican William Knowland. By 1959, the three coastal states had five of six U.S. Senate seats in Democratic hands for the first time ever; and in Oregon, the Democrats controlled both houses of the legislature for the first time since 1879.

Lyndon B. Johnson rounding up a Hereford yearling on the LBJ Ranch, near Stonewall, Texas, on November 4, 1964. Courtesy of A P World Wide Photos.

In the extremely close presidential election of 1960, the West uncharacteristically bucked the national trend when all but three of its states (Texas, New Mexico, and Nevada) voted against the Democratic winner, John F. Kennedy, and for the Republican loser, Richard Nixon. Four years later, however, the region pulled back into the national consensus. In a heated contest pitting two westerners against one another, incumbent liberal Democratic President Lyndon Johnson of Texas versus the archconservative Republican Senator Barry Goldwater of Arizona, the great nationwide Johnson landslide captured every western state except for Goldwater's homeland. Unlike Eisenhower, Johnson did bring a strong western flavor to his presidency (1963–69), particularly with frequent and well-publicized trips back to his Texas "hill country" ranch, complete with wild rides through the mesquite and with big barbeques.

The Johnson administration's "Great Society" program from 1964 to 1969 brought yet another wave of liberal reform and expanding federal power along the lines of the earlier New Deal. The fundamental Great Society programs, such as job training, new federal support for education, and Medicare for the elderly, were national in scope and thus impacted the West as they did all other regions. However, a rising environmental consciousness in the country, which Secretary of the Interior Stewart Udall of Arizona preached but did not always practice, began yielding a series of environmental laws that, as we shall see, would soon prove very important to the West. These included the 1964 Wilderness Preservation Act, which set aside an initial 9.1 million acres, most of them in the West, for permanent safeguard as wilderness; the 1964 Classification and Multiple Use Act, which codified the now well-established system of multiple usage of federal lands; and a succession of tough new air and water quality laws from 1965 through 1970.

The era of the Vietnam War, from the mid-1960s through the early 1970s, witnessed the greatest resurgence of political activism and confrontation since the 1930s; and the West joined fully in the fray. As noted in the preceding chapters, students on western campuses such as the University of California at Berkeley and San Francisco State University vehemently demonstrated against the war and for other social concerns. Following the horrifying Watts riot of 1965, militant California blacks, led by Huey Newton and Bobby Seale, thoroughly frightened white Americans with the sometimes violent and criminal activities of their Black Panthers. Hispanic Americans of the Southwest suddenly became more assertive; and so did western Indians, most notably when "Red Power" extremists occupied Alcatraz Island in 1969 and Wounded Knee, South Dakota, in 1973.

This sudden upsurge of leftist protest and militance soon fueled a conservative reaction. In the very close election of 1968, Republican Richard Nixon captured the presidency and then won a landslide reelection victory against the outspokenly liberal Democratic Senator George McGovern of South Dakota in 1972. Despite his frequent trips to a "western White House" at San Clemente, California, Nixon, like Eisenhower, brought little western flavor to his administration; but his western popularity certainly did outpace his nationwide popularity. Nixon carried every western state except liberal Washington and traditionally Democratic Texas in 1968 and then swept the entire region in his massive landslide victory of 1972. Despite his conservative rhetoric, Nixon's presidency continued to build the prerogatives of the federal government, especially from a western perspective, with further environmental control measures like the creation in 1970 of the controversial Environmental Protection Agency.

From the brief perspective of less than two decades, it appears that the United States entered a long-term conservative phase in the late 1960s, a cyclical departure from the prosperity-born liberalism of the preceding decade. The Watergate scandals that brought down the corrupt Nixon presidency blunted this rightward trend for a time, but it emerged even more clearly by the later 1970s. America was moving away from the long era of political domination by the Democratic party and New Deal liberalism.

Beyond dispute, the states west of the ninety-fifth meridian led by a wide margin this national drift toward the right and the Republican party. The explanations for this phenomenon are subject to dispute, but certain factors are clear enough. Western progressivism had traditionally found its key bases of support not only in the middle classes but also in two other socioeconomic groups: labor unions and family farmers, especially those family farmers that organized in the plains states in the liberal Farmers Union. As we have seen, both of these groups had by the later 1960s dwindled in numbers and influence. As a result, the Democratic parties of the western states, particularly those of the agricultural interior states, saw their liberal wings dwindle and their conservative wings wax in influence. In these same states of the arid interior, the liberal elements of the Republican parties had long ago atrophied; most progressive Republicans had crossed over to the New Deal Democrats years before, leaving the conservatives firmly in control.

The new westerners, especially in the mushrooming Sunbelt, tended to be middle or upper class, suburban, nonunion if not antiunion, and comfortably conservative in outlook. They bore little resemblance to poor homesteaders and blue-collar migrants of earlier days; and they identified less and less with the union-welfare liberalism of the Democratic party, based as it was overwhelmingly on the great cities of the Northeast. As Republican strategist Kevin Phillips wrote in 1969 in *The Emerging Republican Majority*: "So long as the Democrats remain oriented towards the Northeast, their presidential nominees are not likely to carry the old populist Rocky Mountain states. . . . Sparsely populated though they may be, the Rocky Mountains have become pillars of the new national Republicanism." Phillips could just as well have been describing the entire region, not just the mountain states, a region where Democrats still competed well at times but where the Republicans were clearly on the rise. Columnist David Broder would make the same point again in 1987: the liberal Democratic party seemed, more often than not, to ignore the West.

POLITICAL CULTURES IN TRANSITION

Within this context of national and regional political evolution, each subregion and state of the West developed in its own fashion. Every state has a distinct political culture or personality, which arises naturally from its blend of economic and social ingredients and from its history. All the western states, though, moved along the same regional path during these years, some faster than others: away from the angry, old confrontational politics of the era of exploitation and toward the new age of middle-class and suburban rule. In the process, they shed most of the inherited traits of

Oklahoma governor Robert S. Kerr at the unveiling of the Jesse Chisholm Memorial Society marker near Enid, Oklahoma, 1946. Courtesy of the Archives and Manuscripts Division, Oklahoma Historical Society.

frontier and postfrontier times, such as Nonpartisan League radicalism in North Dakota, Anaconda corporate dominance in Montana, Hispanic *patron* politics in New Mexico, or Negro-baiting in Texas. The new politics proved less colorful than the old, lacking the effervescence of the fabled western individualism; but the new politics displayed more structure and efficiency. Like the old, the new western politics faithfully reflected the economic interests and self-interests of the various states and locales.

In no region was this political pilgrimage more stark than in the booming interior Southwest, where big oil and the new industrialists without a flinch pulled the levers of politics. In Oklahoma and Texas, the old-time rustics of the "Alfalfa Bill" Murray and "Pappy" O'Daniel variety now gave way to big-time manipulators like Oklahoma's Senator Robert Kerr, a major power in the U.S. Senate who used his political influence freely to benefit his Kerr-McGee oil firm, to protect the oil depletion allowance, and to siphon federal millions into Arkansas River development.

Like all states, Oklahoma had its liberals, such as the dignified Representative Carl Albert, who rose to become Speaker of the U.S. House of Representatives, or Senator Fred Harris, who ran for the presidency in 1972. But in other respects, Oklahoma seemed strongly wedded to the past; it did not even get around to repealing its antique prohibition statute until 1959. In fact, the Sooner State's postwar political odyssey was typically western. By the 1960s, the state had visibly drifted from its Old South–Democratic majorities and elected its first two probusiness Republican governors, Henry Bellmon and Dewey Bartlett.

Neighboring Texas made this same transition, in a more spectacular manner. Here too the old progressive strain lived on in congressional figures like Representative Maury Maverick and fiery Senator Ralph Yarborough. And here too groups formerly left out of politics found their voice, as seen in the court order striking down the Texas poll tax in 1966, in the real power of Congressman Henry Gonzales of San Antonio, or in the 1972 gubernatorial campaign of feminist leader Frances Farenthold. Yet, the most striking fact of postwar Texas politics, as in Oklahoma, was the manner in which giant economic interests redefined political loyalties.

Thus Democratic Senator Lyndon Johnson, who made himself the most powerful majority leader in U.S. Senate history before becoming vice-president in 1961 and who stressed his liberalism and dedication to civil liberties, also proved himself to be a political broker like Kerr, looking diligently after oil and other vital home-state interests. Many Texas Democrats, who were similarly conservative devotees of local interests, disliked the liberalism of national party leaders such as Adlai Stevenson. Democratic Governor Allan Shivers and his "Shivercrats" openly backed Eisenhower for president and won his support of their claims to offshore oil lands. Johnson's close ally, silver-haired John Connally, served three terms as governor, 1963–69, linking state government to wealth and industry and looking ever more like a Republican. Symbolically, in 1970 Connally joined the Nixon administration as secretary of the treasury and soon thereafter formally joined the GOP. The Texas establishment was mainstreaming, outgrowing the awkward rough edges of its Old South–wildcatter–cattle baron heritage.

New Mexico traveled the road to modernity more slowly than did its neighbors to the east and west. Here, the large Hispanic community was not a new and submissive minority but an old and proud pillar of the state. Long-time Senator Dennis Chávez personified the old order—of Hispanic ties to the majority Democratic party and of the sometimes corrupt *patron* system of Hispanic rural machines—until his death in 1963. And for many years, powerful Democratic Senator Clinton Anderson, who chaired the key Senate Space and Joint Atomic Energy committees, served as the state's typically western reward seeker in Washington. But New Mexico's many new federal and military types frequently tended to vote Republican; and Edwin Mechem, who sat in the governor's chair for much of the 1950s and 1960s, typified the budding marriage of business and Republicanism in the Southwest.

The sudden transformation of Arizona's political culture might truly be termed a sociopolitical earthquake. Since frontier times, the Democratic party had predominated in the old Arizona of copper, cattle, and cotton. Senator Carl Hayden, who represented the state in Washington from territorial days until 1968 and whose seniority gave him the chairmanship of the powerful Appropriations Committee, personified this tradition. Suddenly, the massive influx of conservative retirees, midwesterners, and high-tech employees overwhelmed the old order. Led by archconservatives like Howard Pyle, Barry Goldwater, and newspaper magnate Eugene Pulliam, the Republican party surged forward in 1952, sending John Rhodes to a position of eventual leadership in the House of Representatives and Goldwater to the Senate, where he would soon emerge as the foremost national spokesman of the Far Right. Arizona would remain

a two-party state, producing national Democratic personalities like the Udall brothers, Stewart and Morris; but the
conservative Republicans, allied with equally conservative
"Pinto" Democrats, henceforth dominated the legislature
and state politics in general.

Across the breadth of the interior West, similar trends
emerged, but in a wide variety of manifestations, with
conservatives gaining ever greater control of the state Republican parties and with liberal and conservative wings
competing for control among the Democrats. Normally,
conservatives of either party, or of both parties working
in coalition, dominated the state governments and legislatures, where they could effect their main priorities of cutting spending and taxes. Court-ordered reapportionments
of the state legislatures in the mid-1960s, aimed at ending
the unfair overrepresentation of rural areas and at forcing
"one-man, one-vote" equity, did little to break these patterns
of conservative rule. Meanwhile, liberal Democrats usually
had much better luck in seeking congressional and senatorial offices, where their philosophy of governmental activism
and spending fit well with the desires of western states to
channel federal dollars in their direction.

These tendencies were especially pronounced in those
two least-developed and most classically "western" states,
Wyoming and Montana. More perhaps than any other western state, Montana exhibited a pattern of "political schizophrenia," of a liberal posture in Washington matched by a
conservative coloration in state government. Thus, backed
by powerful mining and railroad unions and the liberal
Farmers Union, the Democrats almost totally monopolized
Montana's selections to the U.S. Senate, perennially electing
such influential progressives as James Murray, Lee Metcalf,
and Mike Mansfield, the latter serving longer as Senate majority leader (1961–77) than any other man in history. Looking at state government, however, especially at the long
lineage of rock-ribbed conservative governors like J. Hugo
Aronson, Donald Nutter, and Tim Babcock, one encountered almost entirely rightist Republicans and Democrats,

the seemingly natural products of an economy in which big agriculture and extractive industries prevailed.

Some attributed this political split-voting to simple self-interest, sending the big spenders to Washington to garner federal dollars while keeping the parsimonious conservatives at home to keep taxes and expenditures down. Admitting that this explanation is too simple, one must also note that this same pattern occurred elsewhere too, although not usually so strikingly as in Montana. Wyoming also sent liberals to the Senate, such as Joseph O'Mahoney, whom John Gunther once described as "one of the two or three ablest men in Washington," and college professor Gale McGee. But with fewer miners and farmers, Wyoming's political culture was far more basically conservative than Montana's. At times, the Wyoming Stock Growers Association could claim over half the members of the state senate as members; and pragmatic conservatives like Governors Milward Simpson, Cliff Hansen, and Stan Hathaway typified the Wyoming point of view.

Westward, in the intermountain desert states, conservatives and Republicans held greater sway than in the Rockies. In Utah and Idaho, Democrats won a share of the pie, with the usual support of family farmers and mining-railroad labor. Idaho Democrats sent the avowedly radical Glen Taylor to a single Senate term and later elected thoughtful liberal Frank Church to a Senate career that eventually spanned a quarter-century. But the traditional mining-lumber-Democratic region of the northern Idaho panhandle steadily lost influence to the more heavily Mormon and conservative lands of the desert south; and it was these voters, primarily, who elected GOP stalwarts like Governor (later Senator) Len Jordan and the highly capable Robert Smylie, who governed the state well for three terms before going down to defeat in 1966 after pushing through a controversial sales tax.

Utah turned early and sharply to the right after the war. Having seen the New Deal curb its prerogatives, the Mormon Church now reasserted itself, successfully opposing New Deal Democrats Governor Herbert Maw in 1948 and

Senator Elbert Thomas in 1950. By the mid-1950s, roughly 95 percent of Utah legislators and state officeholders were Mormon, although the LDS percentage of the population stood at only 70 percent. But, as Frank Jonas points out, the church's role in Utah politics was more one of heavy influence than of real "control." The state's most famous politician, Secretary of Agriculture Ezra Taft Benson, stood well to the right of most Utahns; and its most colorful performer, Governor J. Bracken Lee, was essentially a non-Mormon maverick who successfully wooed Mormon support. Meanwhile, here as elsewhere, Democrats like liberal Senator Frank Moss and successful, probusiness Governor Calvin Rampton proved their ability to penetrate, at least occasionally, the wall of Republican dominance in Utah.

Party labels usually meant little in Nevada, where conservatism stood less for ideological commitment than for a marriage of politics to the state's marginal livestock and mining industries and its predominant gaming trade. Thus the political "machine" of conservative Democratic Senator Pat McCarran ran things in the postwar era, in consort with developer Norman Biltz. The squat and unlovable McCarran allied with Republicans in Washington and at home, even while snatching federal plums for Nevada from a Congress run by his own party. His sway, and that of his protégés, ended in 1966 with the election of Republican Governor Paul Laxalt, who was more of a party regular but still a big business ally. Laxalt, for instance, welcomed billionaire developer Howard Hughes as "the greatest thing that has happened to Nevada since the Comstock Lode."

No subregion of the West had a longer tradition of Republican party loyalty than did the four-state Great Plains tier reaching from North Dakota to Kansas, an area whose GOP affiliation mainly derived from the pioneers' midwestern roots. Here, as throughout the Republican West, progressive party members of the Teddy Roosevelt–William Allen White variety became harder and harder to find; and hard-core conservatives prevailed. In wide-open South Dakota, where stockmen far outnumbered the small farmers who once had voted Populist, men of the Far Right like Senators Karl Mundt and Francis Case usually represented the prevailing wisdom. The minority liberals were now almost exclusively Democrats. They normally slipped into office by vocalizing discontent with Republican farm policies and by hawking their abilities to garner federal funding, as the outspoken progressive George McGovern did, winning a House seat in 1956, later rising to the Senate, and still later becoming the Democratic party nominee for the presidency in 1972.

Of the four states, North Dakota had, in contrast to its southern neighbor, by far the most progressive history. By the 1950s, though, the radicalism and isolationism of the old Nonpartisan League no longer won the vote. In 1956, in a classic instance of political mainstreaming, the NPL coalesced with the minority Democratic party, making for a real two-party system in the state. The Democrats, able to seat only five members of the state assembly prior to the merger, rose to near parity with the GOP afterward. An ex-NPL man, Quentin Burdick, became the state's first Democratic congressman in 1959 and later a U.S. senator; and Democrats William Guy and Arthur Link held the governor's chair through the 1960s and 1970s. Still, the Republicans continued to control most majority votes, represented by staunch conservatives like Senator Milton Young and Congressman Thomas Kleppe, whom President Nixon later appointed secretary of the interior.

The central plains states of Nebraska and Kansas seemed to lose little of their conservative Republican coloration with the passing years. In Nebraska, the memory of old progressive Senator George Norris faded with a long series of arch-conservative GOP senators, like the longtime team of Carl Curtis and Roman Hruska, whom columnist Jack Anderson once impolitely dubbed "dolts" and "the two worst members of the United States Senate." The state manifested its agrarian conservatism in other ways too. It did not adopt an income tax until 1965 or a modern, general state school funding program before 1967; and its unique unicameral legislature, created in 1934, showed few signs of reformism. Lobbyists, in fact, sat on the floor of the assembly behind the lawmakers. But in truth, Nebraskans seemed about as chary of party conformity as other westerners. For example, the most highly regarded of modern governors, Norbert Tiemann, was a Republican, who was preceded by one conservative Democrat, Frank Morrison, and succeeded by another, J. James Exon.

Perhaps no other state outside New England has been more faithfully Republican nor more firmly wedded to cautious conservatism than Kansas. The state voted Republican for president in every election between 1940 and 1988 except once, in 1964; and its legislature normally had lopsided G O P majorities. Not until 1986 did the "rectangle of righteousness" finally end its statewide ban on liquor-by-the-drink. Yet Kansas conservatism seems more traditional and mellow than the fiercely individualist variety that is common south of its borders. The retirement in 1948 of the old farm rebel Senator Arthur Capper seemed to symbolize the eclipse of a once-virulent Populist-progressive tradition. Not until the emergence in 1969 of the suave and astute Senator Robert Dole did the Sunflower State again produce a congressional leader of major importance. And only with luck did Kansas Democrats ever capture much of the political action, as they did with the father and son gubernatorial team of George and Robert Docking; the Democrats who did, like the Dockings, were usually conservative enough to look like Republicans themselves.

Politically, as in so many other ways, the coastal states seemed to be in the West but not fully *of* it. Here, despite the political power of old and new corporations and the impressive muscle of unions in places like greater Seattle and San Francisco, the surging middle classes of a region traditionally urban and now increasingly suburban set the parameters of politics. In this sense, the West Coast stood at the forefront of a national trend. The consensual middle-class politics held less firmly to old party loyalties, focused more intensely on personalities and issues, and was less confrontational. Here, more than in the interior areas, the two parties competed closely, each with a strong liberal and conservative wing. Whereas moderate-progressive Republicans were rare in the deserts and mountains, they seemed to thrive on the Coast, a phenomenon that made the humid Pacific Rim states sometimes look more like the Northeast politically than like the neighboring intermountain area.

Of the three coastal states, Washington had, at least in the recent past, the most liberal tradition. Franklin Roosevelt's political wizard James Farley had once facetiously called it the "Soviet of Washington" because of the far left leanings of certain of its labor-based congressmen. After the war, the radical Washington Commonwealth Federation, also rooted in leftist unions, drew notoriety as an alleged "Communist front" organization. But this isolated radicalism was misleading. Spreading suburbs in booming Seattle-Tacoma, combined with the agrarian conservatism of Spokane and eastern Washington, mellowed and balanced the political order as the years passed. Washington drew the most attention for its progressive Republican governors, like Arthur Langlie and the highly respected Dan Evans, and for its entrenched and powerful Democratic team of Senators Warren Magnuson and Henry "Scoop" Jackson, each of whom sometimes received the label of "Senator from Boeing."

Oregon, a less industrialized and even more middle-class state than Washington, had a long history of progressive Republican prevalence. However, the postwar wave of reaction allowed staunch conservatives like Douglas McKay and Guy Cordon to capture the GOP. This drove the tempestuous, iron-willed maverick Senator Wayne Morse to change parties; and as a Democrat, Morse would continue to go his own way for many years, ending up as a formidable critic of the Vietnam War. The GOP move to the right also allowed the anemic Oregon Democratic Party to resurrect, electing writer Richard Neuberger as senator and Edith Green as the state's first Democrat in Congress in a decade. Soon, however, the pendulum of tradition began to swing back, heralded by attractive, young liberal Republican Mark Hatfield, who captured the governorship in 1958 and a Senate seat in

1966. In 1968, another liberal Republican, Bob Packwood, defeated Morse to join Hatfield in the Senate.

Of the three Pacific States, imperial California best exemplified the postwar politics of middle-class consensus and disregard of party lines. Progressive GOP Governor Earl Warren seemed to dominate the politics of both parties during his two-plus terms (1943–53), until President Eisenhower appointed him chief justice of the United States, from which post he would play a significant role in the shaping of national affairs. Warren's successor, Goodwin Knight, carried on the same progressive-bipartisan policies; but by now, the GOP right wing chafed at it. In addition, the politics of disregarding party lines received a fatal blow when the state finally ended its bizarre system of ballot cross-filing, which had allowed incumbents like Warren the advantage of running as the candidate of more than one party at the same time. In the key election of 1958, rightist Republican ex-Senator William Knowland ran on an antilabor platform against liberal Democrat Edmund "Pat" Brown in an exceptionally bitter campaign. Clearly, the era of consensual politics was coming to an end.

Riding the tide of national liberal resurgence, Brown won; and during his two gubernatorial terms, he pressed through the legislature a sweeping program of reform, featuring higher taxes, massive water development, and increased welfare and unemployment and workmen's compensation benefits. Meanwhile, California's congressional representatives, such as Republican Senator Thomas Kuchel and Democratic Senator Clair Engle, tended toward progressivism. By the later 1960s, however, the liberal tide had begun to ebb. In 1966, Brown lost a third-term bid to the archconservative actor Ronald Reagan. As governor, Reagan quickly won a wider national following among conservatives by defying and taunting radical students on the state's campuses, slashing at welfare budgets, and calling for reduced state spending. That his rhetoric often contrasted with his actions seemed to make little difference to the voters. Nor, apparently, did the fact that, as Garry Wills comments, "the candidate who had run against big spenders quickly became the governor who asked for and got the highest tax raise in the history of California (or any other state)." In the case of Governor Reagan, as in so many others, the California style of personalized, show-business politics seemed to cast an imposing shadow eastward across the nation.

Among all the states of the West, none so well exemplified all of these scattered trends as did centrally located Colorado. Here, the Democrats agonized over the decline in their bulue-collar base in Pueblo and in the state's coal-iron-Hispanic southcentral region, whereas the Republicans grew ever stronger in the sprawling suburbs from Colorado Springs north to Boulder. Actually, Colorado seemed reasonably well balanced politically, with a growing slant to the right. In Colorado, as elsewhere throughout the region, the picking of federal plums usually seemed more important that ideology or party. From his powerful post as chairman of the House Interior Committee, Congressman Wayne Aspinall channeled many millions in water and other appropriations to his home state. Colorado's two equally conservative senators, Democrat "Big Ed" Johnson and Republican Eugene Millikin, worked together so closely in securing federal funds for their state that people spoke of their "practically incestuous" relationship.

So, in one sense, the fast-changing western states of the postwar era were most noteworthy for their diversity, from the slow-moving Old West regions of the northern plains and Rockies to the tumultuous, urban Southwest. In other ways—their shedding of postfrontier, confrontational politics and their gravitation toward a conservatism based on suburban and middle-class values—they seemed more alike. This latter conservative trend would become much more pronounced during the mid-1970s and after.

THE CONTEMPORARY ERA

From this brief vantage, it might be argued that the contemporary era of western history began with the big energy crisis of 1973–74. The prospect of a massive and long-term energy boom, coming atop an already surging economy, was pleasing to some westerners and distressing to others. Thus, it is less incongruous than it might seem at first glance that the hectic 1970s should produce matching western crusades that marched in different directions, toward environmental and wilderness preservation on the one hand and toward opening up federally owned lands for wholesale development on the other.

The increasingly powerful environmentalist-wilderness preservation crusade, which budded in the 1950s and 1960s and then surged in the 1970s, was not unique to the West; but it focused here, where most of the lands in question lay. Building on earlier legislation, like the Wilderness Act of 1964, new programs like the Roadless Area Review and Evaluation Acts of 1971–73 and 1977–79 (RARE I & II) looked beyond the national forests, with their multiple-use harvests of resources, toward a new National Wilderness Preservation System to be maintained forever pristine. These marked signal victories for environmentalist groups like the Sierra Club and the Friends of the Earth; but, since both the Wilderness Act and the RARE laws terminated all mineral exploration on these lands after 1983, they seemed unrealistic to western developers and to others worried about growing American reliance on foreign imports. In 1984, Congress set aside 8.6 million acres of new wilderness; but, under the review process set forth by the Federal Land Policy and Management Act of 1976, 25 million acres of land contained in "Wilderness Study Areas" remained under consideration for future set-asides. Thus, the controversy continued through the late 1980s.

Meanwhile, the environmentalist movement advanced on many fronts, state and local as well as national. As early as the late 1950s, San Franciscans set a new precedent by rebelling against the ugly monstrosity of the Embarcadero Freeway. Other Californians won major victories in securing the creation of Redwood National Park in 1968 (even as Governor Reagan commented that seeing one redwood was as good as seeing them all) and in adding the lovely Mineral King Valley to Sequoia National Park.

Fearing "Californication" from the south, Oregon became an ecological pacesetter. The popular governor Tom McCall advised outsiders to visit but "for God's sake, don't move here"; and the legislature enacted some of the toughest water quality and litter laws in the nation. Washington Governor John Spellman shocked the region by blocking construction of the vaunted Northern Tier oil pipeline when he refused to allow the siting of its terminal at Port Angeles. In Montana, unlikely alliances of young environmentalists and conservative ranchers joined hands in organizations like the Northern Plains Resource Council to oppose unrestrained coal mining. Colorado proved to be an ecological cockpit, where environmentalists and developers, evenly matched, fought head-to-head. Led by flamboyant Governor-to-be Richard Lamm, Coloradans rejected the opportunity to host the 1976 Winter Olympics. Yet, when Lamm became governor, he disappointed some of his ecologist friends by backing federal and other developers.

The heated arguments between developers and conservationists seemed, in a sense, to be a reenactment of the first conservationist crusade, back in the Progressive Era. This time, however, the "beneficial use"–Pinchot types were less the clear winners than before; this time, the preservationist heirs of Muir emerged far more successful, in part because affluent Americans saw the vanishing wilderness as something they needed and could afford. But just as had occurred sixty years earlier, many westerners, especially conservatives and those miners, cattlemen, and others whose livelihood depended on cheap access to federal lands, reacted angrily to such extensions of federal tutelage. After all, three "superbureaus"—the Bureau of Land Management, the U. S. Forest Service, and the National Park Service—between them controlled more than 350 million acres of the West, "virtually as much of the West," in the words of Governor Richard Lamm and Michael McCarthy, "as the West owns of itself." Among all the states east of the Rocky Mountain tier, by contrast,

Richard Lamm, shortly before his election to the governorship of Colorado, strides along a Colorado highway, February, 1974. Courtesy of the *Denver Post*.

the federal government owned no more than 12 percent of any of them.

The most extreme rendering of antigovernment ownership protest emerged in the form of a 1979 Nevada law demanding the cession of 49 million federally owned acres to the state, a state where Uncle Sam owned 86 percent of the land. Other states like Utah, Wyoming, and New Mexico soon joined the fray, which became popularly known as the "Sagebrush Rebellion"; and that fall, Senator Orrin Hatch of Utah introduced legislation to transfer 544 million acres in thirteen western states from federal to home-state hands. This strident antifederalism touched a responsive chord out West. Presidential candidate Ronald Reagan endorsed the cause, stating, "Count me in as a rebel." But, in fact, such a wholesale transfer of public lands to individual states, which lacked the means to maintain them and would presumably sell them off cheaply to private owners, was an irresponsible idea. Many of the Sagebrush Rebels knew as much and simply trumpeted the cause to voice their resentment at federal constraints. Quite accurately, Governor Bruce Babbitt of Arizona dismissed the crusade as one meant to "sell off the land into private ownership, lock the gates, post the no-trespassing sign, and proceed to use and abuse the land."

The Sagebrush Rebels and the "eco-freaks" simply represented the two extremes of the historic dialogue between developers and preservationists that had begun nearly a century ago and promises to extend far into the future. Most westerners occupied positions between these two extremes and identified other issues, mostly national and global, of greater importance to them than were those of the environment and the regional economy. Still, it remains true today, as it did seventy years ago, that the key unifying theme among the eleven states of the Far West is the simple fact that Uncle Sam owns one-third of their land mass. This is not true of the six plains states of the West, however, where almost all of the public lands were long ago alienated. Nebraska, for instance, is only 1.4 percent federally owned.

This theme of federal custodianship ran prominently through the West's relationship with the presidential administrations of Democrat Jimmy Carter (1977–81) and Republican Ronald Reagan (1981–89). Despite his appointment of the able Cecil Andrus, the former and future governor of Idaho, as Interior secretary, Carter quickly demonstrated his political naïveté about the West in 1977 by informing Congress of his intent to cut funding for eighteen western reclamation projects with a total price tag of $5.1 billion. Carter was quite correct in denouncing these projects as "unsupportable" examples of log-rolling politics, produced by political alliances between the Reclamation Bureau and Army Engineers and western politicians and business interests. But he completely underestimated the extent to which these alliances dominated the West's ties to Washington. Liberals and conservatives, Democrats and Republicans alike—even environmentalist critics of the water pork barrel such as Governors Lamm of Colorado and Jerry Brown of California—attacked the Carter "hit list"; and by late 1980, the administration had beat a retreat, approving funding of all but four of the targeted projects.

President Carter stirred up another western hornets' nest in 1979–80 when he announced his controversial plan to base the gargantuan "MX" (Missile Experimental) system in the Great Basin states of Nevada and Utah. This incredible proposal envisioned blanketing thirty to forty-six thousand square miles of desert, an area the size of Pennsylvania, with underground tunnels through which rails would carry a fleet of nuclear missiles so that the Soviets could never be sure where the launchers would be at any specific moment. Its cost came to a mind-numbing $100 billion; and it threatened to engulf the small desert towns with up to 160,000 new inhabitants and to draw off precious groundwater reserves.

In the past, the West had welcomed, or at least scarcely resisted, the staging of nuclear weapons on its wide-open expanses. Few had protested the more than one hundred above-ground nuclear explosions set off at the Nevada Test Site from 1951 to 1963 or the basing of Minuteman missiles in Montana, Wyoming, and North Dakota during the early 1960s. North Dakotans, in fact, joked that if their state should become an independent nation, it would be the world's third-greatest nuclear power. This time, however, environmentally conscious Great Basin folks reacted sharply. Even the conservative and nationalistic Mormon Church opposed the threats to the land and to the fragile social order; and Utahns now realized that horrendous cancer rates in the southern portion of their state probably stemmed in part from radiation fallout from east-drifting clouds produced by long-ago Nevada testing. In 1981 the Reagan administration announced its withdrawal of the plan, and by 1986 the MX missiles were simply being placed in older silos.

President Carter obviously had few ties to the West. He won election in 1976 carrying only one state in the region, Texas; and in his losing effort of 1980, he lost every western state to the landslide winner, Republican Ronald Reagan. The Reagan landslide seemed to mark the cresting wave of neoconservatism in America. Out West, for instance, the Republican tidal wave of 1980 spelled defeat for some of the region's most liberal Democrats, such as Senators Frank Church of Idaho and George McGovern of South Dakota. When Reagan stood for reelection in 1984, he once again swept the West, as he nearly did the entire country.

The Reagan administration came to office in 1981 with a clear, conservative agenda for the resource-rich West: removing the price controls that Carter had earlier imposed on oil and gas (which was immediately done), easing restrictions on oil leases and offshore drilling, cutting back such regulatory bodies as the Environmental Protection Agency, and generally opening up western resources to development. In addition to his appointments of westerners to top-level positions in his administration, like Vice-President George Bush of Texas and Attorney General William French Smith and Defense Secretary Caspar Weinberger of California, Reagan's appointments to lesser positions clearly reflected these priorities.

For secretary of the interior, Reagan chose the vehemently outspoken James Watt, director of the rightist Mountain States Legal Foundation that Colorado brewing millionaire Joseph Coors bankrolled. The Reagan-Watt team demonstrated their proclivities by appointing Colorado rancher-legislator Robert Burford, an archcritic of the whole purpose of the Bureau of Land Management, to head that very organization. Similarly, another Colorado legislator, Anne Gorsuch, received the directorship of the EPA, with the clear intent that she would call off its environmental watchdogs. The director of the Office of Surface Mining, which oversaw the reclamation of strip-mined lands, was an appointee from Indiana who had long argued that such regulations were unconstitutional. It seemed at first that the public resources and lands of the West might indeed be "privatized" along the lines advocated by the Sagebrush Rebels. Secretary Watt, for instance, leased northern plains coal lands at ridiculously low prices to private companies. But in the end, it did not quite happen. In 1983, Anne Gorsuch Burford was forced from office in scandal; and Watt resigned amid heavy criticism and controversy. As before, developers and conservationists continued to checkmate one another.

The tide of conservatism flowed strongly at the state and local levels of government too. In California, Reagan was succeeded as governor by Edmund G. (Jerry) Brown, Jr., the Democratic son of the former liberal governor. Once in office and later as a presidential contender, however, Brown looked and acted more like a conservative, vetoing large legislative appropriations, slashing budgets, and criticizing the state bureaucracy. In 1983, the governorship of this largest of states returned to the custody of a traditionally conservative Republican, George Deukmejian. In 1978, California had captured national attention by enacting via popular vote the controversial Proposition Thirteen, which mandated a whopping 57 percent slash in state property taxes, eliminating the state's treasury surplus and forcing major cutbacks in services. Proposition Thirteen really amounted to a conservative redistribution of the tax burden, in favor of the wealthy. It looked for a time as if this California tax revolt might sweep the nation. But it did not; similar measures failed, for instance, in Nebraska, Oregon, and Colorado, largely because these and other states simply lacked the huge treasury surpluses that California had accumulated.

With less fanfare, Texas, the region's other pacesetter, also seemed headed rightward. Old-style progressive Democrats still appeared on the scene, most notably Fort Worth Congressman Jim Wright, who rose to become House majority leader in 1976 and House Speaker in 1987; but both parties, particularly the fast-rising Republicans, seemed more wedded to the mushrooming Texas megabusiness community. Symbolically, in 1970 wealthy and probusiness Lloyd Bentsen defeated the old Populist-liberal Ralph Yarborough in the Democratic primary, beginning a long and influential Senate career that led to his nomination for the vice-presidency in 1988. William Clements became the first Republican governor of Texas in one hundred years in 1979. As the nation watched in awe, he lost the position to Democrat

Mark White in 1982, despite his campaign expenditure of $12 million, and then regained it in 1986. Meanwhile, farther to the right, the pro-Reagan Democratic ("Boll Weevil") Congressman Phil Gramm abandoned his party to become a GOP senator. Clearly, Texas, that crossroads South-West colossus, had become a two-party state.

Interior states that had, prior to the 1970s, leaned to the right, now leaned even farther. Utah, for instance, had for years balanced its Senate seats between a liberal Democrat and a conservative Republican. Now, both seats fell to outspoken GOP conservatives, Jake Garn and Orrin Hatch. Wyoming did the same thing, retiring liberal Senator Gale McGee in 1976 in favor of rightist Republican Malcolm Wallop, who allied first with fellow conservative Cliff Hansen and then with equally conservative Alan Simpson to form one of the most right-wing Senate teams in Washington. In Idaho, similarly, the archconservative Steve Symms joined James McClure in 1981 to form a Republican Senate tandem, allied with a congressional twosome that has not seen a Democratic face since 1967.

In Nevada, close Reagan associate Senator Paul Laxalt stood about as far to the right as did any prominent western public figure. Political alliances between the Teamsters Union, organized crime, and state politicians drew frequent attention. In New Mexico, as in Texas, Republicans continued to make inroads into what had been a Democrat-dominated political structure, as witnessed in the defeat of the old Democratic warhorse Senator Joseph Montoya by Republican astronaut Harrison Schmitt in 1976 and in the rise of GOP Senator Pete Domenici to the powerful position of chairman of the Senate Budget Committee in 1981.

In many cases, those western Democrats who bucked the conservative Republican trend did so by trimming their progressive sails. Colorado Senator Gary Hart survived the 1980 onslaught by distancing himself from the liberal bent of the national Democratic party and from positions he had earlier embraced, a course that launched him on a nearly successful quest for his party's presidential nomination in 1984 and on a similar, scandal-ridden quest for the 1988 nomination. Widely respected Oklahoma Congressman James Jones, who rose to the chairmanship of the House Budget Committee in 1981, attempted to move his fellow Democrats away from free-spending liberalism while stopping well short of the "Boll Weevil" members of his party who allied with the Reagan administration. Democratic Governors Cal Rampton and Scott Matheson of Utah pragmatically allied themselves with the state business community while maintaining the favor of their party's rank and file.

In the final analysis, however, western politics of the 1970s and 1980s were far too complex and multifaceted to be characterized as simply on a steadily rightward incline. In California, despite the conservative trend obvious in the statehouse, liberal Democratic Senator Alan Cranston, who was elected in 1969 and who became party whip in 1976, continued to hold onto his seat through the years. In Montana, both U.S. Senate seats remained in Democratic hands, those of Max Baucus and John Melcher, until Melcher's defeat in 1988. Despite Republican inroads, New Mexico continued to elect Democratic as well as Republican governors and resisted enactment of a right-to-work law. Conservative Nebraska replaced the old Curtis-Hruska Senate team with a pair of Democrats, Edward Zorinsky and J. James Exon, and in 1982 shocked everyone by voting to restrict corporate farming in the state. Republican Arizona still elected competent Democrats like Congressman Mo Udall, Senator Dennis DeConcini, and Governor Bruce Babbitt; and the travails of Governor Evan Mecham indicated that even the most conservative communities rebelled at true zaniness. And on the West Coast, progressive Republicans continued to demonstrate their vitality. For a time, Washington replaced the venerable Senate team of Magnuson and Jackson with a pair of moderate Republicans, Slade Gorton and Dan Evans; and Oregon maintained the veteran, progressive GOP Senate team of Mark Hatfield and Bob Packwood.

In one sense, especially, the western political order was enriched during the 1970s and 1980s: more and more, the total population, including women and minorities, became directly involved in electoral politics. Here, the West not only followed but in many ways led national trends. By the 1980s, women occupied up to one-third of the seats in the Colorado legislature. Increasingly, females captured the highest offices in the region: the mayoralties of San Francisco, Houston, and Dallas, held respectively by Dianne Feinstein, Kathy Whitmire, and Annette Strauss; the governor's chairs of Washington and Nebraska, won respectively by Dixy Lee Ray and Kay Orr; such prominent congressional posts as those garnered by Barbara Jordan of Texas and Pat Schroeder of Colorado. For a time, Senator Nancy Landon Kassebaum of Kansas served as the only female member of that august body.

The West's largest ethnic groups also asserted their political power with greater success during the years after 1972. Even beyond New Mexico, where they had long held political sway, Hispanic Americans now captured impressive political prizes. By 1985, more than three thousand Hispanics held political offices in America, most of them in the West, including the mayoralties of San Antonio and Denver, the governorship of New Mexico, and thirteen seats in Congress. In California, Japanese Americans proved their full entry into the mainstream with the Senate victory of conservative Republican S. I. Hayakawa and the rise to eminence of the highly respected Democratic Congressman Norman Mineta. The large black population of California elected powerful congressmen such as Ron Dellums and Augustus Hawkins. In addition, black Californians had the satisfaction of seeing Tom Bradley win one reelection after another as mayor of Los Angeles and crafty Willie Brown exercise real power as speaker of the state assembly. Although many political problems remained unsolved, no one could dispute the real broadening of political power to those who had hitherto been denied it.

Speaking generally, western politics of the contemporary era seemed, as was traditional, to be more open and unstructured than those of the nation at large. Aside from California, with its professionalized legislature and staffs, the West was otherwise noted for its "citizen legislators," highly accessible to constituents and notoriously prone to wrangling, special sessions, and party disunity. In contrast to other regions—and reminiscent of frontier territorial times—the states of the West often juxtaposed legislatures under the control of one party with governors from the other party, governors who, in addition, were in many states still closely limited in their authority by the state constitutions. Still, in the final analysis, it remained as difficult as ever to generalize about such a region of diversities. The West Coast and the Rockies continued to support strong environmentalist movements, whereas the arid lands of the interior pressed, more often than not, for development at almost any price. Similarly, though unions continued to lag in influence, especially in the interior states, they remained relatively strong on the Coast, as did other liberal forces.

So, as the final decade of the twentieth century approached, the West was as politically enigmatic as ever, in a sense appearing to lead a national trend toward the right, in another sense seeming to lead a national trend toward integrating all of America's cosmopolitan populations into the political process and democratizing that process as well. The old political order of western "colonial" subservience to the East, and of confrontational politics between exploitative corporations and their allies on the one side and downtrodden farmers and workers on the other, now seemed quaintly historical. The West appeared to be the least tradition-bound of American regions. And the new order, of suburbs and of Sunbelt cities and of the politics of energy, agriculture, and the unending quest for federal dollars, seemed likely to persist far into the future.

Chapter Eight

A New Western Generation,
Mid-1980s–2005

A ll four are westerners. They come from different
subregions, illustrating the West's racial-ethnic, social, and economic diversity. In their varied backgrounds they epitomize major ingredients of the late twentieth-century West. The lives and careers of Dolores Huerta,
Bill Gates, Ben Nighthorse Campbell, and Nancy Landon
Kassebaum also demonstrate once again how much change
and complexity are hallmarks of the modern American West.

Dolores Huerta was born into a Hispanic migrant worker
family in New Mexico in 1930. Successful as a high school
and college student and spurred on by palpable ambition,
she rose above her hardscrabble beginnings. In the 1950s she
began registering Chicano/a voters, and in the 1960s she became a labor organizer and activist César Chávez's most valued colleague. Despite her humble origins and the challenges of mothering eleven children, Huerta achieved notoriety
as the country's best-known Chicana. Her career illustrates
the rising importance of a very small group of women ethnic
leaders in the West in the closing decades of the twentieth
century.

Bill Gates also rose to quick prominence in another sub-
region of the recent West, but by a much different path.
Born in 1955 into an upper-middle-class family in the Pacific
Northwest, Gates gained a superb education in public and

Dolores Huerta served as an organizer and negotiator for Chicano/a farmworkers from the 1950s forward. As a notable woman minority leader, she was an exception in the West. Courtesy Walter P. Reuther Library, Wayne State University.

private schools in the state of Washington before attending Harvard. Early on an addict of technology, he was already experimenting with computers as a teenager and even more so as an undergraduate. Dropping out of Harvard but unable to start up a computer company in New Mexico, he and his computer-nerd buddy Paul Allen retreated to Seattle, their hometown, linked up with IBM, garnered funds for their own company, and were on their way with the hugely successful Microsoft Corporation. Said to be the richest man in the world in 2000, Gates and his extraordinary career reflect the sudden rise of "footloose" or "sunrise" (electronic, computer, and other high-tech) industries and a new economic order in the post-1960s West.

The career of Native American politician Ben Nighthorse Campbell illustrates other facets of a complex modern West. Born in California in 1933 to a Native American father (Northern Cheyenne) and a Portuguese immigrant mother, Campbell was a troubled youth. Spending time in an orphanage, he dropped out of high school and joined the air force. After returning from the service, he graduated from San Jose State College (now University), moved to Colorado, and was a self-employed jewelry designer and trainer of quarter horses. Elected to the Colorado legislature, he served five years before being elevated to the U.S. Senate in 1992. For part of his twelve years in the Senate (1993–2005), he was the only senator of Indian heritage and the first to serve there in sixty years. In his path-breaking political role as one of the few American Indian members of the U.S. Congress, Campbell became known for his legislative efforts in behalf of Native American water rights, public lands and natural resource management, and wilderness protection. In the 1990s, while serving as a grand marshal of the Tournament of Roses, he reminded everyone involved that "we were here first." He also told fellow Natives, "We need to participate and be able to tell our story; that simply can't be done if we drop out of the system." Unusual in his national political position, Nighthorse Campbell faced and overcame many of the barriers that western minority groups continued to battle and sometimes surmounted in the past generation.

The career of Nancy Landon Kassebaum (Baker) both substantiates recent western political trends and reveals path-breaking developments. Born in 1932 as the daughter of Alf Landon, the former Kansas governor and Republican presidential candidate in 1936, Kassebaum—like her father and similar to most Kansas politicians and many wheat-belt voters—supported most Republican and conservative measures in her first years in the U.S. Senate (1978–97). But in other ways her role as western politician broke with tradition. At the time of her election in 1978 she was the only woman in the Senate. She also voted for the Equal Rights Amendment. When the Republicans gained a Senate majority in 1980, Kassebaum was named to the prestigious Senate Foreign Relations Committee. In 1984 and 1990 she won reelection to the Senate but chose not to be a candidate in 1996. In her political allegiances Kassebaum represented the swing to the right that characterized western politics in the post-1960s, but she also represented a newer trend by being one of the first women elected to the Senate and being twice reelected.

As the lives of these four emblematic westerners reveal, persistent change and increasing complexity marked the recent American West. In the two generations following the early 1960s, when California surpassed New York as the most populous state, the West became the nation's most powerful region. A noticeable Western Tilt, booming California, and an expanding Sunbelt were parts of this mushrooming West. From Texas to California, from California to the Canadian border, and in scattered parts of the inland region, the West experienced floods of incoming population. These rising tides of immigrants, from abroad and from the U.S. East and South, washed over and reshaped the social makeup of the region at the end of the twentieth century.

Equally powerful forces of economic change pulsated through the West. While the importance of an older, natural resource–based economy diminished and agriculture changed directions, new footloose technical and sunrise computer industries and amenity tourism expanded in significance. Uncle Sam's continued Cold War expenditures and other government spending, as well as new multinational trade connections, kept the western economy humming.

As western social and economic patterns changed and became more complex, politics in the West swung right. Before 1970, western politicians such as Barry Goldwater and Richard Nixon epitomized these conservative moves. In the next decades Ronald Reagan and George W. Bush captained this Republican triumph from California and Texas to the White House. North from Texas and across much of the interior West, westerners had joined the red-state parade. Only the Pacific Coast states and occasionally New Mexico remained in the blue-state Democratic column.

These social, economic, and political shifts helped to introduce new cultural changes in the modern West. Trends in western literature, historiography, and films reveal that westerners were increasingly uncertain and ambivalent about the changes and expanding complexities that enveloped them. Novelists, historians, and filmmakers increasingly depicted a "New Gray West," overflowing with ambiguities and tensions. Novelists such as Wallace Stegner, Larry McMurtry, Joan Didion, and Cormac McCarthy avoided the lone, strong heroes of the frontier past to portray instead protagonists riven with flaws and uncertainties. Historians, especially the New Western historians, also saw a western past shadowed by racism, environmental problems, and pioneer cupidity. Simultaneously, women and ethnic writers and historians enlarged the western literary and historical landscapes with new kinds of heroines, settings, and autobiographical stories.

URBAN AND RURAL WESTS

Major western social patterns established in the early 1980s persisted over the next two decades. Expanding western urban areas, shrinking rural populations, mounting numbers of minorities, and large challenges to western families all continued. But exceptions appeared within these general patterns, and even a few countertrends surfaced. Above all, though, the American West continued to be a destination region. Americans from other U.S. regions and immigrants from all corners of the globe came to the West, especially to its cities.

Numbers frame several of the most important recent stories about western states. In the nineteenth century many Americans went east to seek their fortunes, but increasingly in the twentieth century they ventured west for jobs and brighter futures. Those dreams often led newcomers to areas

Population of Western States, 1980–2005

State	1980	1990	2000	2005 (est.)
Arizona	2,716,546	3,665,339	5,130,632	5,953,007
California	23,667,764	29,811,427	33,871,648	36,154,147
Colorado	2,889,735	3,294,473	4,301,261	4,663,295
Idaho	944,127	1,006,734	1,293,953	1,429,367
Kansas	2,364,236	2,477,588	2,688,418	2,748,172
Montana	786,690	799,065	902,195	934,737
Nebraska	1,569,825	1,578,417	1,711,263	1,758,163
Nevada	800,508	1,201,675	1,998,257	2,412,301
New Mexico	1,303,302	1,515,069	1,819,046	1,925,985
North Dakota	652,717	638,800	642,200	634,605
Oklahoma	3,025,487	3,145,576	3,450,654	3,543,442
Oregon	2,633,156	2,842,337	3,421,399	3,638,871
South Dakota	690,768	696,004	754,844	774,883
Texas	14,225,513	16,986,335	20,851,820	22,928,508
Utah	1,416,037	1,722,850	2,233,169	2,490,334
Washington	4,132,353	4,866,669	5,894,121	6,291,899
Wyoming	469,557	453,589	493,782	508,798
U. S.	226,542,199	248,790,925	281,421,906	296,507,061

Sources: U. S. Census Bureau, decennial census of population, 1900 to 2000 corrected;
U. S Census, Annual Estimates of the Population.

already experiencing demographic expansion. After 1980 the large-population states of California and Texas continued to outgrow other western areas. California expanded from 23.7 million residents in 1980, to 29.8 in 1990, and 33.9 in 2000. At the opening of the twenty-first century more persons lived in California than resided in the entire United States at the beginning of the Civil War (1861). Texas experienced similar growth, from 14.2 million residents in 1980, to 17 million in 1990, and 20.9 million in 2000. Only Florida grew as rapidly. By 2000 the combined populations of California and Texas made up nearly 20 percent of the country's total number of inhabitants. More telling, of the 91.4 million residents in the West in 2000, nearly 60 percent lived in California or Texas, more than 37 percent in California alone. During these same two decades the population of Nevada doubled and Arizona's nearly so.

At the other end of the demographic spectrum, a few western states experienced much less growth or even lost population. South Dakota, Nebraska, Kansas, Oklahoma, and Wyoming expanded in small numbers. North Dakota's population dropped, from 652,717 in 1980 to 642,200 in 2000. These figures substantiate headline stories about the West since World War II: the growing western areas lay along the southwestern and Pacific rims of the region. With a few exceptions, to be noted, the inland West (chiefly the north-central and east-central states) lagged behind in the western demographic competitions.

Not surprisingly, metropolitan areas in the growing states expanded the most. Las Vegas was the extraordinary example. Gaining large numbers of immigrants—from abroad and from within the United States—to work in its gaming and service industries, Las Vegas more than doubled its residents between 1980 and 2000. Southwestern cities such as Austin and Phoenix nearly doubled in population, and Albuquerque, Tucson, and San Diego gained nearly 50 percent in these two decades. The interior cities of Boise, Colorado Springs, and Sioux Falls jumped at least 50 percent. Of the major western urban areas, only Kansas City, Kansas, lost population. Seen in a national perspective, this growth tells a larger, comparative story. In the half century between the 1940s and 1990s well more than half of the nation's fastest-growing cities were in the West. In those decades 29 percent of all U.S. population expansion came in the West's twelve largest urban areas, with 36 percent in the 1980s alone. What historian Carl Abbott, the country's leading expert on western cities, argued in the early 1990s was still true nearly fifteen years later: "western cities . . . organize the region's vast spaces and connect them to the even larger sphere of the world economy," and "urban growth [in the West] since 1940 has constituted a distinct era in which Western cities have become national and even international pacesetters."

Population of Major Western Cities, 1980–2005

City	1980	1990	2000	2005 (est.)
Albuquerque	332,920	386,988	448,607	494,236
Austin	345,890	494,290	656,562	690,252
Billings	66,818	81,469	89,847	98,721
Boise	102,249	135,150	185,787	193,161
Cheyenne	47,283	50,209	53,011	55,731
Colorado Springs	215,105	283,112	360,890	369,815
Dallas	904,599	1,006,646	1,188,580	1,213,825
Denver	492,686	467,549	554,636	557,917
El Paso	425,259	515,652	563,662	598,590
Fargo	61,383	74,195	90,599	90,672
Fort Worth	385,164	448,181	534,694	624,067
Houston	1,595,138	1,697,873	1,953,631	2,016,582
Kansas City (KS)	161,148	151,344	146,866	144,210
Las Vegas	164,674	259,834	478,434	545,147
Los Angeles	2,968,528	3,485,499	3,694,820	3,844,829
Oakland	339,337	399,886	399,484	395,274
Oklahoma City	404,014	444,605	506,132	531,324
Omaha	313,939	357,807	390,007	414,521
Phoenix	789,704	988,983	1,321,045	1,461,575
Portland	368,149	486,083	529,121	533,427
Salt Lake City	163,034	159,952	181,743	178,097
San Antonio	785,940	997,434	1,144,646	1,256,509
San Diego	875,538	1,110,549	1,223,400	1,255,540
San Francisco	678,974	723,959	776,733	739,426
San Jose	629,400	783,324	894,943	912,332
Seattle	493,846	516,332	563,374	573,911
Sioux Falls	81,343	101,461	123,975	139,517
Spokane	171,300	178,120	195,629	196,818
Tucson	330,537	417,139	486,699	515,526
Tulsa	360,919	367,167	393,049	382,457
Wichita	279,838	308,652	344,284	354,865

Sources: U.S. Census Bureau, decennial census of population, 1900 to 2000, corrected.
Also, http://www.census.gov/popest/cities/. Population for central cities rather than metropolitan areas of core, suburbs, and linked surrounding areas.

Expanding urban centers increasingly dominated the West, but they were not the whole story. Enormous expanses of the West remained thinly populated or dotted with small towns; they were the rural West. During the twentieth century in large sections of the Great Plains, Rockies, Southwest, and noncoastal areas of the far-western states, farms, ranches, and uncultivated areas spread over much of the land. These agricultural, wilderness, and desert landscapes continue as important if less-noticed segments of the most recent American West.

A discussion of each of the nearly eight hundred counties in the American West would alienate even the most devoted fans of things western, but a handful or two of generalizations about the rural sections of the West are useful. In the two generations following 1965, farm populations dwindled year by year, with individual farms and small ranches gobbled up by conglomerate agribusinesses.

The takeover by sprawling agricultural conglomerates set off a series of shrinking actions. When the smaller farm units were replaced by highly mechanized operations, fewer farm or ranch workers were needed. A reduction in necessary agricultural workers undercut the demand for family organizations, health clinics, and schools, thereby squeezing these institutions and reducing the tax base of most farm areas. As some counties in Kansas, Oklahoma, and west Texas became depleted, towns disappeared. More than enough young people were born in these shrinking rural areas to supply the workforce, but as individual farms and ranches diminished in number so did the jobs, sending increasing numbers off to cities and other areas to find employment. Statistics tell a darkening story. In 1940 one in four Americans were part of the farm population; by the late 1980s the farm population had plummeted to less than 2 percent of the U.S. total. In the early twenty-first century farm families made up even less of the national population. The general depopulation of western rural sections seemed to parallel the steady expansion of the region's metropolitan areas.

The density of population also varied throughout the

West. Generally, throughout the twentieth century the West was less densely populated than the East. Only California ranked among the ten states with more than two hundred persons per square mile. Besides California, only Texas and Washington hosted more than seventy-five persons per square mile; all the other western states had less than seventy-five. In fact, in 2000 South Dakota, North Dakota, Montana, and Wyoming featured less than ten persons per square mile. Sometimes these clustered urban areas, spread out populations, and lightly populated expanses gave visitors a false impression that the West was primarily a region of unsettled rural areas.

The populations of western rural areas on the edges of expanding urban areas—but not yet a part of them—also grew rapidly in the 1980s and 1990s. Western residents as well as newcomers to the region, perhaps dreaming of "having a piece of land out in the country," seemed driven to remain close to urban amenities while avoiding central cities and growing suburbs. Areas in the northern West proximate to Denver and Colorado Springs, Marin County in the Bay Area, Seattle, and Bozeman, Montana, for example, swelled with these in-the-country-but-near-the-city residents, blurring distinctions between urban and rural Wests. If they quickly developed all the requisite institutions of cities— businesses, schools, hospitals and clinics, and recreational facilities—they were soon dubbed "edge cities" and no longer part of the rural West.

Some sections of the northern Plains experienced the bleakest trends defining the rural West. In the early 1990s counties in western North Dakota suffered more than a 10 percent dip in population. In the mid-1990s a national moving company reported that two persons were leaving North Dakota for each newcomer. Available young women were so few that some bachelors even resorted to advertising for wives in national farm journals. An "epidemic of bachelorhood" had set in. In South Dakota, beyond the Missouri, the number of farmers in western counties dropped from twenty-one thousand in 1930 to eight thousand in 1992. Similar depletions of farm populations struck rural areas of Kansas and Nebraska, causing some to ask who would "do the reaping" in coming decades.

Exceptions to these depopulating trends in the rural West added to the complexity of the picture. In some areas farmers continued to do well or even expanded in numbers. Some counties in the Dakotas experienced extraordinary rises in per capita income, but primarily because wheat prices remained high, many farmers sold their holdings to larger outfits, and thus fewer residents divided the gross income. That anomaly was particularly true for Sully County in South Dakota, where 1,600 residents enjoyed in excess of $24,000 each from bumper wheat crops. Population growth also occurred where the underground Ogallala Aquifer provided much-needed irrigation water for otherwise dry lands, usually through lengthy, expensive center-pivot sprinklers. Parts of southwestern Kansas, panhandle Texas, and Nebraska's nearby Platte River valley likewise enjoyed modest growth.

Some rural areas attempted to counter depopulation through imaginative means. Dozens of ghost towns, on life support at best, were resurrected as colorful and rip-roaring relics of an Old West that promoters hoped would draw curious, maybe gullible, tourists. Other remote spots, such as Kellogg and Tamarack, Idaho, launched new resort, recreational, or "wilderness" sites to reorient the area's draw and economy. Garden City, Kansas, and Lexington, Nebraska, lured in IBP, Inc., a meatpacking plant that imported thousands of new employees. Among the new workers were several thousand laborers from Mexico and Southeast Asia, thereby expanding these areas and small towns and adding to a growing multicultural West.

A MULTICULTURAL WEST

President John F. Kennedy once defined the United States as a "nation of immigrants." He would have said the same about the American West. Through the region's long history, it has always been a place and society of newcomers.

These incoming tides of immigrants arrive, contact, sometimes conflict with, and just as frequently combine with the region's societies and cultures. But the number and rapidity of the entering multitudes complicated the process of establishing or defining a stable, ongoing regional identity. Even before recognizable signs of a western identity came into focus, a host of newcomers enlivened or redirected the host society. As a result, the western past has been one of persistent change and increasing complexity and diversity. So it has been, and so it has continued since the mid-1980s.

The expanding economy of most sections of the West, the availability of jobs in the region, and discontents and dissatisfactions in their home areas drew and pushed thousands—even millions—of newcomers to the West from the early 1980s forward. Latinos and Asians, for example, found good-paying jobs more plentiful in the trans-Mississippi American West than in their homelands. African Americans and other job seekers within the United States found similar opportunities in the region, especially in Cold War–related, service, and new footloose industries, such as computer and electronic firms. Native Americans, unfortunately, were unable to benefit as frequently as other groups from these opportunities. The numbers of all these minority peoples expanded in the 1980s and 1990s. By 2000 two out of three Native Americans, more than half the country's Hispanics, one in two Asians, and growing numbers of blacks lived in the West. These growing minority populations added notably to the multicultural cast of the region.

Specific legislation, world events, and economic trends were the main spurs to added minority populations coming to the West. The Immigration Act of 1965 and subsequent amendments to the law, the postconflict difficulties following wars and revolutions in Southeast Asia, and expanding job opportunities in western cities, on farms, and in tourist and technology industries beckoned newcomers from Mexico, other Latin American areas, and Asia. Although a strong economy in Japan and restraints in China stemmed the flow from those countries, Korean, Filipino, and East Indian numbers continued to swell.

At the beginning of the twenty-first century, the oldest westerners, American Indians, both moved ahead and continued to suffer from residual inequalities experienced earlier in the twentieth century. By 1980 more than half of the country's Native Americans lived off reservations, often in urban areas such as Los Angeles, Phoenix, Denver, and Albuquerque. Although jobs were plentiful in these and other cities, and unemployment rates were lower in urban areas than the extremely high rates on reservations, several problems continued to plague American Indians. They were poorer, sicker, and less educated than other westerners. One in three Indian families lived below the poverty line, with Native income only two-thirds that of other Americans. They were often beset, too, with diabetes, eye diseases, and alcoholism. Diabetes struck one in eight Indians, with Indian deaths from this illness three times the rate for Caucasians. Alcoholism rates were five to six times those of other Americans.

Still, there were clear reasons to be optimistic. Tribal enrollments were expanding, birthrates were up, and Indian cultural and artistic activities were flourishing. Between 1980 and 1990 the Indian population grew from 1.4 to 2.5 million, a 44 percent gain. Indian numbers expanded in every western state. Indian writers and artists such as Louise Erdrich, Sherman Alexie, and R. C. Gorman became increasingly well known as delineators of Indian history and culture. And, as we have seen, Ben Nighthorse Campbell gained a national reputation in the U.S. Congress as a political spokesman for Natives. So at the beginning of the twenty-first century, despite ongoing problems, many Indians could be much more optimistic about their futures than they were a century earlier.

For Mexican Americans (and also Chicano/as and Hispanics), as well as for immigrant Mexicans and Latinos, the challenges in the post-1980 West were quite different. Growing rapidly because of high birthrates and swelling immigrant waves, Hispanics had become the largest minority in the West—as well as in the United States. In the two decades following 1980, the Hispanic population in the United

States jumped from 14.6 to 35.3 million, with about two-thirds of those persons living in the West. In 2000 California hosted the largest Hispanic population at 10.9 million, with Texas second at 6.7.

This huge influx brought new challenges. Often newcomers crowded into urban barrios, such as the sprawling one in East Los Angeles, which contained more persons of Mexican heritage than any other global city save Mexico City. These barrios sometimes boiled over in violence, often fueled by unemployment, gangs, crime, public school dropouts, and surrounding racism.

Major dilemmas arose from problems inside and outside Chicano communities. Class differences and varied places of origin often led to clashes. Hispanics who could trace their family's arrival in the Southwest two or three centuries earlier frequently saw themselves as Spanish and often expressed hostility toward Mexicans or Chicanos who had arrived in the past few months, sometimes as illegal immigrants. When some Hispanics in Los Angeles, Albuquerque, El Paso, or San Antonio, for example, accumulated enough income to become middle class and attempted to move into non-Hispanic, middle-class suburbs, they often were treated as traitors to *La Raza* (the race) by other Hispanics *and* brushed off by Anglos in those suburbs. Also, when César Chávez died in 1993, Chicanos lost their heroic leader. No one seemed to assume his mantle or that of any other activist who had spoken for Chicano workers in the 1960s through the 1980s.

Other signs indicated Hispanics were making rapid strides forward, however. They made up 13 percent of the total U.S. population and more than 40 percent of the population in New Mexico and California. Writers such as Rudolfo Anaya, Ana Castillo, and Richard Rodriguez gained national—if not international—attention. Hispanics were also flexing their muscles in the area of politics, with more than three thousand Hispanics nationally holding office, including the mayor's post in Denver and San Antonio and twice the governorship of New Mexico. In early 2007 more than a few

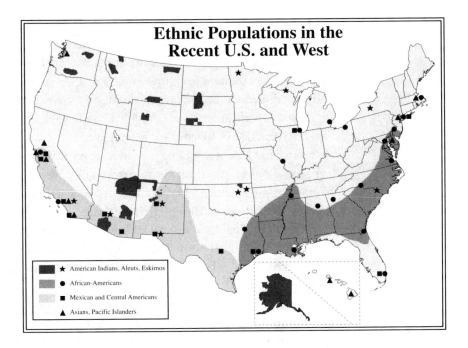

Ethnic Populations in the Recent U.S. and West

Legend:
- ★ American Indians, Aleuts, Eskimos
- ● African-Americans
- ■ Mexican and Central Americans
- ▲ Asians, Pacific Islanders

In the United States most Asians, Hispanics, Indians, and increasing numbers of African Americans resided in the West by the end of the twentieth century. Map taken from Richard W. Etulain, *Beyond the Missouri: The Story of the American West* (Albuquerque: University of New Mexico Press, 2006), 427. Map by Robert Pace. Used by permission of publisher.

observers were touting New Mexico's governor Bill Richardson (Hispanic on his mother's side) as a viable presidential candidate for the 2008 election. That was a first in the American West. So in the face of continuing labor problems in the fields and feedlots, clashes in the barrios, and controversies over immigration along southwestern borders, Hispanics were gaining power and attention in political, economic, and cultural arenas.

The rapid changes and growing complexities that characterized most of the West in the 1980s and 1990s were clearly traceable in the experiences of many Asians living in or immigrating to the region. Intraethnic differences among Asians also helped define their lives in the American West. After 1980 there were huge influxes of Koreans and Filipinos, for example, but dwindling numbers of newcomers from Japan and mainland China. The Immigration Act of 1965 obviously opened the door for Asian immigration, and even the words used to denote these newcomers from Asia changed. They were no longer "Orientals" but now simply "Asians."

A solid, even expanding, economy in Japan kept newcomers from those islands from coming to the United States. In fact, by 1990 the annual influx of Japanese immigrants had dropped to only four thousand of the twenty thousand yearly quota. At the same time, *Sansei* and *Yonsei* (third- and fourth-generation Japanese Americans) were becoming more Americanized; very few spoke Japanese. But the Japanese American Citizens League remained active, seeking redress for the Japanese incarcerated in relocation camps during World War II. After much controversy, Congress agreed to compensate all living internees $20,000 each. As one historian observed, when the congressional caucus of its Asian members agreed to follow JACL leadership, that action was "a prime example . . . of how Asian American elected officials . . . worked hand in hand with community activists toward a common end."

Although the coercive administration of mainland China greatly discouraged immigration to the United States after 1980, unabated flows from Hong Kong and Taiwan continued to swell the Chinese population in the West and other parts of the United States. Indeed, the Chinese have surpassed the Japanese in U.S. numbers since 1980. The Chinese population in the United States jumped from 806,000 in 1980 to about 3.6 million in 2000, with about half living in the West and most of those on the Pacific Coast. San Francisco hosted a large, vibrant Chinatown, known for its restaurants and small shops. Unfortunately, in the early 1980s there were also perhaps as many as 150 sweatshops in San Francisco's Chinatown that employed 3,500 Chinese women, often overworked illegal immigrants who did not appeal their status for risk of endangering their stay in the United States. Similar bittersweet conditions existed among Chinese young people. Although more than one-fourth of all Chinese Americans were college graduates (about twice the national average of other Americans), juvenile delinquency and gang warfare continued to be unanswered problems, particularly in California urban areas.

Korean and Filipino numbers climbed even more noticeably. Expanding population, economic challenges, and large families in the Philippines encouraged immigration to the United States, despite that country's sometimes hostile criticism of America's foreign policies in Asia and reputed mistreatment of minorities in its own homeland. Between 1980 and 2000 Filipino numbers in the United States jumped from 774,000 to 2.5 million. Earlier, many Filipinos had worked on West Coast farms, but the new immigrants from the Philippines primarily crowded into Pacific Coast cities. Two out of three Filipinos in the United States resided in the West Coast states. More educated, coming with families (rather than as the single males of previous Filipino groups), and preferring to work in white-collar jobs, the swelling tides of Filipinos in the 1980s and 1990s threatened to replace the Chinese as the largest Asian group in the United States.

Korean numbers in the United States, although not as large as the Chinese or Filipinos, were nonetheless expanding more rapidly in percentage than either of those groups. In 1970, 70,000 Koreans resided in the United States, 354,000 lived here ten years later, and by 2000 Korean numbers had doubled to more than 700,000. That was the largest percentage growth of any sizeable minority group during those two decades. Like so many other Asians, Koreans chose to live on the West Coast, especially in California, with nearly 20 percent of all Korean Americans residing in Los Angeles County. They worked as grocers, owned liquor stores, or established other small businesses. Korean expansion into many sections of Los Angeles and their competition with other ethnic entrepreneurs sometimes led to clashes, the most violent of which was the riot of 1992.

The newest groups of Asians to come to the West were those arriving from Southeast Asia. Most South Vietnamese came as refugees fleeing the chaos following the Vietnam War of the 1960s and 1970s. At first they were doled out like so many orphans to various parts of the United States, but gradually most of the Vietnamese relocated to the warmer climates of California and Texas. Nearly fifty thousand congregated in Los Angeles. Other newcomers from Cambodia and Laos, escaping their war-ravaged countries, immigrated to the United States and also moved to sunny southwestern cities. Still another group, the East Indians, doubled in population size in the United States between 1980 and 1990 and again in the next decade. By 2000 nearly 1.7 million East Indians lived in the United States. Roughly one-fourth, or about four hundred thousand East Indians, made their homes in the West, particularly on the West Coast and in urban areas. Speaking English and possessing good educations, many of these immigrants from India were professionals and worked as engineers, computer specialists, or doctors and lawyers. Still others from India and Pakistan took positions as hotel and motel workers or, pooling their resources, became family owners of such establishments. American travelers to the West often encountered the pleasant, inviting aroma of curry when they checked into motels in western rural areas and small towns of the region.

Still another minority group, African Americans, clearly experienced gains in the post-1980 West, but those advancements were sometimes shadowed with difficulties. Black populations expanded in Texas and California, where their numbers had been largest in the West since World War II. Jobs in Cold War and support industries continued to attract blacks to Los Angeles, the Bay Area, San Diego, Houston, and Dallas–Fort Worth, but they increasingly moved also into Nevada, Oklahoma, and Kansas for service, technology, and manual labor positions. And the mood of many African Americans seemed to change. They were less inclined to join activist groups such as the Black Panthers and more inclined to gain college or advanced technological training, push for white-collar positions, and, perhaps, climb into the middle class. After the Civil Rights Act of 1964, discrimination in residential neighborhoods and public facilities seemed to lessen. Meanwhile, the black population in the West burgeoned from 2.5 million in 1960 to more than 8 million in 2000.

These developments pointed to clear advancements for African Americans in the West. But other events, chiefly the Los Angeles riot of April 1992, revealed racism lurking just below the surface of western society. A year earlier Los Angeles police had attempted to detain an African American man for speeding, he resisted, and a home video caught the vicious pummeling the police gave the detainee. The next year, after an all-white jury declared the police not guilty of undue violence, a red-hot, four-day riot erupted, leaving fifty-five persons dead and more than two thousand injured. The rioting targeted not only whites but minority groups competing with blacks for jobs and trade in black areas. As Quintard Taylor, *the* expert on African American history of the West, notes, the riot and similar incidents soon thereafter "made the nation aware of the complex relationships between Anglos and people of color in the modern urban West."

These horrendous events in Los Angeles in the early 1990s were symptomatic of the uncertain race relations in the West, as well as in many other parts of the United States from the 1960s forward. Reformist legislation in Congress, sometimes strong presidential direction, charismatic leadership by minority leaders such as César Chávez, Dolores Huerta, and Martin Luther King, and a growing sense of a greater need for fairness all pushed westerners and other Americans toward greater sensitivity and support for peoples of other races and ethnicities. But for others these "multicultural" efforts smacked of reverse discrimination, of racial chauvinism, of "romantic ethnicity." Some westerners, again like many other Americans, wondered if in the country's attempts for a new equality, it hadn't tipped the scales away from white, middle-class America. These doubters pointed to mandated school busing, racial quotas in public schools and colleges, and special legislation allowing casinos on reservations as examples of a new "political correctness" that could undo and undermine the hard work and achievement of nonminorities. As the twenty-first century began, these conflicting attitudes about minorities and new immigrants divided westerners, and the divisions seemed destined not to close in the near future.

A WESTERN PROFILE

As one would expect, the urban expansion of the West and its mushrooming racial and ethnic populations continued to shape the profile of the region's peoples. Those demographic distinctions become clearer when one looks at the West's age and gender indexes, as well as at a few other indicators in the census.

Birthrates in the West often topped those in other U.S. regions. From 1960 to the late 1980s, New Mexico, Utah, Arizona, and Texas, along with Alaska and Hawaii, remained among the ten states with the highest birthrates. A decade later Utah continued to be the highest on the list, but other states were closer to the national average. As was often the case in the past, these high birthrates were linked to migration; migrants were younger, and wives were still in their child-bearing years, meaning they continued expanding their families after moving west. The fecund newcomers, many of them baby boomers, undoubtedly thought of the West as the land of opportunity, freedom, and the California Dream. They and their young families helped keep the West a youthful place. In fact, it replaced the South as the youngest of all American regions.

But this youthfulness was not uniform throughout the West. The twenty and thirtysomethings moved primarily to the Southwest and West Coast, where most of the jobs beckoned. These two areas not only gained hundreds of thousands of newcomers but also fresh crops of babies. The elderly and the very young did not leave their homes, staying put outside the West or within the Plains and Rockies areas. Those less-populated parts of the West received smaller parts of the new influx. The young and energetic—and fruitful— headed off to the expanding areas of the Sunbelt, particularly California and Texas. Their numbers kept the median age down in those regions even though the sunny Southwest and California also became the new hosts to floods of older retirees.

The shifting tides of immigration also markedly influenced family makeup in the West. Between 1920 and 1960 about three-fourths of immigrants to the United States came from Europe and Canada, but the Immigration Act of 1965 changed the flow. The new legislation gave immigration preferences to spouses, children, and parents of citizens and permanent residents and also ended immigration discrimination against Asians. The impact of these changes was quick and direct. During the 1970s and afterward, three-quarters of the new arrivals in the United States were from Latin America (40 percent) and Asia (35 percent) when they had totaled only 22 percent from 1920 to 1960. A consequence of the act of 1965 was the reuniting of Mexican and Asian families. Once spouses, children, and parents of these two groups took advantage of the act's provisions, Mexicans and Asians transitioned from their earlier male-dominated groups to more full-fledged families. Revealingly, Mexican and Asian families, often averaging a half-dozen or more children at the time of immigration, frequently became smaller in the next generation. Quite possibly the traumas of relocation and refugee status as well as the pattern of smaller families in the United States greatly influenced immigrant families; their birthrates plummeted once they arrived.

The census of 2000 provides other revealing facts about the West's populations. As we have seen, westerners were young and had a higher birthrate than most other U.S. areas. The West was also, along with Florida, said to be the destination of swelling numbers of "snowbirds" spending winter months or retiring in the warm Southwest. But the facts tell a more complex story. In 2000 six of the states with the highest percentage of persons under age fifteen were in the West (plus Alaska). In the same year only North Dakota and South Dakota—two parts of the "frost belt"—ranked among the ten states with the highest percentage of their populations over age sixty-five. Importantly, and the reverse of many popular beliefs, the much-acclaimed Sunbelt states with their retirement populations were not among the top ten states in senior citizens, but New Mexico, California, and Arizona did rank fifth, sixth, and eighth among states with the youngest populations. Not surprisingly, Utah and its large families of children was the youngest state, with the lowest age mean. Oregon was the only western state significantly older than the national average, and its state birthrate was low too.

Clearly, seniors were visiting or retiring in California and the Southwest, but even larger groups of young immigrants from abroad or from within the United States were coming, keeping the West youthful and expanding. In 1990 and 2000 the West hosted the highest percentage of persons under age fifteen and the lowest percentage of persons over age sixty-five from 1970 to 2000.

The ratio of men to women also indicates the difference between some areas of the West and the nonwestern regions of the United States. Generally, the West had the highest sex ratio (number of males per one hundred females) throughout the twentieth century. Even when the sex ratio in the United States shifted to more women than men in the twentieth century, the West maintained the highest percentage of men to women, with their numbers about even in 2000. But notably in that year only five noncoastal western states — Colorado, Idaho, Nevada, Utah, and Wyoming (plus Alaska and Hawaii) — had more men than women. It was these landlocked western states, of course, that often prided themselves as the "real West," with shades of mountain men, cowboys, John Wayne, and Louis L'Amour.

How do these numbers add up? Do they provide useful conclusions about men and women's experiences in the recent West? Do they tell us much about the work patterns, the marriages, and the households of these families? Someone said that only fools and statisticians believe that numbers can provide the central plotline of any story. Despite the many missing pieces, however, we can make some generalizations about the experiences of varied peoples in the post-1980 American West.

Change and complexity, for example, continued to play major roles in defining the recent West. Journalists, sociologists, not a few historians, and other students of modern American society have often sounded the death knell of the California Dream and its appeal to newcomers. Nearly all their dire predictions were proved wrong. Despite a few demographic dips, California continued to be a mighty draw. That beckoning to the Golden State, like the pull to other

growing areas of the West, resulted primarily from job opportunities. Uncle Sam continued to funnel funds into the
aerospace industry, military installations, scientific research,
and hundreds of support companies involved in military-industrial complexes. Other job seekers found work in private computer, electronic, and technology companies clustered in areas
such as Silicon Valley, the Pacific Northwest, the Southwest,
and scattered sites of the inland West. Sunny or mild climates
around the southwestern or western edges of the West helped
foster burgeoning tourist industries, adding to employment in
tourism and other service industries. The availability of many
good jobs in amenable, open areas lured millions of people
into the West and continues to do so.

Most of these newcomers moved to western urban or
suburban areas. The West is the most urban region of the
United States, and the largest western growth areas since
World War II have been the expanding metropolitan districts. So expansive are these urban areas that "edge cities"
(mini-cities with all the accoutrements of larger cities—a
downtown, shopping areas, housing, health care and recreation facilities, and schools) have sprung into existence on
the edges of places such as Los Angeles, Phoenix, Denver,
and Dallas–Fort Worth. Often newcomers migrating west
headed for the sprawling suburban developments to avoid
higher home costs and crowded and cluttered central cities.
Within a few years, this movement to the West added to environmental blight in downtown areas, the gobbling up of
surrounding farm areas for new houses, and crisscrossing
freeways and ring roads knifing through older (and sometimes ethnic) neighborhoods.

The population expansion in the West transformed it
into a transregional, transnational, and multicultural place.
The mounting immigration from Latin America and Asia
enlarged and strengthened trade, diplomatic, and sociocultural links with, for example, Mexico, other regions of North
America, China, Korea, the Philippines, and other Asian
countries. Anyone who visits the fastest-growing urban areas
of the West will attest to the plethora of ethnic restaurants,

groceries, and cultural centers as indicators of transnational and multicultural influences. (Conversely, travel to Mexico City and Mexican cities near the U.S. border or to large cities in Japan, China, South Korea, and other parts of Asia, and evidence of western corporate and franchise expansion such as McDonalds, Microsoft, Hewlett-Packard, and Intel can be seen.) Traces of Latin American, Asian, and other immigrant influences are evident everywhere in the urban West—and are expanding.

Sadly, the strains from these demographic changes also reared their ugly heads. Some of the stresses impacted families; still others seemed to influence westerners' outlooks. The rate of divorce in the American West remained extremely high. In fact, historian Glenda Riley, a leading authority on American women and families, asserted that since the nineteenth century the American West "had, and still has, the highest divorce rate in the world." She pointed to the cultural complexities, the failure of intermarriage between mates of opposite racial or ethnic backgrounds, increased urbanization, "women's changing roles" and "liberal attitudes toward divorce," and expanding social, economic, and moral choices as causal factors of the West's very high divorce rate. Another scholar examining statistical information about western women concluded that they were better educated than other American women, more open in their views, less religious, and more optimistic and hence more open to change, including separation, divorce, and singleness.

Other observers concluded that westerners betrayed their essential rootlessness in their tendency to move for nearly any reason. Huge numbers of urban and suburban Californians and Texans had no history, some thought. They lacked the deep-seated traditions that shaped and defined long-time residents of New England and the deep South. Another commentator urged ambitious businesses in the West to invest in U-Haul trailers, short-term rental apartments, motels, and other evanescent industries because westerners were always on the move. Sometimes, as novelist Joan Didion portrayed in her heroine of *Play It As It Lays* (1970), western rootlessness led to lives bereft of a moral or social compass. African American writer Walter Mosley dramatized similar restless wanderings of his black heroes, who migrated from the South to southern California and were unable to locate in their new location any traditions to which they could cling or with which they could identify.

Another type of overnight development created a new kind of chaos in the Highland Ranch area of Douglas County, just south of Denver. In the late 1990s it suddenly experienced a demographic explosion, growing faster than any other county in the United States. Huge houses seemed to drop out of the heavens, covering wide expanses of land that had been open spaces just months prior. Schools were thrown up, houses and businesses followed a riot of architectural styles, with a vapid mix of big box stores and even an ostrich ranch in the carnival mix. But what kind of community was Highland Ranch to be? What kind of regional traditions, if any, would it spawn? Many of the new residents, "lifestyle refugees" working in footloose computer and telemarketer corporations and nourishing their addictions to nearby recreational areas, seemed uninterested in building a new sense of community in Highland Ranch. Perhaps journalist Timothy Eagan had it right when he said that trying to establish community was the major challenge in a frenetic New West. It was like "lasso[ing] the wind." As Eagan explained, "There is no institutional memory in the West, only dawn."

ECONOMIC EXPANSION

Demographic growth and economic expansion went hand in hand in the post-1960s West. Indeed, one might ask the chicken-and-egg question: which one came first, floods of newcomers leading to economic growth or economic expansion drawing new immigrants? Good evidence supports either answer. In the early 1980s, twenty years after California zipped past New York as the most populous state, the American West was becoming the most powerful American economic region. Booming California, the expanding Southwest, and growth of the Sun Belt were all part of this economic explosion.

In the decades following World War II, westerners experienced economic upturns. From Texas to California, from California to Seattle, and from Seattle to scattered spots in the hinterland region, the West pulsated with economic activity, fueled in part by Uncle Sam's spending, the expansion of businesses and manufacturing in the West, and the availability of millions of new workers. Throughout the West, but particularly in the subregions experiencing the most rapid population growth, the region's economic motors purred at high capacity. Even though the Cold War of words between the Americans and the Russians cooled in the early 1990s, federal government monies flooded west. The military metropolises scattered across the region continued to feed on the federal manna descending on them.

Congressional funding was the major fuel stoking the engine of western economic growth in the late twentieth century. The clearest evidence of this "federal landscape" in the West was military installations, plane- and ship-building facilities, and scientific institutions. In every western state federal funding remained a crucial source of financing even though those dollars in 2000 were about half of 1960s levels.

The amount of government spending varied dramatically throughout the West. California, the Pacific Northwest, the Southwest, and interior western places such as Denver and Colorado Springs, Wichita, and Oklahoma City and Tulsa profited from Uncle Sam's largesse. In the Los Angeles area, for example, about one-third of all workers were employed in heavily federally funded aerospace industries. Silicon Valley industries continued to boom. So did companies in Seattle, Boise, Denver, and several urban areas of the Southwest, including Dallas–Fort Worth, Houston, Albuquerque, and Phoenix. But the northern Plains and Rockies states, though recipients of some funding, did not experience the powerful infusion of dollars that continued to rev up the West Coast and Southwest companies. In fact, one eastern scholar and his wife tried to market the controversial idea that large sections of the less-populated and slower-growing upper Plains be transformed into a Buffalo Commons, devoid of people and returned to a natural landscape. In the Dakotas, Montana, and Wyoming that idea played like an all-mutton menu at a cattlemen's convention. In those same states and other western agricultural areas, sprawling agribusinesses continued to usurp huge expanses of farming and grazing areas, pushing aside individual farmers and livestockmen.

But the story of recent western economies is far more complex than booming metropolitan areas and strapped rural sections. Places and the spaces in between displayed a variety of faces. Three midlevel centers in separate western subregions illustrate this diversity. In the intermountain West, Boise shattered previous growth trends by nearly doubling in population from 102,000 in 1980 to an estimated nearly 200,000 in 2005. Profiting from the "California bounce" underway in the 1980s and 1990s, Boise, as Idaho's capital and economic hub, built quickly on new Hewlett-Packard (printers) and Micron Technology plants. Between 1987 and 1993 Boise featured new jobs as rapidly as any place in the United States. At about the same time (from 1990 to 1996), it was the fourth–quickest expanding metropolitan site in the country.

At the other end of the West, Sioux Falls, South Dakota, was also booming. With only 81,000 residents in 1980, it zoomed to an estimated 140,000 in 2005. Lincoln County, home of Sioux Falls, was the second–fastest growing county in the United States in 1997. Primarily known as a strategically located trade center and home of stockyards and meat-packing industries, Sioux Falls changed dramatically when New York Citibank relocated its credit card center there in 1981. Other companies followed, and Sioux Falls thrived as a new business center in the northern West. In 1992 *Money* magazine named Sioux Falls the most desirable community in the country.

Lubbock in the west Texas Llano Estacado country illustrates still another kind of subregional economy. Traditionally an agricultural center and university town, Lubbock expanded as a regional hub from World War II through the Cold War. In the postwar years it also increasingly became a center for agribusiness. By the 1980s and 1990s it was the urban nucleus for west Texas and eastern New Mexico, becoming the world's largest center for the production of cotton seed. Meanwhile, as it grew in population from 174,000 in 1980, to 186,000 in 1990, and to an estimated more than 200,000 in 2005, Lubbock became increasingly multicultural. Much more than Boise or Sioux Falls, the west Texas city attracted greater numbers of minority residents. By the end of the century at least one in four of Lubbock's residents was Hispanic or African American. When a nearby air base closed in 1997, Lubbock was forced to rely more and more on its college and university base (four campuses in total) and its mainstay of agriculture. Boise, Sioux Falls, and Lubbock remain revealing examples of the diverse economies in the West's midsized cities surrounded primarily by agricultural or rural areas.

Other older segments of the western economy declined or nearly collapsed. The timber industry plummeted, particularly in the Pacific Northwest. Lumber and other forest product industries, claiming their escalating costs and shrinking markets had gotten out of hand, abandoned the West or closed. International competition, stricter environmental standards, and higher labor costs were pinching the big operators, but their ruinous past practices of clear-cutting and over-production also caught up with them. Industry giants such as George Pacific, for example, left lumber-rich Oregon and moved to Georgia, where labor costs were lower and less-expensive, fast-growing trees were available.

Similar problems vexed the western mining industry and sent it even farther down the economic ladder. Transnational competitors, especially those headquartered in Latin America, costly adjustments to meet new air and water standards, and labor demands also undercut several mining operations. The downward economic turn for the western mining industry continued after the 1980s. True, coal mining and the petroleum industry did not face the widespread disasters that hard-rock miners experienced in the late twentieth century, but neither did they find a new utopia of riches in the West. It was increasingly clear by the opening years of the twenty-first century that the older extractive industries in the West were diminishing as major forces in the western economy. Taking their places as central players were expanding tourism and high-tech industries in a new economic order.

After 1980 in-place tourism continued to furnish an important source of fuel for the West's economic engine. Tourists had invaded the West for well more than a century, of course, but in the decades following World War II the completion of an extensive freeway system and expanding airline grids covering the region encouraged a greatly expanded crop of travelers. Visitors continued to flood into such popular sites as Disneyland, Las Vegas, the Grand Canyon, and numerous national parks, but their numbers also mounted at the sacred Old West shrines: Deadwood, Tombstone, the Little Bighorn, the cattle towns of Kansas, and rodeo-rich Cheyenne. Not only Americans but increasing hordes of foreign travelers were lured to tourist sites, thereby forging additional transnational connections between the West and other world areas.

This booming tourism also had its downsides. Attempting to slake the worldwide thirst for a mythical Old West, tourist entrepreneurs redoubled their efforts to create a fantasy Wild West, overrun with gallant cowboys, rambunctious outlaws, and renegade Indians. Those who already loved the frontier West wanted it unsettled, adventurous, and thrilling. Tourist brokers happily catered to this hungering for a blood and thunder, mythical West. Any clear-eyed observer should be struck by the huge disconnect between the Old West of frontier aficionados and the powerful, mushrooming urban areas and the computer and high-tech industries that drive the modern West.

Western tourism had negative socioeconomic ramifications as well. In catering so diligently to the desires of visitors, many tourist entrepreneurs made a "devil's bargain," selling their souls for tourist dollars. Expanding recreational areas paved over mountain meadows and valleys, spilled into limpid streams, and encouraged—with funding—sprawling housing developments. Even worse, needing thousands of workers for resorts and gaming establishments, tourist companies hired native or foreign minority workers, paying them minimum or low wages. In the dubious trade-off, an expanding tourism industry provided large amounts of revenue for western states but also exacted ruinous demands on environmental and human resources.

In other areas western economic developments after 1980 moved in new directions or built on relatively new trends. This was especially evident in the case of computer and electronic industries. As historian Gerald D. Nash wrote, "the development of electronic and computer-based industries . . . usher[ed] in the new information age" in the West and spread throughout the world.

In 1975 Bill Gates and his nerdish computer pal Paul Allen moved to Albuquerque and launched a small-scale computer firm. Unable to gain the funding necessary to expand their new company in the Southwest, the two college dropouts returned to their hometown of Seattle, borrowed money, and established Microsoft Corporation in the Seattle area. Immediately successful, Gates and Allen became multimillionaires nearly overnight. By 2000 Gates was the richest man in the world.

Microsoft built on the previous successes of high-tech industries in the West. As we saw in chapter 6, technology and computer firms had emerged in the West soon after World War II and were usually linked to government-funded and military-related companies during the Cold War era. Places such as Silicon Valley in the Bay Area of California, sites proximate to university campuses such as those in Austin, Texas, and southern California, and nuclear laboratories near Albuquerque fostered and funded expansion of electronic, computer, and other defense-related companies. Wichita, Boise, Tulsa, and Portland were other areas that gained reputations for hosting such firms.

But Microsoft did more: it vertically transformed the eco-

Bill Gates cofounded the Microsoft Corporation (with Paul Allen) and made it the world's most powerful computer firm. He was also said to be the world's richest man at the end of the twentieth century. Courtesy Microsoft Corporation.

nomic landscape of Seattle and the north coast of the Pacific Northwest. Seattle, primarily known for its ties to Boeing Aircraft and as a major hub of forestry and mining firms, became the home of Microsoft. Thousands of families of young computer specialists, pulling down six-figure salaries, transferred to Seattle, especially to the suburbs of Bellevue and Redmond. These newcomers profoundly reshaped the economy, sociocultural landscape, and schooling programs of their new home. The Microsoft motto ("A personal computer on every desk and in every home") had caught hold— in Seattle, the Pacific Northwest, the West, the rest of the nation, and in many urban-industrial countries around the world. The billions of dollars in revenue that flooded into the Microsoft treasury illustrates how quickly and thoroughly one economic development might transform a subregion of the American West.

The Microsoft Corporation and Bill Gates both continued and broke from previous trends in the recent West. Similar companies, such as Intel in California; Hewlett-Packard in Boise; Honeywell and Sperry in Albuquerque; Texas Instruments and Electronic Data Systems in Houston, Dallas, and Austin; and other electronic and computer firms in Wichita, Salt Lake City, and Denver, demonstrate how widespread the footloose industries had become in the West. In another way Microsoft epitomized the future, a new economic order in the American West. A century earlier most western laborers were working on a farm or ranch, as a miner or logger, or as a small-town businessman, but at the end of the twentieth century hundreds of thousands of westerners were peering at computer screens, working for U.S. defense-related industries, large new businesses (often with ties to the military-industrial complex), or preparing innovative new systems for small businesses, households, and college students around the world. A new economic system, frequently tied to funding from national, state, and local governmental sources and often linked to high-tech industries such as computers, had invaded and taken over the West by 2000.

POLITICAL PATTERNS

The political stances of many western politicians of the late twentieth century became increasingly clear from the 1960s onward. In addition, western politicos played more important roles in national politics, in the White House as well as in Congress. The swing to the right continued in the red states, especially in the midlands West, whereas the blue-state Democrats kept control in the Pacific Coast areas. But there was evidence of change too in the rising numbers of western women winning office and in the increasing power of minority voters. By 2000 national voters also learned that successful presidential candidates had to win either California or Texas (holding the nation's two largest totals of electoral votes) if they were to gain the White House.

Opening his presidency in 1981, former governor of California Ronald Reagan urged Americans to "believe in ourselves . . . to believe . . . we can and will resolve the problems which now confront us. . . . Why shouldn't we believe that? We are Americans." Most Americans did believe Reagan, supporting his administration, reelecting him to the White House in 1984, and following many of his general political stances. Indeed, no other politician did as much as Reagan to define the agendas that dominated the political West in the quarter-century following 1980. Several of the conservative positions Reagan took derived from the views of earlier western politicians such as Barry Goldwater and Richard Nixon and paralleled the political views held by Nancy Kassebaum. They became distinctly known and adopted as western political viewpoints in the 1980s and 1990s and on into the twenty-first century.

So influential was the role of Ronald Reagan as California's governor (1967–75) and as president (1981–89) that some speak of his national administration as the "Reagan Revolution." Reagan was a superb speaker, a manipulator of his image, and nearly always genial. He also knew how to restore Americans' confidence and stability after the defeat in Vietnam and the disruptions of the 1960s and 1970s. "It's Morning Again in America," a Reagan ad told believers. Willing to compromise, and a man of patience and good humor, Reagan could rally bipartisan support for his bills. Watching Reagan's skillful work behind the scenes, Texan James Wright, majority leader in the House, recorded in his diary: "I stand in awe . . . of [Reagan's] political skill. I am not sure I have seen its equal."

Reagan labeled his economic plans "supply-side economics." He called for cutting taxes, reducing government spending (except for the military), and allowing citizens to keep more of their income, thus encouraging them to save and

Ronald Reagan, as governor of California (1967–75) and president of the United States (1981–89), did more than any other person to engineer the swing to the right in recent western politics. Here he rides a favorite horse on his ranch near Santa Barbara, California. C15871–21A. Courtesy Ronald Reagan Library.

to invest wisely. These political and economic stances, referred to as "Reaganomics," became part of the swing to the right that swept over the United States in the early 1980s, including much of the West. Most westerners leaped on the conservative Reagan bandwagon that rumbled through the country. Reagan's opponents, including not a few historians, have questioned Reagan's achievements, however. There is no evidence that his policies encouraged saving and new wise investments among American citizens. And despite his popular image as a tight-fisted, antitax leader, his administration piled up huge debts from federal spending.

Even though Reagan's first secretary of the interior James Watt grew increasingly unpopular for his willingness to open previously protected lands for new oil drilling, mines, and lumbering, Reagan retained his popularity through his two terms in the White House, including carrying all the western states in the 1984 election. Many of Reagan's enthusiastic supporters gave him credit for having the largest role of any world leader in bringing down the Iron Curtain separating Western and Eastern Europe and ending the Cold War between the United States and the Soviet Union. His naming of the first woman to the Supreme Court—Arizonian Sandra Day O'Connor—also won support in the West. Clearly, westerners liked Ronald Reagan and voted overwhelmingly for him. Perhaps insider Lou Cannon came closest to encapsulating Reagan's greatest attraction to westerners and other Americans: "Because of his ability to reflect and give voice to the aspirations of his fellow citizens, Reagan succeeded in reviving national confidence at a time when there was a great need for inspiration. This was his great contribution as president."

The growing political strength of the West revealed itself in the presidential candidates from 1980 forward. Reagan ran and won in 1980 and 1984, and in 1988 former Texas congressman George Bush gained the presidency as a Republican. In 1992 Bush lost to former Arkansas governor William Clinton, who was reelected in 1996. Then George W. Bush, another Texan, was elected in 2000 and 2004. Billionaire Texas entrepreneur Ross Perot also ran for the presidency in 1992 (as an independent) and in 1996 (as a candidate with the Reform Party). In those same years several vice-presidential candidates and cabinet members hailed from the West. It was becoming increasingly clear that successful presidential candidates not only had to win either Texas or California but also could—and did—look west for running mates or cabinet members.

These elections revealed too that although Republicans, especially conservatives, were doing increasingly well in the West, the region was not solidly red-state territory. Progressive or liberal Democrats who often won in the urban areas of the northeastern United States also fared well on the West Coast. They garnered additional support in blue-collar laboring areas of the Midwest and in some heavily populated minority areas. But they lost out to the rising coteries of conservative voters, especially in inland and scattered Sunbelt areas. As one historian wrote, "A majority of Americans living in the Plains states and in the Mountain West, though benefiting from a range of government programs—notably irrigation and power projects and farm subsidies—continued to complain about the influence, as they saw it, of 'elitist' eastern liberals, environmentalists, and regulatory bureaucrats who told them how to run their lives." Other westerners heatedly confronted legislators who encouraged a more open, accepting policy of legal and illegal immigrants crossing the southwestern borders of the United States.

These divisions of Republican majorities in the Plains and Rockies and Democratic strongholds on the Pacific Coast held sway for much of the twenty-five years following Reagan's first victory in 1980. Although western Republicans liked the moderate to conservative politics of leaders such as Bob Dole and Nancy Kassebaum of Kansas and eschewed the warrior-like, uncompromising tactics of Georgian and House Republican whip Newt Gingrich, Dole and most western Republicans were not much inclined to work out compromises on legislative measures with the popular president Bill Clinton in the 1990s.

Other political issues emerged in specific areas of the West. Non-Mormons in states such as Utah and Idaho—and sometimes in Wyoming and Nevada—criticized what they considered the steamroller tactics of the Latter-day Saints. North Dakota and Wyoming politicians tried to insert feel-good issues into political campaigns to detract from the static or falling populations in those states and, conversely, the increasing populations—and power—in other western areas. The waves of immigrants that spilled over into California, Texas, Colorado, Arizona, and Washington and that added new fire to political conflicts over land, water, reform, and health issues were hardly the major controversies that stirred the hearts of residents of the Dakotas, Montana, and Wyoming. Westerners, like most Americans, could always find something needing their complaints. In the mid-1990s political scientist James Wilson caught the nuances of the paradox: "Today most of us have not merely the hope but enjoy the reality of a degree of comfort, freedom, and peace unparalleled in human history. And we can't stop complaining about it." It wasn't just that westerners wanted their cake and to eat it too; they continued to gripe about the huge, tasty confection even as they downed it.

By and large westerners grumbled and griped about most of the same political issues that stirred up other Americans. Taxes, spiraling prices, housing and gasoline costs, dirty air and sprawling suburbs, inadequate public services—these issues seemed to vex nearly all westerners and often became controversial planks in regional political platforms. But there were other problems that seemed unique to parts of the West. States such as Oklahoma, New Mexico, Oregon, and Colorado saved special political animosity—and sometimes venom—for California and Texas. These behemoths, their neighbors complained repeatedly and loudly, were lording it over them. State legislatures—Oregon's and New Mexico's, for instance—made anti-California and anti-Texas issues central to their political agendas. Arizonians threw darts at Californians, claiming that if given an opportunity to do so, residents of the Golden State would hog all the water set aside for Arizona, Colorado, and Nevada. Dakotans held similar resentments toward Minnesota, arguing that state was like a greedy octopus, squeezing the life out of merchants and companies in the eastern sections of the Dakotas. These political discontents and squabbles in the recent West not only reveal the complexities of the western political scene but also provide other examples of the importance of viewing the West in an intraregional as well as a transnational perspective.

In the years after World War II, particularly during the 1960s, the electorate gradually changed in the West. For example, once anti-Asian attitudes diminished, particularly those on the West Coast, Asians became more active in western politics. For many years Hawaii—as a territory and then as a state—elected Asian governors and U.S. congressional and senatorial leaders of Asian heritage, but Asians' political successes came later on the continent. Early on, perhaps the best known Asian politician was S. I. Hayakawa, the distinguished semanticist and former president of San Francisco State College, who served as a U.S. senator from California (1977–83). But more influential was Robert Matsui, U.S. congressman from California (1979–2005), who was instrumental in the passage of the Japanese-American Redress Act of 1988. Gary Locke, of Chinese ancestry, was elected governor of the state of Washington in 1996, and David Wu of Oregon became the first Chinese and Taiwanese American serving in Congress (1999–). Of Japanese American heritage, Norman Mineta was mayor of San Jose (1967–75) and a U.S. congressman (1975–95) before being named to the Clinton cabinet as secretary of commerce in 2000 and later as secretary of transportation by President George W. Bush, where he served more than five years.

Persons of Spanish, Mexican, or Hispanic heritage began voting in New Mexico after the Mexican-American War (1846–48), but they were slower to do so in large numbers in other parts of the West until much later. For example, California had no Hispanic U.S. legislator between 1910 and 1962. And by 1980, even though California was 20 percent Hispanic or Chicano, Edward Roybal, elected in 1962, was the only California Hispanic serving in Congress. Once César Chávez, Dolores Huerta, the National Farm Workers Association (1962), and United Farm Workers (1973) became active, more Chicanos and Mexican Americans voted in California and throughout the West. Under the inspirational direction of several other Chicano leaders in the 1960s and 1970s, Chicanos and Hispanics became increasingly important as western voters in the 1970s, but as these leaders seemed to become more retiring in the 1980s and 1990s, this voter impact lessened. For the most part Chicanos and

Hispanics voted Democratic; once Reagan gained leadership in California and then the presidency in 1980, the move right did less to attract new Chicano voters to state or national elections. The same quiescence settled on African American voters after the activism of the Black Panthers disappeared in the 1980s.

Native Americans became more involved politically, often in national and western courts of law. Indians were particularly motivated to make certain that treaty rights from the nineteenth century were being recognized. Other court cases attacked abuses of land laws and fishing rights. A few Indians also won state elections. Larry Echohawk, a Pawnee and Mormon, became an Idaho legislator and then its attorney general. In 1994 he ran unsuccessfully for the governorship of the state. Ben Nighthorse Campbell (Northern Cheyenne), as we have seen, served in Congress for western Colorado and then gained a seat in the U.S. Senate in 1993. He turned more conservative in the Senate and switched from the Democratic to the Republican Party once elected.

Women also became more active in recent western politics, both as voters and officeholders. The latter came more slowly. Even as late as the mid-1970s most western state legislatures were nearly all male; only thirteen had more than five women. California had more black legislators than women. By the early 1990s, change was in the air: state legislatures were comprised of 20 percent women nationally, with 26 percent in the West. The state of Washington's legislature was 38 percent women, but Oklahoma's only was 9 percent.

After Nellie Tayloe Ross and Miriam "Ma" Ferguson were elected governors in Wyoming and Texas, respectively, in 1924, no other woman was elected to that position until Dixy Lee Ray in Washington (1977–81). Kay Orr followed in Nebraska in 1987, and Joan Finney in Kansas and Barbara Roberts in Oregon in 1991. In the U.S. Congress Coloradoan Patricia Schroeder served twenty-four years and left undefeated in 1996. When Dianne Feinstein and Barbara Boxer were elected to the U.S. Senate in the 1990s, California became the first U.S. state to have women holding both senatorial positions. In January 2007, as the 110th Congress opened, California congresswoman Nancy Pelosi was sworn in as the first female speaker of the House of Representatives. As such, she became the highest-ranking woman in the two hundred–year history of the federal government. As speaker, Pelosi ranked third in the order of presidential succession, behind two other westerners: President George W. Bush and Vice President Dick Cheney from Wyoming. Secretary of State Condoleezza Rice, an African American woman from Colorado, ranked fourth in that line of succession. At the same time, Senator Patty Murphy of Washington became secretary of the Senate Democrats, the highest-ranking woman in the Senate. She and Maria Cantwell gave another western state two female senators.

Earlier in the twentieth century, women often served as state superintendents of education, county clerks, and even small-town mayors but not often in state legislatures. Although African Americans, Hispanics, and Native Americans became more politically active in the closing years of the twentieth century, women from these minority groups rarely gained state or national office. Barbara Jordan of Texas, Yvonne Braithwaite Burke of California, and Secretary Rice, all African Americans, were exceptions as minority women in the U.S. House of Representatives and president's cabinet. With these exceptions kept in mind, these changes and advancements are further evidence of the gathering strength and prestige of western women political leaders.

Recent national elections also provide striking illustrations of the westward tilt of politics, both in fact and location. In 1996 the Republicans ran Bob Dole, a long-time and well-known moderately conservative Kansas senator. The Democrats, of course, renominated incumbent Bill Clinton of Arkansas. Texan Ross Perot, running under the banner of the Reform Party, entered the race late and although not as much of a factor as in 1992, he nonetheless gained nearly 10 percent of the vote. Clinton won the election with 49 percent over Dole's 41 percent. All three candidates lived west of the Mississippi. Indeed, their homes in Kansas, Arkansas, and Texas were in nearly contiguous states; less than one thousand miles separated the three major presidential candidates. If Massachusetts, New York, Pennsylvania, and Ohio had been home to the country's leading politicians in the first half of the twentieth century, that locus of political power had shifted sharply west in the second half of the century.

The next two presidential elections (2000 and 2004), both won by Texan George W. Bush, are further revelations about recent western politics. In 2000 only the Pacific Coast states and New Mexico (narrowly) voted for the Democratic candidate Al Gore, who won the election's popular vote but lost the electoral vote. The same subregional division of western voters remained in 2004, with the Republicans sweeping the interior West and the Democrats holding on to the Pacific coastal states. The West paraded its growing political strength in still another way. In the half century between 1950 and 2000 the West Coast and southwestern and adjacent states, because of their expanding populations, gained forty-nine electoral votes, which other states lost. Of these new electoral votes thirty-three went to California and Texas. Only twenty-two electoral votes (seventeen of which were in Florida) were gained east of the Mississippi; all other eastern states (save Georgia, Maryland, North Carolina, and Virginia) lost electoral votes or remained the same. By 2004 California with fifty-five and Texas with thirty-four combined to hold eighty-nine electoral votes.

As the West cantered into the twenty-first century, several trends in its political history were becoming clear. The fast-expanding populations and resulting voting power of California and Texas (and of Washington, Arizona, Colorado, and Nevada to a lesser extent) dominated the political scene. Meanwhile, the political controversies of nearly all the upper Plains and Rockies states were taking a backseat to those conflicts that emerged in the booming states, where sprawling urban and metropolitan problems and environmental issues were grabbing national headlines. But other political disputes, such as water issues, land use policies, immigration restriction, and equitable taxation, were red-hot conflicts embroiling most westerners. Regional political trends emerging in the post-1960s West also extended into the new century. Moderates and conservatives, especially in the Republican Party, did well at the national and regional polls; but the Democrats, outside coastal urban areas in California, Oregon, Washington, and sometimes in New Mexico and in additional western metropolitan areas, had difficulty winning support in the West. The legacy of Ronald Reagan and his brand of conservatism remains the most recognizable trend in recent western politics.

CULTURAL CONTOURS

From the 1960s on westerners and other Americans embraced less optimistic, unified, and static views of the West. Novelists, historians, artists, and moviemakers usually depicted the region in less positive terms. This trend led toward a New Gray West that emerged in the 1960s and grew more popular after 1980. At the same time, religious experiences in the West continued to change and to become more complex. As a result, a half dozen years into the new epoch the cultural history of the West remained in flux, its contours difficult to define and pin down.

Novelists and historians at the end of the twentieth and the beginning of the twenty-first centuries portrayed the West far differently than a century earlier. If novelists such as Owen Wister and Zane Grey and historians such as Frederick Jackson Turner and Frederic Logan Paxson featured a rather uncivilized frontier West that needed civilizing agents, those images were nearly nonexistent in the works of leading fiction writers and historians a hundred years later. These more recent writers, such as Wallace Stegner, Joan Didion, Cormac McCarthy, and Patricia Nelson Limerick, painted the West as a region often overcivilized, swarming with greedy newcomers, and fouled by sprawling housing developments and smog, overrun with violent, rudderless residents. Even when they dealt with earlier periods of western history, Robert Utley and Richard White—two quite different western historians—found little to praise in westerners' treatment of Indians and the lands they encountered. In his Pulitzer Prize–winning novel *Lonesome Dove* (1985) Larry McMurtry implied that many of the characters inhabiting his fictional scenes were so flawed, ineffectual, or selfengrossed that they could not serve or save communities with gigantic needs.

Moreover, the standard story line in most recent works of western fiction and nonfiction was nearly always at odds with that of early twentieth-century novels and histories. From Owen Wister and Zane Grey through other writers such as Max Brand, Ernest Haycox, Luke Short, and the giant of them all, Louis L'Amour, plots of popular Westerns nearly always featured courageous white men as agents of social—and perhaps moral—order. The explicit decentering of this core narrative became apparent in the 1960s and 1970s. The appearance of new ethnic or racial heroes or heroines in N. Scott Momaday's *House Made of Dawn* (1968, Native American), Leslie Silko's *Ceremony* (1977, Native American), Rudolfo Anaya's *Bless Me, Ultima* (1972, Chicano), and Maxine Hong Kingson's *The Woman Warrior* (1976, Asian) signaled that the story line of valiant and restorative Anglo males no longer dominated the western literary scene. Other women writers also added new ingredients to western stories. Barbara Kingsolver continued to present lively, inventive women in a series of novels with strong heroines, including *The Bean Trees* (1988), *Animal Dreams* (1980), and *Pigs in Heaven* (1993). Molly Gloss reversed earlier plot organization in her prize-winning novel *The Jump-Off Creek* (1989) by making her female pioneer the central figure and reducing men to supporting roles.

Other recent western novelists also separated themselves from earlier patterns in western fiction. Ivan Doig's quiet, probing works about Montana, including his memorable first work, the autobiographical *This House of Sky* (1978), showed him to be a superb literary craftsman. His first trilogy of Montana fiction, *English Creek* (1984), *Dancing at the Rascal Fair* (1987), and *Ride with Me, Mariah Montana* (1990), were worthy predecessors of Doig's more recent and still poetic *Prairie Nocturne* (2003) and *The Whistling Season* (2006). At the southern end of the West, Cormac McCarthy's brilliant novels, especially *All the Pretty Horses* (1992), *The Crossing* (1994), and *Cities of the Plain* (1998), overflowed with penetrating, disturbing violence, all delivered up in minimalist, Hemingway-like prose. Even more recently Marilynne Robinson proved a worthy descendent of Stegner, McMurtry, and other Pulitzer Prize winners in her disarmingly quiet, deep novel *Gilead* (2004). A polished, literate work of great stylistic power and beauty and overflowing with probing characterization, Robinson's novel clearly revealed the Idaho/Iowa author's first-rank literary talents.

Western historians showed as many complex, divergent faces as their literary brothers and sisters. Moving to center stage in the late 1980s and early 1990s were the New Western historians, including Patricia Nelson Limerick, Richard White, and Donald Worster. Talented writers and scholars, and attentive to the new interests of historians in race, class, and environmental topics, this threesome—and more than a few other like-minded historians—dominated western historical writing in the closing years of the twentieth century. Limerick's stirring and smoothly written work of synthesis *The Legacy of Conquest: The Unbroken Past of the American West* (1997) and White's mammoth analytical overview *"It's Your Misfortune and None of My Own": A History of the American West* (1991) led teachers, students, and layreaders to think more about the dilemmas, shadows, and failures in the western past. These two authors, as well as Worster in his histories such as *Dust Bowl: The Southern Plains in the 1930s* (1979) and *Rivers of Empire: Water, Aridity, and the Growth of the American West* (1985), portrayed a gray western past, in which residents of the West often mistreated minority groups, economic competitors, and western landscapes. In answering what they thought to be the too-positive earlier histories about the American West and countering the myth-driven stories of hundreds of popularizers, the New Western historians depicted a region more shaped by human frailties and faults than pioneers' successes and achievements.

338

Glenda Riley is the most prolific historian dealing with women's experiences in the American West. Her many volumes provide complex, probing, and balanced portraits of western women. Courtesy Glenda Riley.

But other historical stories were less critical and more complex in treating the western past. In his thoughtful and superbly written study *The Contested Plains: Indians, Goldseekers, and the Rush to Colorado* (1998), Elliott West presented a mid-nineteenth-century western Great Plains teeming with complications. First Indians and then whites overloaded a fragile environment with excessive, damaging numbers of humans and animals. West's history was not a new myth of bad whites and good Indians but a nuanced narrative of several groups of humans, driven by needs and cupidity, harming and sometimes destroying the land, water, and trees surrounding them. Social historian Walter Nugent told of a similarly complex West in his sophisticated but clearly presented study of demography, *Into the West: The Story of Its People* (1999). Without overlooking the competitions and clashes that occurred among racial and ethnic groups, Nugent gave a comprehensive view of the migration and mobility of millions of people who uprooted themselves and moved into the West. His engrossing story was a refreshing balance of conflict and community—of people on the move, competing with others, but also attempting to find new homes and identities in the West.

The most prolific historian of women's experiences in the West, Glenda Riley, also subscribed to a West of complexity. In a revealing early monograph, *Women and Indians on the Frontier, 1825–1915* (1984; revised and republished as *Confronting Race: Women and Indians on the Frontier, 1815–1915* [2004]), Riley demonstrated that white women, much more than their menfolk, forged links of trade and friendship with Indians they encountered on their way west. Gender differences likewise informed Riley's study *Women and Nature: Saving the "Wild" West* (1999). As Riley showed, gender expectations may have driven men to "use" and "exploit" the land, but the same social prescriptions urged women to "preserve" and "protect" the land, as they did their families and children. Enlarging her vision, Riley then compared colonizers in the U.S. West and central Africa in her book *Taking Land, Breaking Land: Women Colonizing the American West and Kenya, 1840–1940* (2003). In analyzing the roles of white women and women of color in the West and comparing them with the varied women who colonized Kenya in a parallel period, Riley once again painted an intricate western past without overemphasizing conflict. Riley's heroines searched for "settlement," their actions differing from the more invasive, take-and-run measures of men. Women sometimes competed with and resisted women of other racial backgrounds, but they also strove to find and define themselves in these new settings separated by the Atlantic.

Riley's histories, like those of Elliott West and Walter Nugent, presented a West with changing and complex gender, ethnic and racial, class, and environmental relations. But clashes and conflicts did not crowd out or obliterate successes and nascent communities of agreement. Professor Nugent aptly summarized this mediating, balanced position as "neither triumphant or declensionist." In the past two decades, Nugent added, western historical writing had moved "from a lingering Turnerian dominance, through and possibly beyond the paradigm shift wrought by the New Western

Historians, to a matter-of-fact acceptance and portrayal of the good and the bad, the edifying and the disgusting, the mythic and the fact based." Perhaps these themes will be the hallmarks of a post-New Western history that will flower in the early twenty-first century.

Filmmakers moved in a similar direction; they too presented a more complex and Gray West in their western movies. Once John Wayne and the Vietnam-inspired Westerns galloped off the Hollywood scene, moviemakers faced the question of what to do next. Seemingly puzzled and uncertain about what direction to follow, some directors abandoned the Western, with naive movie critics prematurely declaring the film genre dead. But two award-winning Westerns, *Dances with Wolves* (1990) and *The Unforgiven* (1992), both garnered the first Oscars for a Western in nearly sixty years, proving the naysayers as wrong as those who earlier predicted that the 1960s and the Cold War would not reshape the Western.

These two popular films epitomize the variety of Westerns made from the 1970s forward. *Dances with Wolves*, starring Kevin Costner as a soldier who abandons the frontier army to join an Indian camp, represents the increasingly positive cinematic treatment of Native Americans since the appearance of the film *Little Big Man* in 1970. *The Unforgiven* showcased ambivalent characters played by Clint Eastwood and Gene Hackman. The good guys next door and yet violent killers, the duo provides still another example of the New Gray West's gaining popularity. The film's treatment of gratuitous violence and its undercutting of the mythic qualities of John Wayne Westerns make it wonderfully emblematic of the ongoing search for the cinematic meaning of the Old West.

The quest for a new kind of Western led in several directions at the end of the twentieth century. *Geronimo: An American Legend* (1993), superbly directed by Walter Hill, asked searching questions about "who's right and wrong" in the persisting conflicts between whites and Indians. Even more probing, *Lone Star* (1996), directed by John Sayles, fo-

Deadwood (2004–7). This controversial Western series, made for HBO, depicts frontier Deadwood as a wild, unsettled place devoid of law and dominated by selfish, power-hungry men. The series illustrates well the New Gray West that became increasingly popular in Western films made after the 1960s.

cused on the modern Mexican-U.S. border, covering controversial racial and ethnic, generational, and gender topics. These high-quality Westerns imply that modern Americans ought to look more carefully at both the continual conflicts and the conversations of the western past if they are to formulate workable communities in the present.

Some Westerns, in breaking new ground, sparked extraordinary controversies. The HBO-produced series *Deadwood* (2004–7), loaded with profanity and frequently displaying blatant sexism and unrestrained violence, billed itself as the "real thing" Old West and serves as a revealing example of the New Gray West. Film writer and producer David Milch claimed that the vulgar language of most of his characters, providing realistic content for the series, was historically accurate. Many critics found that argument and Milch's historical research shaky. But many of the same critics applauded his major goal in *Deadwood*: to depict a nascent frontier not yet a settled community, without formal legal organization, and often rife with violent, antisocial, and power-hungry individuals. Another film, *Brokeback Mountain* (2005), the first major Western to deal with homosexual cowboys, stirred up a corral-full of arguments—and won several major film awards. For hardcore traditionalists addicted to a romantic and adventurous Old West, the Ang Lee–directed *Brokeback* seemed to pander more to gay communities than to depict the "real West." (Of course, sheepherders could complain too that once again only out-of-work cowboys would be willing to herd woollies.) Whatever one concludes about the veracity of these two controversial films—the squabbles were akin to red and blue staters at one another's throats—they clearly reveal how much the Western continued to change in the post-1960s decades.

Historian Richard White, viewing the West in national and international circumference, observed that "the boundaries of the American West are a series of doors pretending to be walls" and that therefore the West is "open to the outside and divided within." Recent western artists depicted that complexity. In the late twentieth-century West, European and eastern American artistic traditions continued to course through the region even as other western artists pioneered new artistic ideas and techniques. Still others stubbornly followed the popular frontier and regional legacies of the earlier twentieth century.

More than a few western artists after the 1960s championed postregional emphases, moving beyond the frontier era and place-bound stresses of previous painters. Rather than deal primarily with the shaping power of place and physical landscapes, as regionalists had, postregionalists employed several of the innovative artistic methods of abstract expressionism, pop art and photo realism, and conceptual art. As Georgia O'Keeffe had done, artists such as Jackson Pollock, Clyfford Still, and Mark Rothko emphasized abstract, colorful, and innovative designs to create paintings more *in* than *about* the West. Instead of utilizing western places and scenes, the postregionalists stressed colors, shapes, and flat surfaces that filled up canvasses in mysterious ways rather than merely "meaning something." During the postwar decades Los Angeles and San Francisco—and Santa Fe to a lesser extent—became important art centers. For the first time westerners could argue that significant, trend-setting art was "happening" in the West on its own terms rather than imitating European and eastern U.S. motifs.

Abstract and figurative paintings increasingly dominated the western art scene from the 1950s forward. Clyfford Still and Mark Rothko were leaders among the abstract artists. Still filled his canvases with jagged, brightly colored shapes, seeming to suggest that as in modern existentialism, existence preceded meaning. One art critic linked Still's "freer, more open and electrifying" works to the West, "not . . . in appearance, but in feeling. . . . It is the overwhelming sense of freedom and the lack of any constraining barrier or finite limitation that give these paintings their extra-mundane quality." Like Still, Rothko executed abstract paintings while teaching at the California School of Fine Arts (later the San Francisco Art Institute). Together—and through their numerous artistic disciples—Still and Rothko had established, some onlookers thought, a West Coast school of abstract expressionism. Meanwhile, David Park and Richard Diebenkorn pioneered artworks that included eye-catching figures placed against abstract, colorful backgrounds, such as Park's *Kids on Bikes* (1950) and Diebenkorn's *Woman on Porch* (1958). Unlike Still and the abstractionist guru Jackson Pollack, the figurative painters juxtaposed human figures and other objects in front of abstract backdrops to suggest the figure-space unities so important to figurative artists.

West Coast art was also awash in other forms of experimental painting. One of the most intriguing groups of these innovative artists was the photo realists. Chuck Close and Richard McLean of Washington state and Californians Robert Bechtle and Ralph Goings employed photographs for their paintings of close-ups of human faces, specific car models, and street scenes. By emphasizing the realistic, mundane details of facial features, Pontiacs and Fords, and fast-food restaurants, the photo realists transplanted total reality (the "real") onto their canvases.

Another coterie of painters, the pop artists, utilized artifacts of popular culture as well as the recognizable mediums of mass culture in their artworks. Like Andy Warhol's depictions of Campbell's soup cans and Marilyn Monroe, the paintings of Wayne Thiebaud, Mel Ramos, and Ed Ruscha— all California artists—experimented with popular objects such as gumball and pinball machines, comic book characters, and commercial advertisements in their works of pop art. Attempting to eliminate the previous barriers between so-called elite and mundane art, the pop artists endeavored to use, as well as to comment on, the symbols created by an increasingly standardized urban society.

From the 1960s onward ethnic artists also increasingly came to the fore as important western cultural representatives. Parallel to the rise of activist Chicano/a spokespersons in the 1960s and 1970s, Chicano/a artists began to display their talents and ideologies. Some did so as feminist artists. Texans Santa Barraza and Carmen Lomas Garza and several other artists in California subverted earlier patriarchal artistic traditions, reinterpreting those traditions in the forms of their *abuelas* (grandmothers) and *madres* (mothers) and enlarging the meaning of La Virgen of Guadalupe. Other Chicano artists utilized wall posters and *placas* (graffiti inscriptions) to speak out on the racism, exclusion, conflicts, and squabbles Chicanos faced throughout the Southwest. For still others, building walls, bridge supports, and other large, visible spaces became ideal sites for expansive murals recontextualizing Chicano history and their search for cultural identity. San Diego became especially well known for its many colorful murals. The most notable Chicano mural, however, was *The Great Wall of Los Angeles* (1967–), under the direction of skilled artist Judith Baca. Stretching more than a half mile up the San Fernando Valley, the *Great Wall* became a panoramic history of the Chicano past, a montage of "resistance and affirmation," commenting on injustices as well as celebrating long-held identities.

Native Americans moved in other directions as artists. Some Indian artists, such as Fritz Scholder and T. C. Cannon, chose to satirize white mistreatment of Indians, the environment, or mainstream cultural clichés. Scholder's *Indian with*

Beer Can (1969) and Cannon's *Village with Bomb* (1972) were just such reinterpretations of the past, depicting the disparities between stereotyped images of Indians and the dilemmas and tragedies of their lives. Two other American Indian artists chose different paths. Navajo painter R. C. Gorman, perhaps the best-known of all the Native artists, emphasized the serenity and beauty of Indian figures and scenes in his highly sought-after paintings such as *Old Navajo* (1971) and *Happy Old Navajo* (n.d.). Jaune Quick-to-See Smith, of mixed tribal heritage, utilized Indian ledger art, combined those traditions with the themes of modernist art criticism, and produced hybrid canvases marrying Indian traditions and modern art. These combinations, Smith wrote, "seem as fresh and spontaneous to me as most contemporary art."

These new currents in western art, emerging soon after World War II, continued into the early twenty-first century. Abstract, figurative, pop, and photo realist styles remained popular among western artists. Concurrently, ethnic artists, particularly Chicanos and Native Americans, utilized their murals and paintings to parody the past mistreatment of their peoples as well as to celebrate their cultural traditions. Taken together, these new trends in painting suggest that the American West was coming of age artistically; the region was no longer taking its primary cultural cues from Europe or the American East.

Although secularist historians often overlook the fact, religion remains a centrally important experience for many residents of the American West. But those religious journeys have followed many varied paths. As historian Ferenc M. Szasz, the leading authority on religion in the American West, asserted, religious experiences in the closing decades of the twentieth-century West "splintered into a seemingly endless array of social/theological positions." "The [religious] center," Szasz added, "lost its hold." Mainline Protestant denominations and the Roman Catholic Church were either losing adherents or barely gaining in membership. Conversely, the Latter-day Saints (Mormons) and some evangelical groups were steadily expanding, and several megachurch or parachurch organizations exploded in size. For the first time, too, alternative faiths were attracting more than miniscule numbers. Some of these groups breaking away from traditional Protestant organizations became involved in sensational or even tragic happenings in the West. Viewed together, these diverse trends in western religious affiliations illustrate the aptness of Professor Szasz's observation. The varied spiritual journeys help us to understand how the twin themes of western history—change and complexity—help define religion in the recent American West.

In the late twentieth century, mainline Protestants and Catholics maintained their strength in scattered areas of the West. Methodists were most numerous in the middle and northern Plains, with Lutherans and Presbyterians challenging them for leadership in those locales. Southern Baptists spread across the Southwest from Texas to California and into northern and northwestern areas and were the only mainline (and evangelical) Protestant group to experience notable growth, becoming the largest western Protestant denomination by 2000. Meanwhile, Catholics retained their clear presence in Spanish-heritage parts of the region along the southwestern border, in older mining areas and in the northern Plains, and in western metropolitan locations. But except for the Latino Catholics who immigrated from the south, Catholic numbers seemed to have reached a plateau.

Not so with the Latter-day Saints and evangelicals, who grew more rapidly than any of the other western religious groups in the late twentieth century. So evident and steady was Mormon expansion in the United States and abroad that religion watchers predicted the Salt Lake City–based denomination would become a notable world religion by the end of the twenty-first century. With only 1.5 million adherents around the world in 1960, the Mormons exploded to about 11 million forty years later, with a bit less than half of the Saints living in the United States. By 2000 U.S. Mormons outnumbered American Presbyterians and Jews and were twice as numerous as American Episcopalians.

Evangelicals challenged the Mormons for numerical supremacy in some parts of the West. Southern Baptists, Pentecostals (e.g., Assemblies of God), the Church of the Nazarene, and new nondenominational denominations such as Calvary Chapel and Vineyard Fellowship experienced modest (if not phenomenal) growth in the Southwest, California, and scattered areas of the central and Plains West. As a diverse group of conservative Protestants, fundamentalists and evangelicals numbered larger in the West than in the South if one includes the first range of states beyond the Mississippi as western rather than southern. Recent evangelical organizations such as Bill Bright's Campus Crusade for Christ (1951–), James Dobson's Focus on the Family (1976–), and Bill McCartney's Promise Keepers (1991–) illustrate the parachurch groups that rallied evangelicals in the West and elsewhere. Megachurches such as Robert Schuller's Crystal Cathedral in the Garden Grove suburb of Los Angeles, Joel Osteen's Lakewood Church in Houston, Bishop T. D. Jakes's the Potter's House in Dallas, and Rick Warren's Saddleback Church in California provide examples of the drawing power of dynamic, encouraging evangelical preachers.

Not all westerners interested in religious journeys joined these Protestant, Catholic, or evangelical groups, however. From the 1960s onward, an intriguing assortment of non-Christian, "alternative faith," and experimental religious groups sprang up in the West. These included Muslim, Buddhist, and other Middle Eastern and Far Eastern faiths, particularly in California, across the Southwest, and up the Pacific Coast. Even more attention-grabbing were the Moonie, Scientology, Hare Krishna, and Children of God and People's Temple groups emerging in the Golden State. Others, such as the Rajneeshpuram, began by an East Indian mystic in remote rural Oregon, the Church Universal and Triumphant that relocated to western Montana, and the Branch Davidians near Waco, Texas, attracted a good deal of curiosity. Tragically, the People's Temple, led by the energetic Jim Jones, and the Branch Davidians, headed by David Koresh, ended (respectively) in mass suicide and fiery destruction after engaging in tension-ridden struggles with local, state, and national authorities.

These controversial groups and the more traditional Protestant, Catholic, Mormon, and Jewish groups were spread unevenly across the West. Utah, Idaho, and New Mexico, where Mormon and Catholic adherents were the most numerous, hosted the largest percentages of churchgoers. Evangelicals spread from California across the Southwest and captured growing numbers and influence in midlands cities such as Colorado Springs. But the Pacific Northwest states of Oregon and Washington were intriguingly among the lowest religiously affiliated regions in the entire country. Los Angeles, meanwhile, hosted the largest colony of Jews, with its roughly six hundred thousand representing about 75 percent of the West's Jewish population in 1990. The variety of these religious faiths furnishes yet another sign of the West's complex, diverse cultures.

INCHING INTO THE TWENTY-FIRST CENTURY WEST

Even though westerners have spoken of cataclysmic changes in their region infrequently, they sometimes recognized and commented on less dramatic transformations surrounding them. In the nineteenth century some thought of a trip up the Santa Fe, Oregon, or Mormon trail as the experience of a lifetime. Later, thousands—even millions—of immigrants, relocating to the West to become farmers, small town residents, or new urbanites, thought of these as *the* moves of their lives. But these experiences seemed to be events with time boundaries: a beginning, middle, and end.

What about other periods of the western past in which changes were more dramatic and longer lasting? Three traumatic times of transformation affected the West in the past two centuries: (1) in the 1840s and 1850s, when the Oregon Country opened up, the Mormons fled west, Americans and Mexicans engaged in the vicious Mexican-American War, the nation was divided over the possible expansion of slavery into western territories, and men (primarily) scattered across the West to find mineral riches, building towns overnight, and moving on when the veins played out; (2) in the

1930s and 1940s, when the Great Depression, World War II, and Uncle Sam disrupted, transformed, and redefined the West; and (3) the 1960s and 1970s, when an unpopular war in Southeast Asia, rising student activism on campuses throughout the country, and seismic eruptions of ethnic, racial, and gender consciousness redirected westerners as well as the residents of other American regions. A few historians have pointed to the 1890s as another notable transition period in western history.

The changes westerners experienced in the quarter century following 1980 were of another kind. Although transformations of the West continued during these twenty-five years, they were of a lesser magnitude, like being on a treadmill set at low speed. Indeed, a paradoxical truth comes into focus: westerners in the years surrounding 2000 were learning to live with continuous change. And those persisting changes continued to diversify the West, to make it more complex.

Social patterns in the early twenty-first century followed trends that emerged as early as the 1960s or as recently as the 1980s. The West was becoming increasingly metropolitan, less and less rural and agricultural, and more multicultural. Non-American newcomers were arriving largely from Mexico, other parts of Latin America, and Asia rather than from Europe. The West had also replaced the South as the youngest American region.

Economic trends in the post-2000 West likewise demonstrated unremitting change. A new western economic order based on computer and other high-tech firms and an expanding tourism continued to overturn the earlier economic reliance on extractive industries such as agriculture, mineral resources, and timber. This new, powerful economic grid remained greatly reliant on government funding. Even though the Cold War had ended, Uncle Sam's financial largesse fueled many of the West's economic engines.

Western political power swung to the right in the 1970s and remained there three decades later. Capitalizing on the popularity and enduring conservative legacies of Ronald Reagan, Republicans dominated nearly all the interior, red-state regions. Democrats, meanwhile, remained strong on the West Coast, in some other urban areas, and among some minority groups. Women and racial and ethnic minority voters, as well as their representatives, successfully gained power in state and national elections. Political leaders such as George W. Bush, Vice President Dick Cheney, Senator John McCain, and Governor Bill Richardson also illustrated the growing importance of western politicos on the national scene.

These social, economic, and political shifts continued to make westerners uneasy. Cultural trends in the region betrayed this anxiety. Novelists, historians, and filmmakers, abandoning earlier romantic and heroic images of the West, infused their fiction, histories, and movies with a New Gray West, often featuring antiheroes, racism, and environmental chaos. Similarly, painters embraced innovative artistic techniques that relinquished earlier frontier and regional emphases and adopted expressionistic and other novel painterly approaches. Even religiously affiliated westerners moved in several new directions, often dropping out of mainline Protestant or Roman Catholic churches, joining growing Mormon or evangelical groups, or even experimenting with Far Eastern or alternative faith sects. Cultural change moved into the new century like a horse following new steps that were becoming familiar.

Now, return to the four emblematic westerners who opened this chapter: Dolores Huerta, Bill Gates, Ben Nighthorse Campbell, and Nancy Kassebaum. A half dozen years into the twenty-first century these four persons remain as illustrative participants in recent social, economic, political, and cultural trends in the American West. They continue as revealing symbols of the persisting patterns defining the region. If the recent past and present are reliable indicators, the early twenty-first century is likely to follow these now-recognizable patterns of change and complexity.

Bibliographical Essays

REFERENCE GUIDES AND GENERAL WORKS

Several reference guides are of major importance for the study of the post-1900 American West. The standard bibliography, although somewhat dated, is Richard W. Etulain et al., eds., *The American West in the Twentieth Century: A Bibliography* (Norman: University of Oklahoma Press, 1994), which lists more than eight thousand items. An earlier annotated listing is Dwight L. Smith, ed., *The American and Canadian West: A Bibliography* (Santa Barbara CA: ABC-Clio, 1979). The best index of new publications on the region is the listing of recent articles on the West carried in each quarterly issue of the *Western Historical Quarterly*, supplemented by that journal's annual July listing of recent dissertations and by the book review section carried in each of its issues. Also see the quarterly review sections in such other leading regional journals as *Pacific Historical Review*, *Pacific Northwest Quarterly*, *Southwestern Historical Quarterly*, and *Montana: The Magazine of Western History*. From 1990 to 2002 the Center for the American West (now the Center for the Southwest) at the University of New Mexico published bibliographies listing five hundred or more items on several western topics. Among these bibliographies are listings of women and families, Mexican Americans, African Americans, Indians, Asians, the environment, religion, theatre and drama, comparative studies, and politics. Some citations of these compilations appear below.

The best of the reference guides is Howard R. Lamar, ed., *The New Encyclopedia of the American West* (1977; repr., New Haven CT: Yale University Press, 1998). Another similar, very useful volume is David J. Wishart, ed., *Encyclopedia of the Great Plains* (Lincoln: University of Nebraska Press, 2004). Also helpful are two other works: Charles Philips and Alan Axelrod et al., eds., *Encyclopedia of the American West*, 4 vols. (New York: Simon and Schuster–Macmillan, 1996) and Dan L. Thrapp, *Encyclopedia of Frontier Biography*, 4 vols. (Spokane WA: Arthur H. Clark, 1988, 1994). Both of these latter guides, although emphasizing the pre-1900 period, include some twentieth-century subjects.

Another first-rate reference source is Clyde Milner II et al., eds., *The Oxford History of the American West* (New York: Oxford University Press, 1994). This volume contains twenty-three topically and chronologically organized essays by leading western historians. *A Companion to the American West* (Malden MA: Blackwell Publishing, 2004), edited by William Deverell, is a similar volume, also organized topically and chronologically, and includes thorough bibliographies. Other handy topical reference guides include Stephan Thernstrom et al., eds., *Harvard Encyclopedia of American Ethnic Groups* (Cambridge MA: Harvard University Press and Belknap Press, 1980). A volume particularly useful for scholars and advanced students is Gerald D. Nash and Richard W. Etulain, eds., *Researching Western History: Topics in the Twentieth Century* (Albuquerque: University of New Mexico Press, 1997). Several other volumes provide handy introductions to western historical writing. Two are collections of topical essays: Michael P. Malone, ed., *Historians and the American West* (Lincoln: University of Nebraska Press, 1983) and Roger Nichols, ed., *American Frontier and Western Issues: A Historiographical Review* (Westport CT: Greenwood Press, 1988). Two other volumes contain essays on well-known western historians: John Wunder, ed., *Historians of the American West: A Bio-Bibliographical Sourcebook* (Westport

CT: Greenwood Press, 1988) and Richard W. Etulain, ed., *Writing Western History: Essays on Major Western Historians* (1991; repr., Reno: University of Nevada Press, 2002). The only single-author historiographical overview is Gerald D. Nash, *Creating the West: Historical Interpretations, 1890–1990* (Albuquerque: University of New Mexico Press, 1991).

The pioneering history of the modern West is Gerald D. Nash's well-known *The American West in the Twentieth Century* (1973; repr., Albuquerque: University of New Mexico Press, 1977). The present revised volume of *The American West* is the only other book devoted fully to the post-1900 West. In addition, Gerald D. Nash's final volume, *A Brief History of the American West Since 1945* (Fort Worth TX: Harcourt College Publishers, 2001), deals with the most recent period of western history. Other full-scale histories of the American West devote considerable space to the twentieth century. Among these are Richard White, *"It's Your Misfortune and None of My Own": A History of the American West* (Norman: University of Oklahoma Press, 1991); Robert V. Hine and John Mack Faragher, *The American West: A New Interpretive History* (New Haven CT: Yale University Press, 2000); Richard W. Etulain, *Beyond the Missouri: The Story of the American West* (Albuquerque: University of New Mexico Press, 2006); and Gary Clayton Anderson and Kathleen Chamberlain, *Power and Promise: The Changing American West* (New York: Pearson Longman, 2007). Patricia Nelson Limerick, in her lively volume *Legacy of Conquest: The Unbroken Past of the American West* (New York: W. W. Norton, 1987), illustrates the approach and tone of several New Western histories. *Major Problems in the History of the American West* (Boston: Houghton Mifflin Company, 1997), edited by Clyde A. Milner II et al., provides a useful collection of previously published essays, and Richard W. Etulain, ed., *Western Lives: A Biographical History of the American West* (Albuquerque: University of New Mexico Press, 2004) gathers newly written essays to provide a history of the West through biography.

Several state and subregional studies furnish important

discussions of the twentieth-century West. Among the works that devote the most serious and extensive attention to the post-1900 West are Carl Abbott et al., *Colorado: A History of the Centennial State*, 4th ed. (Boulder: University Press of Colorado, 2005); Leonard J. Arrington, *History of Idaho*, 2 vols. (Moscow: University of Idaho Press, 1994); Richard B. Rice et al., *The Elusive Eden: A New History of California*, 3rd ed. (Boston: McGraw-Hill, 2002); Robert A. Calvert and Arnoldo De Leon, *The History of Texas*, 3rd ed. (Wheeling IL: Harlan Davidson, 2002); Michael P. Malone et al., *Montana: A History of Two Centuries* (Seattle: University of Washington Press, 1991); Russell R. Elliott and William D. Rowley, *History of Nevada*, 2nd ed. (Lincoln: University of Nebraska Press, 1987); and Herbert S. Schell and John E. Miller, *History of South Dakota*, 4th ed., rev. (Pierre: South Dakota State Historical Society Press, 2004).

Several subregional overviews also contain valuable sections on the twentieth-century West. See, for example, Earl Pomeroy's still very useful volume *The Pacific Slope: A History of California, Oregon, Washington, Idaho, Utah, and Nevada* (1965; repr., Reno: University of Nevada Press, 2003). Also consult Carl Frederick Kraenzel, *The Great Plains in Transition* (Norman: University of Oklahoma Press, 1955) and Carlos Schwantes, *The Pacific Northwest: An Interpretive History* (Lincoln: University of Nebraska Press, 1996). D. W. Meinig's several monographs on western subregions and especially the fourth volume of his magnum opus *The Shaping of America: A Geographical Perspective on 500 Years of History, Global America, 1915–2000* (New Haven CT: Yale University Press, 2004) provide the invaluable perspective of a historical geographer.

INTRODUCTION

Most of the broad themes and subjects introduced here, such as western social, economic, and cultural topics, are addressed more fully in subsequent chapters. Therefore the bibliographical essays for those chapters may be appropriately referenced. The life and influence of Frederick Jackson Turner are brilliantly narrated in Ray Allen Billington's *Frederick Jackson Turner: Historian, Scholar, Teacher* (New York: Oxford University Press, 1973). More evaluative and stronger on Turner's ideas is the recent study by Allan G. Bogue, *Frederick Jackson Turner: Strange Roads Going Down* (Norman: University of Oklahoma Press, 1998). The essence of Walter Prescott Webb's controversial interpretations is contained in his *The Great Plains* (Boston: Ginn, 1931) and "The American West: Perpetual Mirage," *Harper's* 214 (May 1957): 25–31.

Most of the standard frontier histories of the region depict the 1890s as a watershed, if only implicitly, at the close of the frontier process. See, for example, Ray Allen Billington and Martin Ridge, *Westward Expansion: A History of the American Frontier* 6th ed., abr. (Albuquerque: University of New Mexico Press, 2001). The most provocative questionings of the concept of closing frontiers are Patricia Nelson Limerick, *The Legacy of Conquest: The Unbroken Past of the American West* (New York: Norton, 1987) and Richard White, *"It's Your Misfortune and None of My Own": A History of the American West* (Norman: University of Oklahoma Press, 1991).

1. THE EMERGING POSTFRONTIER ECONOMY, 1900–1930

A first-rate study of modern American agriculture is Gilbert C. Fite, *American Farmers: The New Minority* (Bloomington: Indiana University Press, 1981). The most recent helpful study is R. Douglas Hurt, *Problems of Plenty: The American Farmer in the Twentieth Century* (Chicago: Ivan Dee, 2002). Other valuable overviews are John T. Schlebecker, *Whereby We Thrive: A History of American Farming, 1607–1972* (Ames: Iowa State University Press, 1975) and John Opie, *The Law of the Land: 200 Years of American Farmland Policy* (Lincoln: University of Nebraska Press, 1987).

Homesteading is best addressed in western state-subre-gional studies, but see too Mary Wilma M. Hargreaves, *Dry*

Farming in the Northern Great Plains, 1900–1925 (Cambridge MA: Harvard University Press, 1957); D. W. Meinig, *The Great Columbia Plain: A Historical Geography, 1805–1910* (Seattle: University of Washington Press, 1968); and Lawrence J. Jelinek, *Harvest Empire: A History of California Agriculture* (San Francisco: Boyd and Fraser, 1979). For an interesting study examining the contacts and occasional conflicts between governmental regulation and individual ownership, see Karen R. Merrill, *Public Lands and Political Meaning: Ranchers, the Government, and the Property Between Them* (Berkeley: University of California Pres, 2002).

The rise of western reclamation is discussed in Donald Worster, *Rivers of Empire: Water, Aridity and the Growth of the American West* (New York: Pantheon, 1985); Marc Reisner, *Cadillac Desert: The American West and Its Disappearing Water* (New York: Viking Press, 1986); Donald E. Green, *Land of the Underground Rain: Irrigation on the Texas High Plains, 1910–1970* (Austin: University of Texas Press, 1973); Donald J. Pisani, *From the Family Farm to Agribusiness: The Irrigation Crusade in California and the West, 1850–1931* (Berkeley: University of California Press, 1984); Pisani, *Water and the American Government: The Reclamation Bureau, National Water Policy, and the West, 1902–1935* (Berkeley: University of California Press, 2002); William L. Kahrl, *Water and Power: The Conflict over Los Angeles's Water Supply in the Owens Valley* (Berkeley: University of California Press, 1982); Robert Righter, *The Battle Over Hetch Hetchy: America's Most Controversial Dam and the Birth of Modern Environmentalism* (New York: Oxford University Press, 2005); and Norris Hundley, jr.'s exceptional *Dividing the Waters: A Century of Controversy Between the United States and Mexico* (Berkeley: University of California Press, 1966) and *Water and the West: The Colorado River Compact and the Politics of Water in the American West* (Berkeley: University of California Press, 1975).

Stockgrowers are treated in John T. Schlebecker, *Cattle Raising on the Plains, 1900–1961* (Lincoln: University of Nebraska Press, 1963); Jimmy M. Skaggs, *Prime Cut: Livestock Raising and Meatpacking in the United States, 1607–1983*

(College Station: Texas A&M University Press, 1986); and Alexander C. McGregor, *Counting Sheep: From Open Range to Agribusiness on the Columbia Plateau* (Seattle: University of Washington Press, 1982). James H. Shideler treats an important topic in *Farm Crisis: 1919–1923* (Berkeley: University of California Press, 1957). A fine study is Terry G. Jordan, *North American Cattle-Ranching Frontiers: Origins, Diffusion, and Differentiation* (Albuquerque: University of New Mexico Press, 1993).

On modern western mining, begin with Duane Smith, *Mining America: The Industry and the Environment, 1800–1980* (Lawrence: University Press of Kansas, 1987). Ira B. Joralemon provides a start on one subject with *Copper*, 2nd ed. (Berkeley CA: Howell-North, 1973). More focused studies include Leonard J. Arrington and Gary B. Hansen, *"The Richest Hole on Earth": A History of the Bingham Copper Mine* (Logan: Utah State University Press, 1963); James W. Byrkit, *Forging the Copper Collar: Arizona's Labor-Management War of 1901–1921* (Tucson: University of Arizona Press, 1982); Michael P. Malone, *The Battle for Butte: Mining and Politics on the Northern Frontier, 1864–1906* (Seattle: University of Washington Press, 1981); and Clark Spence, *Mining Engineers and the American West: The Lace-Boot Brigade, 1849–1933* (New Haven CT: Yale University Press, 1970).

On western lumbering, see Thomas R. Cox et al., *This Well-Wooded Land: Americans and Their Forests from Colonial Times to the Present* (Lincoln: University of Nebraska Press, 1985) and several works by William G. Robbins, including *American Forestry: A History of National, State, and Private Cooperation* (Lincoln: University of Nebraska Press, 1985), *Lumberjacks and Legislators: Political Economy of the U.S. Lumber Industry, 1890–1941* (College Station: Texas A&M University Press, 1982), and "The Western Lumber Industry: A Twentieth-Century Perspective," in Gerald D. Nash and Richard W. Etulain, eds., *The Twentieth-Century West: Historical Interpretations* (Albuquerque: University of New Mexico Press, 1989), 233–56.

For the rise of fossil fuel industries we have relied heavily on state histories, such as S. S. McKay and O. B. Faulk, *Texas after Spindletop* (Austin: University of Texas Press, 1965). Also useful are Gerald D. Nash, *U.S. Oil Policy, 1890–1964: Business and Government in Twentieth-Century America* (Pittsburgh PA: University of Pittsburgh Press, 1968); Nash, "Oil in the West: Reflections on the Historiography of an Unexplored Field," *Pacific Historical Review* 39 (May 1970): 193–204; Carl C. Rister, *Oil: Titan of the Southwest* (Norman: University of Oklahoma Press, 1949); and Gerald T. White, *Formative Years in the Far West: A History of the Standard Oil Company of California and Its Predecessors Through 1919* (New York: Appleton-Century-Crofts, 1962). See also Roger M. Olien and Diana D. Olien, *Oil Booms: Social Change in Five Texas Towns* (Lincoln: University of Nebraska Press, 1982).

General works on railroads include John F. Stover, *The Life and Decline of the American Railroad* (New York: Oxford University Press, 1970); Glenn C. Quiett, *They Built the West: An Epic of Rails and Cities* (New York: D. Appleton-Century, 1934); and Ira G. Clark, *Then Came the Railroads: The Century from Steam to Diesel in the Southwest* (Norman: University of Oklahoma Press, 1958). Among the best studies of individual roads and road builders are Robert G. Athearn, *Union Pacific Country* (New York: Rand, McNally, 1971); Keith L. Bryant Jr., *History of the Atchison, Topeka and Santa Fe Railroad* (New York: Macmillan, 1974); Maury Klein, *Union Pacific: The Rebirth, 1894–1969* (Garden City NY: Doubleday, 1990); Richard Orsi, *Sunset Limited: The Southern Pacific Railroad and the Development of the American West, 1850–1930* (Berkeley: University of California Press, 2005); and Michael P. Malone, *James J. Hill: Empire Builder of the Northwest* (Norman: University of Oklahoma Press, 1996).

Two generalized studies of the coming of the automobile age are John B. Rae, *The Road and the Car in American Life* (Cambridge MA: MIT Press, 1971) and James J. Flink, *America Adopts the Automobile, 1895–1910* (Cambridge MA: MIT Press, 1970). See also the most recent study by Mark S. Foster, *A Nation on Wheels: The Automobile Culture in America Since 1945* (Belmont CA: Wadsworth/Thomson, 2003). The classic study of western tourism is Earl Pomeroy, *In Search of the Golden West: The Tourist in Western America* (New York: Alfred A. Knopf, 1955). See also John A. Jakle, *The Tourist: Travel in Twentieth-Century North America* (Lincoln: University of Nebraska Press, 1985) and Hal K. Rothman, *Devil's Bargains: Tourism in the Twentieth-Century American West* (Lawrence: University Press of Kansas, 1998). On one key topic in western tourism, consult Lawrence R. Bourne, *Dude Ranching: A Complete History* (Albuquerque: University of New Mexico Press, 1983). The contours of western aviation can be discerned in Carl Solberg, *Conquest of the Skies: A History of Commercial Aviation in America* (Boston: Little, Brown, 1979) and Joseph K. Corn, *The Winged Gospel: America's Romance with Aviation, 1900–1950* (New York: Oxford University Press, 1983). The best recent study of transportation in the modern West is Carlos Arnaldo Schwantes, *Going Places: Transportation Redefines the Twentieth-Century West* (Bloomington: Indiana University Press, 2003).

Exceptional among the histories of the motion picture industry is Robert Sklar, *Movie-Made America: A Cultural History of American Movies*, rev. ed. (New York: Vintage, 1994). The first westward extension of the steel industry is the subject of Lee Scamehorn, *Pioneer Steelmaker in the West: The Colorado Fuel and Iron Company, 1872–1903* (Boulder CO: Pruett Publishing, 1976).

The national profile of American labor is depicted in such works as James R. Green, *The World of the Worker: Labor in Twentieth-Century America* (New York: Hill and Wang, 1980) and Gary M. Fink, ed., *Labor Unions* (Westport CT: Greenwood Press, 1977). Many aspects of western labor history remain unexplored, but two interrelated subjects, mining and labor, have attracted considerable attention. On the Colorado "war," see George S. McGovern and Leonard F. Guttridge, *The Great Coalfield War* (Boston: Houghton Mifflin, 1972) and the more recent model monograph by Elizabeth Jameson, *All That Glitters: Class, Conflict, and Community in Cripple Creek* (Urbana: University of Illinois Press, 1998). On mining company and labor conflicts in

Idaho and the resulting Haywood Trial in Boise in 1907, see the extensive and dramatically written volume by J. Anthony Lukas, *Big Trouble: A Murder in a Small Western Town Sets Off a Struggle for the Soul of America* (New York: Simon and Schuster, 1997). Among the several volumes on the IWW or Wobblies, see especially Melvyn Dubofsky, *We Shall Be All: A History of the Industrial Workers of the World* (Chicago: Quadrangle Books, 1969) and Joseph R. Conlin, *Bread and Roses Too: Studies of the Wobblies* (Westport CT: Greenwood Press, 1969). For one especially innovative study of labor, race, and ethnicity, see Neil Foley, *The White Scourge: Mexicans, Blacks, and Poor Whites in Texas Cotton Culture* (Berkeley: University of California Press, 1997).

Studies of mining labor include Ronald C. Brown, *Hard-Rock Miners: The Intermountain West, 1860–1920* (College Station: Texas A&M University Press, 1979); Joseph H. Cash, *Working at the Homestake* (Ames: Iowa State University Press, 1973); Russell R. Elliott, *Radical Labor in the Nevada Mining Booms—1900–1920* (Reno: University of Nevada Press, 1961); George G. Suggs Jr., *Colorado's War on Militant Unionism: James H. Peabody and the Western Federation of Miners* (Detroit: Wayne State University Press, 1972); and Mark Wyman, *Hard-Rock Epic: Western Miners and the Industrial Revolution, 1860–1910* (Berkeley: University of California Press, 1979).

2. POLITICS OF THE POSTFRONTIER ERA, 1900–1930

We now have a number of sound histories of western progressivism, particularly those focused on progressivism at the state level. George E. Mowry set the standard long ago with his *The California Progressives* (Berkeley: University of California Press, 1951). His study accentuates the reformers' middle-class–urban roots rather than the legacies of populism. See also Walton Bean, *Boss Ruef's San Francisco: The Story of the Union Labor Party, Big Business, and the Graft Prosecution* (Berkeley: University of California Press, 1952); Spencer Olin, *California's Prodigal Sons: Hiram Johnson and the Progressives, 1911–1917* (Berkeley: University of California Press, 1968); and William Deverell and Tom Sitton, eds., *California Progressivism Revisited* (Berkeley: University of California Press, 1994). Michael McGerr, *A Fierce Discontent: The Rise and Fall of the Progressive Movement in America, 1870–1920* (New York: Free Press, 2003) puts western progressivism in a national perspective.

Other states' experiences are treated in Robert W. Cherny, *Populism, Progressivism, and the Transformation of Nebraska Politics, 1885–1915* (Lincoln: University of Nebraska Press, 1981); Danney Goble, *Progressive Oklahoma: The Making of a New Kind of State* (Norman: University of Oklahoma Press, 1980); Robert S. La Forte, *Leaders of Reform: Progressive Republicans in Kansas, 1900–1916* (Lawrence: University Press of Kansas, 1974); and Robert D. Johnston, *The Radical Middle Class: Populist Democracy and the Question of Capitalism in Progressive Era Portland* (Princeton NJ: Princeton University Press, 2003). Three helpful articles elaborate on western political perspectives: Paul Kleppner, "Politics without Parties: The Western States, 1900–1984," in Gerald D. Nash and Richard W. Etulain, eds., *The Twentieth-Century West: Historical Interpretations* (Albuquerque: University of New Mexico Press, 1989), 295–338; Mark Harvey, "James J. Hill, Jeannette Rankin, and John Muir: The American West in the Progressive Era, 1890 to 1920," in Richard W. Etulain, ed., *Western Lives: A Biographical History of the American West* (Albuquerque: University of New Mexico Press, 2004), 283–304; and Robert C. Woodward, "William S. U'Ren, A Progressive Era Personality," *Idaho Yesterdays* 4 (Summer 1960): 4–10.

Book-length studies of key political personalities of the era include Paolo E. Coletta, *William Jennings Bryan*, 3 vols. (Lincoln: University of Nebraska Press, 1964–69); Michael Kazin, *A Godly Hero: The Life of William Jennings Bryan* (New York: Alfred A. Knopf, 2006); Richard Lowitt, *George W. Norris: The Making of a Progressive, 1861–1912* (Syracuse NY: Syracuse University Press, 1963); Marian C. McKenna, *Borah* (Ann Arbor: University of Michigan Press, 1961); and James

Lopach and Jean A. Luckowski, *Jeannette Rankin: A Political Woman* (Boulder: University Press of Colorado, 2005).

For various western manifestations of the prohibition experiment, consult Robert S. Bader, *Prohibition in Kansas: A History* (Lawrence: University Press of Kansas, 1986); Norman H. Clark, *The Dry Years: Prohibition and Social Change in Washington* (Seattle: University of Washington Press, 1965); Lewis L. Gould, *Progressives and Prohibitionists: Texas Democrats in the Wilson Era* (Austin: University of Texas Press, 1973); and Gilman M. Ostrander, *The Prohibition Movement in California, 1848–1933* (Berkeley: University of California Press, 1957). Kevin Starr deals with progressivism, prohibition, and other notable cultural topics in his *Inventing the Dream: California Through the Progressive Era* (New York: Oxford University Press, 1985).

Much remains to be written about the woman's suffrage movement in the West. An earlier study is Beverly Beeton, *Women Vote in the West: The Woman Suffrage Movement, 1869–1896* (New York: Garland Publishing, 1986). A recent examination of this important subject is the book by Rebecca J. Mead, *How the Vote Was Won: Woman Suffrage in the Western United States, 1868–1914* (New York: New York University Press, 2004). The important essays on western woman suffrage by historian T. A. Larson, numbering nearly a dozen, are listed in the previously cited Etulain et al., *The American West in the Twentieth Century: A Bibliography*.

Historians have produced an increasingly bountiful literature regarding the environmental-conservation-wilderness-ecological movements. For early works, see Samuel P. Hays, *Conservation and the Gospel of Efficiency: The Progressive Movement, 1890–1920* (Cambridge MA: Harvard University Press, 1959); Roderick Nash, *Wilderness and the American Mind*, 4th ed. (1967; repr., New Haven CT: Yale University Press, 2001); Michael P. Cohen, *The Pathless Way: John Muir and American Wilderness* (Madison: University of Wisconsin Press, 1984); Joseph M. Petulla, *American Environmentalism: Values, Tactics, Priorities* (College Station: Texas A&M University Press, 1980); and Donald Worster,

Nature's Economy: The Roots of Ecology (San Francisco: Sierra Club Books, 1977). Recent studies include Donald Worster, *An Unsettled Country: Changing Landscapes of the American West* (Albuquerque: University of New Mexico Press, 1994); Philip Shabecoff, *A Fierce Green Fire: The American Environmental Movement* (New York: Hill and Wang, 1993); William G. Robbins, *Landscapes of Promise: The Oregon Story 1800–1940* (Seattle: University of Washington Press, 1997); and Ted Steinberg, *Down to Earth: Nature's Role in American History* (New York: Oxford University Press, 2002).

The national parks are covered in several useful volumes. Among these are John Ise, *Our National Park Policy: A Critical History* (Baltimore: Johns Hopkins University Press, 1961); Alfred Runte, *National Parks: The American Experience*, 2nd ed. (1979; repr., Lincoln: University of Nebraska Press, 1987); Richard A. Bartlett, *Yellowstone: A Wilderness Besieged* (Tucson: University of Arizona Press, 1985); Robert W. Righter, *Crucible for Conservation: The Creation of Teton National Park* (Boulder: Colorado Associated University Press, 1982); Chris J. Magoc, *Yellowstone: The Creation and Selling of an American Landscape, 1870–1903* (Albuquerque: University of New Mexico, 1999); Thomas Cox, *The Park Builders: A History of the State Parks in the Pacific Northwest* (Seattle: University of Washington, 1988); and Duane A. Smith, *Mesa Verde National Park: Shadows of the Centuries* (Lawrence: University Press of Kansas, 1988).

Western radical movements are dealt with in Garin Burbank, *When Farmers Voted Red: The Gospel of Socialism in the Oklahoma Countryside, 1910–1924* (Westport CT: Greenwood Press, 1976); James R. Green, *Grass-Roots Socialism: Radical Movements in the Southwest, 1895–1943* (Baton Rouge: Louisiana State University Press, 1978); Robert L. Morlan, *Political Prairie Fire: The Nonpartisan League, 1915–1922* (Minneapolis: University of Minnesota Press, 1955); Carlos A. Schwantes, *Radical Heritage: Labor, Socialism, and Reform in Washington and British Columbia, 1885–1917* (Seattle: University of Washington Press, 1979); Gibbs Smith, *Joe Hill* (Salt Lake City: University of Utah

Press, 1969); and the previously mentioned volumes on the Industrial Workers of the World.

For the political repression of 1917 to 1920, we have relied on the above-noted state and labor histories and on such general works as H. C. Peterson and Gilbert C. Fite, *Opponents of War, 1917–1918* (Madison: University of Wisconsin Press, 1957); Joan M. Jensen, *The Price of Vigilance* (Chicago: University of Chicago Press, 1968); and Robert K. Murray, *Red Scare: A Study in National Hysteria, 1919–1920* (Minneapolis: University of Minnesota Press, 1955). More focused studies include Robert L. Friedheim, *The Seattle General Strike* (Seattle: University of Washington Press, 1964); John McClelland Jr., *Wobbly War: The Centralia Story* (Tacoma: Washington State Historical Society, 1987); and, on the Bisbee deportation, James W. Byrkit, *Forging the Copper Collar: Arizona's Labor-Management War of 1901–1921* (Tucson: University of Arizona Press, 1982). Clearly, we need a wide-reaching study of the impact of World War I on the American West.

The impact of religious fundamentalism on nativistic movements is discussed in the bibliographical essay for chapter 5. On the Ku Klux Klan, see the state-by-state assessments in David M. Chambers, *Hooded Americanism: The History of the Ku Klux Klan* (New York: Doubleday, 1965). See also Charles C. Alexander, *The Ku Klux Klan in the Southwest* (Lexington: University of Kentucky Press, 1965); Robert A. Goldberg, *Hooded Empire: The Ku Klux Klan in Colorado* (Urbana: University of Illinois Press, 1981); Shawn Lay, ed., *The Invisible Empire in the West: Toward a New Historical Appraisal of the Ku Klux Klan of the 1920s* (Urbana: University of Illinois Press, 1991); as well as the valuable articles by Eckard V. Toy on right-wing movements listed in the previously cited *The American West in the Twentieth Century: A Bibliography*.

For other political movements and personalities of the 1920s, consult LeRoy Ashby, *The Spearless Leader: Senator Borah and the Progressive Movement in the 1920s* (Urbana: University of Illinois Press, 1972); J. Leonard Bates, *The*

Origins of Teapot Dome: Progressives, Parties and Petroleum, 1909–1921 (Urbana: University of Illinois Press, 1963); Norman D. Brown, *Hood, Bonnet, and Little Brown Jug: Texas Politics, 1921–1928* (College Station: Texas A&M University Press, 1984); and Richard Lowitt, *George W. Norris: The Persistence of a Progressive, 1913–1933* (Urbana: University of Illinois Press, 1971). Among the most recent useful studies are David H. Stratton, *Tempest over Teapot Dome: The Story of Albert B. Fall* (Norman: University of Oklahoma Press, 1998) and Richard Lowitt, *Bronson Cutting: Progressive Politician* (Albuquerque: University of New Mexico Press, 1992).

3. DEPRESSION, NEW DEAL, AND WAR, 1930–1945

There is no thorough, multifaceted overview of the American West during the 1930s, but the beginning place for a helpful study of the impacts of federal policies and expenditures on the region during the New Deal is Richard Lowitt, *The New Deal and the West* (Bloomington: Indiana University Press, 1984). The terrible consequences of the Great Depression can be examined in Richard Lowitt and Maurine Beasley, eds., *One Third of a Nation: Lorena Hickok Reports on the Great Depression* (Urbana: University of Illinois Press, 1981).

On the Dust Bowl, Paul Bonnifield argues in *The Dust Bowl* (Albuquerque: University of New Mexico Press, 1979) that catastrophe arose mainly from natural causes, but Donald Worster's conclusion that the Dust Bowl was primarily human-caused is more convincing in his prize-winning *Dust Bowl* (New York: Oxford University Press, 1979). The Dust Bowl refugees are treated in Walter J. Stein, *California and the Dust Bowl Migration* (Westport CT: Greenwood Press, 1973) and incisively in James N. Gregory, *American Exodus: The Dust Bowl Migration and Okie Culture in California* (New York: Oxford University Press, 1989). Journalist Timothy Egan won a Pulitzer Prize for the most recent study of the Dust Bowl, *The Worst Hard Time: The Untold Story of Those Who Survived the Great American Dust Bowl* (Boston: Houghton Mifflin, 2005). Howard R. Lamar provides an interesting perspective in his essay "Comparing Depressions: The Great Plains and Canadian Prairie Experiences, 1929–1941," in Nash and Etulain, *The Twentieth-Century West*, 175–206.

For New Deal agricultural and land policies, see William D. Rowley, *M. L. Wilson and the Campaign for the Domestic Allotment* (Lincoln: University of Nebraska Press, 1970) and E. Louise Peffer, *The Closing of the Public Domain: Disposal and Reservation Policies, 1900–1950* (Stanford CA: Stanford University Press, 1951). For the New Deal's impact on extractive industries, consult Gerald D. Nash, *U.S. Oil Policy, 1890–1964: Business and Government in Twentieth-Century America* (Pittsburgh PA: University of Pittsburgh Press, 1968) and John Brennan, *Silver and the First New Deal* (Reno: University of Nevada Press, 1969).

Two illuminating studies of the New Deal's impact on Indians are Graham D. Taylor, *The New Deal and American Indian Tribalism: The Administration of the Indian Reorganization Act, 1934–1945* (Lincoln: University of Nebraska Press, 1980) and Donald L. Parman, *The Navajos and the New Deal* (New Haven CT: Yale University Press, 1976). Vernon H. Jensen's *Nonferrous Metals Industry Unionism, 1932–1954: A Story of Leadership* (Ithaca NY: Cornell University Press, 1954) offers a ponderous look into the labor turmoil of the decade.

We now have a number of solid state studies of the New Deal's impact on the West. They include Robert E. Burke, *Olson's New Deal for California* (Berkeley: University of California Press, 1953); Michael P. Malone, *C. Ben Ross and the New Deal in Idaho* (Seattle: University of Washington Press, 1970); Francis W. Schruben, *Kansas in Turmoil, 1930–1936* (Columbia: University of Missouri Press, 1969); and James F. Wickens, *Colorado in the Great Depression* (New York: Garland, 1979). John Braeman et al., eds., *The New Deal, Vol. 2: The State and Local Levels* (Columbus: Ohio State University Press, 1975) contains essays on New Deal programs in several western states. See also the *Pacific Historical Review* 38 (August 1969), a special issue devoted to the New Deal in the West. For another key essay, consult

Leonard J. Arrington, "The Sagebrush Resurrection: New Deal Expenditures in the Western States, 1933–1939," *Pacific Historical Review* 52 (February 1983): 1–16.

Key political personalities of the period are treated in Robert A. Caro, *The Years of Lyndon Johnson: The Path to Power* (New York: Random House, 1981); Richard Lowitt, *George W. Norris: The Persistence of a Progressive, 1913–1933* (Urbana: University of Illinois Press, 1971); and Donald R. McCoy, *Landon of Kansas* (Lincoln: University of Nebraska Press, 1966).

Two important studies by Gerald D. Nash on the impact of World War II on the West are *The American West Transformed: The Impact of the Second World War* (Bloomington: Indiana University Press, 1985) and *World War II and the West: Reshaping the Economy* (Lincoln: University of Nebraska Press, 1990). Roger W. Lotchin adds much to our understanding of the modern West in *Fortress California 1910–1961: From Warfare to Welfare* (New York: Oxford University Press, 1992) and *The Bad City in the Good War: San Francisco, Los Angeles, Oakland, and San Diego* (Bloomington: Indiana University Press, 2003). Mark S. Foster deals with a key western figure of wartime in *Henry J. Kaiser: Builder in the Modern American West* (Austin: University of Texas Press, 1989). Another important participant is profiled in Gerald D. Nash, *A. P. Giannini and the Bank of America* (Norman: University of Oklahoma Press, 1992).

Among the numerous studies of the birth of atomic weaponry and atomic sites in the West, see especially Ferenc M. Szasz, *The Day the Sun Rose Twice: The Story of the Trinity Site Nuclear Explosion, July 16, 1945* (Albuquerque: University of New Mexico Press, 1984); Richard Rhodes, *The Making of the Atomic Bomb* (New York: Simon and Schuster, 1986); and Jon Hunner, *Inventing Los Alamos: The Growth of an Atomic Community* (Norman: University of Oklahoma Press, 2004).

Karen Anderson treats an important subject in *Wartime Women: Sex Roles, Family Relations and the Status of Women during World War II* (Westport CT: Greenwood Press, 1981).

On this topic, also see Sherna Berger Gluck, *Rosie the Riveter Revisited: Women, the War, and Social Change* (Boston: Twayne Publishers, 1987) and Amy Kesselman, *Fleeting Opportunities: Women Shipyard Workers in Portland and Vancouver During World War II and Reconversion* (Albany: State University of New York Press, 1990).

Several historians deal with the tragic Japanese relocation. The earlier accounts include two books by Roger Daniels: *The Politics of Prejudice: The Anti-Japanese Movement in California and the Struggle for Japanese Exclusion* (Berkeley: University of California Press, 1962) and *Concentration Camps USA: Japanese Americans and World War II* (New York: Holt, Rinehart and Winston, 1971). A more recent study is Brian Masaru Hayashi, *Democratizing the Enemy: The Japanese American Internment* (Princeton NJ: Princeton University Press, 2004). For general trends in wartime politics, consult the state histories previously noted.

4. SOCIAL PATTERNS IN THE MODERN WEST

The social history of the modern West, especially its demographic, ethnic, and family patterns, lacks a one-volume synthetic overview. Instead, the main ingredients of western social history must be drawn together from a number of books and essays. But Walter Nugent provides a valuable account of one strand of the story—the demographic history of the West from its origins to the present—in his smoothly written *Into the West: The Story of Its People* (New York: Alfred A. Knopf, 1999). Those interested in further statistical information on urban and rural populations, western ethnic diversity, and families in the West should consult the handy annual compilations in U.S. Bureau of the Census, *Statistical Abstract of the United States* (Washington DC: U.S. Government Printing Office).

Several major studies of western urbanization or individual cities are now available. The best overview is Carl Abbott, *The Metropolitan Frontier: Cities in the Modern American West* (Tucson: University of Arizona Press, 1993), which lists the western urban biographies published through the early 1990s. Western suburbs are discussed in Kenneth T. Jackson's prize-winning *Crabgrass Frontiers: The Suburbanization of the United States* (New York: Oxford University Press, 1985). See also two books by journalist Joel Garreau: *The Nine Nations of North America* (Boston: Houghton Mifflin Company, 1981), an impressionistic and lively study of urbanization in the United States and Canada, and *Edge City: Life on the New Frontier* (New York: Doubleday, 1991), a provocative study of a new urban phenomenon in the United States.

Among the notable studies of western cities are Robert M. Fogelson, *The Fragmented Metropolis: Los Angeles, 1850–1930* (Cambridge MA: Harvard University Press, 1967) and William Issel and Robert W. Cherny, *San Francisco, 1865–1932: Politics, Power, and Urban Development* (Berkeley: University of California Press, 1986). More recent examinations of western cities include Marilynn S. Johnson, *The Second Gold Rush: Oakland and the East Bay in World War II* (Berkeley: University of California Press, 1993); Carl Abbott, *Greater Portland: Urban Life and Landscape in the Pacific Northwest* (Philadelphia: University of Pennsylvania Press, 2001); and Hal Rothman, *Neon Metropolis: How Las Vegas Started the Twenty-First Century* (New York: Routledge, 2003).

The best overview of American Indian policy in the twentieth century is the second volume of Francis Paul Prucha, *The Great Father: The United States Government and the American Indians*, 2 vols. (Lincoln: University of Nebraska Press, 1984). Donald L. Parman provides a briefer but very useful overview of Native Americans in the recent West in his *Indians and the American West in the Twentieth Century* (Bloomington: Indiana University Press, 1994). Two other studies help to understand John Collier and his major role in New Deal policies involving Indians: Lawrence Kelly, *The Assault on Assimilation: John Collier and the Origins of Indian Policy Reform* (Albuquerque: University of New Mexico Press, 1983) and Kenneth R. Philp, *John Collier's Crusade for Indian Reform: 1920–1954* (Tucson: University of Arizona Press, 1977). Donald L. Fixico treats a later period in his *Termination and Relocation: Federal Indian Policy, 1945–1960* (Albuquerque: University of New Mexico Press, 1986). The best recent study of one of the largest tribal groups is Peter Iverson's authoritative *Diné: A History of the Navajos* (Albuquerque: University of New Mexico Press, 2002).

On Mexican Americans, one should begin with the classic but now dated study by Carey McWilliams, *North from Mexico: The Spanish-Speaking People of the United States* (Philadelphia: J. B. Lippincott, 1949). Much more pronounced in viewpoint is the widely adopted text by Rodolfo Acuña, *Occupied America: A History of Chicanos*, 5th ed. (New York: Pearson Longman, 2004). Several model monographs published earlier remain instructive: Albert Camarillo, *Chicanos in a Changing Society* (Cambridge MA: Harvard University Press, 1979); Mario T. García, *Desert Immigrants: The Mexicans of El Paso, 1880–1920* (New Haven CT: Yale University Press, 1971); Sarah Deutsch, *No Separate Refuge: Culture, Class, and Gender on an Anglo-Hispanic Frontier in the American Southwest, 1880–1940* (New York: Oxford University Press, 1987); and David Montejano, *Anglos and Mexicanos in the Making of Texas, 1836–1986* (Austin: University of Texas Press, 1987). Recent volumes of note include George J. Sánchez, *Becoming Mexican American: Ethnicity, Culture, and Identity in Chicano Los Angeles, 1900–1945* (New York: Oxford University Press, 1993); Juan Gómez-Quiñones, *Roots of Chicano Politics, 1600–1940* (Albuquerque: University of New Mexico Press, 1994), as well as several other works by the same author; David G. Gutiérrez, *Walls and Mirrors: Mexican Americans, Mexican Immigrants, and the Politics of Ethnicity* (Berkeley: University of California Press, 1995); and Oscar J. Martínez, *Mexican-Origin People in the United States: A Topical History* (Tucson: University of Arizona Press, 2001). See also the important writings of Vicki L. Ruiz, listed later.

Material on other ethnic groups in the modern West is more sparse. The most satisfactory study of black experience in the West is Quintard Taylor, *In Search of the Racial Frontier: African Americans in the American West, 1528–1990* (New York: W. W. Norton, 1998), which includes an extensive bibliography. On Asian Americans, see the earlier works on Japanese relocation; the outspoken discussions in Ronald Takaki, *Strangers from a Different Shore: A History of Asian Americans* (Boston: Little, Brown and Company, 1989); Roger Daniels, *Asian America: Chinese and Japanese in the United States since 1850* (Seattle: University of Washington Press, 1988); and Sucheng Chan, *Asian Americans: An Interpretive History* (Boston: Twayne Publishers, 1991).

All the major western ethnic groups receive attention in the still very useful essays in Stephan Thernstrom, ed., *Harvard Encyclopedia of American Ethnic Groups* (Cambridge MA: Harvard University Press, 1980). The histories of several groups are treated in a collection of essays edited by Frederick C. Luebke, *European Immigrants in the American West: Community Histories* (Albuquerque: University of New Mexico Press, 1998). Two other thoughtful essays remain helpful: Frederick C. Luebke, "Ethnic Minority Groups in the American West," in Michael P. Malone, *Historians and the American West* (Lincoln: University of Nebraska Press, 1983), 387–413 and Richard White, "Race Relations in the American West," *American Quarterly* 38 (Bibliography 1986): 396–416. The most recent study of immigration into the West is Elliott Robert Barkan, *From All Points: American's Immigrant West, 1870s–1952* (Bloomington: Indiana University Press, 2007).

The study of families, a fairly recent topic for most American historians, is even more unfamiliar to specialists in twentieth-century western history. Indeed, many of the useful generalizations about families in the modern West are to be found in national rather than regional studies. Especially helpful overviews are Carl N. Degler, *At Odds: Women and Family in America from the Revolution to the Present* (New York: Oxford University Press, 1980) and William H. Chafe, *The Paradox of Change: American Women in the Twentieth Century* (New York: Oxford University Press, 1991).

Ironically, though much western mythology has centered on "tough guy" John Wayne images, little is really known about masculinity in the West. For useful sources on national coverage of this topic, see Joe L. Dubbert, *A Man's Place:*

Masculinity in Transition (Englewood Cliffs NJ: Prentice-Hall, 1979); the collected essays in Elizabeth H. Pleck and Joseph H. Pleck, eds., *The American Man* (Englewood Cliffs NJ: Prentice-Hall, 1980); Robert L. Griswold, *Fatherhood in America: A History* (New York: Basic Books, 1993); and E. Anthony Rotundo, *American Manhood: Transformations in Masculinity from the Revolution to the Modern Era* (New York: Basic Books, 1993).

More good works are increasingly available on women's experiences in the modern West. Some of the essays in Susan H. Armitage and Elizabeth A. Jameson, eds., *The Women's West* (Norman: University of Oklahoma Press, 1987) and Elizabeth Jameson and Susan Armitage, eds., *Writing the Range: Race, Class, and Culture in the Women's West* (Norman: University of Oklahoma Press, 1997) touch on the modern period, as do all the essays in Sandra K. Schackel's collection *Western Women's Lives: Continuity and Change in the Twentieth Century* (Albuquerque: University of New Mexico Press, 2003). The most prolific author on western women's experiences, Glenda Riley, has written numerous books and essays on the subject. They are listed in *The American West in the Twentieth Century: A Bibliography* and in the bibliography for chapter 8. Karen Anderson emphasizes women's ethnic, urban, and occupational experiences in her brief overview "Western Women: The Twentieth-Century Experience," in Nash and Etulain, *The Twentieth-Century West*, 99–122.

Although now a generation old, one pathbreaking article remains central to writing about women and families in the West. See Joan M. Jensen and Darlis A. Miller, "The Gentle Tamers Revisited: New Approaches to the History of Women in the American West," *Pacific Historical Review* 49 (May 1980): 173–213. Another more recent overview is Elizabeth A. Jameson, "Toward a Multicultural History of Women in the Western United States," *Signs* 13 (Summer 1988): 761–91. See too the collected essays in Joan Jensen, *Promise to the Land: Essays on Rural Women* (Albuquerque: University of New Mexico Press, 1991). For a model monograph, consider Peggy Pascoe, *Relations of Rescue: The Search for Female Moral Authority in the American West, 1874–1939* (New York: Oxford University Press, 1990). Vicki L. Ruiz provides an overview of one group of ethnic women in *From Out of the Shadows: Mexican Women in Twentieth-Century America* (New York: Oxford University Press, 1998). We badly need a full-scale overview of women's experiences in the twentieth-century West.

Several of these studies include material on children and adolescents in the West, but these topics deserve much more attention. For national experiences with regional ramifications, consult Paula S. Fass, *The Damned and the Beautiful: American Youth in the 1920s* (New York: Oxford University Press, 1977). Richard Griswold del Castillo provides an additional vista on western families in his *La Familia: Chicano Families in the Urban Southwest: 1848 to the Present* (Notre Dame IN: University of Notre Dame Press, 1984). Scott G. McNall and Sally Allen McNall, *Plains Families: Exploring Sociology through Social History* (New York: St. Martin's Press, 1983) and Judith Stacey, *Brave New Families: Stories of Domestic Upheaval in the Late Twentieth-Century America* (New York: Basic Books, 1990) are also helpful.

5. CULTURE IN THE MODERN WEST

In the absence of full-scale studies of the cultural history of the modern American West, we must piece together the story from diverse sources. Two overviews of selected cultural topics are Richard W. Etulain, *Re-imagining the Modern American West: A Century of Fiction, History, and Art* (Tucson: University of Arizona Press, 1996) and Michael L. Johnson, *New Westers: The West in Contemporary American Culture* (Lawrence: University Press of Kansas, 1996). Keith L. Bryant provides a useful survey of the cultural history of one western subregion in his *Culture in the American Southwest: The Earth, the Sky, the People* (College Station: Texas A&M University Press, 2001).

The seven volumes in Kevin Starr's Americans and the California Dream series (all published by the Oxford

University Press in New York)—from *Americans and the California Dream, 1850–1915* (1973) to *Coast of Dreams: California on the Edge, 1990–2003* (2004)—are an unmatched source on that state's, or any other state's, cultural history. They treat literature, art, architecture, and popular culture and contain as well briefer sections on religion, education, and other cultural topics.

Readers interested in tracing the shifting tides of western historiography should consult the volumes listed earlier in the "Reference Guides and General Works" section. In addition to the collections of essays mentioned there, scholars and students should consult two especially strong essays on Frederick Jackson Turner: William Cronon, "Revisiting the Vanishing Frontier: The Legacy of Frederick Jackson Turner," *Western Historical Quarterly* 18 (April 1987): 157–65 and Michael C. Steiner, "The Significance of Turner's Sectional Thesis," *Western Historical Quarterly* 10 (October 1979): 437–66. Nor should one overlook two stimulating works on western historiography: Kerwin Lee Klein, *Frontiers of Historical Imagination: Narrating the European Conquest of Native America, 1890–1990* (Berkeley: University of California Press, 1997) and Gary Topping, *Utah Historians and the Reconstruction of Western History* (Norman: University of Oklahoma Press, 2003). Still another rewarding study is David M. Wrobel, *The End of American Exceptionalism: Frontier Anxiety from the Old West to the New Deal* (Lawrence: University Press of Kansas, 1993).

Less numerous than the works on Turner, writings about historians such as Walter Prescott Webb, Herbert E. Bolton, and others also illuminate the major trends of western historiography. On Webb, see Necah Stewart Furman, *Walter Prescott Webb: His Life and Impact* (Albuquerque: University of New Mexico Press, 1976) and Gregory M. Tobin, *The Making of a History: Walter Prescott Webb and "The Great Plains"* (Austin: University of Texas Press, 1976). Both are much more positive on Webb than the classic negative interpretation: Fred A. Shannon, *An Appraisal of Walter Prescott Webb's "The Great Plains: A Study in Institutions and*

Environment" (New York: Social Science Research Council, 1940). On Bolton, see John Francis Bolton's narrative, uncritical study *Herbert Eugene Bolton: The Historian and Man, 1870–1953* (Tucson: University of Arizona Press, 1978).

Western literature has received far more attention from scholars than has regional historiography. For more than forty years the Western Literature Association, through its *Western American Literature*, has fostered numerous discussions of literary topics. The association has sponsored two huge studies, which, although more reference guides than literary histories, are nonetheless immensely useful for understanding the subject: [J. Golden Taylor and Thomas J. Lyon et al., eds.,] *A Literary History of the American West* (Forth Worth: Texas Christian University Press, 1987) and [Thomas J. Lyon et al., eds.,] *Updating the Literary West* (Fort Worth: Texas Christian University Press, 1997). The best study of western popular fiction from dime novels to Louis L'Amour Westerns is Christine Bold, *Selling the Wild West: Popular Western Fiction, 1860–1960* (Bloomington: Indiana University Press, 1987), whereas Robert L. Dorman provides the premier study of American regionalism with strong sections on the West in his *Revolt of the Provinces: The Regionalist Movement in America, 1920–1945* (Chapel Hill: University of North Carolina Press, 1993). For a stimulating reading of western literature from a feminist perspective, see Krista Comer, *Landscapes of the New West: Gender and Geography in Contemporary Women's Writing* (Chapel Hill: University of North Carolina Press, 1999). Richard W. Etulain deals with novels, histories, biographies, and films in his brief study *Telling Western Stories: From Buffalo Bill to Larry McMurtry* (Albuquerque: University of New Mexico Press, 1999). Thousands of essays and books about western American literature are listed in Richard W. Etulain and N. Jill Howard, eds., *A Bibliographical Guide to the Study of Western American Literature*, 2nd ed. (Albuquerque: University of New Mexico Press, 1995).

The only book-length attempt to trace the major contours of western art in the twentieth century is Patricia Janis

Broder, *The American West: The Modern Vision* (Boston: Little, Brown, 1984). William H. Goetzmann and William N. Goetzmann include several chapters on western art, along with sections on other facets of western culture, in their lavishly illustrated *The West of the Imagination* (New York: W. W. Norton, 1986). Discussions of frontier, regional, and postregional western art appear in Richard W. Etulain, *Re-imagining the Modern American West*. On early twentieth-century western art, see the stimulating essays in Charles C. Eldredge et al., eds., *Art in New Mexico: 1900–1945: Paths to Taos and Santa Fe* (New York: Abbeville Press, 1986) and the less probing but nonetheless helpful volume by Patricia Janis Broder, *Taos: A Painter's Dream* (Boston: New York Graphic Art Society, 1980). The most useful anthology of western regional art, with instructive commentaries, is Nancy Heller and Julia Williams, *The Regionalists* (New York: Watson-Guptill, 1976).

Artists of the Pacific Northwest are treated in *Northwest Traditions* (Seattle: Seattle Art Museum, 1978), and those in northern California in Thomas Albright, *Art in the San Francisco Bay Area, 1945–1980* (Berkeley: University of California Press, 1985). Those interested in western ethnic art will benefit from Dorothy Dunn, *American Indian Painting of the Southwest and Plains Areas* (Albuquerque: University of New Mexico Press, 1968) and Ralph T. Coe, *Lost and Found Traditions: Native American Art 1965–1985* (Seattle: University of Washington Press, 1986).

Not many extensive studies are available on religion and education in the modern West, but the beginning place for the study of religion in the post-1900 West is Ferenc Morton Szasz, *Religion in the Modern American West* (Tucson: University of Arizona Press, 2000). Useful religious statistics and growth trends appear in the county-by-county enumeration by Bernard Quinn et al., *Churches and Church Membership in the United States 1980* ... (Atlanta: 1982); Martin B. Bradley, ed., *Churches and Church Membership in the United States 1990* ... (Atlanta: 1992); and Dale Jones and Douglas W. Johnson, eds., *Religious Congregations and Memberships in the United*

States in 2000 . . . (Nashville TN: 2002). All three were compiled and published by the Glenmary Research Center. For a general history of religion in the United States, with some comments on the American West, see Sydney E. Ahlstrom, *A Religious History of the American People* (New Haven CT: Yale University Press, 1972).

Other scholars are beginning to study specific western leaders and religious groups. Ferenc Morton Szasz, *The Divided Mind of Protestant America, 1880–1930* (University: University of Alabama Press, 1982) and Szasz, *The Protestant Clergy in the Great Plains and Mountain West, 1865–1915* (Albuquerque: University of New Mexico Press, 1988) touch on most of the major Protestant groups and their leaders. The best study of the most well-known woman religious leader is Edith L. Blumhofer, *Aimee Semple McPherson: Everybody's Sister* (Grand Rapids MI: William B. Eerdmans Publishing Company, 1993). We need more interpretative volumes like John W. Storey, *Texas Baptist Leadership and Social Christianity, 1900–1980* (College Station: Texas A&M University Press, 1986) and Daniel R. Carnett, *Contending for the Faith: Southern Baptists in New Mexico, 1938–1995* (Albuquerque: University of New Mexico Press, 2002). Other fundamentalist-evangelical groups are analyzed in Vinson Synan, *The Holiness-Pentecostal Movement in the United States* (Grand Rapids MI: Eerdmans, 1971) and Timothy L. Smith, *Called Unto Holiness* (Kansas City MO: Nazarene Publishing House, 1962).

We still lack extensive studies of Catholic and Jewish experiences in the recent West. For brief comments, see John Tracy Ellis, *American Catholicism*, 2nd ed., rev. (Chicago: University of Chicago Press, 1969) and the more extensive coverage in Timothy M. Dolan, ed., *The American Catholic Parish: A History from 1850 to the Present*, vol. 2, *Pacific States, Intermountain West, Midwest* (New York: Paulist Press, 1987). Henry J. Tobias provides focused studies in two books on Jews: *The Jews of Oklahoma* (Norman: University of Oklahoma Press, 1980) and *A History of the Jews of New Mexico* (Albuquerque: University of New Mexico Press, 1999). See too the essays collected in Moses Rischin and

John Livingston, eds., *Jews of the American West* (Detroit: Wayne State University Press, 1991).

For thorough studies of the Latter-day Saints or Mormons in the early twentieth century, consult Thomas G. Alexander, *Mormonism in Transition: A History of the Latter-day Saints, 1890–1930* (Urbana: University of Illinois Press, 1986) and the appropriate sections of Leonard J. Arrington and Davis Bitton, *The Mormon Experience: A History of the Latter-day Saints* (New York: Alfred A. Knopf, 1979).

David B. Tyack, a leading educational historian, deals with urban schools in the West in his stimulating overview *The One Best System: A History of American Urban Education* (Cambridge MA: Harvard University Press, 1974). Also helpful for a general background are Lawrence A. Cremin, *American Education: The Metropolitan Experience, 1876–1980* (New York: Harper and Row, 1988) and his earlier *The Transformation of the School: Progressivism in American Education, 1876–1957* (New York: Alfred A. Knopf, 1961).

Nearly all western state and regional histories include abbreviated sections on schools and colleges, but educational developments in one crucial state are chronicled in Irving G. Hendrick, *California Education: A Brief History* (San Francisco: Boyd and Fraser, 1980). Two model monographs are also worthy of note: Guadalupe San Miguel Jr., *"Let All of Them Take Heed": Mexican Americans and the Campaign for Educational Equality in Texas, 1910–1981* (Austin: University of Texas Press, 1987) and Judith Rosenberg Raftery, *Land of Fair Promise: Politics and Reform in Los Angeles Schools, 1885–1941* (Stanford CA: Stanford University Press, 1992). Another facet of recent schooling in the West is treated in Margaret Connell Szasz, *Education and the American Indian: The Road to Self-Determination Since 1928*, 3rd ed., rev. and enl. (1977; repr., Albuquerque: University of New Mexico Press, 1999).

Unfortunately, there is no counterpart to Henry Nash Smith's brilliant study of nineteenth-century attitudes toward the West *Virgin Land: The American West as Symbol and Myth* (Cambridge MA: Harvard University Press, 1950). Another scholar of American studies, Richard Slotkin, attempts something similar in his mammoth *Gunfighter Nation: The Myth of the Frontier in Twentieth-Century America* (New York: Atheneum, 1992), which includes dozens of critical readings of well-known Western films. The best survey of Hollywood and the American film is Robert Sklar, *Movie-Made America: A Cultural History of American Movies*, rev. ed. (New York: Vintage, 1994). John H. Lenihan studies Westerns as cultural artifacts in *Showdown: Confronting Modern America in the Western Film* (Urbana: University of Illinois Press, 1980), whereas Lee Clark Mitchell extensively employs critical theory in his study *Westerns: Making the Man in Fiction and Film* (Chicago: University of Chicago Press, 1996).

Another collection of essays, *The Hollywood West* (Golden CO: Fulcrum Publishing, 2001), edited by Richard W. Etulain and Glenda Riley, approaches the Western through minibiographies of Western stars from the silent heroes to Clint Eastwood. The most useful reference volume on this popular film genre, by far, is Edward Buscombe, ed., *The BFI Companion to the Western* (New York: Atheneum, 1988).

William W. Savage, *The Cowboy Hero: His Image in American History* (Norman: University of Oklahoma Press, 1983) remains the most useful study of that ubiquitous figure. Lawrence R. Borne provides the standard account of another aspect of western popular culture in *Dude Ranching: A Complete History* (Albuquerque: University of New Mexico Press, 1983). On a closely related topic, see Kristine Fredericksson, *American Rodeo: From Buffalo Bill to Big Business* (College Station: Texas A&M University Press, 1985) and Elizabeth Atwood Lawrence, *Rodeo: An Anthropological Look at the Wild and the Tame* (Knoxville: University of Tennessee Press, 1982).

Few if any modern western topics need more attention from scholars and students than does cultural history. Three essays that examine the general field and point out accomplishments and needs are Howard R. Lamar, "Much to Celebrate: The Western History Association's Twenty-Fifth Birthday," *Western Historical Quarterly* 17 (October 1986): 397–416; Richard W. Etulain, "Shifting Interpretations of Western

American Cultural History," in Malone, *Historians and the American West*, 414–32; and Etulain, "Research Opportunities in Twentieth-Century Western Cultural History," in Gerald D. Nash and Richard W. Etulain, eds., *Researching Western History: Topics in the Twentieth Century* (Albuquerque: University of New Mexico Press, 1997), 147–66.

6. THE MODERN WESTERN ECONOMY

On this topic, readers should begin with two very helpful books by Gerald D. Nash: *World War II and the West: Reshaping the Economy* (Lincoln: University of Nebraska Press, 1990) and *The Federal Landscape: An Economic History of the Twentieth-Century West* (Tucson: University of Arizona Press, 1999). The huge roles of the military and other federal governmental influences on the West are treated in a helpful collection of essays, Kevin J. Fernlund, ed., *The Cold War American West, 1945–1989* (Albuquerque: University of New Mexico Press, 1998). Still useful is another essay: James L. Clayton, "Impact of the Cold War on the Economies of California and Utah, 1946–1965," *Pacific Historical Review* 36 (November 1967): 449–73. See also Adam Yarmolinsky and Gregory D. Foster, *Paradoxes of Power: The Military Establishment in the Eighties* (Bloomington: Indiana University Press, 1983).

Federal reclamation is well depicted in Donald E. Green, *Land of Underground Rain: Irrigation on the Texas High Plains, 1910–1970* (Austin: University of Texas Press, 1973); Norris Hundley, jr., *Dividing the Waters: A Century of Controversy Between the United States and Mexico* (Berkeley: University of California Press, 1966); Hundley, *Water and the West: The Colorado River Compact and the Politics of Water in the American West* (Berkeley: University of California Press, 1975); Marc Reisner, *Cadillac Desert: The American West and Its Disappearing Water* (New York: Viking Penguin, 1986); and Donald Worster, *Rivers of Empire: Water, Aridity, and the Growth of the American West* (New York: Pantheon, 1986).

The beginning place for understanding transportation

history in the modern West is Carlos Arnaldo Schwantes, *Going Places: Transportation Redefines the Twentieth-Century West* (Bloomington: Indiana University Press, 2003). Most railroad histories do not approach the present, but see John F. Stover, *The Life and Decline of the American Railroad* (New York: Oxford University Press, 1970); Keith L. Bryant Jr., *History of the Atchison, Topeka and Santa Fe Railroad* (New York: Macmillan, 1974); Don L. Hofsommer, *The Southern Pacific, 1901–1985* (College Station: Texas A&M University Press, 1986); and Richard C. Overton, *Burlington Route: A History of the Burlington Lines* (New York: Alfred A. Knopf, 1965).

The best treatment of the impact of automobiles on the recent United States is Mark S. Foster's *A Nation on Wheels: The Automobile Culture in America Since 1945* (Belmont CA: Wadsworth/Thomson, 2003). See also John B. Rae, *The Road and the Car in American Life* (Cambridge MA: MIT Press, 1971); Richard O. Davies, *The Age of Asphalt: The Automobile, the Freeway, and the Condition of Metropolitan America* (Philadelphia: J. B. Lippincott Company, 1975); and Mark H. Rose, *Interstate: Express Highway Politics, 1941–1956* (Lawrence: Regents Press of Kansas, 1979). The standard works on tourism and aviation are listed in chapter 1.

For an examination of farmers and farming in modern America, begin with R. Douglas Hurt, *Problems of Plenty: The American Farmer in the Twentieth Century* (Chicago: Ivan Dee, 2002). Earlier studies include Gilbert C. Fite, *American Farmers: The New Minority* (Bloomington: Indiana University Press, 1981); John T. Schlebecker, *Whereby We Thrive: A History of American Farming, 1607–1972* (Ames: Iowa State University Press, 1975); and John Opie, *The Law of the Land: 200 Years of American Farmland Policy* (Lincoln: University of Nebraska Press, 1987). See too Thomas D. Isern, *Custom Combining on the Great Plains: A History* (Norman: University of Oklahoma Press, 1981); John T. Schlebecker, *Cattle Raising on the Plains, 1900–1961* (Lincoln: University of Nebraska Press, 1963); and Paul F. Steers, *Let the Cowboy Ride: Cattle Ranching in the American West* (Baltimore: The Johns Hopkins University Press, 1998).

The many works of Duane Smith deal authoritatively with western mining. See especially his *Mining America: The Industry and the Environment, 1800–1980* (Lawrence: University Press of Kansas, 1987). A well-informed source on western mining is the earlier work by Thomas R. Navin, *Copper Mining and Management* (Tucson: University of Arizona Press, 1978). See too Leonard J. Arrington and Gary B. Hansen, *"The Richest Hole on Earth": A History of the Bingham Copper Mine* (Logan: Utah State University Press, 1963). Michael P. Malone provides a key overview essay in "The Collapse of Western Metal Mining: An Historical Epitaph," *Pacific Historical Review* 55 (August 1986): 455–64.

A rich body of scholarship has emerged on modern western lumbering and forest policy. See Thomas R. Cox et al., *This Well-Wooded Land: Americans and Their Forests from Colonial Times to the Present* (Lincoln: University of Nebraska Press, 1985); Harold K. Steen, *The U.S. Forest Service: A History* (Seattle: University of Washington Press, 1976); and William G. Robbins, *American Forestry: A History of National, State, and Private Cooperation* (Lincoln: University of Nebraska Press, 1985). Consult too Robbins's helpful essay "The Social Context of Forestry: The Pacific Northwest in the Twentieth Century," *Western Historical Quarterly* 16 (October 1985): 413–27.

Historians have also produced a number of important studies of the oil industry in the West. Anthony Sampson offers a global perspective in *The Seven Sisters: The Great Oil Companies and the World They Shaped* (New York: Viking Press, 1975). Also of value and interest are the special issue on "The Petroleum Industry," *Pacific Historical Review* 39 (May 1970) and Roger M. Olien and Diana D. Olien, *Wildcatters: Texas Independent Oilmen* (Austin: Texas Monthly Press, 1984).

Most studies of western coal are localized. The best of these studies is the important story of one mineral in one state, A. Dudley Gardner and Verla R. Flores, *Forgotten Frontier: A History of Wyoming Coal Mining* (Boulder CO: Westview Press, 1989). For a larger context, see Wallace E. Tyner and Robert J. Kalter, *Western Coal: Promise or*

Problem (Lexington MA: Lexington Books, 1978); Frederic J. Athearn, "Black Diamonds: A History of Federal Coal Policy in the Western United States, 1862–1981," *Journal of the West* 21 (October 1982): 44–50; and, on a related subject, Paul L. Russell, *History of Western Oil Shale* (East Brunswick NJ: Center for Professional Management, 1980).

The western energy crisis and boom attracted a good deal of attention from journalists and historians. See the polemical account in K. Ross Toole, *The Rape of the Great Plains: Northwest America, Cattle and Coal* (Boston: Atlantic Monthly Press—Little, Brown, 1976) and Richard D. Lamm and Michael McCarthy, *The Angry West: A Vulnerable Land and Its Future* (Boston: Houghton Mifflin, 1982). Also helpful are Lynton R. Hayes, *Energy, Economic Growth, and Regionalism in the West* (Albuquerque: University of New Mexico Press, 1980); Kirkpatrick Sale, *Power Shift: The Rise of the Southern Rim and Its Challenge to the Eastern Establishment* (New York: Random House, 1975); and Peter Wiley and Robert Gottlieb, *Empires in the Sun: The Rise of the New American West* (New York: G. P. Putnam's Sons, 1982).

Scholars are just beginning to deal with the emergence of high-technology and service industries in the American West. A handy overview volume is Everett M. Rogers and Judith K. Larsen, *Silicon Valley Fever: Growth of High-Technology Culture* (New York: Basic Books, 1984). For studies of two giants in the computer industry, consult James Wallace and Jim Erickson, *Hard Drive: Bill Gates and the Making of the Microsoft Empire* (New York: Wiley, 1993) and Laura Rich, *The Accidental Zillionaire: Demystifying Paul Allen* (New York: Wiley, 2002).

Western labor in the modern era remains largely unexamined by historians. Among general studies of value are James R. Green, *The World of the Worker: Labor in Twentieth-Century America* (New York: Hill and Wang, 1980) and, for reference purposes, Gary M. Fink, *Labor Unions* (Westport CT: Greenwood Press, 1972). On one important labor leader, see Charles P. Larrowe, *Harry Bridges: The Rise and Fall of Radical Labor in the United States*, 2nd ed., rev. (New York:

L. Hill, 1977). Several useful studies also focus on Chicano/a laborers. For one, consult Vicki L. Ruiz, *Cannery Women/Cannery Lives: Mexican Women, Unionization, and the California Food Processing Industry, 1930–1950* (Albuquerque: University of New Mexico Press, 1987). The most accessible biography of César Chávez is Richard Griswold del Castillo and Richard A Garcia, *César Chávez: A Triumph of Spirit* (Norman: University of New Mexico Press, 1995).

7. POLITICS OF THE MODERN ERA, 1945–1987

Given the relative paucity of monographic studies of this recent period, it is especially necessary to pay heed to national studies. Particularly helpful are James T. Patterson's two well-written and thoroughly researched overviews of recent American history: *Grand Expectations: The United States, 1945–1974* (New York: Oxford University Press, 1996) and *Restless Giant: The United States from Watergate to Bush v. Gore* (New York: Oxford University Press, 2005). Two standard guides to national electoral trends are Arthur M. Schlesinger Jr. and Fred L. Israel, eds., *History of American Presidential Elections*, 10 vols. (New York: Chelsea House, 1971) and Schlesinger, ed., *History of American Presidential Elections: 1972–1984* (New York: Chelsea House, 1985). See also two overviews of the 1960s: Allen J. Matusow, *The Unraveling of America: A History of Liberalism in the 1960s* (New York: Harper and Row, 1984) and David Farber, *The Age of Great Dreams: America in the 1960s* (New York: Hill and Wang, 1994).

Journalists provided several impressionistic surveys in the 1960s and 1970s that helped illuminate international-national-regional connections in western politics. See, for example, the volumes by Neal R. Peirce, all of which are published by W. W. Norton: *The Pacific States of America* (1972), *The Mountain States of America* (1972), and *The Great Plains States of America* (1973). Similar in approach are Neil Morgan, *Westward Tilt: The American West Today* (New York: Random House, 1963); Jerry Hagstrom with Neal R. Peirce, *The Book of America: Inside Fifty States Today* (New

York: W. W. Norton, 1983); and Hagstrom, *Beyond Reagan: The New Landscape of American Politics* (New York: W. W. Norton, 1988).

Several collections of essays also help explain recent western politics. See, for instance, Thomas C. Donnelly, ed., *Rocky Mountain Politics* (Albuquerque: University of New Mexico Press, 1947); Frank H. Jonas, ed., *Politics in the American West* (Salt Lake City: University of Utah Press, 1969); and Richard Lowitt, ed., *Politics in the Postwar American West* (Norman: University of Oklahoma Press, 1995).

Many of the major political personalities of the modern era have now attracted their biographers. These life stories help to illuminate the subject of regional politics. Among the most extensive are Stephen E. Ambrose, *Eisenhower*, 2 vols. (New York: Simon and Schuster, 1983–84); Ambrose, *Nixon*, 3 vols. (New York: Simon and Schuster, 1987–91); Robert Caro's first volume of his multivolume biography of another western political giant, *The Path to Power: The Years of Lyndon Johnson* (New York: Alfred A. Knopf, 1982); Garry Wills, *Reagan's America: Innocents at Home* (Garden City NY: Doubleday, 1987); Peter Iverson, *Barry Goldwater: Native Arizonian* (Norman: University of Arizona Press, 1997); and Robert A. Goldberg, *Barry Goldwater* (New Haven CT: Yale University Press, 1995).

Biographies of lesser-known political figures help to fill in some of the missing details in modern western politics. They include G. Edward White, *Earl Warren: A Public Life* (New York: Oxford University Press, 1987); A. Robert Smith, *Tiger in the Senate: The Biography of Wayne Morse* (Garden City NY: Doubleday, 1962); LeRoy Ashby and Rod Gramer, *Fighting the Odds: The Life of Senator Frank Church* (Pullman: Washington State University Press, 1994); and Mary Beth Rogers, *Barbara Jordan: American Hero* (New York: Bantam, 1998).

Scholars and students, after a bit of searching, will soon learn how much is yet to be done in tracing the main contours of western politics since World War II.

8. A NEW WESTERN GENERATION, MID-1980S–2005

Historians are just beginning to turn their attention to the post-1980 American West. Journalists, memoirists, and other writers have already laid down the first layer of oral histories, autobiographies, and memoirs for this very recent period, but only a very few general historical works venture into the twenty-first century.

For overarching interpretations of U.S. history from 1980 onward, one might start with James T. Patterson, *Restless Giant: The United States from Watergate to Bush v. Gore* (New York: Oxford University Press, 2005); William Chafe, *The Unfinished Journey: America Since World War II*, 5th ed. (New York: Oxford University Press, 2003); or examine a geographer's insightful approach in D. W. Meinig, *Global America, 1915–2000*, vol. 4, *The Shaping of America: A Geographical Perspective on 500 Years of History* (New Haven CT: Yale University Press, 2004). In addition, all the overviews mentioned at the beginning of this bibliographical listing venture past 1980 in their narratives.

Recently published collections of essays also add important information on the West in the 1980s and 1990s. These collections include Patricia Nelson Limerick's anthology of her own essays, *Something in the Soil: Legacies and Reckonings in the New West* (New York: W. W. Norton, 2000); David M. Wrobel and Michael C. Steiner, eds., *Many Wests: Place, Culture, and Regional Identity* (Lawrence: University Press of Kansas, 1997); Kevin J. Fernlund, ed., *The Cold War American West, 1945–1989* (Albuquerque: University of New Mexico Press, 1998); and Richard W. Etulain and Ferenc M. Szasz, eds., *The American West in 2000: Essays in Honor of Gerald D. Nash* (Albuquerque: University of New Mexico Press, 2003). Journalist Timothy Egan's *Lasso the Wind: Away to the New West* (New York: Alfred A. Knopf, 1998) is impressionistic but also provocative and evocative in its coverage of the modern West. Only Gerald D. Nash provides a historical study devoted to the postwar half century in his *A Brief History of the American West since 1945* (Fort Worth TX:

Harcourt, 2000). Kevin Starr's *Coast of Dreams: California on the Edge, 1990–2003* (New York: Alfred A. Knopf, 2004) is an extensive, invaluable overview of recent California.

The most useful study of demographic patterns in the American West, including illuminating sections on the post-1945 period, is Walter Nugent, *Into the West: The Story of Its People* (New York: Alfred A. Knopf, 1999). This chapter owes much to this invaluable, invitingly written volume. The best of the western urban histories is Carl Abbott, *The Metropolitan Frontier: Cities in the Modern American West* (Tucson: University of Arizona Press, 1993). See too the innovative treatment of Disneyland, Stanford Industrial Park, Sun City, Arizona, and Seattle's World Fair in John M. Findlay's thoughtful *Magic Lands: Western Cityscapes and American Culture* (Berkeley: University of California Press, 1992). The recent rural and agricultural Wests are covered in R. Douglas Hurt, ed., *The Rural West since World War II* (Lawrence: University Press of Kansas, 1998) and Hurt, *Problems of Plenty: The American Farmer in the Twentieth Century* (Chicago: Ivan Dee, 2002).

We lack a one-volume study of racial and ethnic groups in the modern West, but a useful book on those subjects and immigration to the United States is James S. Olson, *Equality Deferred: Race, Ethnicity, and Immigration in America Since 1945* (Fort Worth TX: Harcourt Brace, 2003). Oscar Martínez's *Mexican-Origin People in the United States: A Topical History* (Tucson: University of Arizona Press, 2001) provides a helpful overview, as does Vicki L. Ruiz's *From Out of the Shadows: Mexican Women in Twentieth-Century America* (New York: Oxford University Press, 1998). The most useful brief study of American Indians in the United States since World War II is James J. Rawls, *Chief Red Fox Is Dead: A History of Native Americans Since 1945* (Fort Worth TX: Harcourt Brace, 1996). The concluding section of Quintard Taylor's superb synthesis *In Search of the Racial Frontier: African Americans in the American West, 1528–1990* (New York: W. W. Norton, 1998) deals with African Americans in the recent West.

No one has dealt extensively with families in the contem-

porary West, but all the pertinent books and essays are list-
ed in Cindy Tyson, comp., *Families in the Twentieth-Century
American West: A Bibliography* (2001) and Suzanne Sermon,
comp., *Women in the Twentieth-Century American West:
A Bibliography* (2000), both issued by the Center for the
American West, University of New Mexico, Albuquerque.

Glenda Riley is, by far, the most prolific scholar study-
ing western women. Of her many books see, for example,
Women and Indians on the Frontier, 1825–1915 (1984; rev., repr.,
Confronting Race: Women and Indians on the Frontier, 1815–1915
[Albuquerque: University of New Mexico Press, 2004]); *The
Female Frontier: A Comparative View of Women on the Prairie
and the Plains* (Lawrence: University Press of Kansas, 1988);
The Life and Legacy of Annie Oakley (Norman: University of
Oklahoma Press, 1994); and *Taking Land, Breaking Land:
Women Colonizing the American West and Kenya, 1840–1940*
(Albuquerque: University of New Mexico Press, 2003).

The most helpful volume on economic developments in
the modern West is Gerald D. Nash, *The Federal Landscape:
An Economic History of the Twentieth-Century West* (Tucson:
University of Arizona Press, 1999). Here and elsewhere
Nash clearly shows the importance of federal government
funding to the post–World War II West. Two helpful stud-
ies of transportation are Carlos Arnaldo Schwantes, *Going
Places: Transportation Redefines the Twentieth-Century West*
(Bloomington: Indiana University Press, 2003) and Mark
S. Foster, *A Nation on Wheels: The Automobile Culture in
America Since 1945* (Fort Worth TX: Harcourt, 2003). Hal
Rothman's imaginative overview of recent tourism *Devil's
Bargains: Tourism in the Twentieth-Century West* (Lawrence:
University Press of Kansas, 1999) deserves close attention.

Several authors treat the multifaceted environmental controversies sweeping through the recent West. Ted Steinberg
includes comments on many of the contested issues in his
extensive overview *Down to Earth: Nature's Role in American
History* (New York: Oxford University Press, 2002). See also
the numerous writings on varied environmental topics of
Donald Worster, Richard White, Patricia Nelson Limerick,

William Cronon, Donald Pisani, William G. Robbins, and Dan Flores listed in Richard W. Etulain et al., eds., *The American West in the Twentieth Century: A Bibliography* (Norman: University of Oklahoma Press, 1994).

Historians and other scholars are just beginning to treat the impact of computers and other "footloose industries" on the newest West. On early computer industries, consult James Wallace, *Overdrive* (New York: John Wiley and Sons, 1997). For accounts of Bill Gates and Paul Allen, see James Wallace and Jim Erickson, *Hard Drive: Bill Gates and the Making of the Microsoft Empire* (New York: Wiley, 1993) and Laura Rich, *The Accidental Zillionaire: Demystifying Paul Allen* (New York: Wiley, 2002). Carl Abbott perceptively traces the influences of computer industries on the modern West in his essay "Paul Allen: High Technology and the High Country in a New West," in Richard W. Etulain, ed., *Western Lives: A Biographical History of the American West* (Albuquerque: University of New Mexico Press, 2004), 385–411.

The pertinent chapters in James T. Patterson's *Restless Giant* (2005) provide illuminating backgrounds for examining trends in recent western politics. Two helpful books for understanding Ronald Reagan's shaping influences on regional, national, and international politics are insider Lou Cannon's *President Reagan: The Role of a Lifetime* (1991; repr., New York: Public Affairs, 2000) and Robert Dallek, *Ronald Reagan: The Politics of Symbolism* (1984; repr., Cambridge MA: Harvard University Press, 1999).

Two collections of essays are also valuable for a study of western politics. The chapters in Clive S. Thomas, ed., *Politics and Public Policy in the Contemporary American West* (Albuquerque: University of New Mexico Press, 1991), primarily by political scientists, focus as much on public policy as on politics, whereas the nineteen essays in Richard Lowitt, ed., *Politics in the Postwar American West* (Norman: University of Oklahoma Press, 1995) treat the political history of individual western states. In his widely cited essay "Politics without Parties: The Western States, 1900–1984," in Gerald D. Nash and Richard W. Etulain, eds., *The Twentieth-Century*

West: Historical Interpretations (Albuquerque: University of New Mexico Press, 1989), 295–338, Paul Kleppner makes the case for the weakening of party loyalties in the twentieth-century West.

Generally, we lack studies providing an overview of western politics since World War II. Opportunities for research on broad regional topics, transnational subjects, state politics, as well as studies of individual politicians are available to dozens of researchers. For a helpful discussion of these possibilities, see Robert W. Cherny, "Research Opportunities in Twentieth-Century Western History: Politics," in Gerald D. Nash and Richard Etulain, eds., *Researching Western History: Topics in the Twentieth Century* (Albuquerque: University of New Mexico Press, 1997), 83–118. A thorough listing of the books and essays published about post-1900 western politics appears in M. David Key, comp., *Political History in the Twentieth-Century American West: A General Bibliography* (Albuquerque: Center for the American West, University of New Mexico, 2000).

Most historians have been slower to study western cultural history than topics in economic, political, and social history. But several writers have produced important works on the literature, historiography, religions, and popular culture of the West since the mid-1980s. In addition to the previously mentioned *Coast of Dreams* by Kevin Starr, Keith L. Bryant provides a cultural overview of another region in his *Culture in the American Southwest* (College Station: Texas A&M University Press, 2001). A thorough, sweeping account of Americans' fascination with a wilderness West and its cultural transformations appears in Michael L. Johnson, *Hunger for the Wild: America's Obsession with the Untamed West* (Lawrence: University Press of Kansas, 2007).

Two recent studies are models for the kinds of work that can be done with western historical writing. Kevin Lee Klein uses broader strokes to deal with the philosophies and ideologies shaping western historiography in his probing, challenging volume *Frontiers of the Imagination: Narrating the European Conquest of Native America, 1890–1990* (Berkeley:

University of California Press, 1997). On the other hand, Gary Topping in his valuable volume *Utah Historians and the Reconstruction of Western History* (Norman: University of Oklahoma Press, 2003) looks closely at major historians and writers in Utah (including, for example, Wallace Stegner, Bernard DeVoto, and Fawn Brodie) to scrutinize the predilections and biases of these authors, which unfortunately limited the insights of their histories and novels.

Michael L. Johnson's lively volume *New Westers: The West in Contemporary American Culture* (Lawrence: University Press of Kansas, 1996) roams over several topical areas to deal with western literature, historiography, film, art, and popular culture. Richard W. Etulain treats similar topics in two of his recent books: *Re-imagining the Modern American West: A Century of Western Fiction, History, and Art* (Tucson: University of Arizona Press, 1966) and *Telling Western Stories: From Buffalo Bill to Larry McMurtry* (Albuquerque: University of New Mexico Press, 1999).

Ferenc M. Szasz, the preeminent authority on religion in the American West, displays his command of that subject in his pioneering volume *Religion in the Modern American West* (Tucson: University of Arizona Press, 2000). Valuable insights from that study are summarized in Szasz, "Organized Religion and the Search for Community in the Modern American West," in Etulain and Szasz, *The American West in 2000*, 127–42. For a case study of one state's alternative faiths, see Stephen Fox, "Boomer Dharma: The Evolution of Alternative Spiritual Communities in Modern New Mexico," in Ferenc M. Szasz and Richard W. Etulain, eds., *Religion in Modern New Mexico* (Albuquerque: University of New Mexico Press, 1997), 145–70.

Finally, for a valuable collection of entertaining essays on several manifestations of popular culture in the American West, see Richard Aquila, *Wanted Dead or Alive: The American West in Popular Culture* (Urbana: University of Illinois Press, 1996).

Index

About the Authors

Richard W. Etulain (1938–) is professor emeritus of history and former director of the Center for the American West at the University of New Mexico, where he taught from 1979 to 2001. He also served on the faculties at Northwest Nazarene College (University) and Idaho State University. Etulain is the author or editor of more than forty books, most of which focus on the history and cultures of the American West. His most important books include *Conversations with Wallace Stegner* (1983, 1996), *Writing Western History* (editor, 1991), *Re-imagining the Modern American West: A Century of Fiction, History, and Art* (1996), *Telling Western Stories: From Buffalo Bill to Larry McMurtry* (1999), and *Beyond the Missouri: The Story of the American West* (2006). Etulain has been president of both the Western Literature and Western History associations. He has lectured abroad in several countries, most recently as a Fulbright Lecturer in Ukraine. He is currently working on a study of Abraham Lincoln and the American West.

Michael P. Malone (1940–99) was a well-known specialist in western history and a long-time college administrator at Montana State University, Bozeman. After gaining his doctorate in American studies at Washington State University, Malone became part of the faculty at Montana State, where he served as department head, dean of graduate studies, and university president (1991–99). Malone authored or edited nine books and numerous essays. Among his most important books are *C. Ben Ross and the New Deal in Idaho* (1970), *Montana: A History of Two Centuries* (coauthor, 1976, 1991), *The Battle for Butte: Mining and Politics on the Northern Frontier, 1864–1906* (1982), *Historians and the American West* (editor, 1983), and *James J. Hill: Empire Builder of the Northwest* (1996). He was a widely cited and much-praised historian of Montana and the modern American West.